In this book Mark Harrison rebuilds and analyses the Soviet economy's wartime statistical record, examining its prewar size and composition, and wartime changes in GNP, employment, the defence burden, and the role of foreign aid. Complementing classic long-run growth studies the book compares the Soviet experience with that of other great powers. It emphasises the severity of current costs and capital losses arising from the war, which had a negative effect on GNP which persisted well after 1945. The results are based on a comprehensive analysis of hitherto closed official documents, throwing new light on the dimensions of the Soviet war effort, the comparative economics of the war, and its long-term impact on the Soviet economy.

ACCOUNTING FOR WAR

Cambridge Russian, Soviet and Post-Soviet Studies

99 MARK HARRISON
Accounting for war
Soviet production, employment, and the defence burden, 1940–1945

98 KAZIMIERZ Z. POZNANSKI
Poland's protracted transition
Institutional change and economic growth, 1971–1993

97 ANITA J. PRAZMOWSKA
Britain and Poland, 1939–1943
The betrayed ally

96 JOHN DOYLE KLIER
Imperial Russia's Jewish question 1855–1881

95 DON C. RAWSON
Russian rightists and the revolution of 1905

94 GRAEME GILL
The collapse of a single party system
The disintegration of the Communist Party of the Soviet Union

93 DONALD FILTZER
Soviet workers and the collapse of *perestroika*
The Soviet labour process and Gorbachev's reforms, 1985–1991

92 PETER GATRELL
Government, industry and rearmament in Russia, 1900–1914
The last argument of tsarism

91 LINDA RACIOPPI
Soviet policy towards South Asia since 1970

90 WENDY GOLDMAN
Women, the State and the family
Soviet family policy and social life, 1917–1936

89 JONATHAN C. VALDEZ
Internationalism and the ideology of Soviet influence in Eastern Europe

88 PETER RUTLAND
The politics of economic stagnation in the Soviet Union
The role of local party organs in economic management

87 DONALD FILTZER
Soviet workers and de-Stalinization
The consolidation of the modern system of Soviet production relations 1953–1964

86 MILIC UVALIC
Investment and property rights in Yugoslavia
The long transition to a market economy

85 AVRIL PITTMAN
From Ostpolitik to reunification: West German/Soviet political relations since 1974

Series list continues on page 339

ACCOUNTING FOR WAR

Soviet production, employment, and the defence burden, 1940–1945

MARK HARRISON
University of Warwick

CAMBRIDGE
UNIVERSITY PRESS

Published by the Press Syndicate of the University of Cambridge
The Pitt Building, Trumpington Street, Cambridge CB2 1RP
40 West 20th Street, New York, NY 10011–4211, USA
10 Stamford Road, Oakleigh, Melbourne 3166, Australia

First published 1996

Printed in Great Britain at the University Press, Cambridge

A catalogue record for this book is available from the British Library

Library of Congress cataloguing in publication data

Harrison, Mark, 1949–
Accounting for war: Soviet production, employment and the defence burden, 1940–1945 / Mark Harrison.
p. cm. – (Cambridge Russian, Soviet and post-Soviet studies; 99)
Includes bibliographical references and index.
ISBN 0 521 48265 8 (hardcover)
1. Soviet Union – Economic conditions – 1917–1945. 2. Soviet Union – – Economic policy – 1938–1942. 3. Soviet Union – Economic policy – 1942–1945. 4. World War, 1939–1945 – Economic aspects – – Soviet Union. I. Title. II. Series.
HC335.6.H36 1996 95–40147 CIP

ISBN 0521 48265 8 hardback

KS

Contents

Figures

Tables

In all tables, data are given for economic activity within contemporary Soviet frontiers, or, in wartime, territory under *de facto* Soviet rule, unless otherwise specified.
'Tons' are metric tonnes. 'Billions' are thousand millions. Rows or columns may not sum to totals because of rounding.
Nil and insignificant values are signified by 0 *or* 0.0
'Not applicable' and 'not available' are signified by –

Preface

This book has been in preparation for nearly a decade. In 1986 Mary McAuley invited me to present a paper on the comparative economics of World War II to the annual conference of the National Association for Soviet and East European Studies in Cambridge the following spring. Trying for the first time to arrive at well-founded comparisons among Germany, Britain, the United States, and the Soviet Union brought home to me how inadequate were existing measures (mostly based on official statistics) of the Soviet war effort. After hearing my paper, Peter Wiles introduced himself to me, giving me to understand that he approved intensely of what I had done, while at the same time disbelieving it completely. From that moment I was drawn inexorably into a task which has lasted twice as long as the war which provided its subject.

The whole thing would have been impossible without the work of Abram Bergson and others in the two postwar decades, sponsored by the RAND Corporation of the United States Air Force. I am grateful to Bergson himself, and also to his former collaborators Janet Chapman and Lynn Turgeon, for their recollections, advice, and comments.

One of the features of western independent evaluations of Soviet economic progress was always the creative tension between American can-do and British scepticism. More recently, Russian economists have joined the fray. I benefited more than I can say from the steadfast support and friendship of Julian Cooper, Bob Davies, and Peter Wiles. Michael Ellman, Peter Gatrell, Phil Hanson, Holland Hunter, Grigorii Khanin, and the late Alec Nove read my work, criticised it, and encouraged me in it.

At Warwick I was lucky to find myself in a sympathetic, research-minded, intellectual environment. The University supported my work with regular periods of study leave. My Department's economic history workshop, including in particular Stephen Broadberry,

Nick Crafts, and Bryan Sadler (the latter also drawing on his experience as a corporal in charge of warlike stores for the British Army), heard reports of my progress and discussed the issues with me. My colleague Jeffrey Round used his wide knowledge of social accounting for developing economies to help me round many awkward corners, especially for the purposes of appendix F. Nick Crafts and his collaborator Terry Mills advised me on the subject matter of appendix N.

I am grateful to the Centre for Russian and East European Studies, University of Birmingham, the intellectual home of Bob Davies and Phil Hanson, and of its director Julian Cooper. Over many years I have drawn freely on its unrivalled human resources, as well as the resources of the Baykov Library. John Dunstan kindly helped me with data on Soviet education for appendix M. The Centre circulated several preliminary stages of my research as discussion papers in the Soviet Industrialisation Project series. I am particularly grateful to Betty Bennett, the Project secretary, for her efficient and friendly assistance.

When I was half way through, Nick Crafts (then Professor of Economic History) suggested the advantages of external research finance. For two crucial years, from September 1991, to August 1993, the Leverhulme Trust funded my research under the title 'Soviet production, employment, and the defence burden, 1937 and 1940–5'. Ken Wallis (then chairman of my department) helped me through the process of application, and then to hire an assistant. I was exceptionally lucky to be able to appoint Edwin Bacon (now of the Centre for Russian and East European Studies, University of Birmingham) to the project. For two years he worked with me, travelled for the project, represented the project, and produced outstanding results. In the present book his work is reflected in evaluations of wartime Soviet civilian industrial production (appendix C), and of the contribution of forced labour to Soviet wartime labour supplies (appendix I). It is a sign of his energy and talents that his own excellent book, *The Gulag at war: Stalin's forced labour system in the light of the archives* (Macmillan), appeared well before this one in 1994. I would also like to acknowledge my gratitude to the Leverhulme trustees, and especially the officers of that time, Sir Rex Richards and Mr D.A. Thompson, who not only approved my original application but also, at short notice, agreed additional funds to take advantage of the new situation in Russian archives which took shape in 1991.

During my research I learnt deep respect for the work of Russian colleagues. Their publications of the Soviet period formed the indispensable starting point of my research. Their archival skills, informed by tradition, training, and wide knowledge, gave my work a dimension which was completely unanticipated from the vantage point of its origins in the mid-1980s. I wish to thank first of all Nikolai Simonov for his invaluable advice and support, as well as for many companionable hours in his uncomplaining company; his ability to locate the significant detail of the Russian historical landscape in its sweeping vastness never failed to astonish me. I am also indebted to Gennadii Kostyrchenko, Georgii Kumanev, Elena Tiurina (director of the Russian State Economic Archive), and Margarita Zinich, who has written recently:

> In the conditions of today's process of critically rethinking all the periods of the Soviet state, it is becoming obvious that the history of the Great Patriotic War also requires deep study and objective analysis of all factors determining both the victory of the Soviet people, and the burden of the ordeals, the bitterness of defeats, the tragedy of irreplaceable losses. The past war will for a long time move the hearts of people, and will evoke in them the pain of bereavement and the joy of victories. And of course the memory of the terrible misfortune which fascism inflicted on millions of families.[1]

The real rethinking of World War II history is just beginning in Russia. 'Why did the victors in the war lose the peace?' is a novel question for Russians. It was posed recently by Andrei Illarionov, who criticised the 'propaganda of uniqueness' in Russian history.[2] Illarionov argued that the Russian experience is too often portrayed in terms of exceptional achievements and incomparable suffering. Systematic comparison with the parallel success and failure of other countries' economies and institutions can throw much light on Russia's postwar economic development. The unique drama of the Russian story makes for a good play in a darkened theatre; but it also shuts out the light.

Thus I gained many unexpected insights from involvement with the international workgroup on 'Economic mobilisation for World War II: six great powers in international comparison, 1937–5', funded by the Volkswagen Foundation during 1993–4. Those who participated in its meetings in Bielefeld and at Warwick included Werner Abelshauser, Stephen Broadberry, Vladimir Busygin, Nick Crafts, Akira Hara, Peter Howlett, Grigorii Khanin, Stefan Merl, Alan Milward, Avner Offer, Richard Overy, Rolf Petri, Hugh Rockoff, Bryan Sadler, and Vera Zamagni, and to all of them I would like to express my sincere thanks.

I owe much to John Barber for the years over which we have collaborated in various projects; his experience of Russian life, his deep knowledge of Russian society and history, and his friendship, have contributed greatly to my work.

I am grateful to Lyn Chatterton, John Haslam, and Michael Holdsworth of Cambridge University Press for their professional support, and to Barbara Docherty for her watchful editorial skill.

Arithmetic is the essence of national accounts, which are basically exercises in addition. My work depended on the computer technology which enabled repeated revision of GNP estimates, taking into account every minor change in basic data and assumptions. To press a button can now replicate arithmetic in a few seconds which, four decades ago, would have faced teams of workers with months of painstaking labour. I am grateful to my Department for its technical support, and to my colleague Graham Wright for his technical skill and forbearance.

The present work rests on many assumptions, approximations, and interpolations. Other researchers will find many mistakes. Many of the mistakes will make little or no difference, or will offset each other, but some will matter. As far as I am aware, the critical reader will find most scope for misgiving or scepticism in appendices D, E, and F. On many matters I have received much good advice, but my advisers are not responsible for the results, because I have also allowed my own instincts to guide me. When all is said and done, I alone am responsible for all errors and omissions, suspected and unsuspected, large and small.

When I began this work, one of my children was a toddler, the other a baby. Now they are both young persons. Sam and Jamie have grown up with this book. I am grateful to them for lighting my life, if not lightening my work.

From my own childhood I remember my father at home in the evenings, auditing company accounts, adding and balancing columns of figures with accounting paper and a silver propelling pencil. This book is dedicated to my father, Roger Harrison, and also to the memory of my mother, Betty Harrison.

Acknowledgements

Chapter 2 is a revised version of work previously published as Harrison (1995a).

Parts of chapter 6 previously appeared in Harrison (1995b). Earlier stages of the research project on which this book is based also gave rise to a number of other working papers and publications: Bacon (1992a), (1992b), (1993a), (1993b), (1994); Bacon and Harrison (1993); Gatrell and Harrison (1993); Harrison (1989a), (1989b), (1990a), (1990b), (1990c), (1991), (1992), (1993a), (1993b), (1994c), (1994e), (1994f), (1994g).

Abbreviations and acronyms

CIA	Central Intelligence Agency
GARF	*Gosudarstvennyi arkhiv Rossiiskoi Federatsii* (State Archive of the Russian Federation), formerly TsGAOR SSSR (the USSR Central State Archive of the October Revolution)
GDP	gross domestic product (see the Guide to national accounts, p. xxvi)
GKO	*Gosudarstvennyi komitet oborony* (State Defence Committee, the war cabinet)
GNP	gross national product (see the Guide to national accounts)
Goskomstat	*Gosudarstvennyi komitet statistiki* (State Committee for Statistics), formerly known as TsSU (q.v.)
Gosplan	*Gosudarstvennaia planovaia komissiia* (State Planning Commission)
GSP	gross social product (see the Guide to national accounts)
GULAG	*Glavnoe upravlenie ispravitel'no-trudovykh lagerei* (Chief administration of corrective-labour camps of the NKVD (q.v.))
kolkhoz	*kollektivnoe khoziastvo* (collective farm)
MBMW	machinebuilding and metalworking
MPS	Material Product System (of accounts, of which the GSP and NMP (q.v.) were the fundamental concepts; see further the Guide to national accounts)
narkomat	*narodnyi komissariat* (people's commissariat), renamed *ministerstvo* (ministry) in 1946

Narkomtsvetmet	*Narodnyi komissariat tsvetnoi metallurgii* (People's Commissariat of Nonferrous Metallurgy)
Narkomugol	*Narodnyi komissariat ugol'noi promyshlennosti* (People's Commissariat of the Coal Industry)
Narkomvneshtorg	*Narodnyi komissariat vneshnei torgovli* (People's Commissariat of External Trade)
NKO	*Narodnyi komissariat oborony* (People's Commissariat of Defence, responsible for the army, including the air force)
NKVD	*Narodnyi komissariat vnutrennykh del* (People's Commissariat of Internal Affairs, responsible for internal security, internal troops, prisons, labour camps and colonies, and labour settlements)
NKVMF	*Narodnyi komissariat voenno-morskogo flota* (People's Commissariat of the Navy)
NMP	net material product (see the Guide to national accounts)
NNP	net national product (see the Guide to national accounts)
OECD	Organisation for Economic Cooperation and Development
Politburo	*Politicheskii biuro* (Political Bureau of the All-Union Communist Party of Bolsheviks Central Committee)
PPP	*promyshlenno-proizvodstvennyi personal* (industrial-production personnel), comprising both manual and nonmanual employees, inclusive of engineering and technical personnel, apprentices and 'junior service personnel' (*mladshii obsluzhivaiushchii personal*), and security staff
RGAE	*Rossiiskii gosudarstvennyi arkhiv ekonomiki* (Russian State Economics Archive), formerly TsGANKh SSSR (the USSR Central State Archive of the National Economy)
RTsKhIDNI	*Rossiiskii tsentr khraneniia i izucheniia dokumentov noveishei istorii* (Russian Centre for Conservation and Investigation of Documents of Recent History), formerly TsPA-IML (the Central Party Archive of the Institute of Marxism-Leninism)
SNA	System of National Accounts (of which GDP or GNP (q.v.) were the fundamental concepts; see further the Guide to national accounts)

SNIP	Soviet National Income and Product (the title of Abram Bergson's postwar research project at the RAND Corporation of the United States Air Force)
SNK *or* Sovnarkom	*Sovet narodnykh komissarov* (Council of People's Commissars)
TFD	total final demand
TsK	*Tsentral'nyi komitet* (Central Committee of the All-Union Communist Party of Bolsheviks)
TsSU	*Tsentral'noe statisticheskoe upravlenie* (Central Statistical Administration), previously known as TsUNNKhU (Central Administration of National Economic Accounts), later renamed Goskomstat (q.v.)

Guide to national accounts

The material product system of accounts

A standard methodology of the material product system (MPS) of accounts was published by the United Nations only in 1971.[1] This description of the MPS deals only with Soviet practice of the 1940s; while the general principles were also followed in postwar decades and in other state socialist countries, details were subject to revision, and the treatment of defence outlays remained particularly uncodified.

Under the MPS, the net material product (NMP) can be calculated from the output side, the income side, and the expenditure side. On the output side, the NMP PRODUCED was calculated as the GROSS SOCIAL PRODUCT (GSP) of the sphere of material production (industry, agriculture, construction, freight transport, and trade), *less* PRODUCTIVE CONSUMPTION.

The gross (sometimes 'total' or 'global') social product was the sum of the gross outputs of material products of firms. It therefore double-counted intermediate transactions both within the production branch, and between branches of the material production sphere. 'Material production' refers to the production of all goods, and of intermediate services, but final services are excluded. Freight transport was considered productive, but passenger transport was not. Military services were considered final services, so were not counted; the transport of parts for assembly into weapons in a defence factory was productive, but the transport of soldiers and weapons to the front was not counted as material production.

'Productive consumption' refers to the sum of intermediate transactions, double-counted in the gross social product of the material production sphere. The utilisation of parts and materials for the manufacture of machinery, including weapons, was of course productive consumption. The utilisation of heating, lighting, and paper in the director's office of a defence factory counted as productive consumption, but the same in the office of the director of a hospital, or of the commanding officer of a regiment, counted as final use, not productive consumption.

On the income side, material production generates the primary incomes of society: the wages, profits, and indirect taxes yielded by agencies engaged in the production of goods (*less* government subsidies paid to them). Since taxes on the turnover of goods are part of this primary income, the NMP is measured at prevailing prices, including net indirect taxes. After redistribution through the fiscal and credit system, and the adjustments described below, these incomes also form the total of material uses.

On the expenditure side, the NMP UTILISED is calculated on a material resources-available basis as the NMP PRODUCED, *less* LOSSES, *plus* NET IMPORTS.

Losses involved the unforeseen depreciation of material resources arising from exogenous insurable contingencies (fires, floods, etc.); being 'exogenous', they excluded losses normally arising in the course of production and consumption; being 'insurable', they excluded acts of war.

In the national accounts, net imports were merchandise imports, *less* exports, measured at domestic ruble prices. In published trade statistics, exports were measured at the usually lower 'foreign-trade' ruble prices set before conversion to dollars at the official dollar/ruble exchange rate, and imports were measured at the usually lower foreign-trade ruble prices found by conversion from dollars, again at the official rate. The difference between net imports in domestic rubles and foreign-trade rubles (i.e. the import tariff, *less* the export subsidy) was counted as a secret revenue to the state budget, as well as part of the primary incomes generated in the production sphere.

On the expenditure side, the material resources available were utilised under various headings. They could be consumed or accumulated, or added to reserves. The *material consumption fund* normally consisted of the material consumption of households (sometimes including the subsistence of military personnel) and of 'nonproductive' institutions supplying final services (including the materials and fuels used in military operations and defence construction). The *material accumulation fund* normally consisted of net additions to fixed capital (depreciation being counted as productive consumption), inventories, and farm stocks. The other use of material resources available was for additions to the *reserve fund* (sometimes 'state reserves'). 'Reserves' were an often shadowy concept which could include military stockpiles along with strategic reserves of commodities and precious metals.

The precise location of *defence outlays* on material products, and the relationship between defence outlays recorded in the state budget and the material consumption and accumulation of the armed forces, remained notoriously ill defined and subject to revision. If defence were to be treated like any other activity in the 'nonproductive' (service) sector, defence uses of material products would be classified under the *personal material consumption* of soldiers (their subsistence and kit, and the portion of their pay used for purchases of goods, but not personal spending on consumer services, personal savings, or tax payments); *institutional material consumption* (e.g. outlays on fuel and other consumable materials; the material cost of drugs and the consumption of heating and lighting by military clinics and cinemas; but not the wages of employees hired to entertain and educate the troops, and prevent or cure their diseases); and *accumulation* (fixed capital items such as buildings and base facilities, and perhaps also military fortifications; but weapons and equipment tended to receive special treatment).

The System of National Accounts

The System of National Accounts (SNA) methodology was first published in 1953, with major revisions in 1968 and 1993.[2] The basic concept of the SNA is the *gross domestic product* (GDP). Like its material product counterpart, GDP may be measured from the point of view of output, income, and expenditure. On the output side, GDP is the total of *value added* in the domestic production of final goods and services. Being 'gross', it includes the value added to products from capital consumption.

The measure of value added is the incomes generated in production. On the income side, GDP at factor cost is therefore equal to the *factor incomes* (wages and gross profits, including depreciation) generated in the domestic production of goods and services.

On the expenditure side, GDP is distributed among various final uses: *household consumption, government consumption, gross domestic investment*, and *net exports*. Such outlays are carried out at prevailing prices; the adjustment to factor cost involves subtraction of *indirect taxes, net of subsidies*.

GDP may be converted to the *gross national product* (GNP) which, being 'national', includes factor incomes (wages and profits) earned in other countries and remitted to the home country by nationals. For the

Soviet Union in the 1940s, foreign factor incomes were negligible or zero, so GNP and GDP may be used interchangeably. In this book I refer usually to GNP rather than GDP for the sake of continuity with previous scholarship. If one were starting from scratch, it would be more in line with modern conventions to refer to GDP.

The *net national product* (NNP) used to be simply called the 'national income'; it is found by subtracting *capital consumption* from GNP. It is also a convenient link to the MPS accountancy. Subtracting net factor incomes from abroad converts NNP to the net domestic product. The net domestic product at factor cost in the SNA, and NMP produced at prevailing prices in the MPS, are identically equal on the condition that purchases of final services are exactly matched by indirect taxes on purchases of final goods.

In some circumstances a still broader concept than GNP can be useful. This is TOTAL FINAL DEMAND (TFD), measured by GNP *plus* NET IMPORTS, which is also equivalent to total outlays on household consumption, government consumption, and gross investment, including outlays on net imports. TFD therefore corresponds to a total resources-available concept, and is the SNA equivalent of NMP utilised.

In the SNA accountancy, *defence outlays* are outlays on the supply of military services, comprising the *pay and subsistence* of military personnel, the *procurement of weapons*, the *cost of military operations* (e.g. fuel and transport), and *defence construction* (e.g. barracks, airfields, fortifications). All defence outlays are counted as government consumption, even when they involve defence construction or additions to military stockpiles. Investment in defence factories, on the other hand, adds to the productive capacity of society, and is counted as firms' gross investment, not in the defence budget.

The MPS and SNA compared

The material product system (all at prevailing prices)

NMP produced	=	gross social product (GSP) of industry, agriculture, freight transport and communications, construction, and trade, *less* productive consumption
	=	value of final goods at prevailing prices
	=	primary incomes of the productive sphere
NMP utilised	=	NMP produced, *less* losses, *plus* net imports
	=	material consumption by households and nonproductive institutions, *plus* material accumulation, *plus* change in reserves

The System of National Accounts (all at factor cost)

GDP = gross domestic value added (the final output of goods and services)
= domestic wages, *plus* gross domestic profits (factor incomes)
= household consumption, *plus* government consumption, *plus* gross domestic investment, *plus* net exports (all at prevailing prices), *less* net indirect taxes (final expenditures)
GNP = GDP, *plus* net foreign factor incomes
NNP = GNP, *less* capital consumption
= NMP produced, *plus* the value of final services, *plus* net foreign factor incomes, *less* net indirect taxes
TFD = GDP, *less* net exports
= household consumption, *plus* government consumption, *plus* gross domestic investment (all at market prices), *less* indirect taxes

Gross and net

The words 'gross' and 'net' are used in economics in many contexts, and with many distinct meanings. This book is no exception.

The word 'net' may be used to indicate that a balance has been struck. *Net imports* are the value of imports, net of exports (so *net exports* are the value of exports, net of imports). *Net indirect taxes* are indirect taxes, net of subsidies.

Gross may mean 'gross of capital consumption'. Thus, in the SNA, net value added is *gross value added*, net of capital consumption; likewise, net national product is the *gross national product*, net of capital consumption, and net investment is *gross investment*, net of capital consumption

The most complex meanings of gross versus net arise in an input/output context. Here gross means 'gross of outlays on intermediate products'. Thus, in the MPS, net material product is the *gross social product*, net of productive consumption.

More generally, net output (value added) is *gross output*, net of intermediate utilisation. Consider an input/output table with an inter-industry matrix of intermediate uses (the **U**-matrix) of $m \times m$ sectors $(1,\ldots,i,j,\ldots m)$; x_{ij} is the i,jth element of **U**. There are column matrices **F** for total final demand, **M** for net imports, **X** for gross outputs (so that $\mathbf{X} = \mathbf{U} + \mathbf{F} - \mathbf{M}$) and **V** for value added (so that $\mathbf{X} = \mathbf{U} + \mathbf{V}$). Then gross output and value added of the ith good are calculated as:

$$v_i = x_i - \sum_j x_{ji}$$

$$x_i = \sum_j x_{ij} + f_i - m_i$$

Note that gross output in this input/output sense involves double-counting of intermediate transactions involving intra-industry uses of the *i*th good within the *i*th sector, x_{ii}. Thus, the greater the vertical disintegration of the *i*th sector, the greater will be its gross output. Eliminating the double-counting gives that part of gross output which leaves the *i*th sector for final or intermediate use elsewhere, $x_i - x_{ii}$. We will call this *finished output* (not necessarily final output, but at least 'finished with' by the sector of most recent origin).

When *ex ante* final demands (including the demand for net exports, –**M**) are known, **K** may be calculated as the matrix of Leontief multipliers given by $(\mathbf{I} - \mathbf{A})^{-1}$, where **I** is the identity matrix, and **A** is the matrix of technical coefficients $a_{ij} = x_{ij}/x_j$. In this case, *gross output* (of the *i*th good) *required* directly and indirectly from domestic sources for the *n*th use in final demand is calculated from:

$$\sum_j k_{ij} \cdot (f_{jn} - m_j)$$

In the above case, the requirement for gross output is calculated 'net of imports'. However, gross may also be used in the sense of 'gross of imports'. *Gross output* (of the *i*th good) *required* directly and indirectly from all sources, domestic and foreign, for the *n*th use in final demand, is calculated simply as:

$$\sum_j k_{ij} \cdot f_{jn} \text{ (i.e. gross of imports)}$$

Gross available output of the *i*th good is used in this book in two different contexts, and with two different meanings. First, in the material-balance sense, gross available output of the *i*th good is used to mean:

$$x_i + m_i - \Delta s_i$$

where Δs is stockbuilding; when stockbuilding is negative, it means all the units of commodity *i* which were made physically available from any source (domestic production, imports, or stocks).

Second, in the direct-plus-indirect requirements sense, commodity *i* is made 'available' to satisfy final demands either directly as a final product, or indirectly embodied in other products from domestic production, net imports, or stocks released. In this sense, gross available output of the *i*th good is given by:

$$\sum_j k_{ij} \cdot (f_j - \Delta s_j)$$

A final complication arises when gross and net output have to be qualified with respect to capital consumption. As stated above, net output is gross output, net of intermediate utilisation; but each may be gross or net of capital consumption. In this book, gross output is always gross of capital consumption, as well of intermediate purchases. Net output is sometimes gross, sometimes net of capital consumption. To avoid confusion I avoid the term 'net output' altogether and write 'value added' in its place; *gross and net value added* are both net output, respectively gross and net of capital consumption.

Note on index number relativity

Consider an index of the current, nominal value of GNP in 1937 expressed as a per centage of 1928 (we call 1928 the *base year*, and 1937 the *current year*; p_t is the set of prices, and q_t the set of quantities produced, in year t):[1]

$$\textit{Nominal GNP index} = \frac{\sum p_{37} \cdot q_{37}}{\sum p_{28} \cdot q_{28}}$$

To find the change in real GNP in 1937 (the current year), compared with 1928 (the base year), this index must be divided ('deflated') by a price index. The price index can be weighted by the structure of output either in the base year (a *Laspeyres index*) or in the current year (a *Paasche index*). In conformity with the Gerschenkron effect, we expect the Laspeyres index to show a large increase, because the prices of food and consumer products grew rapidly over the period, and in 1928 agriculture and light industry had the largest weight in the structure of output. The Paasche price index will show a smaller increase, because machinery prices were relatively stable, and the weight of machinery in the structure of output in 1937 was relatively large.

Real GNP, measured by the nominal value of output, deflated by the Laspeyres price index, will therefore appear to grow more slowly. In fact, it will form a Paasche index of volume, weighted in this case by the current (1937) structure of output, as the following expression shows:

$$\textit{Paasche volume index} = \frac{\textit{nominal value index}}{\textit{Laspeyres price index}}$$

$$= \frac{\Sigma p_{37} \cdot q_{37} / \Sigma p_{28} \cdot q_{28}}{\Sigma p_{37} \cdot q_{28} / \Sigma p_{28} \cdot q_{28}}$$

$$= \frac{\Sigma p_{37} \cdot q_{37}}{\Sigma p_{37} \cdot q_{28}}$$

In this book, the converse is always preferred. Index numbers of real output are always Laspeyres, with 1937 or 1940 as the base year, and price indexes are always Paasche. Where necessary, the nominal value of output is deflated by a Paasche price index to give real output in the Laspeyres form:

$$\textit{Laspeyres volume index} = \frac{\textit{nominal value index}}{\textit{Paasche price index}}$$

$$= \frac{\Sigma p_{37} \cdot q_{37} \,/\, \Sigma p_{28} \cdot q_{28}}{\Sigma p_{37} \cdot q_{37} \,/\, \Sigma p_{28} \cdot q_{37}}$$

$$= \frac{\Sigma p_{28} \cdot q_{37}}{\Sigma p_{28} \cdot q_{28}}$$

Introduction

'A statistic is just a collection of anecdotes' (Peter Wiles)

National accounts are traditionally the concern of the élite. It was when men and taxes were to be levied for the king's service that enumeration became a prerequisite of government. Consecutive millennia may have separated the Roman census takers who required Mary and Joseph to return to Bethlehem to be taxed from the Norman authors of the Domesday Book, and from the Russian local government statisticians of a century ago, but they were all driven by the same imperative of state. Their censuses of population and wealth all contributed to the calculation of national resources potentially available to government.

Quantities are the essence of high level decisions. Generals in charge of operations decide how many thousand soldiers and guns they need, and how many casualties can be expected. Chancellors decide sums to be spent, raised in taxes, and borrowed. Police officials base their deployments (in numbers of personnel) on numbers of crimes reported and awaiting detection. Hospital administrators wrestle with numbers of patients, beds available, and the length of waiting lists for admission.

The view from below is often very different. Popular views of national statistics commonly embody distrust. The distrust has at least two distinct origins. One is the use of statistics by officials to claim authority for a self-serving lie. The lie may serve the legitimacy of the government (for example, to support a claim that unemployment has fallen when, on a consistent definition, it has actually risen). The lie may also serve particular ends of policy (for example, by claiming that households are better able to bear a tax than they are in reality). This view of statistics was expressed in the well known observation of Benjamin Disraeli: there are 'lies, damned lies, and statistics'.

Another source of popular distrust is that statistics based on large numbers of observations are an abstraction from lived personal experience. Aggregation necessarily involves the destruction of specific detail. Every person's experience of unemployment or access to goods and services is individual; when aggregated with others', some essential aspect is always lost. To the person who hasn't got a job, unemployment is 100 percent; this idea expresses the loss of the quality of specific truth involved in statistical aggregation.

When we turn to the statistical systems of state socialism in the USSR and postwar eastern Europe, we find all these problems compounded in layer upon layer. First, the government régime attached extraordinary importance to quantification. Its control of society and the economy rested upon the administrative capacity to allocate resources in physical quantities from the centre. The régime's legitimacy rested upon claims about the level and rate of growth of national output, productivity, and living standards. Not only were figures the stuff of policy, but the practice of statistics was rendered largely subservient to political ends.

In consequence, popular distrust of official statistics was hugely magnified. Of course this was just part of a larger pattern of popular distrust of all the pronouncements of government and party officials in a system which rested in part on secretiveness. Thus, official figures tended to claim a higher level and faster growth of living standards than could readily be perceived by ordinary people. Official secrecy under state socialism created a privileged class within the circle of light cast by information 'for official use', and an unprivileged class in the outer darkness beyond. Secrecy in resource allocation underpinned the discretionary powers of officialdom. The suppression of figures both on the distribution of cash incomes, and on privileged access to goods and services not readily available for cash, also kept ordinary people in the dark about the lifestyle of the élite.

The two origins of popular distrust of official figures gave rise to distinct popular responses. One was the belief that all aggregate statistics are lies; the material of popular experience is impossible to quantify, and the only objective reality is the raw, unprocessed experience of personal witness. This is a view which the quantitative economist is professionally bound to reject. By definition, large scale historical processes such as long-run economic growth and the impact of world wars had an inescapable quantitative dimension. Ultimately, World War II was decided by quantities – that side won the war which had the largest combined GNP at the outset, and which was willing and able to throw the greatest quantity of men and munitions into the battlefield.

Another response, less unsympathetic to us, was the idea that there is truth in numbers, only not in the official numbers: the official figure is a lie, beneath which is concealed the true figure. The lie is shown to be a lie because it conflicts with popular experience, which is also the criterion for acceptance of the truthful figure. This view was taken, for example, by the Hungarian economist János Kornai in his work on shortage economics:

> In many cases the conclusive 'evidence' supporting a proposition is provided by those who live in a socialist country. Do they recognise the situation described ... ? Does what is written coincide with what they experience day after day as consumers or producers, managers or employees, buyers or sellers? I also see myself as a 'witness' of this kind. Moreover, I have spoken over several decades with many other 'witnesses' and read many case studies, accounts, minutes and written reports, interviews, and sociographical studies that can be taken as pieces of 'evidence'.[1]

And in a footnote Kornai continued:

> Many researchers airily dismiss such 'evidence' as merely anecdotal and beneath the attention of men of science. In fact, this kind of evidence often leads much closer to an understanding of the truth than many more ambitious analyses on a higher plane that rest upon distorted official data.

Philip Hanson, observing the 'combat of émigré truth-tellers against western specialists', acknowledges the strength of such witness testimony, and points out that 'In understanding what is happening in a closed society, it is no small advantage to have lived in it'.[2]

The Russian economist G.I. Khanin, presenting his own, unofficial estimates of Soviet long-run economic growth, listed various criteria by which alternative figures should be judged. The last, but not the least, states that 'the resulting evaluations should not contradict the daily living experience of the broad masses, whether in the sphere of production or of consumption'.[3] Continuing more recently in the same vein, Khanin commented on the postwar efforts of the American economists led by Abram Bergson to rebuild Soviet national accounting aggregates to western specifications:

> It seems to me the biggest mistake in the investigations of Bergson's school was their exclusive concentration on purely statistical problems. [The study of] statistics was often disarticulated from the economy as a whole, and, especially, from the character of society itself. Such seclusion within a narrow sphere of investigation, for such a specific object as the Soviet economy, could not proceed without consequences. Nowhere could I find evidence that the authors of this school had read the daily Soviet press, satirical works about Soviet

> reality, the magazine *Krokodil*, émigré writers' books, i.e. that literature which yields a more or less truthful description of Soviet reality.[4]

Since this book largely follows the footsteps of the Bergson school, there is an issue here which we cannot avoid.

I hope that the results of this book will not find themselves at variance with 'living experience'. But the task of economic history is to account for trends, averages, and dispersions among whole populations, not the unique specificities of each individual's life. Therefore, I do not regard experiential data as evidentially superior to quantitative records. Paul Gregory, the economic historian of pre-revolutionary Russia, has warned against reliance on anecdotal evidence for the study of economic trends. Anecdote is selective by nature, and tends to give undue prominence to what is extraordinary and dramatic, not to what is typical or humdrum. Anecdote makes an unreliable guide to the average. Events, not trends, are the subject of anecdote, and Gregory warns that contemporary observers – even professional economists – are 'notoriously poor interpreters of economic events'.[5]

Life does not speak for itself. The facts are made to speak by those who construct them. No privilege can be accorded to the testimony of insiders and witnesses just because they were there. The sum of experience does not speak with a single voice, any more than do statistical sums. The aggregated testimony of witnesses is a social artefact, just like statistical truth. There is no single, objective truth waiting to be discovered beneath the surface of the lie. The Soviet GNP is not a hidden number awaiting discovery, but an aggregation of assumptions and hypotheses about a multi-dimensional reality which resists reduction to a unique figure.

The structure of this book is as follows. In chapter 1, I propose some research issues in light of the nature of warfare on the eastern front, the economic background to the war, the unexpected resilience of the Soviet economy under German attack, and the heavy current costs and capital losses of the war to the Soviet economy. Chapter 2 presents 'an inside view' – the official accounts of Soviet national income and product drawn up in wartime or just after the war. In chapter 3, I discuss the main western precedents for independent reconstruction of Soviet economic statistics and evaluation of economic performance. Chapters 4 and 5 proceed with the substantive work of rebuilding series for industrial production (chapter 4), and GNP (chapter 5). Trends in employment and productivity are analysed, along with changes in the role, composition, and requirements of wartime outlays. Soviet trends are also presented in international comparison. Chapter 6 gives special attention to the vexed question of the role of foreign aid. In chapter 7, I review the evidence of Soviet capital losses arising from the war and their long-term consequences. In chapter 8, I briefly present some overall conclusions.

1 The research agenda

The Eastern Front

Hitler's war against the Soviet Union began on 22 June 1941. His orders to the German Army were to destroy the Red Army defenders and secure Soviet territory up to the 'AA' (Archangel–Astrakhan) line, which ran south-east from Archangel in the White Sea to Moscow's rear, then south along the Volga river to Astrakhan on the Caspian Sea.

Huge German forces swept into the Soviet Union's Baltic republics, Belorussia, the Ukraine, and Russia itself. By the end of September, having advanced more than a thousand kilometres across a front more than a thousand kilometres wide, they had captured Kiev, established a stranglehold around Leningrad, and stood at the gates of Moscow.

In the autumn of 1941, by means of nationalist appeals and harsh discipline, Stalin and his generals rallied their people. The battle of Moscow denied Hitler his chance of a quick victory. Moscow was saved, and Leningrad did not surrender. There followed a year of inconclusive moves and counter-moves on each side, but the German successes appeared more striking. In the spring and summer of 1942 German forces advanced more hundreds of kilometres across the south of Russia towards Stalingrad and the Caucasian oilfields.

But these forces were destined for physical destruction in the Red Army's defence of Stalingrad, and its winter counter-offensive. Their position now untenable, the German forces in the south began a long retreat. In the summer of 1943, Hitler staged his last great offensive in the east on the Kursk salient; the offensive failed, and was answered by a more devastating counter-offensive. The German Army could no longer force even a stalemate, and its final defeat became certain. Even so, the liberation of Soviet territory from German occupation (including the final relief of Leningrad) took a further eighteen months. The

German army did not collapse in defeat. As a result, the Red Army's journey from Kursk to Berlin occupied two years of bloody fighting.

The economic aspect of the war was fundamental to it. On the eastern front it involved each side in the sending of tens of millions of soldiers into battle, their arming with hundreds of thousands of aircraft, tanks, and field guns with billions of shells, and tens of millions of rifles with tens of billions of cartridges. Just to create these forces required the expenditure of colossal resources; each in turn largely destroyed the other, at the same time imposing additional mortality and destruction on an unprecedented scale upon the civilian population and assets of the territories over which they fought.

This book is not about events or personalities, and very little happens in it. It is almost devoid of anecdotes. It is about trends and processes. Of course the processes which it describes were the result of human activity, and it enumerates millions of human beings, but even the people are numbered only to the nearest thousand, or hundred thousand, and there are hardly any named individuals. It reveals only trends and averages; it deals with what was typical, not what was particular or individual. At the same time, the individual and the particular have not disappeared from it; every statistic in it contains a distillation of some essential aspect of the lives of thousands upon thousands of individuals, each with their own unique experience of extraordinary events. Warfare on the eastern front changed the lives of hundreds of millions of people. Tens of millions died prematurely, whether in combat, through genocide, or from undernourishment and overwork. Those who were left behind could never forget the terrible events which have shaped the subject matter of this book.

An Economic Background

World War II was the culminating event of thirty years' violent restructuring in the world economy. During the century from 1815 to 1914, bounded at each extremity by war, the world economy expanded on the basis of relatively unrestricted trade and movements of capital and labour. By the end of the nineteenth century, however, leaders of several newly industrialising countries were turning to the idea of economic stabilisation through tariff protection, and the regulation of trade on lines of greater national economic self-sufficiency. German leaders aimed at the pursuit of Germany's national economic security through trade within a closed economic space based on a colonial empire. The naval arms race which they launched in support of this objective ended in Germany's military and diplomatic encirclement by Britain, France, and Russia, the powers of the Triple Entente; Germany's attempt to break out of containment by attacking France and Russia precipitated World War I.

After World War I, the world economy entered an era of far greater instability and uncertainty than had been customary for the nineteenth century. Its integration was now threatened by the economic weakness of Britain, and by the isolation of Germany and Russia. The trend to disintegration was enormously accelerated by the slump of 1929, which sent deflationary shock waves rippling around the world. In their wake the great powers joined in a fierce competitive struggle for national shares in a world market which was now much smaller than before. In the 1930s the world economy disintegrated into a number of relatively closed trading blocs. The British, French, and Dutch reorganised their trade on colonial lines. With the rise of Hitler, Germany resumed the perspective of regulated trade within a colonial empire in central and eastern Europe, setting in motion a new rivalry with other interested regional powers. Italy and the states of the former Austro–Hungarian Empire established closer, more exclusive trading links; Italy's sights were also set on an African empire. The Americans and Japanese competed for influence in East Asia and the Pacific. The Soviet Union, largely shut out of western markets, also developed a closed economic space within the frontiers of the old Russian Empire.

In the worldwide economic disintegration which followed the slump lay some of the causes of World War II. The economies of Germany, Italy, and Japan were too small, too lacking in diversity, to be viable commercial units on their own in the absence of external trade. In varying proportions they depended on others for the supply of food, fuel, and other industrial materials. Acquisition of the purchasing power necessary to acquire these supplies depended upon the competitiveness of their products in foreign markets. One common thread in their course of external aggression was the attempt to secure these supplies and markets by the forcible imposition of a colonial régime upon trading partners. Germany's wars against first Czechoslovakia, then Poland (which drew in France and Britain), and eventually the Soviet Union, were designed in part to establish the conditions for such a colonial régime. Italy's war against France and Britain was waged for a share of colonial assets and markets in Africa. The Japanese campaign in the Far East was both a grab at the British, French, and Dutch colonies, and a counter-measure against American commercial warfare. In these ways, World War II stands in continuity with preexisting trends in the global economy, as their culminating phase.

Of course, World War II was also more than just a continuation of the trends at work in the world since 1914. It marked a moment when the struggle for regional domination took on a global character, and when the dirty business of genocide took its place beside loftier motives of traditional statecraft.

During the interwar years, the Soviet Union began to implement a strategy of national economic development which showed both similarities and differences in comparison with Germany, Italy, and Japan. Among the differences were its paternalistic multinational ethic of the Soviet family of nations with the Russians as 'elder brother', and the modernising goals imposed by bureaucratic decree upon the Soviet economic space. But there were also similarities. One similarity lay in the administrative regulation of external trade; the early Bolsheviks were keen on trade with western Europe and the United States, but only so long as the trade was state-regulated, and did not pose a competitive threat to Soviet industry. After 1931, conditions at home and in the world economy, and the terms of trade, became so unfavourable that regulated trade gave way to almost no trade at all, and the Soviet Union became a virtually closed economy. Another similarity lay in the fact that the closed space within which the Soviet Union pursued economic security during the 1930s, like the economic spaces of Germany, Italy, and Japan, was organised on colonial lines. In the Soviet case the colonies had been inherited from the old Russian Empire; force had been used to establish the Soviet right to the Russian legacy in the wartime years of 1918–21, but by the interwar years this right no longer needed military reinforcement.

Among the factors which drove several powers towards the idea of self-sufficient economic development within a controlled economic space in the first half of the twentieth century were military–economic considerations. War potential was generally seen as determined by the size and self-sufficiency of the economic unit. The country's size was seen as contributing directly to the size of the armed forces which the economy could support. Self-sufficiency was important because it provided guarantees against commercial disruption of the economy in wartime; for example, supply of the army from within a self-sufficient economy could not be interrupted by the enemy's external blockade. Size and self-sufficiency were also mutually connected because, the larger the country, the more likely it was to contain the broad range of minerals and land resources, and large-scale industrial and scientific establishments, necessary for self-sufficient supply of modern industries and armed forces.

Table 1.1. *Population, gross domestic product, and territory of the great powers within contemporary frontiers, 1940*

	Population, million	GDP, international dollars and 1985 prices		Territory	
		total, $ bn	per head, $	total, 000 sq. km	sq. km per 000 people
	(1)	(2)	(3)	(4)	(5)
1 USA	132.1	850.9	6440	7839	59.3
2 UK	48.2	236.8	4910	244	5.1
3 USSR	194.0	345.3	1780	21629	111.5
4 Allied subtotal	374.3	1433.0	3830	29712	79.4
5 Germany	69.8	273.1	3910	469	6.7
6 Italy	45.0	115.1	2560	310	6.9
7 Japan	73.0	139.4	1910	382	5.2
8 Axis subtotal	187.8	527.5	2810	1161	6.2
9 Allies/Axis	2.0	2.7	1.4	25.6	12.8

Sources: Population and (for the market economies) GDP are as Davies, Harrison and Wheatcroft (1994), 270, recalibrated in international dollars and 1985 prices by 1985 GDP/head from Summers Heston (1991), data disks. Soviet GDP/head in 1937 is fixed at 40 per cent of the UK, from Harrison (1994c). Territory is from League of Nations (1938), 16–23, adjusted for Soviet gains of 453,400 square km in 1939–40.

In the respect of size, the Soviet Union was in a more fortunate situation than Germany, Italy, or Japan. The Soviet Union had inherited large size as the successor state to Imperial Russia, whereas the countries of the Axis could only aim to achieve such size by means of territorial annexations. As table 1.1 shows, in comparison to each of Germany, Italy, or Japan, and not counting their colonial territories, the Soviet Union had two and a half to five times the population of each country, one and a half to three times the gross national product, and twenty times the territory. The leaders of the Axis countries believed, however, that the advantages of size and self-sufficiency did not have to be realised beforehand, before the launching of their first aggressive campaigns; size and self-sufficiency could be achieved through expansion, as a by-product (deliberate, not accidental) of the war's initial stage.

The sorry experience of Russia in World War I suggests, however, that the Soviet advantage of size was unlikely to prove decisive on its own.[1]

Russia was 'mighty and impotent'.[2] In World War I her huge territory and population had proved to be assets of doubtful military value. The large Russian army was necessitated in part by nothing more than lengthy frontiers and the difficulty of moving troops from one part to another. A primitive supply system locked up too many soldiers in logistical tasks, compared with the numbers available for frontline duties. In wartime Russia's factory workers and soldiers went hungry, and the army relied to a significant extent upon imported weapons. Thus, even in Russia's case, securing a closed economic space was not only not sufficient for the wartime effectiveness of Russian military power, but was unsustainable in practice.

The Russian Empire was poor. There were several disadvantages to a low GDP per head in wartime. Russia's low prewar GDP per head limited the surplus of resources over basic subsistence which could be diverted from civilian to war uses; it was easier for a rich country than a poor one to commit 50 per cent or more of GDP to military outlays. Low GDP per head also limited the scope for specialisation in the metallurgical and engineering branches of industry essential to manufacture of modern munitions.

Moreover, low GDP per head was associated with a lack of development of technological, commercial and administrative services; these were especially important for purposes of wartime regulation, and their absence limited the scope for wartime economic mobilisation. Low GDP per head was also associated with poorly commercialised agriculture based on peasant farming. Before 1914, it was commonly assumed that the sophisticated infrastructure (and especially external trading links) of the advanced industrial powers was highly fragile and vulnerable to disruption. It was thought that countries specialised in agriculture could more easily survive blockade. With its limitless plains, apparently rugged agrarian economy and export surplus of food, Russia seemed immune to external disruption. However, World War I proved the opposite: a sophisticated infrastructure gave toughness and resilience to more industrialised economies. Without it, less developed, agrarian economies tended to disintegrate under the stress of total war.

In Russia as in Germany the urban populations were deprived, while in the United Kingdom dietary standards of the mass of the population improved, and civilians lived longer, healthier lives. Under the pressure of mobilising resources into combat, urban–rural trade broke down, and the German and Russian countrysides tended to disintegrate into self-sufficient regions, witholding food surpluses from the food-deficit sectors of towns and industries.

Thus in World War I Russia's apparently favourable possession of a large agricultural sector and peasant population was fatally associated with low GDP per head. It was better for a country to have a high GDP per head than food self-sufficiency. Stalin understood the significance of this gap, and had set the goal 'to catch up and overtake' the advanced capitalist countries in output per head. But by World War II, despite more than a decade of rapid, forced-march industrialisation and rearmament under the five-year plans, the gap between Soviet and western incomes had been far from made up. Table 1.1 shows that in 1940 Soviet GNP per head was still the lowest of the great powers: one quarter of American, one third of British, half German, 70 per cent of Italian, and 90 per cent of Japanese incomes.

From a wartime perspective, table 1.1 also shows the overwhelming economic strength of the Allied coalition. On average the three Allied powers outpointed the Axis powers by 2:1 in demographic resources; by nearly 3:1 in overall GNP, and therefore also 1.4:1 in GNP per head; by more than 20:1 in territorial resources, and therefore more than 10:1 in territory per head. Once these economic factors came into play, there was no question but that the Allies could win.

First, however, the Allies had to neutralise three strategic factors on which the Axis powers relied for their early advantage. One was the superior combat organisation of the Germans and Japanese; the attack of their fighting forces had first to be blunted and ground away by prolonged defensive campaigns. Another was the distance of Britain and America from key theatres in Europe, the Mediterranean, and the Pacific; the Axis leaders relied in part on the fact that to a lesser extent British, and more especially American forces had to be projected over great distances, limiting their size and supply, before they could make contact with the enemy. Last was the traditional status of Russia as a second-rate military power based on a third-rate economy. This alone made the concentration of the German attack upon Russia entirely rational. Hitler believed that he could attack the Soviet Union with impunity, in the reasonable expectation of an early Soviet military and economic collapse, while keeping the British and the Americans at a distance, and in the process secure major German war aims.

The research agenda

In World War II, regardless of the military performance of the Red Army, the Soviet economy should have collapsed. This is what poor, agrarian economies, even large, relatively self-sufficient ones, normally did under the impact of a massive attack. The failure of the Soviet economy to conform to this expectation constitutes the background against which this book's research agenda may be considered.

At the same time, in order not to be disappointed, the reader should bear in mind that this book does not explain *all* the reasons why the Soviet economy did not collapse. After all, why the economy did not collapse is just a part of a much bigger question – why the Soviet state, armed forces, and society at large did not collapse, however close they came to the brink, but continued to function under conditions of deep penetration by invading forces. This question has of course been much discussed, and various hypotheses have been advanced.

The interpretation of the Soviet history of World War II is divided in several ways. For example, some consider that the Soviet Union won its war against Germany because of Stalin, his prewar industrialisation and rearmament policies, his wartime leadership, his ability to invoke Russian national feeling and traditions, his strength of strategic purpose, others – in spite of Stalin, his despotic rule, his alienation of the peasantry, his prewar purges, his disastrous errors of wartime generalship:

> A colleague once said: 'The result of the battle of Stalingrad showed that Stalin's basic line had been correct.' An unsympathetic critic retorted: 'Perhaps, if a different policy had been followed, the Germans would not have got as far as Stalingrad.'[3]

And among Stalin's critics there is a further division between some who attribute the German defeat to the military and economic achievements of the Soviet people (in some versions, their 'heroic achievements') despite poor leadership in appalling circumstances, and others who attribute it to Hitler's unforced errors of racial policy (which discouraged collaboration and pushed the anti-German resistance into a unified camp) and military miscalculation (which endangered the German army and disaffected its officer corps). In all these interpretations, as 1995, the year of fiftieth anniversaries, has shown us, the desire to find moral value in the suffering and deaths of millions, and poetic justice in the outcome of the war, remains very strong.[4]

I do not try to find fresh answers to these questions, which deal in events, personalities, and anecdotes, and are therefore (in Paul Gregory's terms) the business of historians, not of *economic* historians.[5] But my task is still of essential interest. It is to define more clearly than before the balance of resources within which such issues were practically resolved – the balance of resources between the USSR and

Germany, among the Allies, and within the Soviet economy between competing civilian and military uses. It was these balances which decided the scope and significance of Hitler's or Stalin's discretion; for example Seweryn Bialer once argued, on the basis of Allied superiority in resources available, that Roosevelt, Churchill, and eventually Stalin too, but not Hitler, could afford mistakes and miscalculations.[6]

The process and outcome of the war also decided the balance of resources with which the Soviet economy would emerge from it. And this would have persistent long-range effects on its postwar development.

This book aims to rebuild the Soviet wartime national accounts. In doing so, it shows in quantitative terms what the Soviet economy looked like under a deep invasion; it aims to describe the process whereby a large but poor, newly industrialising but still in large part agrarian economy survived the experience, went on working, and mobilised its resources. It also enumerates the costs and losses incurred in doing so, and suggests their long- term consequences.

My project began when the means of completing it were still very limited. Far greater detail and reliability than appeared likely at the outset were made possible by the collapse of the Soviet state in 1991, which opened up a new documentary base to independent research. Among the most important resources utilised for this study are the wartime archives of Gosplan and the Ministry of Finance held partly by the State Archive of the Russian Federation (GARF), and partly by the Russian State Economics Archive (RGAE); and wartime documents of the State Defence Committee (GKO) held by the Russian Centre for Conservation and Investigation of Documents of Recent History (RTsKhIDNI), all in Moscow. Significant use has also been made of the original wartime statistical handbook produced afterwards by the USSR Central Statistical Administration (TsSU SSSR), previously available only in limited circulation.

A main product of the rebuilding of the Soviet wartime national account is the light thrown on various conventional formulae to be found in traditional Soviet historiography, which summed up the lessons drawn officially from the wartime economic experience. Best known of these was Stalin's idea that war provides 'an all-round test of a nation's material and spiritual forces', and that the Soviet state had passed this test in economic as in other respects:

> the Soviet system proved not only the best form of organizing the economic and cultural development of the country in the years of peaceful construction, but also the best form of mobilizing all the forces of the people for resistance to the enemy in time of war.[7]

Other conventional formulae, only slightly less well known, ascribe Soviet wartime economic success to a planned economy. The mobilisation of resources, even in the apparently chaotic months after June 1941, is said to have proceeded 'according to a unified plan (*po edinomu planu*)'.[8] Stalin himself remarked that, with the 'fundamental turning point (*korennyi perelom*)' of 1943, the Soviet state had acquired 'a coherent (*slazhennoe*) and rapidly growing war economy'.[9] Such formulae acquired a life of their own and continued to dominate the language of Soviet historiography long after Stalin's name was no longer mentioned.

Economic relationships among the wartime allies can also be studied in sharper focus through the medium of the Soviet wartime national accounts. In a book published at the end of 1947, which remained for fifteen years the only authoritative account of the Soviet war effort, Voznesenskii wrote of the growth of Soviet imports in 1942–3, mainly from Britain and America, compared with the much lower level of 1940:

> a comparison between the amount of these allied deliveries of industrial goods to the U.S.S.R. and the volume of industrial production at the Soviet Socialist enterprises in the same period will show that these deliveries amounted to only about 4 per cent of the domestic production during the war economy period.[10]

This formula ('only 4 per cent'), a source of much American anger, immediately became and remained compulsory for postwar Soviet historians, but its origins were never demonstrated and western scholars contested it.

Evaluations of the long-term consequences of the war were similarly engraved on tablets, which proved to be made of plaster rather than stone. Here the central issue was the number of war deaths, which Stalin put at 7 million, Khrushchev at 20 million, and Brezhnev at 'more than 20 million'.[11] The war was also said to have resulted in capital losses amounting to 'about 30 per cent of national wealth'.[12]

Among the results of the present work are assessments of such issues which start not from uncritical acceptance or reflex rejection of traditional Soviet figures, but from independent evaluation. For the first time, the traditional figures themselves, their meaning and derivation, can be investigated in depth. In the light of past western experience of Soviet GNP evaluations, we can render an account of the Soviet productive effort in World War II, year by year, which is directly comparable with statistical measures of the wartime economic mobilisation of other powers. It will be possible, therefore, to measure and compare the margin by which the Soviet economy passed the 'test' of war. A more detailed view of the wartime evolution of supply of final and intermediate products and their uses can throw independent light on the degree of harmony and coherence in Soviet wartime economic mobilisation, and on the extent and character of its dependence upon foreign aid. Soviet losses of both physical and human capital can also be evaluated and compared with those of other countries, and their long-term consequences suggested with a firmer basis in fact.

In the process of analysing this material, I hope to make a worthy contribution to the western postwar experience of independent measurement of Soviet economic performance. The Soviet Union's war years are a long-standing gap in the western record. Standard unofficial time series of the Stalin period, for example the industrial production estimates of Hodgman, Nutter, Moorsteen, and Moorsteen and Powell, show a break in 1940 or 1941, and continuity is not resumed until 1945. Bergson incorporated 1944 as a benchmark year for GNP intermediate between prewar 1940 and postwar 1948, but he acknowledged that the wartime year provided a less robust estimate. It is now possible to come to a firmer view of wartime trends and results, although the violence of structural change in the war years, especially in 1941–3, must still make unambiguous evaluations impossible.

2 An inside view

First releases of wartime data

Official assessments of the scale and degree of wartime economic mobilisation began to appear in print in 1945. They were accompanied by release of the most limited selection of figures from the official wartime national accounts of aggregate production and utilisation. Only recently has it become possible to reconstruct these accounts with any precision.

In 1945 a leading official of Gosplan published an article in its monthly journal, and then a short pamphlet, devoted to the Soviet Union's economic experience of World War II.[1] Their author, B. Sukharevskii, was wartime head of the Gosplan section responsible for overall national economic balances. His work served as an official summary of the pattern of Soviet wartime economic mobilisation, at least in its main dimensions, until the appearance of N.A. Voznesenskii's more celebrated *War economy of the USSR in the period of the Patriotic War* at the end of 1947.[2] Voznesenskii, a member of Stalin's war cabinet and Politburo, was head of Gosplan and Sukharevskii's immediate boss; Voznesenskii's text was later said to have been approved personally by Stalin.

Sukharevskii's published work, although brief, contained some noteworthy ideas. He developed a distinction between transient and permanent sources of wartime economic mobilisation. He argued that in the first phase of the war, in 1941–2, the Soviet supply of war had grown by transferring resources out of civilian material production, out of the nonproductive sphere, and out of stockpiles. Workers had worked longer hours, while subsisting at a lower level than in peacetime. By 1943 these sources of mobilisation had exhausted their possibilities, once and for all. After this point, new internal sources had to be found for expansion of the war economy, in restored output per worker, resource-saving technical change, and rising output of heavy industry.

At the time Sukharevskii gave few details. Later publications, beginning with Voznesenskii's, put some flesh on the bones, but Sukharevskii's name disappeared, and soon even Voznesenskii's book appeared to be a false start. Publication of *The war economy of the USSR* coincided with a clampdown on the release of all other statistical information pertaining to the Soviet war effort, and was followed within 15 months by the arrest of Voznesenskii; publication of new data was resumed only in the 1960s.

The release of further information about the wartime national accounts began in 1965. The new figures were consistent, at least, with Sukharevskii's assessment. They showed 1941–2, when output shrank, as a period of transfer of resources out of the civilian economy into defence uses. After this, output recovered, and civilian and defence uses of resources grew together; the defence share peaked in 1943 and then declined. But there were unexplained contradictions. One set of figures suggested that the share of military outlays (*voennye raskhody*) in 'national income' had risen from 11 per cent in 1940 to 40 per cent in 1942 and to a peak of 44 per cent in 1943. Others indicated that the share of resources allocated to 'war needs' (*voennye nuzhdy*) from the same national income had risen from 15 per cent in 1940 to 55 per cent in 1942 or even '57–58 per cent'; the latter figure was attained 'in the course of the war' according to some, but in 1942 according to others.[3]

Such figures posed as many questions as they answered. They were clearly unsatisfactory in terms of detail, definition, and presumed reliability. What was the national income concept employed, and what was the scope of military outlays and 'war needs'? What had been done to account for external military resources supplied in mutual Allied aid – were they counted in the measure either of defence outlays, or of national income? What was the standard of valuation – current or prewar prices and, if prewar, then of which year? Doubts were also raised by more general reservations concerning the Soviet national product concept, measure, and deflation procedures, none of which turned out to be beyond question, and additionally by the postwar military–economic context, which saw a trend to systematic concealment of contemporary Soviet defence outlays.

In this chapter I trace the published figures back to the work carried out under Sukharevskii in Gosplan documents. I show the underlying ruble values, and suggest what they meant and why they differed. I point to conceptual developments found in the work of Gosplan

Table 2.1. *Net material product, 1940 and 1942–3, from Sukharevskii (billion rubles and current prices)*

		1940	1942	1943	Change, 1940–2	1942–3
1	NMP produced	376	291	330	–85	39
2	Losses	–12	–11	–5	1	6
3	Net imports	2	12	17	10	5
4	NMP utilised	366	292	342	–74	50
4.1	nondefence outlays	297	167	202	–130	35
4.1a	accumulation	59	15	41	–44	26
4.1b	consumption	238	152	161	–86	9
4.2	defence outlays	69	125	140	56	15

Source: GARF, f. 3922/4372, op. 4, d. 115, ll. 35–9. NMP utilised (row 4) is the sum of rows 1–3, also the sum of rows 4.1 (itself the sum of rows 4.1a and 4.1b) and 4.2. For definitions and further detail see the Guide to national accounts (p. xxvi).

officials such as Sukharevskii, including study of the phasing of economic mobilisation and sources of war finance, the influence of relative price effects on measures of the defence burden, and the reconciliation of production and expenditure accounts.

I do not present the figures below as trustworthy. They reveal the picture only as it was seen in Moscow at the time within a narrow circle of officials. Part of the context of these developments was the poor quality of basic statistics, which led to divergent estimates of wartime economic burdens.

National income at current prices

Figures for Soviet wartime national income at current prices have never been released. They were compiled, however, and were used in Gosplan to analyse the overall sources and uses of resources at critical stages of the war effort.

At the end of 1943 Sukharevskii reported to Voznesenskii on the financing of the Soviet war effort.[4] In 1942 the net material product of the domestic economy had fallen by 85 billion rubles compared with 1940 and at current prices. At the same time nominal defence outlays had risen by 56 billion rubles. Table 2.1 shows that the rise in defence outlays over 1940–2 was reconciled with shrinking domestic supply to only a small extent by the addition to total supply from other sources –

Table 2.2. *Defence outlays, 1940 and 1942–3, from Sukharevskii (billion rubles and current prices)*

		1940	1942	1943
1	Consumption in cash and kind by personnel	29.3	65.6	71.2
2	Accumulation of defence industry fixed assets	7.4	5.6	4.1
3	Other defence outlays	32.3	53.8	65.0
4	Defence outlays, total	69.0	125.0	140.3
4.1	% of NMP utilised	19%	43%	41%

Sources: Rows 1–4: as table 2.1. Row 4.1: row 4, divided by table 2.1, row 4. The source itself includes several minor variations on this row.

10 billion rubles' worth of net imports, plus 1 billion rubles arising from a reduction in the flow of 'losses'. The main source of finance of the increase in defence outlays was a huge diversion of resources from non-defence uses – 130 billion rubles; two thirds of this sum came out of civilian consumption, although the squeeze on accumulation was proportionally more severe.

In 1943, in contrast, defence outlays would rise by a modest 15 billion rubles, and Sukharevskii pointed to significant recovery in overall resources as the means of financing this increase. The net material product (NMP) produced was 39 billion rubles higher than in 1942, and the excess of NMP utilised over NMP produced was increased by additional net imports and reduced losses of 11 billion rubles, making 50 billion rubles of additional resources in total.[5] In fact, most of this increase in total supply was allocated to civilian uses, accumulation benefiting much more than consumption. The continued expansion of the war economy, Sukharevskii's report argued, was itself forcing a significant increase in accumulation, especially in metallurgy, where supply was lagging far behind the capacity of defence industry to process metals.

What was Sukharevskii's concept of defence outlays? Here he was superficially helpful; in addition to annual totals he provided a breakdown (table 2.2) which accounted separately for consumption by personnel, fixed investment in defence industry, and 'other' outlays. On this basis, the defence burden could be measured as the ratio of such outlays to NMP utilised: 19 per cent in 1940, rising sharply to a peak of 43 per cent in 1942, then relaxing to 41 per cent in 1943.

Table 2.3. *Net material product, 1940 and 1942–5, from Sukharevskii (billion rubles and current prices)*

	1940	1942	1943	1944	1945
(A) Billion rubles					
1 Social product	670	498	602	680	727
2 Productive consumption	285	169	187	227	252
3 NMP produced	385	329	415	453	475
4 Other sources	2	4	22	36	34
5 NMP utilised	387	333	437	489	509
5.1 accumulation	66	33	10	44	53
5.2 consumption	286	250	372	383	392
5.3 defence outlays	30	49	55	61	62
5.4 reserve fund	5	0.8	0.5	1	2
(B) Per cent of NMP utilised					
6 Defence outlays	8%	15%	13%	12%	12%

Source: GARF, f. 3922/4372, op. 4, d. 115, ll. 10-15, except as below. For definitions and further detail see the Guide to national accounts (p. xxvi). Defence outlays (row 5.3) exclude the consumption of military personnel, which is located in the general consumption fund (row 5.2). Row 4, equivalent to net imports, less insurable asset losses: row 5, less row 3. Row 6: row 5.3, divided by row 5.

At the end of the war, Sukharevskii's section produced revised series for wartime national economic balances, including national income and expenditure. The rows which concern us are reproduced in table 2.3. Two things are immediately obvious. First, the revised figures for domestic supply (NMP produced – row 3) were much higher for every year, but especially for 1942 (38 billion rubles) and 1943 (85 billion rubles), than those accepted during the war. Second, a major portion of defence outlays had been transferred from the reported 'defence' heading (row 5.3) to general 'consumption' (row 5.2). This marked the beginning of the practice which subsumed wartime defence outlays attributable to the material consumption of personnel under consumption outlays generally, while reporting the remaining part of defence outlays as 'other' defence outlays, or as outlays on 'the means of waging war', 'armament', or other vague phrases.

Of course, the result of these changes was that the burden of defence outlays appeared much lower than the percentages previously shown in table 2.2. On the basis of table 2.3, the defence burden exclusive of consumption by personnel was no more than 8 per cent of NMP utilised in 1940, rising to a peak of 15 per cent in 1942.

The scope of military outlays

In evaluating wartime defence burdens we must deal with two measures of military expenditures which were conceptually quite different, one derived from the budget account and the other from the material product account. To make matters worse we do not always know for sure which is being used, but in tables 2.1 and 2.2 a budgetary concept was probably applied, while in table 2.3 we find the material-product accounting concept. The two concepts can be further explained as follows.

Defence outlays in the budget

The budget definition should have been straightforward. It normally covered spending on the army (including the air force) and navy under the defence and navy commissariats. These were outlays on goods and services alike, the main items being as follows:

- armament and combat equipment (*vooruzheniie i boevaia tekhnika*)
- maintenance (*soderzhanie*) of the Army and Fleet, comprising pay (*denezhnoe soderzhanie*) and rations (*prodovol'stvie*) of personnel, their personal kit (*veshchevoe imushchestvo*), and outlays on transport and fuel
- capital construction (*kapital'noe stroitel'stvo*), i.e. outlays on capital items with a directly military use such as barracks, airfields, naval installations, fortifications, but not outlays on defence industry investment; and
- other outlays, of which most significant were probably the costs of repairing and maintaining equipment.

This budgetary concept was roughly comparable with a western SNA concept of defence outlays – a flow of goods and services either consumed or stockpiled by the armed forces. One departure from western practice was that minor sums were charged against the Soviet defence budget for officers' pensions.[6] A more important difference is that outlays on military research, development, testing and experimentation were excluded from the Soviet budget concept, being financed from the general science budget. On the other hand, in the USSR as in the west, outlays on defence industry construction were excluded, since they were attributable to civilian capital formation. Subject to a few such qualifications, and despite periods of budgetary deception in the early 1930s and from the 1950s onward, the military budget of the time of World War II 'told the truth'.[7]

Table 2.4. *Outlays of the defence and navy commissariats, 1940–5 (billion rubles and current prices)*

	1940	1941	1942	1943	1944	1945
(A) Terpilovskii						
1 Total	56.8	83.0	108.4	125.0	137.8	128.2
(B) Zverev (July 1941–June 1945)						
2 Munitions	–	16.2	36.2	41.9	46.1	22.8
3 Maintenance						
3.1 pay	–	10.3	28.2	34.0	37.1	22.0
3.2 food	–	8.9	22.6	26.2	26.6	9.7
3.3 personal kit	–	5.7	10.2	8.4	10.1	4.6
3.4 fuel	–	1.5	3.0	3.4	4.0	2.3
3.5 transport	–	1.2	2.4	4.8	5.9	2.7
4 Construction	–	2.6	2.4	1.4	1.9	0.9
5 Other	–	3.1	6.1	5.8	7.0	3.4
6 Total	–	49.5	111.0	125.9	138.7	68.4

Sources: Row 1: Terpilovskii (1967), 29. Rows 2–6: RGAE, f. 7733, op. 36, d. 1892, l. 86; 1941 is July–December, and 1945 is January–June.

Table 2.4 shows that defence outlays on this definition amounted to 57 billion rubles in 1940, rising to 108 or 111 billion rubles in 1942 and a peak of 138 or 139 billion rubles in 1944.

Defence uses of the net material product

In the national accounts, which were based upon the material product system, a more restrictive concept of defence outlays was employed. For a start, the net material product (NMP) covered the utilisation of final goods or material products only, to the exclusion of final services, although intermediate services were included in the value of final goods.

If defence were to be treated like any other activity in the 'nonproductive' (service) sector, the NMP would include defence outlays classified under three headings.[8]

- The *personal material consumption* of employees. In the defence sector, this should have covered troops' subsistence and kit, and the portion of their pay used for purchases of goods; thus personal spending on consumer services, personal savings, and tax payments were excluded.

- The *institutional material consumption* of the service agencies, which might include depreciation of the stock of nonproductive capital. The most important objects of institutional consumption in the defence sector were outlays on fuel and other consumable materials; the material cost of drugs and the consumption of heating and lighting by military clinics and cinemas would be taken into account, but the wages of employees hired to entertain and educate the troops, and prevent or cure their diseases, would not.
- *Accumulation* – the net increment to the stock of nonproductive capital. The defence sector accumulated recognisable fixed capital items such as buildings and base facilities, and perhaps also military fortifications, but weapons and equipment tended to receive special treatment. Under conditions of rapid wartime expenditure, weapons were treated as a consumption flow, much like household durables; in peacetime a special heading of state 'reserves' was used to accommodate additions to military stockpiles along with strategic reserves of strategic commodities and precious metals.[9]

Like the budgetary account, the material product account could be manipulated. One example was the tendency to lose the material personal consumption of service personnel in the general consumption account. Another was to be deliberately vague about where the institutional material consumption of the armed forces was being counted, whether in with purchases of weapons and equipment ('accumulation', or 'reserves'), or in with consumption by personnel.

In principle both defence uses of material products, and defence outlays on a budgetary basis, could be legitimately compared with the overall net material product to measure the national defence burden, although the budget concept would always yield the larger percentage since it included defence uses of final services. In the NMP these services were seen as supported by activities within the material sphere; the 'primary incomes' of workers and firms engaged in material production had to be redistributed through the budget to finance these service sector activities, which were therefore a burden on material production just like the procurement of aircraft, tanks, and fuels.

Which methodology defined the defence outlays reported in tables 2.1 and 2.2 – that of the budget, or of the NMP? The combination of defence outlays with consumption and accumulation to add up national income (table 2.1) implies an NMP methodology. But the same series (69 billion rubles in 1940, and so on, table 2.2) is used in the same document to show the share of defence outlays in budget spending. Besides, the sums reported are too large to be accounted for by the

Table 2.5. *Defence outlays, 1940 and 1942–3: the Sukharevskii gap (billion rubles and current prices)*

	1940	1942	1943
1 Outlays in budget	56.8	111.0	125.9
2 Outlays from Sukharevskii	69.0	125.0	140.3
2.1 less defence industry construction	7.4	5.6	4.1
2.2 on budgetary basis	61.6	119.4	136.2
3 Sukharevskii gap	4.8	8.4	10.3
3.1 consumption of personnel	–	4.6	–
3.2 other outlays	–	3.8	–

Sources: Row 1: table 2.4, row 1 (1940), row 6 (1942–3). Row 2: table 2.2, row 4. Row 2.1: table 2.2, row 2. Row 2.2: row 2, less row 2.1. Row 3: row 2.2, less row 1. Row 3.1: table 2.2, row 1, less table 2.4, the sum of rows 3.1–3.3 Row 3.2: row 3, less row 3.1.

defence expenditure of material products alone, and exceed budget series for allocations to the Army and Navy (table 2.4) by a large and stable margin. Part of this margin is explained by outlays on defence industry construction, which entered the budget under outlays on the economy, not defence, but an unexplained residual still remains.

Sukharevskii can be roughly reconciled with the budget on two assumptions, that both series had their origins in a budget concept (outlays on goods and services), and that the remaining gap is associated at least in part with outlays of the NKVD on internal security. The 'Sukharevskii gap', illustrated in table 2.5, rises from 4.8 billion rubles in 1940 to 8.4 billion rubles in 1942, and 10.3 billion rubles in 1943. The gap may correspond to internal security outlays. The NKVD's planned budget allocation for 1940 was 7.1 billion rubles, part of which would have been spent on internal security.[10] The rough composition of the gap can be established for 1942 (for 1940 table 2.4 is insufficiently detailed, and for 1943 figures in tables 2.1 and 2.2 are clearly very preliminary). Sukharevskii apparently included an extra 4.6 billion rubles' worth of personal consumption over budget outlays of the army and navy on pay, subsistence, and kit, and 3.8 billion extra rubles of 'other' outlays compared with budget outlays of the army and navy on remaining items. Total outlays of the NKVD in 1942 stood at 7.1 billion rubles, although no more than 1.6 billion rubles were accounted for by maintenance of internal security troops.[11]

Sukharevskii almost certainly misleads us when he claims that the military outlays shown in tables 2.1 and 2.2 *exclude* the value of military goods imported under Lend-Lease and British mutual aid. Both the budgetary and the NMP accounts could be expected to have included outlays on such resources, and it will be shown in chapter 6 that they did so in practice.

The 'real' defence burden

The figures shown in table 2.1 imply a sharp increase in the defence share of national income, from 19 per cent in 1940 to 43 per cent in 1942, and little less in 1943. At the same time, provided we set to one side the salient fact that Soviet national income was falling, the increase shown in the defence burden (+24 per cent) is not particularly dramatic by World War II standards, as will be shown in chapter 5. Moreover, subsequent estimates raised the figures for wartime national income, further lowering the measured increase in the defence share.

One reason for the apparently modest wartime increase in the Soviet defence burden is that the Soviet economy encountered relative price changes of huge dimensions. In a further report to Voznesenskii dated January 1945, Sukharevskii pointed out that

> The share of military spending ... does not express the degree of mobilisation of the national economy for the needs of the war ... This is associated with the fact that, in contrast with the wartime increase in prices of commodities for personal consumption, prices of military equipment have fallen.[12]

The strong relative price effects to which Sukharevskii referred are shown in table 2.6, and further documented in appendix A. By 1943, prices of munitions (row 1) had fallen by roughly 40 per cent compared with 1940, while average prices of consumer goods (row 6) had grown 3.5-fold, making a 6-fold shift in relative prices on a bilateral comparison.[13] The obstacle which this represented to an unambiguous evaluation of the Soviet defence burden was completely neglected for many years after Sukharevskii.

When Sukharevskii's office considered the defence burden from revised figures of national income and outlays at current prices, they found a still more modest increase in the defence burden than might have been inferred from table 2.1. The figures in table 2.7 (row 2.1) show the defence burden rising from 19 per cent in 1940 to a peak of 38 per cent (+19 per cent) in 1942. But this did not reflect the much larger change in real volumes of defence and civilian outlays, which was

Table 2.6. *Prevailing prices of goods and services, 1941–44 (per cent of 1940)*

		1941	1942	1943	1944
1	Munitions	85%	66%	61%	59%
2	Civilian machinery	–	–	–	104%
3	Basic industrial goods	–	–	–	106%
4	Construction materials	–	–	–	115%
5	Railway freight	–	–	–	126%
6	Retail trade	215%	357%	352%	267%
6.1	official markets	130%	150%	177%	196%
6.2	kolkhoz markets	561%	1016%	823%	466%
7	Consumer services	–	–	–	120%

Sources: Row 1: table A.2, row 3. Rows 2, 3, 5: Bergson (1961), 367–8. Row 4: Bergson (1961), 350. Rows 6, 6.1, 6.2: table A.5, rows 7–9. Row 7: Chapman (1963), 81, 350.

Table 2.7. *Defence outlays and national income, 1940–3, from Sukharevskii (billion rubles and current or constant 1940 prices)*

		1940	1941	1942	1943 prelim.
(A) At current prices					
1	Net material product	368	350	329	416
2	Defence outlays	70	98	125	146
2.1	% of NMP	19%	28%	38%	35%
(B) At 1940 prices					
3	Net material product	368	335	224	252
4	Defence outlays	70	98	128	147
4.1	% of NMP	19%	29%	57%	58%

Source: GARF, f. 3922/4372, op. 4, d. 115, ll. 50–3.

obscured by the increased relative price of the latter. Wartime defence outlays recalculated in prewar prices looked little different from nominal outlays, apparently because the effects of relative prices changes on the defence budget were mutually offsetting (munitions had become cheaper while other costs had risen). But, since civilian goods weighed much more heavily in national income as a whole than in defence outlays, the effect of deflating wartime national income to prewar prices was dramatic. As a result, wartime change in the defence burden recalculated in prewar prices looked quite different. Table 2.7

shows that by 1942 the 'real' defence burden had risen from 19 per cent of NMP utilised to 57 per cent (+38 per cent), and to 58 per cent in 1943.

These figures correspond numerically to the 'true' defence burden in 1942 as it will be estimated in chapter 5,[14] but the correspondence is accidental, since it will be shown that at 1940 prices the wartime trends of both defence outlays and NMP utilised were each understated by official measures. The most likely causes of official bias are surveyed in chapter 4. One was the tendency of Soviet price indices to lag behind changes in the ratio of price to user characteristics when product assortment and product quality were also changing. This tendency was manifest in peacetime over many decades; it operated in wartime as well, and caused official measures of real output to understate both the wartime growth of military supplies (where prices were falling) and the wartime decline of civilian production (where prices were rising).

With hindsight it is worth stressing that both current-price and prewar-price measures of the defence burden are significant. The high ratio of defence spending to national income at prewar prices in 1943 tells us about the great change in relative volumes of war-related and civilian output. The much lower ratio in current values reminds us of the extraordinary scarcity and high cost of civilian goods (especially foodstuffs) in that year, which set an effective upper limit on the degree of mobilisation.

More on national income at prewar prices

In 1946 more detailed accounts of national income in wartime, but at prewar prices of 1940, were compiled in preparation for drafting the fourth (postwar) five-year plan. The results were released piecemeal over many years, beginning in 1947, with revealing details appearing in 1971 and 1990.

In 1947 Voznesenskii announced that 'the share of war expenditures [in national income], exclusive of the personal consumption of servicemen, increased from 7 per cent in 1940 to 29 per cent in 1942'.[15] It was these figures which were augmented in 1965 by figures for consumption by military personnel, and extended first to 1943–4, then to 1945. They suggested that military consumption and nonconsumption outlays together rose from 11 per cent of national income in 1940 to 40 per cent in 1942, and 44 per cent at the 1943 peak.

The reader will find these figures set out in neat rows and columns in table 2.8 (rows 1–3). There it is stated that they are percentages of NMP utilised at 1940 prices. But when they first appeared, none of this was

Table 2.8. *Net material product, 1940 and 1942–5, from Goskomstat (per cent and 1940 prices)*

	1940	1942	1943	1944	1945
(A) Per cent of NMP utilised					
1 Accumulation	19%	4%	7%	15%	13%
2 Consumption	74%	69%	60%	61%	69%
2.1 by military personnel	4%	13%	11%	11%	7%
3 Other military outlays	7%	27%	33%	24%	18%
4 Defence subtotal	11%	40%	44%	35%	25%
(B) Per cent of 1940					
5 Accumulation	100%	12%	24%	63%	55%
6 Consumption	100%	53%	54%	66%	72%
6.1 by military personnel	100%	191%	191%	216%	135%
7 Other military outlays	100%	202%	287%	262%	180%

Source: A full set of figures (with the exception of row 4) is published in Goskomstat (1990), 29, but note further as follows: Rows 1–3: these figures were released piecemeal over many years, starting with Voznesensky (1948), 56, followed by Chadaev (1965), 380, Kravchenko (1970), 125, 228, IVMV, vol. 6 (1976), 340, and IVMV, vol. 12 (1982), 161. Row 4: row 2.1, plus row 3.

made explicit. What was included in defence outlays was also left in the shadows by Voznesenskii and his followers. It was at least reasonably clear from the context that this was a material product concept of defence uses, not a budget concept; if so, then a classification of material outlays might be expected under the three headings listed above for final-service activities: personal and institutional material consumption, and the increment to the capital stock.

Defence, however, would always be different. Voznesenskii's 'personal consumption of servicemen' (table 2.8, row 2.1) was clear enough. But there was considerable ambiguity surrounding his 'war expenditures exclusive of the personal consumption of servicemen' (table 2.8, row 3), which should have comprised both institutional consumption and military stockbuilding; later authorities referred to it first as 'the means of waging war' (*fond sredstv vedeniia voiny*), then simply 'armament' (*vooruzhenie*), before returning most recently to a residual concept – 'other' military outlays.[16]

'Armament', interpreted literally, implied no more than the increment (whether net or gross) to the stock of weapons; if so, where then was the institutional material consumption by the armed forces of such items as fuel and transport services? Where was military construction? Were these a part of 'the means of waging war'? Not if the latter covered 'armament' alone. Were they concealed under consumption by personnel? Surely there was not enough room under this item. Had they been omitted from 'military outlays' altogether, perhaps buried in the much larger civilian parts of the consumption and accumulation funds?

'Other' outlays, on the other hand, suggest inclusiveness – everything not already counted under the pay and maintenance of personnel, from weapons to costs of operations and construction. But if this was an inclusive measure, why did it not show a larger defence burden by 1943?

Nor did the complications end there. Military outlays were reported in percentages, but per cent of what? Presumably, of NMP utilised, which includes net imports among resources available for utilisation. But there was never any indication of how imported supply of military equipment, and imported army rations, uniforms, and other items attributable to the consumption of personnel, had been treated in the measure of military outlays. Worse still, Voznesenskii and his followers left the all-important question of the price set used to value both spending and national income (whether current or constant prices and, if constant, then of what year) undefined.

In 1990 Goskomstat (the successor to TsSU) at last published an abbreviated version of the official limited-circulation handbook of wartime economic statistics originally prepared in 1959; this included index numbers of the main components of NMP by end-use, as well as the NMP shares already published (table 2.8), which were now stated to have been calculated at 1940 prices; thus the price set, and the NMP denominator of the figures previously released were now known.

The final piece of the jigsaw was to be found in the Gosplan archive. Table 2.9 shows national income in rubles, at current and constant 1940 prices, in rubles at last, for 1940 and 1944. Here are material consumption distributed among civilian households, civilian institutions, and the armed forces; the material accumulation of fixed capital, farm stocks, and other inventories; and, in a third category all by itself, outlays on 'military equipment and materials'. These are postwar estimates of TsSU, set out in a 'Balance of the social product for 1940, 1944, and 1945', dated March 1946.[17] The proportions between the uses of NMP according to the TsSU 'Balance' of 1946, and according to the others from Voznesenskii (in 1947) to Goskomstat (in 1990), are close enough to suggest a common genetic inheritance. Their shared origin is demonstrated beyond any doubt in table 2.10.

Table 2.9. *Net material product and implicit expenditure deflators, 1940, 1944, and 1945, from TsSU (billion rubles at current or constant 1940 prices and per cent)*

		Material product:					Current prices, % of 1940:	
		at current prices:			at 1940 prices:			
		1940	1944 prelim.	1945	1944 prelim.	1945	1944 prelim.	1945
	(1)	(2)	(3)	(4)	(5)	(6)	(7)	
1	Annual social product	682.3	708.6	640.4	473.7	467.0	–	–
2	Productive consumption	296.1	219.0	199.0	204.1	196.5	107%	101%
3	NMP produced	386.2	489.6	441.4	269.6	270.5	–	–
4	Losses	–11.5	–11.1	–10.5	–10.7	–10.0	104%	105%
5	Other sources	4.1	44.7	36.5	45.6	39.7	98%	92%
6	NMP utilised	378.8	523.2	467.4	304.5	300.3	–	–
7	Accumulation	71.1	10.6	28.0	44.6	45.0	–	–
7.1	of fixed assets	40.6	29.1	34.7	23.8	28.1	122%	123%
7.2	of farm products	7.0	–35.1	–23.5	4.6	2.8	–	–
7.3	of other stocks	18.5	14.6	14.8	13.9	11.8	105%	125%
7.4	of reserves	5.0	2.0	2.0	2.3	2.3	87%	87%
8	Consumption	279.3	457.5	400.1	185.6	204.4	–	–
8.1	by households	244.5	404.7	357.7	141.6	169.1	286%	212%
8.2	by institutions	19.9	14.2	16.8	11.8	14.0	120%	120%
8.3	by the army and navy	14.9	38.6	25.6	32.2	21.3	120%	120%
9	Outlays on military equipment and materials	28.4	55.1	39.3	74.3	50.9	74%	77%
10	Defence subtotal	43.3	93.7	64.9	106.5	72.2	–	–
10.1	per cent of NMP utilised	11%	18%	14%	35%	24%	–	–

Source: RGAE, f. 4372, op. 95, d. 168, l. 45, except as noted below. Price deflators (cols 6–7) are calculated from ruble totals (col. 2 divided by col. 4, and col. 3 divided by col. 5). Row 3: row 1, less row 2. Row 6: the sum of rows 3–5, also the sum of rows 7, 8, 9. Row 10: the sum of rows 8.3, 9. Row 10.1: row 10, divided by row 6.

Table 2.9 (columns 6 and 7) also reveals the implicit price index numbers used to deflate the main material expenditure components to prewar prices. (Not all are calculated; in some cases, e.g. farm products, it is not clear what the calculation would mean.) For most items, a gentle wartime inflation between 1940 and 1944 is suggested, ranging from 4 to 22 per cent. The price level applying to material household con-

Table 2.10. *Uses of net material product, 1940 and 1944: TsSU and Goskomstat compared (per cent and 1940 prices)*

	% of NMP utilised:				1944, % of 1940:	
	1940: Goskomstat (1)	TsSU (2)	1944: Goskomstat (3)	TsSU (4)	Goskomstat (5)	TsSU (6)
1 Accumulation	19%	18.8%	15%	14.6%	63%	62.7%
2 Consumption	74%	73.7%	61%	61.0%	66%	66.5%
2.1 by military personnel	4%	3.9%	11%	10.6%	216%	216.1%
3 Other military outlays	7%	7.5%	24%	24.4%	262%	261.6%

Sources: Cols 1, 3, 5: table 2.8. Cols 2, 4, 6: table 2.9; row 2.1 is from table 2.9, row 8.3.

sumption is shown to have nearly trebled, however, in contrast with a 26 per cent fall in the prevailing price of 'military equipment and materials'. As a result of applying these varying deflators, the combined share of defence items in NMP utilised (row 10.1) is shown to have been 11 per cent in 1940, rising to 35 per cent in 1944 at prewar prices, compared with only 18 per cent at current values. However, a comparison with wartime commodity price indexes suggests that the official deflators used in table 2.9 understate wartime change, whether positive or negative, in virtually every case. Weapon prices in 1944 are estimated at 59 per cent of 1940 in table 2.6 (row 1), compared with 74 per cent for 'military equipment and materials' in table 2.9 (row 9); the price level applying to households' retail purchases in official and unofficial markets in 1944 is estimated at 3.5 times 1940 in table 2.6 (row 7), compared with 2.1 times for households' material consumption in table 2.9 (row 8.1). Therefore, the figures in table 2.9 for NMP and material defence outlays in 1944 at prewar prices must also understate the wartime increase in the defence burden.[18]

It is also possible that the material outlays on defence shown in table 2.9 (row 10) are underreported. This is difficult to prove, because they are hard to compare with the budget figures (table 2.4); 1940 is the only year when the two series are measured in common prices, and there is not yet an official breakdown of the defence budget for 1940 itself. A reasonable guess, though, is that in that year budget outlays on munitions, repairs, and construction together amounted to 26 billion rubles, a little

Table 2.11. *Net material product, 1940 and 1942–5, from Goskomstat and TsSU (billion rubles and 1940 prices)*

	1940	1942	1943	1944	1945
1 NMP utilised	378.8	213.9	249.4	303.5	291.3
2 Accumulation	71.1	8.5	17.1	44.8	39.1
3 Consumption	279.3	148.0	150.8	184.3	201.1
3.1 by households and civilian institutions	264.4	119.6	122.4	152.2	181.0
3.2 by the army and navy	14.9	28.5	28.5	32.2	20.1
4 Other military outlays	28.4	57.4	81.5	74.4	51.1
5 Defence subtotal	43.3	85.8	110.0	106.6	71.2
5.1 % of NMP utilised	11%	40%	44%	35%	24%

Sources: Row 1: the sum of rows 2, 3, 4. Rows 2, 3, 3.2, 4: for 1940, as corresponding rows in table 2.9; other years are extrapolated from 1940 on the basis of table 2.8, rows 5–7. Row 3.1: row 3, less row 3.2. Row 5: the sum of rows 3.2, 4. Row 5.1: row 5, divided by row 1.

less than the 28.4 billion rubles allocated to 'military equipment and materials' in the 1946 version of the NMP account. But budget outlays on soldiers' pay, food, and personal kit alone probably reached nearly 30 billion rubles, far above the 15 billion rubles allowed for material consumption by the armed forces in the NMP account.[19] The NMP account appears to leave little or no room for institutional military consumption on items such as fuel and transport. The conclusion seems inevitable, therefore, that significant material outlays on defence are still hidden from view.

By combining the TsSU 'Balance' of 1946 (table 2.9) with the Goskomstat index numbers of material outlays published in 1990 (table 2.8, rows 5–7), it is possible to deduce the official figures for NMP utilised, in rubles and 1940 prices, for each year of the war (table 2.11). Defence outlays of material products are shown to have risen from 43 billion rubles in 1940 to a peak of 110 billion prewar rubles in 1943.

But the light shed by these figures on the defence burden has its limits. Important elements of defence outlays may be concealed under other headings. The major items of civilian material outlays also appear inadequately deflated. Both of these result in overstatement of the real value of civilian uses relative to military uses (especially of munitions). Moreover, there is a discrepancy between the evidence of these tables and other much higher figures published in the mid-1960s on the share of output utilised for meeting 'war needs' (*voennye nuzhdy*) in 1940 and 1942. These figures have special interest for us, and they too can be traced back to Sukharevskii's department.

Reconciling production and utilisation

Although more limited than the national utilisation accounts in years covered, published figures relating to 'war needs' were considerably more detailed in showing the utilisation of output by main productive sector of the economy – and for industry and transport they were also much higher in output percentage terms. The previously published figures reported in table 2.12, rows 1–9, claimed that in 1940 some 15 per cent of national income was utilised for 'war needs', rising to 55 per cent in 1942, or even '57–58 per cent'. (These compare with figures of 11 and 40 per cent from table 2.11.) On a production branch basis, the peak proportions were higher still for industry (68 per cent) and transport (61 per cent), lower for agriculture (24 per cent).

As with preceding data, crucial details were omitted. The reader did not know how 'war needs' were defined in relation to either budget outlays or the NMP methodology. Because they were larger, they could be presumed to be more inclusive than the NMP categories; were missing outlays on institutional consumption of the armed forces involved? Nor did we know how the national income concept was defined; NMP produced and utilised were close in 1940, but by 1942 foreign aid must already have been introducing a widening gap. Once again, the price set was undefined.

Archival documents originating in Sukharevskii's office show that these figures were based on product supply and utilisation balances for each branch of the productive economy.[20] Resources procured to satisfy 'war needs' were measured by the value of products delivered to the armed forces, and the value of intermediate goods and raw materials delivered to defence industry (table 2.13). Some intermediate goods and raw materials (the 'productive consumption' of the defence industry) were therefore counted twice in the top line of the defence-burden ratio. Since the bottom line of the fraction here was the global social product (the sum of gross outputs of all the productive branches), there should have been equal double-counting in both numerator and denominator – in principle, at least. In practice, however, there was too little double-counting on the top line, because the productive consumption of civilian suppliers of 'war needs' was neglected, resulting in understatement of the defence burden.

Table 2.12. *The use of gross output for 'war needs', by production branch, 1940 and 1942–43 (per cent of total)*

	1940	1942	1943 prelim.	During the war
(A) From IVOVSS				
1 Agriculture	9%	24%	–	–
2 Industry	26%	68%	–	–
3 National income	15%	55%	–	–
(B) From Sorokin				
4 Industry	26%	–	–	65–68%
5 National income	15%	–	–	57–58%
(C) From ISE				
6 Agriculture	9%	24%	–	–
7 Industry	26%	68%	–	–
8 Transport	16%	61%	–	–
9 National income	15%	57–58%	–	–
(D) From Sukharevskii				
10 Agriculture	9%	24%	24%	–
11 Industry	26%	68%	66%	–
12 Construction	13%	26%	18%	–
13 Transport	16%	60%	66%	–
14 Trade	6%	31%	32%	–
15 Total social product	17%	48%	48%	–

Sources: Rows 1–3: IVOVSS, vol. 6 (1965), 46. Rows 4–5: Sorokin (1971), 87–8. Rows 6–9: ISE, vol. 5 (1978), 183. This source also gave 70–80 per cent as the share of industrial output allocated to war needs in 1942, taking into account 'military orders fulfilled by civilian industry establishments'; the latter range had previously been attributed to the first half of 1942 alone in IVMV, vol. 4 (1975), 162, where it was also stated that at the same time (i.e. in the first half of the year) the share of war needs had reached 50 per cent of industrial output, counting only the output of the defence industry commissariats. Rows 10–15: calculated from table 2.13; see also GARF, f. 3922/4372, op. 4, d. 115, ll. 50–3.

There was a noteworthy attempt at consistency in pricing. Since defence procurement agencies purchased goods at government prices, total output was also valued and, if necessary, revalued at government prices. This primarily affected agricultural products. Since government prices were more stable than prices generally in wartime, at least those relative price effects stemming from the huge kolkhoz market inflation were eliminated. Thus an attempt was made to render the numerator and denominator of the defence burden comparable in terms of prices, although practical transgressions may have influenced the result.

Table 2.13. *The use of gross output for 'war needs', by production branch, 1940 and 1942–3, from Sukharevskii (billion rubles and prevailing official prices)*

		Total:			For war needs:		
		1940	1942	1943 prelim.	1940	1942	1943 prelim.
1	Agriculture, total	294.0	165.0	173.0	25.0	39.0	42.0
1.1	to defence industry	–	–	–	22.0	32.0	34.0
1.2	to other war needs	–	–	–	3.0	7.0	8.0
2	Industry, total	378.8	231.0	257.0	97.5	156.2	169.0
2.1	group A	145.8	110.0	122.0	49.5	84.2	93.0
2.1a	MBMW	30.6	7.3	12.0	28.5	47.7	54.0
2.1b	industrial materials	–	–	–	11.0	23.0	25.0
2.1c	fuel, power	18.8	10.1	12.1	3.5	7.5	8.0
2.1d	construction materials	12.1	5.7	5.9	3.5	2.6	2.0
2.1e	other group A	–	–	–	3.0	3.4	4.0
2.2	group B	233.0	121.0	135.0	48.0	72.0	76.0
3	Construction, total	38.7	18.3	18.4	5.2	4.8	3.3
4	Transport, total	24.1	12.1	17.5	3.8	7.3	11.6
4.1	military shipments	–	–	–	1.1	2.3	4.6
4.2	to defence industry	–	–	–	2.7	5.0	7.0
5	Trade, mark-up	38.5	22.5	23.6	2.5	7.0	7.5
6	Other	10.9	7.1	8.5	3.0	3.7	4.6
7	Total social product	785.0	456.0	498.0	137.0	218.0	238.0

Source: GARF, f. 3922/4372, op. 4, d. 115, ll. 19–22; figures for 1944 plan are omitted. 'War needs' specified in the source but not apparent from the table are defined as follows: Row 2.1a: supply of military equipment to the armed forces. Row 2.1b: supply of industrial materials to the defence industry. Row 2.1c: supply of fuel and power to the defence industry. Row 2.1d: supply of construction materials to the defence industry and other war needs. Row 3: construction for the defence industry and other military construction. Row 5: the trade markup on products procured on account of defence outlays.

Mysteriously, in the original version authorised by Sukharevskii, the bottom line (table 2.12, row 15) made no mention of national income, or of a defence burden of 15, 55, or '57–58' per cent. Defence uses of resources, with limited double-counting, were compared with the total social product (table 2.13, row 7), rising from 17 per cent in 1940 to 48 per cent in 1942 and the same in 1943.

Where then did the other figures in table 2.12 come from? The '57–58' per cent is clearly from table 2.7, row 4.1: the 'real' defence burden at constant prewar prices in 1942 and 1943, comparing budget outlays on defence and maybe the NKVD troops as well with NMP. The 15 per cent is the precise ratio of the 56.8 billion rubles of official budget outlays on the army and navy, from table 2.4, row 1, to the 379 billion rubles of NMP utilised in 1940, from table 2.9, row 6. Neither has anything in common with the other figures in tables 2.12 and 2.13, nor do they have much in common with each other.

The language of planning

Sukharevskii's reports supply an interesting insight into the concepts and measures available to Soviet planners in wartime for evaluating the overall strains on the macroeconomy. They leave the impression of considerable ingenuity, and a capacity for analytical development, most of which was absorbed by a need to improvise on the basis of poor basic skills and materials. Those at the centre of the information system had to make bricks without much statistical straw. This was probably an inherent feature (not restricted to wartime) of a system of economic regulation which concentrated its scarce talent at the centre.

Sukharevskii and his colleagues could go only part of the way towards an objective picture of the pattern of wartime economic mobilisation. They could improve their concepts and methodologies, but could do little to overcome the poor quality and instability of the statistical underlay. Did this have practical consequences? Not in an obvious sense, since there is no evidence that the documents under review fed directly into practical decisions about resource allocation. But if 'statistics is the language of planning', then those conversant with policy issues were fettered by poor statistics, no matter whether they regarded themselves primarily as practical politicians or as professional economists. For 'planning decisions, being essentially choices between expected outcomes, are almost always quantitative and call for an intimate knowledge of the magnitudes involved'.[21]

The potential for error was present in abundance, and the effects of getting such magnitudes wrong were probably all bad. Understatement and overstatement both carried negative consequences. Exaggerating the achievements of economic mobilisation was dangerous if it led to complacency; but the evidence suggests that this danger was not realised. On the contrary, official understatement of war burdens was normal; it extended also to military and demographic losses.[22] Which was the more realistic measure of the wartime defence burden – 15, or 44, or 48, or '57–58' per cent? As following chapters will show, it was the highest official estimates of the defence burden which corresponded most nearly with the reality. Official measures which underplayed the degree to which resources had already been mobilised invited the régime to censure society for insufficient effort, and prompted politicians to call an exhausted people to fresh, maybe unbearable sacrifices.

Nonetheless, in the wartime reports of Gosplan officials we can find clear evidence of repeated attempts to find more informative and consistent concepts and measures of wartime economic burdens. These efforts began with study of the phasing of economic mobilisation and sources of war finance at current prices; they were extended to examination of concepts of the 'real' defence burden, to seek to compensate for the downward influence on measures of the defence burden arising from relative price effects, and to consider how the production and expenditure accounts could be reconciled. Such efforts were hindered in a variety of ways by the quality of the statistical raw materials, and by the restrictions of established methodologies. Nonetheless they invite our respect, even if we do not choose to give automatic credence to the results.

3 Measuring Soviet GNP

The Bergson school

Western distrust of Soviet official statistics became widespread in the 1930s; the first serious independent reevaluation of Soviet growth was published in 1939 by Colin Clark.[1] These concerns did not have much practical importance until World War II, when western evaluations of Soviet economic strength suddenly acquired major policy implications. And of course this motivation gathered force in the formative years of the Cold War when US–Soviet rivalry became entrenched. After World War II a number of individual scholars made major contributions to western reevalution of the Soviet national income and product. First among them was Naum Jasny (two other notable early studies limited to industrial production were by Donald R. Hodgman and G. Warren Nutter).[2]

Pride of place, however, in terms of the scale of the research effort, the quantity and quality of research output, and its historical legacy, belongs to Abram Bergson and the team which he assembled in the late 1940s and 1950s.

Abram Bergson began work on the reevaluation of Soviet national income in the US Office of Strategic Services (the forerunner of the CIA) during World War II, and continued after the war at Columbia University in New York City. At this time he was approached by the RAND Corporation of the United States Air Force to extend his work, which became known as the SNIP (Soviet national income and product) project. Bergson drafted in Raymond Powell from Yale, and a number of graduate students at Columbia (Abram S. Becker, Roman Bernaut, Janet Chapman, Jerzy F. Karcz, Richard Moorsteen, and Lynn Turgeon).

As has been seen, Bergson's team were not the first or only players. Nor did their work pass without criticism, as will be seen below. But the

SNIP project captured the middle ground of American scholarship. Its intermediate stages were represented by many working papers, articles, and preliminary volumes. Its final product took the form of four weighty monographs covering national income by end-use (Bergson), machinery production (Moorsteen), consumption and living standards (Chapman), and the capital stock (Moorsteen and Powell), all published in the 1960s.[3] The SNIP project also left the most enduring institutional legacy, since its methodology was inherited by the CIS's Office of Soviet Analysis, led successively by Rush Greenslade, Thad Alton, and Laurie Kurtzweg.[4]

Thus Bergson's research began when the Americans and Russians were still wartime allies, expanded through the most traumatic episodes of the Cold War, including the Berlin blockade, the Korean War, and the McCarthy period, and continued (in its original form) far into the era of 'peaceful coexistence'. All the SNIP participants were given security clearance for classified work, except for Turgeon who chose not to be cleared. But the polarised context of military and intelligence insecurity had little impact upon the quality of the research. Turgeon recalls the atmosphere as 'cordial', a word which he also applies to his relations with Bergson, 'despite the fact that we didn't see "eye-to-eye", to use Bergson's description. When I sent away for my FBI files, there was a supportive reaction from Bergson to my having had dinner with a Russian at the United Nations.' Turgeon remembers Bergson as 'very objective and I could detect no bias in our research'.[5] And Bergson also recalls the research context as free from unwarranted external pressures:

> RAND's interest in SNIP and its willingness to fund it through the years doubtless reflected in a degree the internal U.S. preoccupation with the USSR at the time, but remarkably I never had any sense that RAND expected results from our research to be shaped in any way by extra-scholarly concerns. On the contrary, due in part no doubt to the remarkable environment created in the RAND Economics Department under the leadership of [Charles J.] Hitch, it was quite clear from the outset that RAND's interest, like mine, was simply to ascertain the facts, whatever their implications politically or otherwise.[6]

The aims of the SNIP project eventually embraced a wide-ranging reassessment of Soviet economic performance using a GNP system of accounts, and revaluing Soviet outlays, products, and factor productivities at constant prices and costs, together with relevant US–Soviet comparisons. Real GNP by end-use in selected years, 1928–55, was Bergson's own province; Richard Moorsteen and Raymond Powell produced annual series for Soviet GNP, 1928–67, by sector of origin, as a by-product of their work on the capital stock.

The main principles underlying this work can be summed up as follows: that a GNP accountancy measured national income better than the Soviet net material product concept; that Soviet national income was measurable in terms of 'productive potential', if not of social welfare; that Soviet official statistics were not freely invented, but distorted systematically, the distortions arising from index number relativity combined with so-called *pripiski* (fictitious claims to nonexistent output) and hidden inflation; that official figures could therefore be used with appropriate care and discrimination for a root-and-branch reconstruction of Soviet statistical aggregates. Since these principles also underlie the present work, the following questions are discussed below in detail: Why prefer a GNP accountancy? What does GNP mean in a Soviet institutional context? Are Soviet data reliable enough to allow the construction of GNP series? Given good enough data, can we arrive at unambiguous measures of real GNP?

Products and utilities

Much of this book is about measurement of the Soviet national income and product in real terms. Few intellectual disappointments match the student's first discovery of just how artificial a concept is 'real' income. Real income sounds solid and unequivocal. Yet its meaning is burdened with theoretical luggage. Moreover, it turns out to be incapable of unambiguous measurement.

Why prefer a GNP accountancy? The western concept of national income is GNP, the gross national product or GDP, the gross domestic product, which, in the Soviet case, come to the same thing. 'Gross' means including replacement investment to cover capital depreciation, which is hard to measure for purposes of deduction, uses resources and generates employment, and is generally a part of the total flow of resources available to society – three reasons for including it, not deducting it. GNP is further defined by three identities: the sum of *incomes* of the factors of production, which must match both the sum of final *outlays* on goods and services produced, and the sum of final *products*, each valued at factor cost (i.e. at prevailing prices, *minus* indirect taxes, *plus* subsidies). This is the SNA (System of National Accounts) concept adopted in 1953 by UN agencies, and subsequently by the IMF, World Bank, OECD, and other international agencies.[7]

The Soviet national accounts, first drawn up in the 1920s, were organised on the basis of an alternative concept, the Material Product System (MPS).[8] The MPS acquired more limited international status, becoming widespread after World War II in the eastern European and Chinese statistical agencies, and subsequently in Vietnam and Cuba too. National income according to the material product accountancy is not comparable with the GNP concept, but with enough information it is possible to convert between them. The net material product (NMP) is based on a distinction between primary and secondary incomes. 'Primary' incomes are generated in the production of final goods, including only intermediate services (for example, transport services embodied in goods), valued at prevailing prices, including net indirect taxes; their total makes the NMP. Incomes generated in the supply of final services (the nonproductive sphere) are termed 'secondary', and are generated as a result of redistribution of the primary incomes already formed. Lastly, NMP is net of depreciation, where GNP is gross.[9]

In western economics, real income is usually taken to measure two things, the scale of production of things, and the degree of satisfaction of wants. Which of these comes first is an issue which has beset economists since the utilitarians' attack on the labour theory of value. For present purposes I take it for granted that the scale of production of things, and the degree of satisfaction of wants, are both important. The difference between GNP and NMP is that only GNP can be presumed to measure both. The problem with NMP lies in the exclusion of final service products, which represent both uses of productive potential, and activities which satisfy social wants.

Under the well known assumptions of competitive general equilibrium, GNP measures both the production of things and the satisfaction of wants. If prices are proportional to marginal costs, then they give us what Bergson called an *efficiency standard* for measuring productive potential (i.e. profit-maximising producers will allocate resources between uses so that the total value of output cannot be increased by means of reallocation). If prices are proportional to marginal utilities, then they also give us Bergson's *welfare standard* (i.e. consumers will allocate their outlays so that reallocation cannot increase the social welfare derived from output).[10] If the prevailing prices of products and factors of production adjust flexibly to equate marginal costs with marginal utilities, then prevailing prices can be presumed to provide an appropriate standard of value for measuring both the satisfaction of society's wants and the sum of products at their factor cost.

A case can be made for the NMP as a measure of productive potential. A long tradition of western economics sees a prosperous services sector arising only on the basis of success in material production. Moreover, it can be argued that many services defined as final consumption in the GNP concept are really intermediate uses of resources which should be netted out – for example, the provision of defence and security services. Nonetheless, a national income concept which defines three fifths of the economic activity in today's OECD economies as 'non-productive' is certainly unhelpful, and probably obsolete. Moreover, the NMP concept clearly does not meet the requirement of a measure of social welfare, since it excludes a wide range of service-sector activities which satisfy social wants.

A variant of this argument was suggested recently by Robert Higgs, who proposed (in an article concerned with the United States war economy) that GNP should be measured exclusive of defence activity. Citing such past authorities as Simon Kuznets, William Nordhaus, and James Tobin, he maintained that defence spending is not a final demand, since the objects of military spending (defence industry products and military services) do not contribute directly to the satisfaction of wants, but only indirectly as intermediate products, which should therefore be netted out of GNP.[11] Thus, during World War II, American GNP on the conventional measure inclusive of defence outlays rose spectacularly, but there was no increase in social welfare.

This argument has potentially wide implications for evaluating Soviet economic performance both in peacetime and in time of war. As far as wartime is concerned, I believe it to be wrong, because it supposes mistakenly that GNP is the only determinant or measure of social welfare. In fact there is a wide range of noneconomic factors which also enter into the determination of social welfare, including natural disasters and wars. As the authors of the 1993 SNA point out, real GNP may be expected to rise in response to such factors, but because of them total welfare could fall even though GNP has risen:

> Given that a state of war exists, any consequential increase in the production and consumption of armaments or defence services may well increase welfare by affording extra protection to the community. Whether such increased welfare is sufficient to compensate for the loss of welfare caused by the war itself is quite another matter. The fact that the volume of GDP may increase as a result of the outbreak of war when the consumption of individual goods and services by households may be falling does not expose a deficiency in national accounts concepts, as is sometimes maintained. It has been argued that collective defence services should be classified as intermediate rather than final consumption, but there are in fact no further processes of production in which such services are consumed...

> When production and consumption increase in order to compensate for the loss of welfare created by damage or 'bads' that did not previously exist, the community may be no better off than if the damage had not occurred. However, this should not be allowed to obscure the fact that without the extra production and consumption the community would actually be worse off still. The extra production and consumption, in itself, actually increases welfare.[12]

The argument appears a little different with regard to peacetime, but the difference is purely superficial. Kuznets, for example, argued that war spending should be excluded from the determinants of welfare, but only in peacetime (with a great war in progress, the welfare of individuals must necessarily give way to the life or death of a society).[13] Naturally one may question whether the four postwar decades of Soviet military spending contributed much to the welfare of Soviet citizens. But the proposition that Soviet society reaped a poor return on its defence outlays rests on arguments about the efficient allocation of final goods, not the proposition that military goods and services are only intermediate goods. On this count, too, I believe that the revisionist case is weak.

For such reasons Bergson's research began with conversion of Soviet accountancy to a conventional GNP concept. In following chapters I adopt the same preference for GNP, and I do not anticipate great controversy at least on this score. Nonetheless, this decision necessarily plunges us into a further morass of issues arising from the fact that GNP was designed to measure activity in market economies, not in economies of the Soviet type.

Adjusted factor cost

What does GNP mean in a Soviet institutional context? Above it was pointed out that, for GNP to measure both the production of things and the satisfaction of wants, the assumptions of a competitive general equilibrium are required. Without competitive, well-functioning markets, this presumption breaks down. Its absence deprives us of a standard by which to value national income, and the heterogeneous assortment of goods and services produced and utilised cannot then be summed to make up a total, whether of products or of utilities.[14] Market failure in factor markets deprives us of the efficiency standard, the failure of product markets deprives us of the welfare standard, and failure in either destroys the supposition that the two standards give the same result.

Perhaps one should not make too much of this. No economy has ever perfectly matched the exacting standards of neoclassical general equilibrium theory, yet this does not stop practical people from valuing real income and judging policy and performance by their measures. In market economies, divergence between the efficiency and welfare standards is induced by market failures and endogenous taxes. In the Soviet case, of course, we are not even dealing with a basically market economy which suffered from particular market failures. The greater part of the Soviet resource allocation process was governed by quantitative controls administered by the centralised hierarchy of party and state institutions. This would suggest a need for great caution in calculating Soviet income at Soviet prices. At the same time, the cause is not absolutely hopeless, and previous generations of western scholars went to considerable lengths to make careful use of Soviet price and cost data for purposes of real product evaluation.

Bergson's instrument for solving the problem was his *adjusted factor cost* standard of valuation.[15] Prevailing Soviet prices were converted to adjusted factor cost by deducting turnover taxes and adding subsidies, then adding imputed interest and rent.[16] The result was intended to be a measure of Soviet real national product on an efficiency standard; it could also be understood as a measure of *productive potential*, not in the broad sense of a production possibilities frontier, but in the sense of a more restricted feasibility frontier subject to constraint by given institutions.

The adjusted factor cost standard was based on several empirical propositions. First, Soviet prices and wages were not as irrational as might appear. Product prices in the official sector were set administratively on the basis of average variable costs, at least in some recent year, *plus* a rough mark-up for overheads, *plus* the turnover tax on most final and some intermediate products. Second, to calculate average costs, the unit cost of wages and materials was taken into account. Traditionally there was little or no attempt to calculate capital costs or land rentals, but Bergson reckoned that a uniform capital charge would have been distributed roughly in line with actually reported profits.[17] The authorities tried to base prices on costs defined in this way, although there was an inevitable time-lag given the complexities of administrative price determination. Third, as for the determination of wage costs, Bergson found both institutional and empirical grounds to argue that wages were fixed by the authorities' need to attract workers into their best employment and compensate them for the disutility of their labour, so that the structure of wage costs and the adjusted factor cost standard did not diverge.[18] Thus, prices reflected average variable resource costs of the current year (*plus* the mark-up) at least for new goods, or in the event of a periodic price review. But there was no attempt to make prices reflect scarcity to industrial users or household consumers.[19]

There were troublesome implications for the possibility of a welfare standard by which to measure the satisfaction of wants in the Soviet economy. The pattern of production was determined administratively, without too much regard to user or consumer choice. There was a 'sellers' market', in which the seller had power over the buyer, and the buyer had to wait upon the supplier's convenience, or offer a bribe or illicit swap, or behave ingratiatingly, or make do with whatever the seller offered. Official prices bore a lagged relationship to variable costs, but had little or nothing to do with use-values. Under sellers' market conditions, industrial and household purchasers alike were unable to find an optimum because of the lack of availability of some goods at the ruling price, and the restricted range of choice between others which were available, giving rise to a pattern of frustrated purchases and forced substitutions.

As for the unofficial sector, prices fluctuated freely, but supplies were often constrained by quantities of intermediate goods available from the official sector. Here prices reflected scarcities (including scarcities generated by the shortage mechanism), but not marginal social costs. Bergson believed, however, that discrepancies between official and unofficial retail prices were less, and that official prices came nearer to clearing the retail market, in 1937 than in other prewar years.[20]

The adjusted factor cost standard cannot be adopted without reservation. For example, one may adjust the structure of prevailing prices to allow for the cost of factors of production not charged for; but if these factors of production were actually charged for in a market, and supplied and demanded on the basis of a market price, the allocation of resources and the structure of factor costs might look very different from what actually happened under quantitative controls. However, this reservation does not dissuade us from trying. Perhaps it is more relevant to cross-country comparisons of GNP levels than to intertemporal comparisons.[21] The GNP relativities between the USSR and the market economies employed in this book (tables 1.1 and 5.18) do not depend on adjusted factor cost comparisons.

Over-reporting and hidden inflation

Are Soviet data reliable enough to allow the construction of GNP series? Bergson's project began at a time of widespread suspicion about the validity of officially released Soviet economic data. This was partly the result of the first western reevaluations of Soviet economic growth by Clark and Jasny, which already tended to suggest that Soviet claims were greatly exaggerated, but distrust was also fuelled by the virtual blackout on publication of economic statistics operated at the time by the Soviet authorities. This blackout dated back to 1937, was lifted only momentarily with the 1947 publication of Voznesenskii's book about the war economy (which tantalised by as much as it revealed),[22] and would be maintained until 1956.

Bergson himself distinguished carefully between the 'methodological deficiencies' to be found everywhere in Soviet statistics, and 'free invention' which he believed to be rare. 'In the case of free invention', he wrote, 'research on the Soviet economy clearly is practically ruled out at once. In the case of methodological deficiencies, there is at least a core of fact from which to start and one may hope to detect and even correct the deficiencies.' The SNIP researchers were encouraged in their belief that official data were not freely invented by a number of factors, including access to the 1941 Soviet national economic plan, captured in wartime first by the Germans, then the Americans.[23] Comparison of secret plan figures with published documents showed that the two versions coincided, showing that the Soviets did not superimpose published fictions on secret facts. What the Soviets wished to conceal, they made secret, and did not directly fabricate. Withholding from publication was a substitute for free invention; Bergson described the withholding of information, which had become more or less commonplace in the two decades before 1956, as itself 'something of a testimonial to the reliability of what actually is published'.[24]

The quality of basic data was influenced by two main kinds of methodological deficiency: the over-reporting of output, and hidden inflation. Over-reporting involved distortion of the *level of output* at a point in time; hidden inflation, on the other hand, resulted in distortion of its *rate of growth*.

What was the main source of such methodological deficiencies? Output was produced by public-sector firms, and the output figures which they reported were used by higher authority to judge success at every level. Workers' wages were formed on the basis of reported individual or work-team output. Management bonuses and bonuses for distribution amongst the workforce were formed by the reported percentage fulfilment of the output plan, which also influenced career prospects for managers. This gave an incentive for lower levels to overstate performance. A variety of means was available for this. Statistical returns denominated in physical units (for example, of relatively homogeneous industrial materials) could be inflated by inclusion of defective or nonexistent output (*pripiski*); the number of physical units produced for given effort and resources could also be increased by reducing the quality of materials used or making the product to a lower specification. The increase in the quantity of products would exceed the increase in use-values available to society. Conversely, where success was measured by the ruble value of output (for example, of complex machinery), needlessly increasing the quality of materials used or making the product to a higher specification could inflate ruble values without contributing additional use-values.

If the desire to make false claims for output was widespread, there were also countervailing forces. In the short run, machinery producers supplied with defective steel found their own prospects of output quota fulfilment jeopardised, and could and did complain. So did equipment users supplied with inappropriately designed, excessively complex and unreliable machinery. Within the limits of the official system, household consumers could express discontent in reponse to retail shortages and deficiencies, and labour productivity could be influenced by low consumer morale.

The countervailing forces were not always decisive. Ministers and their deputies watched the output fulfilment records of firms aggregated under chief administrations and other ministerial divisions, for similar reasons of personal reward and promotion. At higher levels, therefore, officials were often motivated to collude with the overstatement arising at lower levels. The statistical apparatus itself was too heavily involved in the allocation of resources and rewards to have an independent voice within the ministerial system; the central statistical administration (TsUNKhU, later TsSU), was subordinate to the planning board (Gosplan) from 1932, and from 1941 did not even have a separate local apparatus. Uncovering the inflation of claimed achievements sometimes invited official retribution, and the very uncertainty surrounding official responses to whistle-blowing was itself often an effective deterrent. For firms suffering the deficiencies of the supply system, collusion with others' exaggerated claims might sometimes prove the better strategy in the long run; the firm which covered for the defective performance of suppliers acquired a handle on others through knowledge of their secret violations, and collusion might also buy goodwill and better supplies in the future. Individual consumers either suffered the discrepancies between claims and realities in silence, or sought private solutions to private problems.

Nonetheless, some claims were more easily inflated than others. Grigorii Khanin has proposed recently that official data may be classified in two ways: by the *pressure for distortion*, which was essentially a function of the use to which they were put, and by the *ease of distortion*, which depended on the relationship of the data to stocks and flows which are visible and physically homogeneous.[25] The pressure for distortion applied to all series used as success indicators such as the value and volume of output; this also means that data passed upwards into the administrative hierarchy were more likely distorted than data compiled for internal use within the firm. Since aggregation was a necessary aspect of passing data up the hierarchy, more highly aggregated data were also more liable to distortion. Data relating to nonstandardised, quality-sensitive engineering products or nonresidential construction objects were more easily distorted than figures for basic industrial goods or agricultural commodities. Thus Khanin identified machinery, construction, and road transport as sectors particularly vulnerable to hidden inflation.

However, the ease of distortion remained greater for value-of-output series than for physical volumes; *pripiski* were directly punishable by law, and more easily exposed by dissatisfied customers. Therefore, independent evaluations of Soviet production have generally been ready to use physical output data as a foundation for alternative estimates, even accepting that some distortion did take place.

Were there significant variations in the degree of distortion over time? It used to be the common view that false reporting could influence comparisons of levels, but not growth rates; 'If the degree of … misreporting is constant', Peter Wiles wrote, 'it does not affect growth measurement'; in some notorious years the inflation of claims was particularly widespread but 'if we neglect such bad years and concentrate on the rate of growth over a period, rather than on absolute levels at a date, they are insignificant'.[26] Alec Nove's 'law of equal cheating' followed the same spirit: 'False reporting at two different dates does not affect growth rates, unless there is more false reporting at one date than at another.'[27] But the cheating may not have remained equal; Khanin, for example, has argued that there were two big waves of distortion of physical output, one in the prewar years which resulted from the Stalinist excess of optimism, and was corrected in the 1950s, and another in the late

1980s, associated with the final disintegration of old-style Soviet economic discipline.[28] As we have seen, interwar Soviet agricultural production data were distorted by officially approved *pripiski* over an extended period. This distortion went entirely unpunished, and the power of dissatisfied food consumers to expose it was absolutely negligible.

Indicators of output based on value aggregates were on the whole more vulnerable to distorting pressures. This applied typically to manufactured products characterised by qualitative heterogeneity and assortment change, and gave rise to 'hidden inflation'. The hidden inflation mechanism operated in negotiation between the firm and the higher administrative levels which set prices in relation to the unit costs and use characteristics of products, and which monitored firms' performance. Sometimes it was the quality of firms' existing products which was allowed to fall, while the price was maintained, resulting in an unreported rise in the ratio of price to qualitative characteristics. Sometimes the firm falsely claimed an improvement in product quality; the authorities permitted a rise in price, which was offset against an illusory increase in product quality, while the product's true technical specifications remained unaltered, or were amended in ways which added useless detail to the product. New products were also introduced into the assortment range at prices and costs raised out of proportion to real use characteristics; in reality, the overall price level was inflated, but in official statistics the increase was again offset against the false claim of quality improvement, giving the illusion of price stability.

Soviet official figures for real product growth in the 1930s and 1940s were typically weighted by the so-called 'unchanged prices of 1926/27'. Jasny and Hodgman showed that these supposedly constant prices were not constant but rose through time with a consistent bias towards hidden inflation of machinery prices. Evidence from both the interwar and the postwar years suggested that, in practice, current and '1926/27' prices of Soviet engineering products tended to move together.[29] Since the turnover of assortment was more rapid in engineering than in other branches, by 1940 machinery was heavily over-represented in industrial production measured at so-called '1926/27' prices.[30] Similarly, Hodgman established that in the 1941-plan, engineering products accounted for 43 per cent of total industrial production at '1926/27' prices, but only 25 per cent at current production costs.[31] This implied an overvaluation of machinery relative to other industrial products, when '1926/27' prices were used in place of current costs, by a factor of more than 2:1.

This led the western researchers along two complementary courses. One was the search for output measures based on the most detailed possible information about physical output series. For example, Hodgman's index of industrial production utilised serial data for some 140 industrial products; Nutter's used data for more than 200 products.[32] The other was specialised study of the machinery sector and construction sectors, thought to be the prime source of hidden inflation. Construction was one of Powell's specialities.[33] Machinebuilding attracted particular attention in Hodgman's and Nutter's studies, and was also the subject of a substantial monograph by Moorsteen, who built a machinery index based on 210 product series.[34]

One curious result was the 'Moorsteen paradox', which has been identified by R.W. Davies. Moorsteen's index of machinery production at 1928 prices appeared to confirm the validity of the official index based on the 'unchanged prices of 1926/27' – no hidden inflation there. To judge from Nutter's index numbers of industrial production in different branches, statistical distortion in official figures was most pronounced for food products and other consumer goods.[35]

The Gerschenkron effect

Given good enough data, can we arrive at unambiguous measures of real GNP? Even if prevailing prices do equate marginal costs with marginal utilities, comparisons of real income through time and across countries cannot be done without ambiguity. The structure of prevailing prices does not form a universal standard, but changes systematically with real income, because the patterns of costs and wants change as incomes rise. The usual situation is that a given increase in physical output appears more desirable, and is more highly valued in terms of real income, before the change than after. This gives rise to index number relativity, also known as the 'Gerschenkron effect'. The effect can be observed both over time as a given country becomes richer, and at the same time comparing the real income of a rich country with that of a poor one.

The difficulty of making unambiguous comparisons of real output through time or across countries when there is substantial change in the structure of prices and quantities is well known. In the early 1950s, Alexander Gerschenkron suggested the particular form which this difficulty was likely to take in the Soviet case, when the structure of prices and quantities was changing rapidly.[36] Compare the Soviet economy in 1928 and 1937. (Note that for 'the Soviet economy in 1937' we could equally substitute another, richer country such as the United States.) In the USSR in 1928 machinery was expensive compared with food which was relatively cheap. This reflected many factors, among them the fact that machinery is capital-intensive, and Soviet capital was scarce, and therefore costly. Food was labour-intensive, and labour was cheap, so food was cheap. From the standpoint of 1928 values, therefore, expanding machinery output looked exceptionally desirable.

By 1937, things had changed. Between 1928 and 1937, Soviet machinery output had grown much faster than other branches. Capital was more abundant, and so was machinery, which had become relatively much cheaper; labour, and food, were both more scarce, and relatively more expensive. Food had become more expensive, and machinery cheaper. As a result, when Soviet goods and services are valued at constant prices of 1928, the growth of total output is dominated by high-value machinery, and grows with exceptional rapidity. When 1937 prices are used, however, total output is dominated by more slowly growing food and consumer goods, and the index of real output grows more slowly. In other words, from the *ex post* standpoint of 1937 values, the increased output achieved since 1928 looked rather less valuable than it had appeared *ex ante*.

By the same token, the development gap between the Soviet economy and the United States economy tended consistently to look far wider when goods and services are valued by Soviet standards; these gave a high ruble value to machinery, abundant in America and scarce in the USSR. On the other hand, from the standpoint of United States values the gap looked much narrower, given the relatively high dollar valuation of food, industrial materials, and labour-intensive goods in which the Soviet economy was relatively well endowed.

Index number relativity also applied to measures of the price level. A price index covering all goods and services, weighted by the structure of output in 1928 (when the economy was still dominated by agriculture and light industry) would show much sharper increases over the period to 1937, in line with spiralling inflation in consumer markets. A price index weighted by the 1937 structure of output would be correspondingly more influenced by machinery prices, and would rise more slowly.

As we have seen, Soviet official figures for real product growth of the period were typically weighted by the so-called 'unchanged prices of 1926/27'. By the late 1930s, 1926/27 was already far distant; even without any *pripiski* or hidden inflation, the Gerschenkron effect alone ensured that official index numbers showed very high growth rates.

This was not a bias in the sense of statistical distortion, but it was biased in the sense of a deliberate preference for an upper-bound estimate, while lower figures were suppressed.

At the same time, there were distorting practices at work, which meant that '1926/27' prices were not truly unchanged, but were liable to hidden inflation. By 1937 or 1940 the relative prices of '1926/27' diverged markedly not only from relative unit costs of the time, but also from the relative unit costs which would have been actually incurred had the the late 1930s' nomenclature of industrial commodities been produced in 1926/27. The reason was that new products introduced after 1926/27 were incorporated into the list of '1926/27' prices using the unit costs of the period of first production, which were usually much higher than they would have been in 1926/27; this gave a further boost to relative machinery prices, compounding the Gerschenkron effect.

The response of the SNIP methodology to these problems meant building new index numbers which were not only based on more exacting measures of product and price change, but also used a variety of weighting schemes, including fixed weights with several alternative base years (typically 1928, 1937, and 1955), and variable weights. At the same time, 1937 was often preferred for purposes of presentation and comparison, the reason being that this was the prewar year which Bergson had identified as giving the nearest to market-clearing prices.

The critics

The SNIP methodology never convinced everyone. Roughly speaking, the critics fell into two groups: the competitors, and the sceptics.

Competing conclusions of the various groups of independent researchers about the size of Soviet real national income in 1928, 1937, and 1940, within pre-1939 frontiers, are compared with Soviet official figures in table 3.1. These figures also illustrate nicely the extent of the various biases and distorting influences which the western researchers believed they had uncovered. According to TsSU, the real national product had quadrupled by 1937 and quintupled by 1940. Among the independent researchers, all were agreed that the official figures were too high, with the excess over western estimates attributed to a mixture of statistical distortion and index number relativity. But perceptions of the extent and mixture of these two influences diverged, often to the accompaniment of much bad temper.

Consider for a baseline Bergson's estimates of growth over 1928–37,

Table 3.1. *Soviet real national income within pre-1939 frontiers, 1937 and 1940 (growth over 1928, per cent per year) : alternative estimates*

Source	Concept	Standard of value	1937	1940
1 TsSU	NMP	'Unchanged' ruble prices of 1926/27	16.2%	14.6%
2 Clark	Real product	'International' dollars	3.2%	3.1%
3 Jasny	NNP	'Real' ruble prices of 1926/27	6.2%	5.4%
4 Bergson	GNP	Ruble factor costs of 1928	11.9%	–
5 Bergson	GNP	Ruble factor costs of 1937	5.5%	5.0%
6 Moorsteen/ Powell	GNP	Ruble factor costs of 1937	6.2%	5.4%
7 Khanin	Real product	Wage fund, expenditure, various years	–	3.2%

Sources: Row 1: TsSU (1962), 597. Row 2: Clark (1957), 247. Row 3: Jasny (1961), 444. Rows 4, 5: Bergson (1961), 128, 153. Row 6: Moorsteen, Powell (1966), 622. Row 7: Khanin (1988), 85.

5.5 per cent annually using 1937 weights, and 11.9 per cent based on 1928. These figures implied that the high TsSU figure for real product growth, 16.2 per cent annually over 1928–37, was made up roughly as follows: one part hidden inflation (16.2 – 11.9 = 4.3 per cent), one part index number relativity (11.9 – 5.5 = 6.4 per cent), and one part growth at current weights (5.5 per cent).

Jasny argued that Bergson had understated hidden inflation and had gone too high as a result; Jasny's own figure of 6.2 per cent in 'real' 1926/27 prices fell far below Bergson's 11.9 per cent based on 1928. But a mistake in Jasny's computation meant that, for comparisons between the late 1920s and late 1930s, the structure of his mis-named 'real' 1926/27 prices was similar to that of Bergson's 1937 factor costs;[37] therefore, Jasny's figure (6.2 per cent) inadvertently confirmed Bergson's, and cast further doubt on Clark's much lower one.

Clark (3.2 per cent), it was agreed by other western studies, had gone too low. The lone Russian estimate by Khanin, however, agrees with Clark's.

The sceptics proved to be a more lasting source of discomfiture than the competitors. They were disproportionately British; 'It is something of a British speciality, in Sovietological economics', writes Philip Hanson, to draw attention to conceptual shortcomings in monumental US studies. We share with the Russians a readiness to credit methodological problems with being insoluble; also a readiness to believe that common sense and common observation are not made ineffective either by their commonness or by their being unquantifiable.[38]

The sources of scepticism varied. Among welfare-oriented economists such as Peter Wiles, Bergson's adjusted factor cost standard evoked disbelief. Prevailing prices (Wiles argued), not factor costs are relevant to a welfare standard. The ultimate goal should be to measure 'the output of utility, not goods'; valuing physical products at cost, regardless of their variety, quality, and availability, could only overstate their welfare significance.[39]

Among economic historians could be found a more generalised unease; here Alec Nove provided a representative voice of compelling authority. When *all* the pitfalls of quantification are taken together, they make a daunting list: index number relativity; the inherent difficulty of accounting for product assortment and quality change in product and price indices; the problems of compensating for *pripiski* and hidden inflation, and for the withholding of information in the defence sector; the sincere disagreements among western experts. Better, perhaps, to scan the unadorned figures of coal, steel, and textiles produced, and make do with them.[40]

Khanin, a sceptic as well as competitor, has recently published a substantial critique of the RAND–CIA tradition. One theme of his work is that, in the absence of a feeling for Soviet reality, methodological complexity and the aspiration to comprehensiveness lead only to the multiplication of errors. Monumental studies executed without insight make monumental mistakes. Better the unstudied intuition of Clark and Jasny; better, perhaps, in Jasny's case, to get it right by mistake, than to miss the target despite following correct procedures.[41]

I acknowledge the force of these criticisms, but I am not one of the sceptics. Of course, I accept that every element of the SNIP methodology should be scrutinised, tested, and rejected if found wanting. The original knowledge base of the RAND studies was also characterised by many uncorrected distortions and lacunae. But the original aspiration, with its practical conception in Bergson's work, was sound. This conviction is reinforced when one considers the alternatives.

The weighting and aggregation of physical product series is always, inherently, problematic. But it is no solution simply to present the reader with tables of bare, apparently unweighted series for millions of tons of steel and coal, megawatt-hours of electricity, thousands of machine-tools and vehicles, and metres of cotton cloth. For one thing such figures always involve prior weighting and aggregation, since the true heterogeneity even among basic industrial commodities such as steel products, or petroleum products, is always much greater than such figures suggest. Then, the act of scanning such an array of figures and drawing conclusions from it also involves weighting and aggregation, but impressionistically, in the mind's eye, and therefore incorrectly. A suit, a car, and a ton of coal may occupy equal space in a column of figures, but do not have equal weight in the economy, and do not even have the same value as another suit, another car, and another ton of different coal.

The social scientist who simply throws her or his hands up in the face of uncertainty about 'true' weights, betrays a scientific responsibility to the truth. This truth is not the one true figure which remains obstinately hidden from us ignorant observers; it is the truth that all such figures are necessarily and inherently artefacts, constructed after the historical event, embodying values which are historical and relative as well as the less obviously constructed 'facts'.

Nor is it the answer to resort to intuition and personal experience to overturn scientific methodology. The individual may be convinced that a 'scientific' methodology has given the wrong answer, for example, that the estimated growth rate of GNP is too high, and that personal experience is right to suggest a lower growth rate. But what is the test of experience? Here the goal of social science is surely to unify the testimony of witnesses and experts into a coherent whole. This cannot be done without scientific method. For example, in 1950 Bergson suggested (on the basis of highly incomplete information, it is true) that '[Soviet] living standards in 1937 were higher than in any year since 1928 ... and according to many indications may even have surpassed those of the earlier year'.[42] For this he was roundly attacked by Jasny, who argued from more piecemeal evidence of the 'unweighted' sort that living standards for each sector of the population, urban and rural, had declined.[43] It was left to Bergson to explain that it was precisely the aggregation of different sectors of the population, while their weights were changing under the impact of rapid movement from country to town, which allowed aggregate living standards to remain unchanged despite decline in each sector considered in isolation.[44]

Official secrecy, statistical distortion, index number relativity, and the divergence between welfare and efficiency standards are all difficult problems which cannot be made to go away. These problems are challenges, not obstacles. The scholar's duty is not to lie down in front of them, but to try to analyse and quantify them as essential steps towards indicating their importance. These are also steps towards a more general evaluation of Soviet economic performance. In the same spirit, I approach the tasks of filling the gap left by World War II in the Soviet economic record, analysing Soviet wartime economic experience, and evaluating the impact of the war on the Soviet economy, as challenges which should excite, not daunt the present-day economic historian.

4 Industry

Official and unofficial biases

In World War II, industry supplied the means of warfare: not only guns, shells, tanks, ships, and planes, but also radios and radar, signalling equipment, vehicles, fuels, food rations, uniforms, and footwear. These things in turn required machinery, instruments, chemicals, metals, fibres, and electric power. By the mid-twentieth century Mechanisation had enhanced almost beyond measure not only the productive forces of modern societies, but also the forces of destruction. Two hundred years of scientific and technical revolution had stamped their influence on every aspect of warfare. The economic focus of this revolution was industry. It is with industry that the process of compiling a measure of Soviet wartime GNP by sector of origin begins.

In this chapter new measures of the scale and dynamic of wartime industrial production are presented. These are compared with the findings of previous authorities (the official TsSU figures, and subsequent estimates of Raymond Powell), together with the reasons for disagreement. Industrial employment and productivity trends are estimated. Defence industry output, productivity, and employment grew while civilian industry output, productivity, and employment fell.

The present chapter refers to 'industry' in the Soviet parlance, which corresponds roughly with the production industries on a western classification, so the main branches of extractive and manufacturing industries (including the fuel and power sectors) are included; construction and transport are treated separately in chapter 5. GNP originating in industry means value added, which is gross output, *less* intermediate purchases. In this chapter value added is net of capital depreciation, since depreciation is also treated separately in chapter 5.

The competing estimates agree that the German invasion of 1941 set off a sudden decline of Soviet industrial production. The composition of

Table 4.1. *Industrial production, 1941–5: alternative estimates (per cent of 1940)*

	1941	1942	1943	1944	1945
1 Harrison	98%	86%	101%	113%	96%
2 Powell	93%	63%	70%	78%	69%
3 TsSU	98%	77%	90%	104%	92%

Sources: Row 1: table 4.8, row 4 (net value added, at 1937 factor cost). Row 2: Powell (1968), 7 (net value added, at 1937 factor cost). Row 3: TsSU (1959), 8–9 (gross output, at 1926/27 prices).

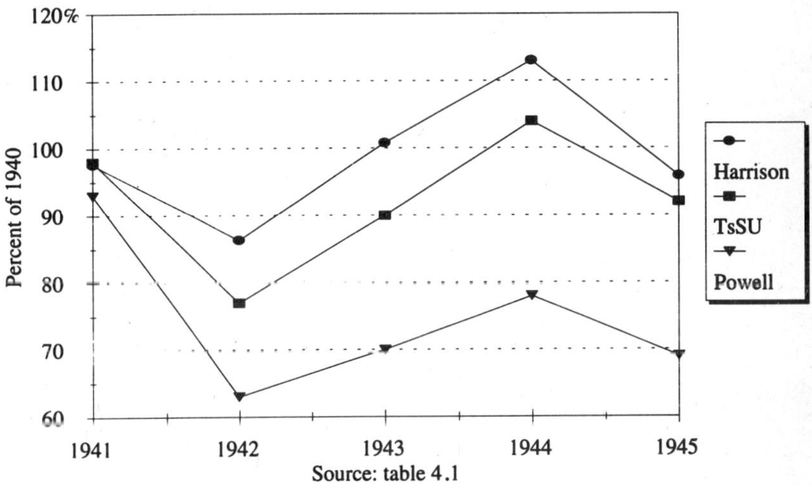

4.1 Industrial production, 1941–5: alternative estimates

industrial production also changed sharply away from civilian products towards military goods. Beyond these simple generalisations, however, there are wide-ranging disagreements, which are illustrated in table 4.1.

According to the official figures, despite the growth of defence industry output, the gross output of industry as a whole (measured in 'unchanged' 1926/27 prices) fell by a quarter between 1940 and 1942, and did not recover until 1944. In 1945 there was another sharp setback to industrial activity as the reconversion of defence industry to civilian production got under way. Powell's subsequent, independent estimate (net value added in Soviet industry, at 1937 factor costs) was even more pessimistic; he believed that in the 1942 trough industrial production fell short of the 1940 benchmark by 30 per cent. Even at the 1944 peak, Powell estimated, Soviet industry still fell short of 1940 output by one fifth. The present estimate is not only more sanguine than Powell's, but is also more optimistic even than official figures. There was a temporary drop in the 1942 level of industrial production to 86 per cent of 1940; recovery to the prewar level had been achieved by 1943, and at the peak of the war effort industrial production exceeded the prewar level by one eighth. However, the subsequent decline associated with reconversion at the war's end was very sharp.

The differences among the various estimates are explicable in terms of two sets of factors – differences in the underlying knowledge base, and differences in the degree of correction of various distortions affecting the processing of the statistical data. The knowledge base of the official figures was naturally the most complete, but its processing was seriously distorted. Powell's estimate was reached on the basis of very poor knowledge under the conditions of widespread official secrecy which still prevailed at the time, and his attempts to rectify the biases then recognised in the west resulted, ironically, in an even more distorted picture. The knowledge base of present estimates is far from complete, but vastly improved. Our methodological procedures can recognise and avoid or correct a much wider range of biases than before. But there are still some areas of obscurity and procedural difficulties. The measurement of industrial output, comprising in particular the procedure for valuing defence products relative to civilian products, proves to be the most sensitive step in the entire exercise of GNP estimation.

In order to provide an overview of the potential for statistical distortion, we shall consider the official figures for wartime gross output of industry at 'unchanged' 1926/27 prices for a baseline. These figures incorporated five main distortions (see p. 61). The first three had a common source in prewar and wartime hidden inflation and deflaction. Bias 1 involved an upward distortion arising from the excessive *initial weight attributed to machinery* (including defence industry products) in the official measures of wartime industrial production and NMP. Bias 2 involved an upward distortion of the *trend of civilian output*, and bias 3 involved a downward distortion of the wartime *trend of defence industry output*. The other two originated elsewhere, in the official gross output concept used to value industrial production, and both created downward distortions. Bias 4 involved attribution of an excessive *initial weight to intermediate products* compared with products for final use; bias 5 arose from neglect of wartime divergence between defence industry trends in

Distortions in evaluation of wartime industrial production

Bias	direction	via ...	induced by ...
1	upward	overstated prewar weight of machinery	prewar hidden inflation
2	upward	overstated wartime trend of civilian output	wartime hidden inflation
3	downward	understated wartime trend defence industry output	wartime hidden deflation
4	downward	overstated prewar weight of intermediate products	use of gross output value to weight products
5	downward	understated wartime trend defence industry output	use of value added to weight products

gross output and value added, resulting in understatement of the wartime *trend of defence industry value added* (its contribution to GNP).

Bias 1

In the prewar years, the so-called 'unchanged' prices of 1926/27 concealed inflation in the machinery sector. As new machinery products with a higher price/quality ratio replaced old machines with a lower ratio, they were incorporated into the serial data at relatively high current costs and prices, not the lower costs and prices which would notionally have prevailed in 1926/27. By the late 1930s this had resulted in a large overstatement of the value of machinery (including military machinery) relative to other kinds of product where the assortment range had changed less rapidly.

Since machinery was the only substantial product group to expand in wartime, bias 1 tended to inflate the growth of official wartime figures of real output of industry as a whole, and is therefore classed as an upward bias.

Bias 2

Another upward bias stemmed from wartime hidden inflation which continued to operate as usual, at least in civilian branches. As in peacetime, changes in product assortment and quality were apparently used by producers to raise the price/quality ratio compared with the ratio which would notionally have applied in 1926/27. One may suppose that in wartime it was the downgrading of product quality and the introduction of new, inferior products which provided the main opportunities for hidden inflation. Reclassified or downgraded products, incorporated into the measure of real output at inflated price/quality ratios, lent an upward bias to official index numbers of real output. Below it will be shown that, by 1944, the official index of gross output of civilian industry products based on 1940 was some 20 per cent above a more realistic estimate of gross output.

Bias 3

In defence industry, however, there were two offsetting downward biases, the first as follows. The war years saw the exact converse of the peacetime trend of hidden inflation. Prices of weapons *fell* by roughly 40 per cent according to official figures between 1940 and 1944, at the same time as the quality of weaponry improved.[1] The relative speed of introduction of new weapons, combined with the large wartime deflation of weapons prices, meant that by 1944 the increase in real output of military machinery compared with 1940 was considerably understated. Modernised, cheaper weapons took the place of obsolete, expensive ones; they were incorporated into official index numbers but, because their price/quality ratio was well below the previous level, they did not receive their due weight. Below it will be shown that, by 1944, the official index of gross output of defence industry products based on 1940 was nearly 15 per cent below a more realistic estimate of gross output.

Bias 4

A further downward bias arose from the gross output concept used to measure the results of industrial activity. Official index numbers measured gross output (*valovaia produktsiia*); even without any hidden inflation or other distortions, this alone was sufficient to bias the official valuation of industrial activity from the point of view of its contribution to GNP. Gross output sums the products leaving the factory gates, regardless of their destination – to other users in the same branch, to users in other branches, or to final use for consumption, investment, or export. When production involves many distinct stages, the same commodities are counted more than once as they pass through the various stages. This double-counting of intermediate goods exaggerates their importance relative to final products, and the weight attached to more finished or highly fabricated goods is too small.

The proper weights to apply to gross output series are, of course, gross output values multiplied by the share of final products in gross output which, in the case of sectors supplying intermediate products, is zero.

Despite the theoretical bias, under normal circumstances and over a short run of years, the trend in gross output can be expected to give a reasonable approximation to the trend in value added. Provided that each branch's gross output and value added move roughly in step, and provided that there are no violent changes in the structure of industry, so that incorrect weights do not matter much, a gross output index will not diverge much from an index of real value added.

Wartime circumstances, however, were not normal. In wartime the output of military machinery (representing finished goods) grew by three or four times, while the output of civilian goods (including most intermediate products) shrank to relatively small percentages of the prewar level. If official measures exaggerated the prewar weight of intermediate goods, and understated the weight of finished goods (such as military machinery), the result was to understate the wartime trend of industrial production as a whole.

Bias 5

A procedure for partially rectifying bias 4, which was actually even more distorting, was practised by some of the western pioneers in revision of Soviet industrial statistics. Hodgman, Nutter, Kaplan, Moorsteen, and Powell diligently identified the pitfalls associated with the 'unchanged' prices of 1926/27, and strove in their own work to eliminate the associated biases.[2] They used serial product data, confident that their widening knowledge base would largely eliminate hidden inflation from the trend of output.

All that remained was to combine the new measures of branch output, using sector value added (usually represented by adjusted wage-fund or employment figures) rather than gross output value to weight them. Their updating of base-year value-added weights also aimed to eliminate the distorting effects of hidden inflation in the 'unchanged' prices of 1926/27 on relative machinery prices since the latter year.

There was a conceptual mismatch, however, between products and weights, which Hodgman and his successors were unable to resolve. Weights were *net* (i.e. proxies for value added), while products were *gross* (of intermediate requirements). Under normal circumstances this was hardly a terrible crime, and most index-number practitioners are probably guilty of it at one time or another. The reason for it is that, for computing base-year weights, net output of the different branches of industry can be measured at a point in time from wages and profits at current factor costs, at least in market economies, although not without effort; and in the Soviet case we have to resort to Bergson's 'adjusted factor cost', or a proxy such as branch shares in employment or the wage fund. But calculating the trend in 'real' value added in subsequent years is usually ruled out altogether, because of the difficulty of carrying out the necessary double deflation of nominal values of gross outputs and intermediate purchases separately. So the practitioner takes what is practically measurable, rather than what is theoretically desirable, uses real gross output as a proxy for real value added, and combines branch gross outputs using net (value-added) weights.

Everything is all right as long as gross output trends are representative of net output. But in wartime Soviet industry this proves not to have been the case, and the procedure becomes yet another source of distortion. The distortion is even larger than for a conventional gross output index. The problem with the conventional gross output index was that it gave excessive weight to intermediate products (bias 4). When gross outputs are given net weights, the relative weight attached to fabricated goods is further reduced, so that the excessive weight of intermediate goods is actually increased.

Again, under normal circumstances and over a short run of years, when the input/output structure of industry does not change markedly, no great damage may result. Hodgman, Nutter, Kaplan, and Moorsteen did not try to compute measures of industrial production under the abnormal circumstances of wartime. But Raymond Powell did subsequently make such an estimate, reported above (table 4.1). Noting the uncertainties surrounding his figures (he regretted that 'for industrial production, physical output data have not been published in enough volume to permit estimates based on them, which lack is much the largest one remaining in the official data'), Powell suggested that they might be on the low side, and this appears to have been an accurate presentiment.[3] The official wartime index and Powell's figures rise and fall in phase, but the decline according to Powell's was much more marked.

Given the paucity of the serial data for physical output then available, Powell had to rely heavily on official index numbers of gross output as a basis for interpolating an industrial production series between 1940 and 1945. He stated that his index was weighted by 1950 prices for civilian industry, and 1937 prices for munitions relative to both machinery and industry as a whole; exactly what this means is not clear, but it was most certainly an improvement on '1926/27' prices, and must have largely removed bias 1.[4] However, Powell was unable to correct the other three biases; indeed, in the absence of any detailed product or price series, he had no basis to anticipate them.

So, having corrected the excessive prewar weight of machinery (bias-1) in the official figures, Powell continued to calculate industrial production by combining index numbers of civilian and defence industry output, which were distorted respectively by hidden inflation (bias 2) and deflation (bias 3); the index numbers measured gross output (bias 4), and may have been combined using net weights (bias 5). Thus, having removed one upward bias, without affecting the other upward and downward ones, Powell's estimate was consequently still more understated than the official one.

The evidence points to a substantial wartime fall in the defence industry ratio of intermediate purchases to gross output, so that value added in the specialised manufacture of weapons rose much faster than index numbers of gross output suggest. It will be shown below that, by 1944, the excess of an index of value added over a gross output index based on 1940 was nearly 30 per cent. The evidence is indirect and somewhat fragmentary, but cumulatively compelling. There is, moreover, one undisputed observation of trend which drives us to consider it. When war broke out, the production of industrial materials declined precipitously. (The same was true of supply of nonindustrial materials to industry from other sectors.) The output of fabricated goods fell by much less; civilian lines fell roughly in proportion with the decline in availability of materials, while the supply of munitions increased. Some (not all) of the gap between output of intermediate and fabricated goods can be accounted for by release of materials from stocks (especially in 1942), and by supply of material requirements from abroad (in 1943–4). On balance, however, regardless of how the different sectors are weighted, and of different sources of supply, there must have been a substantial rise in the ratio of fabricated products to intermediate materials used. With it therefore rose the share of industry value added in gross output.

To summarise the impact of the various biases, consider the formula for V^*_t, a Laspeyres index of value added in year t, calculated as a weighted average of index numbers of real value added V^*_{jt} over j

sectors of industry (j = 1, 2, 3).[5] Sector 1 produces intermediate goods, sector 2 finished civilian goods, and sector 3 finished military goods. The GNP contributed by the three sectors is valued using weights μ_{jt} ($\mu_{1t} + \mu_{2t} + \mu_{3t} = 1$) of a base year ($t = 0$), so that:

$$V^*_t = \sum_j \mu_{j0} \cdot V^*_{jt}$$

$$= \mu_{10} \cdot V^*_{1t} + \mu_{20} \cdot V^*_{2t} + \mu_{30} \cdot V^*_{3t}$$

Bias 1 led to the understatement of μ_{10} and overstatement of μ_{20} and m_{30}. Bias 2 led to the overstatement of V^*_{1t} and V^*_{2t}, and bias 3 to the understatement of V^*_{3t}. Bias 4 had effects converse to those of bias 1, and bias-5 reinforced bias 3. Given that in wartime V^*_{3t} rose sharply while V^*_{1t} and V^*_{2t} fell, the various biases thus had the potential to offset each other in the aggregate, and in fact did so to some extent, but we shall find that in practice the downward biases predominated in previous estimates, both official and western.

Real gross output by sector

For 1941 through to the end of the war, the present index of industrial production is completely reconstructed. Estimates of output of the production industries are based on 248 individual civilian and military product series. These are used to generate 11 industrial sector indexes of real gross output. The data sources, the product series, and the prices and other weights used to combine them, are shown in appendices B (defence industry) and C (civilian industry).

Defence industry

The data for defence industry, newly derived from archival documents of the former Soviet government, cover the main types of ground and air weapons supplied to the Soviet Army during World War II. They are broadly consistent with the much more aggregated figures published in the 1970s and early 1980s, but throw additional light on the volume of wartime munitions output in two main respects. First, individual models of weapon are identified in great detail, allowing much finer judgement of the changing assortment. Where previously we knew series only for 'bombers', or for 'medium and large calibre guns', we now have data by model and calibre. Second, the range of weapons covered is wider than before, extending to the significant and hitherto neglected category of small arms ammunition.

The new data include 15 types of fighter aircraft, assault aircraft (2 types), bombers (11), and other aircraft including training, transport, and reconnaissance (16), tanks (9) and self-propelled artillery (6), field guns (11), anti-tank guns (2) and tank guns (5), guns for self-propelled artillery (6), anti-aircraft guns (6), aircraft guns, small arms (5), small arms ammunition (4), and other ammunition comprising separately artillery shells, bombs, mortar shells, aircraft shells, mines, and grenades, making 105 series in total. Other than aircraft, each series has 5 annual observations beginning in 1940, and 19 quarterly figures starting from January 1941. In some cases monthly figures through 1941 are also available. The aircraft series are more aggregated, with annual data only (1937–45) for individual aircraft models, and half-yearly data for the war years (quarterly from mid-1941 to mid-1943) for broad types only ('fighters', 'bombers', etc.), requiring some interpolation. A summary of the new data is included in table 4.2. Their main defect is the lack of adequate series for supply of naval munitions. Even so, they are far more comprehensive than the data set underlying the author's previous evaluation of wartime munitions output, which relied on only 15 series in physical units observed over five full years (1940–4) and one half year (the first six months of 1945), with more than 30 interpolations to cover missing observations.

To supplement new serial data for output, we also have a much wider sample of defence industry product prices gathered from various wartime years.[6] They confirm the exceptionally sharp price deflation of the war years, especially in 1942 compared with 1941. Their range is narrower than the product sample for which production is known; frustratingly, no prices appear to be accessible as yet for ammunition.

Civilian industry

The real volume of Soviet civilian industrial production in the years of World War II is estimated from output data for 143 products in physical units, and ruble prices from 1937 or closely adjacent years.[7] The price data were assembled some years ago by Jasny, Moorsteen, Chapman and, more recently, Zaleski.[8] Despite their efforts, however, data for prices are now less abundant than for quantities, and gaps in the price data are one constraint on our ability to make use of available product series.

The civilian series are comprehensive, and contain no interpolations. They include 45 types of machinery, fuels (10 products), iron and steel products (9), chemicals and rubber products (4), timber and

Table 4.2. *Industrial production, selected series, 1940–45 (units)*

		1940	1941	1942	1943	1944	1945
1	Defence industry						
1.1	combat aircraft	8331	12377	21681	29877	33205	–
1.2	armoured vehicles	2794	6590	24719	24006	28983	–
1.3	guns	15343	40547	128092	130295	122385	–
1.4	shells, million	43	83	133	175	184	–
1.5	small arms, '000	1916	2956	5358	5081	4045	–
1.6	cartridges, million	3006	4335	4117	5956	7406	–
2	Iron, steel						
2.1	crude steel, '000 tons	18317	17893	8070	8475	10887	12252
2.2	pig iron, total, '000 tons	14902	13816	4779	5591	7296	8803
2.3	rolled metal, total, '000 tons	13113	12588	5415	5675	7278	8485
3	Nonferrous metals						
3.1	copper, '000 tons	139	185	118	130	140	136
3.2	aluminium, '000 tons	60	68	52	62	83	87
4	Fuel industry						
4.1	coal, '000 tons	165923	151428	75536	93141	121470	149333
4.2	oil, '000 tons	31121	33038	21988	17984	18261	19436
5	Electric power, million kWh	48309	46698	29068	32288	39214	43257
6	Chemical industry						
6.1	soda ash, '000 tons	536	463	62	105	158	235
6.2	mineral fertiliser, '000 tons	3238	2674	364	539	776	1121
6.3	toluene, '000 tons	38	58	38	40	38	34
7	MBMW						
7.01	lathes	58437	44510	22935	23281	34049	38419
7.02	presses	4668	3119	2210	2423	2691	2871
7.03	steam turbines	57	45	3	4	6	8
7.04	steam boilers	1784	854	141	267	426	726
7.05	diesel engines	1329	1016	142	100	105	452
7.06	steam turbine generators	27	13	0	7	19	22
7.07	electric motors >100kW	3067	2570	209	453	1797	3237
7.08	electric motors <100kW, '000	259.5	184.2	12	27.4	73	110.7
7.09	power transformers	3506	3004	960	1086	1559	1848
7.10	trunkline steam locomotives	914	708	9	43	32	8
7.11	trunkline freight cars	30880	33096	147	108	13	819
7.12	automobiles	145390	124176	34976	49266	60549	74657
7.13	bearings, million	45	38	22	30	33	34
8	Timber, paper						
8.1	commercial timber, million cu. m.	117.9	115.1	48.2	43.4	52.4	61.6
8.2	firewood, million cu. m.	128.2	114.2	84.5	110	108.2	106.8
8.3	sawn timber, million cu. m.	34.8	29.7	15.1	13.1	13.2	14.7
9	Construction materials						
9.1	cement, '000 tons	5675	5514	1133	980	1490	1845
9.2	bricks, million	7454.7	5574.7	1572.2	1316.6	1558	2026

Table 4.2 (contd.)

		1940	1941	1942	1943	1944	1945
9.3	window glass, '000 sq. m.	44690	38487	6333	7184	13533	23309
10	Light industry						
10.1	cotton textiles, million m.	3954	3824	1644	1635	1779	1617
10.2	leather footwear, '000 prs	211033	157687	52675	55804	67423	63115
10.3	clocks and watches, '000	2796	1838	61	417	355	336
10.4	sewing machines , '000	175	200	0	0	0	0
10.5	bicycles , '000	255	142	0	0	1	24
11	Food industry						
11.01	sugar, granulated, '000 tons	2165	523	114	117	245	465
11.02	meat, excl. kolkhoz, '000 tons	1501	1172	723	614	543	663
11.03	fish, '000 tons	1404	1281	962	1208	1235	1125
11.04	butter, '000 tons	226	205	111	101	106	117
11.05	vegetable oil, '000 tons	798	685	253	215	238	292
11.06	beer, million dcl.	121	97	30	31	33	41
11.07	salt, million tons	4	3	1	3	3	3
11.08	tea, '000 tons	25	20	14	18	20	18
11.09	cigarettes, billion	100	74	4	6	7	25
11.10	flour, million tons	29	24	16	13	13	15

Sources: Rows 1.1–1.6: as table B-1. Rows 2.1–11.10: as table C-1.

paper products (7), nonferrous metals (5), construction materials (5), and electric power, as well 17 food products and 10 products of light industry. A selection is reproduced in table 4.2. Their scope (113 civilian products, which together with 105 defence products make 218 series in total) is sufficient for a reliable measure. It is comparable with Nutter's 203-product index, which spanned 1928–58 with a break between 1940 and 1945.[9] It exceeds that of the 104-product index used by Khanin for 1928–80; Khanin is said to have also calculated parallel indexes covering approximately 400 and 1,000 products respectively, finding almost no divergence among the three series.[10]

Some civilian branches receive adequate coverage for the first time in a western study, for example, nonferrous metallurgy. At the same time it is clear that not all branches are covered equally well; as well as products whose wartime supply is still secret, such as gold and uranium, there are also many products not included in the quantity data presented here. This is particularly the case with branches such as machinebuilding, light industry, and food products, where the assortment range was most varied. For example, in the case of light industry there is no mention of cutlery, crockery, and cooking utensils.

Sector gross output

At this stage, 218 products are grouped under 11 industrial branch headings:

- defence industry
- civilian MBMW
- iron, steel
- nonferrous metals
- fuels
- electric power
- chemicals
- timber, paper
- construction materials
- light industry
- food industry

This makes for a commodity classification of industrial production, rather than one based on establishments and ministries.

It would be perfectly possible in terms of computation to short-cut the process of calculating sector index numbers, by assembling the annual ruble values of the 218 product series at 1937 prices, and summing arithmetically without any further adjustment. However, this would ignore two problems. First, some correction needs to be made for uneven representativeness. The branch-by-branch coverage of the raw data is not at all uniform across industry (for example, it was much more comprehensive for the fuel and electric power industries than for chemicals and machinebuilding); in the raw data, the more comprehensively represented sectors carry an undue weight. Second, we shall find that the ratio of value added to gross output (which depended on the degree of fabricatedness of products) varied significantly across industry, and in the case of the defence industry through time; simply adding up products multiplied by prices assumes that these ratios were uniform and constant.

The gross output of each branch is calculated separately. For civilian branches, the computation is done in constant prices of 1937 or some near equivalent. For defence products, 1942 is the year of most abundant price data, so series are valued in prices of 1942; special allowance is made for ammunition (for which there are product series but no prices) and naval munitions (for which deflated outlays must take the place of product series). Generally, for both civilian and military goods, gaps in the price data are filled with prices taken or extrapolated from other years, or by informed guesswork, making abundant use of the

Table 4.3. *Gross output of industry, by branch of origin, 1941–5 (1937 prices and per cent of 1940)*

	1941	1942	1943	1944	1945
1 Defence industry	148%	307%	365%	389%	263%
2 Civilian MBMW	83%	21%	25%	35%	45%
3 Iron, steel	96%	41%	44%	57%	65%
4 Nonferrous metallurgy	121%	84%	86%	102%	103%
5 Fuels	91%	45%	55%	70%	72%
6 Power	97%	60%	67%	81%	90%
7 Chemicals, rubber	100%	54%	70%	79%	61%
8 Timber, paper	91%	50%	56%	58%	62%
9 Construction materials	83%	19%	17%	26%	35%
10 Light industry	87%	35%	37%	40%	38%
11 Food industry	78%	44%	37%	39%	46%

Sources: Row 1: table B-9, row 3.1. Rows 2–11: table C-3, rows 1–10.

principle (demonstrated many years ago by Peter Wiles) that 'it is better to guess a weight than to omit a growth series'.[11]

The constant-price values of output of each branch are then expressed as index numbers, in percentages of output of the base year 1940. Results are shown in table 4.3. The divergence between trends in defence industry and civilian industry is obvious and striking. While the output of defence industry products multiplied, reaching 3.9 times the prewar level in 1944, civilian output tended to collapse.

Within the overall pattern, there were some significant differences in civilian industry performance. To judge from table 4.3, civilian branches can be considered in three groups. The first group, which best maintained output levels through 1942–3, included the civilian branch most closely involved in supply of defence industry, *nonferrous metals*, and also the *electric power* industry. In 1942 their output fell roughly 20–40 per cent below prewar levels before recovering strongly in 1943.

In an intermediate group are found the basic industries supplying *iron and steel, fuels, chemicals,* and *timber products.* These branches, despite their key significance not only for defence industry and the army, but also for the infrastructure of the whole economy, suffered a crushing blow, and in 1942 their output fell 45–65 per cent below prewar levels before subsequent recovery. The chemical industry, however, made a strong recovery in 1943. Also in this intermediate group can be found the *light* and *food* industries supplying retail products

Table 4.4. *Industrial production, by branch of origin, 1944: alternative estimates (per cent of 1940)*

	Present estimates of gross output, at 1937 prices, classified by commodity	TsSU figures of gross output at 1926/27 prices, classified by	
		establishment	commodity
	(1)	(2)	(3)
1 MBMW	–	158%	–
1.1 defence industry	389%	251%	–
1.2 civilian MBMW	35%	–	–
2 Metallurgy	–	88%	–
2.1 iron, steel	57%	–	–
2.2 nonferrous metals	102%	–	–
3 Fuels	70%	71%	–
4 Power	81%	81%	–
5 Chemicals, rubber	79%	133%	–
6 Timber, paper	58%	55%	–
7 Construction materials	26%	35%	–
8 Light industry	40%	64%	–
9 Food industry	39%	47%	–
10 Defence products	389%	251%	312%
11 Civilian products	50%	–	61%

Sources: Col. 1: table 4.3. Col. 2: IVOVSS, vol. 6 (1965), 45 (four defence industry commissariats: aircraft industry, armament industry, ammunition industry, shipbuilding), 59 (six heavy industries), 63 (the light and food industries). Col. 3: TsSU (1959), 28.

to the consumer market; their performance was distinguished from that of the basic industries because recovery was delayed until after the war.

A third group comprising *civilian machinebuilding*, and the *construction materials* industry, saw output fall in 1942 by 80 per cent, with noticeable recovery delayed until 1944 or 1945.

It is also possible to make more detailed comparisons with the official branch index numbers of gross output. Present estimates show a much sharper increase in the output of defence industry and reduction in the output of civilian industry during the war years than official measures (table 4.4). In all civilian branches supplying fabricated goods, the fall in real output was typically much greater than was officially reported.

Table 4.5. *Gross output of civilian industry, by branch of origin, 1944 (per cent of 1940): standard deviations of product relatives*

	Number of products (1)	Standard deviation (2)
1 Civilian MBMW	53	0.41
2 Iron, steel	11	0.20
3 Nonferrous metals	6	0.46
4 Fuels	13	0.35
5 Power	1	–
6 Chemicals, rubber	8	0.42
7 Timber, paper	7	0.22
8 Construction materials	8	0.06
9 Light industry	12	0.19
10 Food industry	23	0.33
11 Civilian industry	142	0.41

Source: Calculated from table C.1.

Only the indices for products which were highly homogeneous, or relatively unfabricated (timber, fuels, and electric power) show a close fit between the official measure and present estimates.

Of course, one possibility is that present estimates are in error. Our results may be distorted if the underlying serial data are unrepresentative, or if the commodity prices selected to evaluate branch products are unrepresentative. I believe neither of these to be the case. First, the product series underlying present estimates are both relatively comprehensive, and relatively robust. Second, results for each branch are not very sensitive to the particular prices selected to value individual products. This is demonstrated by the standard deviations of 1944 index numbers for the 110 individual civilian product series used in our estimates, by branch, and across industry, reported in table 4.5. Within each branch, the degree of variation in the trend of output of individual products was generally no greater than, and often less than, the degree of variation across industry as a whole. Most branch products behaved in a relatively uniform way, meaning that wrong relative prices can have had little distorting effect on branch index numbers.

Therefore, the more probable explanation of the discrepancies shown in table 4.4 is that the official figures are distorted. The main likely sources of distortion are wartime hidden inflation, and accounting for sideline military products of civilian industry.

Sideline military products

Present estimates are commodity-based, while official index numbers were establishment-based. It may be that, in wartime, civilian establishments in the iron and steel, chemical, and light industries produced sideline military products which accounted for a rising share of their output. If sideline military products are represented in official figures for civilian branch output, but excluded from present, commodity-based estimates for civilian industry, this may explain some proportion of the discrepancies with official data.

How much can be explained in this way is not clear. For example, before the war ammunition production was widely subcontracted to civilian establishments,[12] and in wartime this practice continued. But in 1944, when war production was at its peak, the iron and steel, chemical, and timber industries together contributed no more than 6.4 per cent of the nationwide supply of ammunition.[13]

Table 4.4 displays not one but two official index numbers for defence industry production in 1944. Both are in the 'unchanged' prices of 1926/27. The lower one (251 per cent of 1940) has been well known since it was first published in 1965 as representing the gross output of four defence industry commissariats (aircraft, armament, ammunition, and shipbuilding).[14] Much defence industry activity was therefore omitted, for example, work carried on under the auspices of the tankbuilding and mortar armament commissariats, as well as orders subcontracted to civilian industry. (This activity was therefore counted elsewhere in industrial production under nominally civilian agencies.) The proportion of omitted activity may well have been higher in 1944 than in 1940. Even for the limited range of establishments included, though, the official index was, surely, a ludicrous underestimate.

The second figure for defence industry output in 1944 became available to us only recently; originally put in limited circulation in 1959, it claims to represent 'military output' (*voennaia produktsiia*), beside a parallel index of 'civilian output', which implies that it is based on a more inclusive commodity classification. Its trend is indeed higher: 312 per cent of 1940, instead of 251 per cent, in 1944. The difference between the two may well provide a measure of the rising wartime importance of sideline military products of civilian industry.

However, even 312 per cent still falls far short of the 361 per cent calculated for 1944 from the present relatively comprehensive sample of robust serial data for defence products. Thus, the role of sideline military products of civilian industry does not explain the full scope of the discrepancy between official and revised estimates of defence industry output.

In the same spirit, the parallel official figure for 'civilian output' (*grazhdanskaia produktsiia*) in 1944, 61 per cent of 1940, is also presumably based on a commodity classification which excludes the sideline military products of civilian industry. But this figure is still excessive compared with the 50 per cent of 1940 obtained by summing present estimates of the trend in value added across civilian industry.

Hidden inflation

The remainder of the discrepancy between present estimates and official figures must be attributed to wartime hidden inflation and deflation in the official data. In peacetime, civilian establishments supplying fabricated goods, where the product range was characterised by regular change in assortment and quality, used such changes to raise the ratio of price to product quality compared with the 1926/27 ratio (bias-2). These were also exactly the branches showing the widest discrepancies in table 4.4. However, in civilian industry the wartime mechanism was probably somewhat different. It was more likely to be the downgrading of product quality, rather than the introduction of new or apparently upgraded products, which provided the opportunity for hidden inflation. New, lower-quality, and downgraded civilian products, incorporated into the measure of real output at higher prices and higher price/quality ratios, lent an upward bias to official index numbers of real output.

In defence industry, bias 3 ('hidden deflation') operated. Prices of weapons fell while quality improved. Cheaper, more effective weapons took the place of expensive, outmoded ones in official index numbers, but were underweighted because of their lower price/quality ratio at the time of their introduction. Consequently, even the official commodity index of war production understates the real growth of output.

Hidden inflation and deflation in official figures, combined with official failure to account for sideline military products of civilian industry, appears likely to explain the discrepancies observed in table 4.4. Thus we should certainly have greater confidence in present estimates than in those traditionally reported by Soviet officials.

From sector gross output to value added

How serious were wartime divergences of trend between industry's gross output and its value-added contribution to GNP? The extent of divergence can be gauged very roughly from trends in sector prices, costs, and sources of distortion in price/cost ratios. These suggest that real value added and gross output evolved roughly in parallel in basic industry and light industry; in defence industry, in contrast, the ratio of value added to gross output rose sharply.

I begin from the proposition that the general intention of the price fixing authorities was to maintain proportionality between prices of industrial products and average variable costs (labour costs, the costs of materials, components, commercial and transport services, and so on). Variable costs were at the focus, fixed costs being poorly represented in the Soviet unit-cost accountancy (*sebestoimost'*) of the period. There was a zero capital charge, with minimal depreciation allowances,[15] and overheads were covered by an arbitrary mark-up.[16] There is little information on the profitability of wartime industry.[17] Therefore, the trend of variable costs makes the first contribution to explaining price trends.

While the general intention of the price-fixing authorities was to maintain price/cost proportionality, this intention was implemented only from time to time. In between, there were many sources of disturbance in the price/cost relationship. Some were temporary and local. There were also systematic disturbances, of which three were practically important in wartime. These were *turnover taxation*, raised almost entirely on the retail sales of industrial consumer products; *budget subsidies*, which were used on an increasing scale to hold down the prices of basic industrial materials produced domestically; and *subsidised imports* of basic industrial materials (goods lend-leased from the United States, and priced before transfer to Soviet industry at the official, overvalued ruble/dollar rate, which was inadequately compensated by an import levy paid to the budget). Despite such disturbances, the spirit of this approach is that, provided they are sufficiently interpreted, trends in Soviet industrial product prices were meaningful, not arbitrary.

A simple methodology can account roughly for the change in real value added per unit of real gross output in terms of trends in prices, direct costs of labour and materials, and the impact of disturbing factors. This methodology is set out in appendix D. Applied at the lowest practicable level of aggregation, it involves a division of industry into three branches, defence industry, basic industry, and light industry. Defence industry comprises military machinery and metal products, but it is not possible to arrive at a separate estimate either for the machinery sector as a whole, or for civilian machinebuilding and metalworking separately. The spirit of the methodology is as follows. Any change in wartime product prices must be associated either with a

Table 4.6. *The estimated trend in real value added relative to real gross output of industry, 1941–4 (per cent of 1940)*

	1941	1942	1943	1944	1945
1 Defence industry	108%	120%	125%	128%	132%
2 Basic industry	–	137%	112%	101%	–
3 Light industry	–	103%	97%	87%	–

Note: Figures show the estimated ratio in each year of an index number of real value added to an index number of real gross output, when both are expressed as % of 1940.

Sources: Row 1: table D.3, row 6. Rows 2, 3: table D.1 (A), (B), row 7.

change in wartime variable costs (the cost of labour and materials per unit of output), or with one of the three disturbance factors.

From the evidence of wartime product prices, gross output and employment, wages and hours worked, and the prewar share of value added in gross output, combined with the wartime behaviour of disturbance factors, it is possible to infer how real value added must have behaved in wartime. Results are shown in table 4.6. On the wartime evidence, value added in civilian branches may have been quite variable in relation to gross output; between 1940 and 1942 the ratio of value added to gross output rose (rows 2, 3), slightly in the case of light industry, substantially in basic industry, but in each case the increase was followed by correction in 1943 and overshooting in 1944. But both data and methodology are rather fragile; I interpret the results rather weakly, as a failure to refute the nil-divergence hypothesis. The rather jagged movements do not show a permanent break in the ratio of value added to gross output, and do not support any strong inference about systematic change in this ratio in either case.

The defence industry trends suggested by table 4.6 were quite different for those observed in civilian branches. It is implied that the ratio of value added to gross output rose continually, steeply at first, reaching a level one third in excess of 1940 by 1945. I take this suggested trend as a stronger finding, partly because of its monotonic character, partly because of its consistency with other synchronous trends, Soviet and comparative; the latter are detailed, and the implications considered in appendix E.

Table 4.7. *The branch composition of industrial production and employment, 1940: alternative measures*

		Net value added, billion rubles at 1937 factor costs (1)	(%)	Gross output, billion rubles at 1926/27 prices (2)	(%)	Employment, millions (3)	(%)
1	MBMW	21.2	28.2%	50.3	36.3%	3.519	25.6%
1.1	defence industry	10.5	14.0%	–	–	–	–
1.2	civilian MBMW	10.6	14.2%	–	–	–	–
2	Iron, steel	3.0	4.0%	4.8	3.5%	0.526	3.8%
3	Nonferrous metals	1.8	2.4%	2.2	1.6%	0.497	3.6%
4	Fuels	12.8	17.0%	5.8	4.2%	0.923	6.7%
5	Power	1.6	2.2%	2.6	1.9%	0.164	1.2%
6	Chemicals	1.4	1.9%	8.7	6.3%	0.414	3.0%
7	Timber, paper	5.7	7.6%	6.9	5.0%	2.166	15.7%
8	Construction materials	1.2	1.6%	1.9	1.4%	0.483	3.5%
9	Light industry	11.2	15.0%	23.5	17.0%	2.853	20.7%
10	Food industry	11.7	15.6%	23.7	17.1%	1.568	11.4%
11	Other industry	3.3	4.4%	1.1	0.8%	0.642	4.7%
12	Industry, total	75.1	100.0%	138.5	100.0%	13.755	100.0%
12.1	of which, civilian	64.5	86.0%	–	–	–	–

Sources: Col. 1: as table F.8, col. 5. Col. 2: taken or calculated from TsSU (1959), 70, 72. Col. 3: public-sector employees, as table G.1, col. 2 (reallocating employees in nonferrous metallurgy from 'other' industry as explained in the corresponding note to the latter table), combined with employees in NKVD industrial establishments, as table G.4.

Value Added: Industry as a whole

At the final stage, we have the 11 sector indexes of gross output shown above in table 4.3. For the 10 civilian branches, the trend of gross output is taken as an adequate proxy for value added. For defence industry, index numbers of gross output must first be corrected by the changing ratio of value added to gross output, the estimation of which was shown in table 4.6 (row 1).

The 11 branch indexes are weighted by the share of each branch in 1940 industry net value added (measured at 1937 factor cost); the weights are shown in table 4.7 (column 1). Estimating appropriate

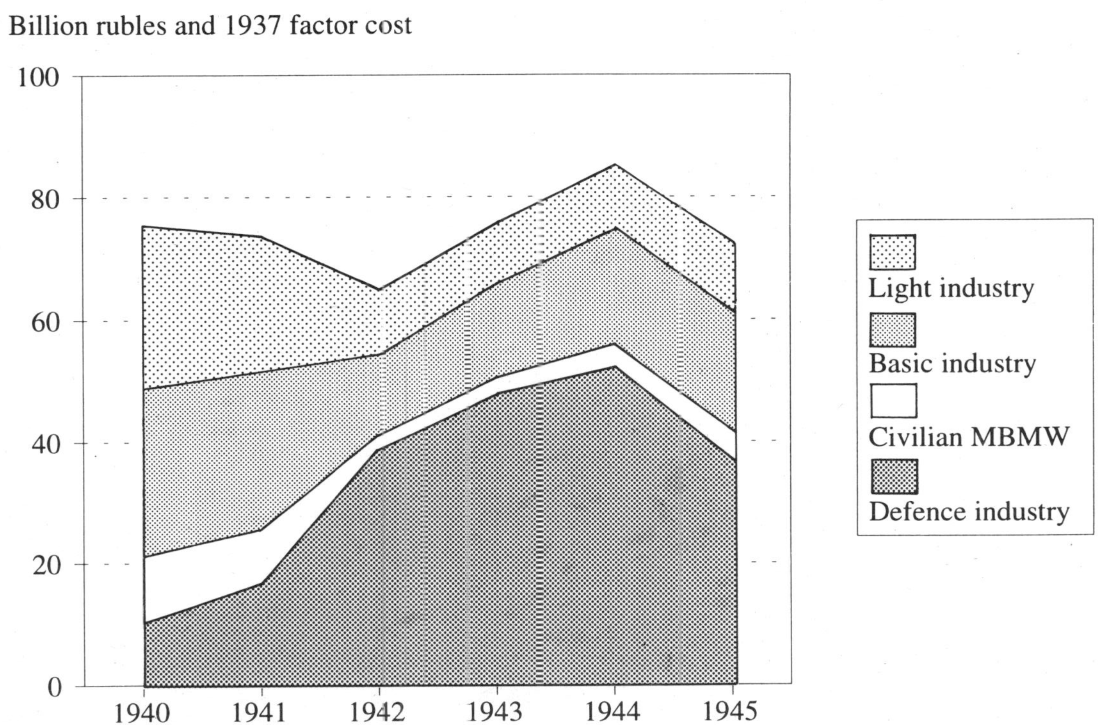

Source: table 4.8

4.2 Net value added in industry, by branch, 1940–5

weights is a problem in input/output. For this purpose I use an input/output table, compiled originally in 1952 by a group at the RAND Corporation under Norman Kaplan on the basis of the captured 1941 national economic plan; various revisions, extensions, and applications of the table are explained in appendix F. Table 4.7 also shows the importance of estimating value-added weights directly, rather than relying on proxies such as gross output weights based on 'unchanged' 1926/27 prices (column 2) or employment weights (column 3). Gross output weights would greatly overstate the importance of the machinery sector relative to the extractive industries, whereas employment weights would have an exactly converse effect.

When combined with 1940 final demands estimated by Abram Bergson, the revised input/output table produces detailed figures for industry value added by branch of origin, in a degree of detail sufficient to calculate the real output of industry as a whole year by year, the results being shown in table 4.8 (see also figure 4.2).

This table shows clearly the huge gap which quickly opened up in wartime between defence industry and civilian branches. By 1942 defence industry value added (row 1.1) had grown to 3.7 times the 1940 level, while value added in civilian industry (row 4.1) had fallen by three fifths, making a near ten-fold change in relative magnitudes. In 1940 civilian industry had contributed 85 per cent of total industry value added; by 1942 its share had fallen to 40 per cent. This proportion was maintained through 1944, because, while civilian industry began to recover, defence industry was expanded further. Thus, by 1944 defence industry value added had grown to five times the 1940 level, while the shortfall of value added in civilian industry still stood at 50 per cent, maintaining the ten-fold change of relativity. The gap between them began to close only with 1945.

Table 4.8 (row 4) also shows the trend of real industry value added, at 1937 factor costs, 1940–5, initially reported above in table 4.1. While the present estimate rises and falls in phase with the official index, the degree of change over 1940 diverges markedly. The present estimate is more optimistic over 1942–4, but falls back to the officially estimated trend with the onset of defence industry reconversion in 1945. As was indicated above, the official figures suffered from four distinct biases, but in practice bias 1, bias 2, and bias 3 largely offset each other. The major part of the gap in 1942–4 must be attributed to the correction of bias 4 in present estimates.

Table 4.8. *Value added in industry, by branch of origin, 1940–5 (billion rubles at 1937 factor cost and per cent of 1940)*

	1940	1941	1942	1943	1944	1945
(A) Per cent of 1940						
1 MBMW	100%	121%	194%	239%	264%	196%
1.1 defence industry	100%	159%	367%	454%	496%	348%
1.2 civilian MBMW	100%	83%	21%	25%	35%	45%
2 Basic industry	100%	94%	48%	56%	67%	70%
2.1 iron, steel	100%	96%	41%	44%	57%	65%
2.2 nonferrous metallurgy	100%	121%	84%	86%	102%	103%
2.3 fuels	100%	91%	45%	55%	70%	72%
2.4 power	100%	97%	60%	67%	81%	90%
2.5 chemicals, rubber	100%	100%	54%	70%	79%	61%
2.6 timber, paper	100%	91%	50%	56%	58%	62%
2.7 construction materials	100%	83%	19%	17%	26%	35%
3 Light, other industry	100%	83%	40%	37%	39%	42%
3.1 light industry	100%	87%	35%	37%	40%	38%
3.2 food industry	100%	78%	44%	37%	39%	46%
3.3 other industry	100%	83%	40%	37%	39%	42%
4 Industry, total	100%	98%	86%	101%	113%	96%
4.1 of which, civilian	100%	88%	40%	43%	50%	55%
(B) Billion 1937 rubles						
1 MBMW	21.2	25.6	41.0	50.5	56.0	41.4
1.1 defence industry	10.5	16.8	38.7	47.8	52.3	36.7
1.2 civilian MBMW	10.6	8.8	2.3	2.7	3.7	4.7
2 Basic industry	27.6	26.0	13.4	15.4	18.5	19.4
2.1 iron, steel	3.0	2.9	1.2	1.3	1.7	2.0
2.2 nonferrous metallurgy	1.8	2.2	1.5	1.6	1.8	1.9
2.3 fuels	12.8	11.6	5.8	7.0	8.9	9.2
2.4 power	1.6	1.6	1.0	1.1	1.3	1.5
2.5 chemicals, rubber	1.4	1.4	0.8	1.0	1.1	0.9
2.6 timber, paper	5.7	5.2	2.9	3.2	3.3	3.6
2.7 construction materials	1.2	1.0	0.2	0.2	0.3	0.4
3 Light, other industry	26.3	21.7	10.4	9.7	10.4	11.1
3.1 light industry	11.2	9.8	3.9	4.1	4.5	4.3
3.2 food industry	11.7	9.2	5.2	4.4	4.5	5.4
3.3 other industry	3.3	2.8	1.3	1.2	1.3	1.4
4 Industry, total	75.1	73.3	64.8	75.7	84.9	71.9
4.1 of which, civilian	64.5	56.5	26.1	27.8	32.6	35.2

Sources: (A) Index numbers are taken from corresponding rows in table 4.3, except that for defence industry table 4.3 (row 1) is first multiplied by table 4.6 (row 1), for reasons given in the text; rows 1, 2, 3, 4, 4.1 are calculated from part (B). (B) Calculated as index numbers in part (A), weighted by 1940 net value added from table 4.7, col. 1, with exceptions as follows. Row 1 is the sum of rows 1.1, 1.2; row 2 is the sum of rows 2.1–2.7; row 3 is the sum of rows 3.1–3.3; row 4 is the sum of rows 1, 2, 3; row 4.1 is row 4, less row 1.1.

Employment and output per worker

Official figures for employment and hours worked in Soviet industry in wartime do not arouse the intense scepticism due to Soviet measures of output volume. Counting heads generates much less ambiguity than counting rubles of '1926/27'. Their central problem is that they are seriously incomplete, and archival documentation is of limited use. The process of accounting for the gaps is shown in appendix G.

The Soviet wartime employment record is incomplete in several respects. The available figures exclude employment in artisan industry (often) and in NKVD establishments (always). Subject to these exclusions, there are series for wartime employment in public-sector industry as a whole. Other figures show the employment of manual workers in industry both as a whole (omitting several million nonmanual employees), and in a few selected branches (the machinery sector, iron and steel, the light industry, and food processing). Hours of work of manual workers are available on a similar basis. But there are no figures for employment of all employees by branch of industry, or distinguishing civilian from war-related employment.

Detailed employment records were of course maintained during the war period. But these were compiled on an establishment or commissariat basis; there, workers employed in industrial production, and construction, transport, and service sector employees were numbered without distinction. Consequently, the mass of wartime records does not provide us with figures for industrial employment on a basis comparable with the classification of output.

Below I approach the measurement of employment and productivity from two different angles. First, I consider manual employment, for which the greatest detail is available – but without the possibility of directly contrasting trends in civilian and defence industry. At the same time, it can be recognised that the machinery sector supplied the central core of the defence industry's fixed assets and employees, and (if the decline in civilian machinery output shown in table 4.8 is any guide) by 1942 effectively *was* the defence industry. Secondly, I approach the issue of civilian versus defence industry employment directly.

Table 4.9 shows trends in the numbers and hours of employment of manual workers in industry, including allowance both for labourers in artisan industry and for industrial labourers in NKVD establishments (see also figure 4.3). Overall, between 1940 and 1942 employment fell by nearly two fifths, and the decline in the total was also expressed in a fall in employment within each branch. But while employment in the

Table 4.9. *Employment of manual workers in industry, 1940–5*

	1940	1941	1942	1943	1944	1945
(A) Millions of employees						
1 MBMW	2.395	2.304	1.874	2.092	2.186	2.261
2 Basic industry	4.074	4.150	2.767	2.707	3.054	3.694
2.1 iron, steel	0.332	0.286	0.166	0.193	0.244	0.298
2.2 other basic	3.742	3.864	2.601	2.514	2.810	3.396
3 Light industry	4.609	3.930	2.338	2.418	2.860	3.299
4 Industry, total	11.078	10.383	6.979	7.217	8.100	9.254
(B) % of total						
1 MBMW	22%	22%	27%	29%	27%	24%
2 Basic industry	37%	40%	40%	38%	38%	40%
2.1 iron, steel	3%	3%	2%	3%	3%	3%
2.2 other basic	34%	37%	37%	35%	35%	37%
3 Light industry	42%	38%	34%	34%	35%	36%
4 Industry, total	100%	100%	100%	100%	100%	100%
(C) Hours per worker						
1 MBMW	2106	2538	2863	2908	2868	2372
2 Basic industry	2053	2307	2565	2687	2647	2401
3 Light industry	2012	2264	2308	2448	2499	2332
4 Industry, total	2056	2364	2600	2708	2684	2374
(D) % of 1940						
1 MBMW	100%	121%	136%	138%	136%	113%
2 Basic industry	100%	112%	125%	131%	129%	117%
3 Light industry	100%	113%	115%	122%	124%	116%
4 Industry, total	100%	115%	126%	132%	131%	115%

Source: (A), (B): table G-5, rows 5–5.3. (C), (D): table G-6, rows 5–8.

machinery sector fell by one fifth, and in basic industry by one third, employment in light industry fell by one half. Consequently, there was a sharp increase in the share of the machinery sector, corresponding to the decline in the light industry share.

In western market economies in peacetime, the postwar record shows that 48 hours marks the point at which output per week reaches a maximum; persistently working longer hours does not increase total output.[18] In the Soviet economy in wartime, hours of work of labourers in the public sector rose everywhere; by 1944 the typical industrial worker was working more than 9 hours a day, after taking into account time off for sickness and absenteeism, and nearly 6 days a week,

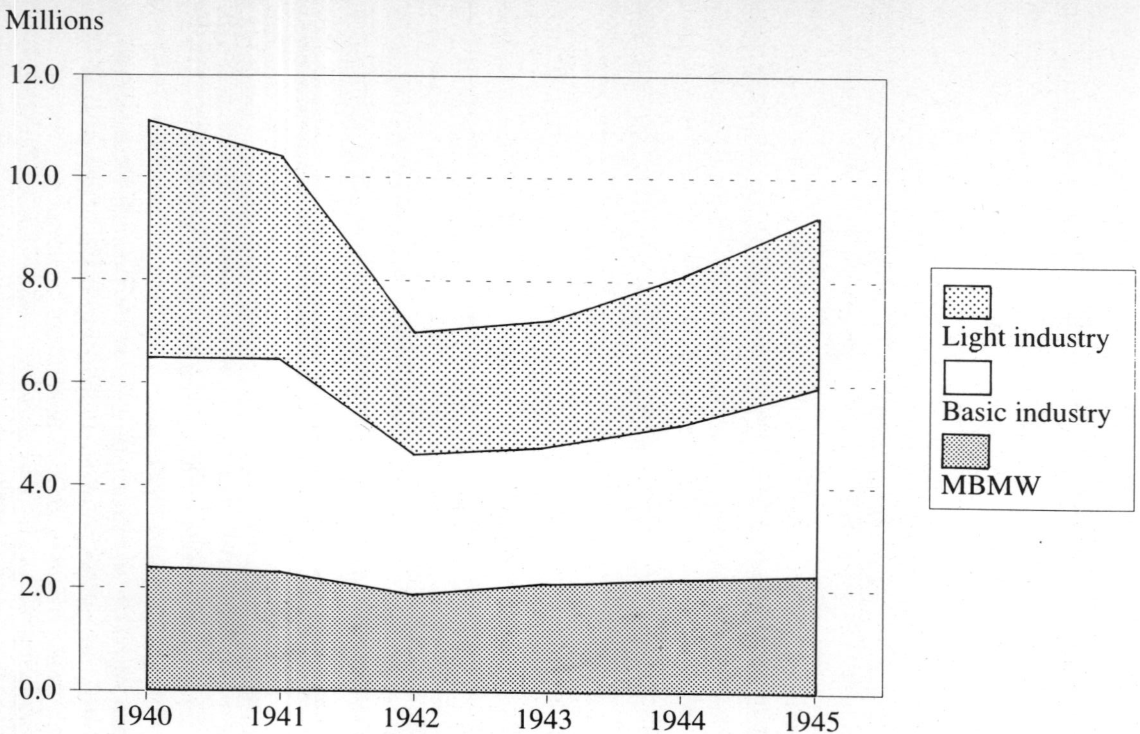

Source: table 4.9

4.3 Manual workers in industry, by branch, 1940–5

Table 4.10. *Labour productivity in industry, 1940–5 (manual workers and net value added at 1937 factor cost)*

	1940	1941	1942	1943	1944	1945
(A) Rubles per worker						
1 MBMW	8843	11115	21870	24162	25614	18324
2 Basic industry	6771	6254	4832	5696	6070	5250
2.1 iron, steel	9076	10139	7445	6877	7008	6618
2.2 other basic	6566	5966	4665	5605	5989	5130
3 Light industry	5709	5527	4468	4012	3622	3367
4 Industry, total	6777	7057	9285	10485	10480	7773
(B) % of 1940						
1 MBMW	100%	126%	247%	273%	290%	207%
2 Basic industry	100%	92%	71%	84%	90%	78%
2.1 iron, steel	100%	112%	82%	76%	77%	73%
2.2 other basic	100%	91%	71%	85%	91%	78%
3 Light industry	100%	97%	78%	70%	63%	59%
4 Industry, total	100%	104%	137%	155%	155%	115%
(C) Rubles per hour worked						
1 MBMW	4.20	4.38	7.64	8.31	8.93	7.73
2 Basic industry	3.30	2.71	1.88	2.12	2.29	2.19
3 Light industry	2.84	2.44	1.94	1.64	1.45	1.44
4 Industry, total	3.30	2.99	3.57	3.87	3.91	3.27
(D) % of 1940						
1 MBMW	100%	104%	182%	198%	213%	184%
2 Basic industry	100%	82%	57%	64%	70%	66%
3 Light industry	100%	86%	68%	58%	51%	51%
4 Industry, total	100%	91%	108%	117%	118%	99%

Source: Value added (table 4.8) is divided by numbers in manual employment and hours worked (table 4.9).

without holidays. They had substantially exceeded the 48-hour limit. The increase was greatest in the machinery sector, least in light industry. If labour inputs are measured by time worked, it is probable that total labour inputs (i.e. numbers multiplied by hours) were more than maintained in the machinery sector, falling elsewhere.

The implications for output per worker and per hour worked are shown in table 4.10 and figure 4.4. Between 1940 and 1944 value added per worker in machinebuilding nearly trebled, but in basic industry it fell sharply, recovering in 1943–4; in light industry it fell less sharply, but

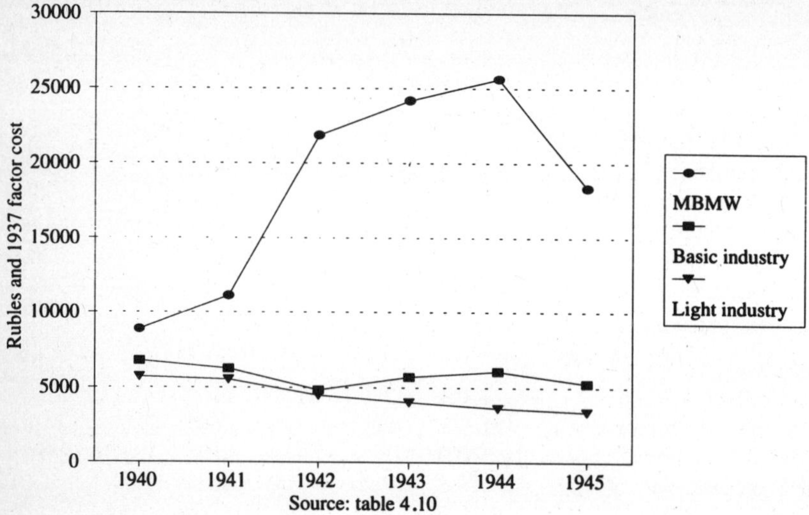

4.4 Net value added per manual worker in industry, 1940–5

more continuously. As a result, by 1944 the productivity gap between the machinery sector and other branches, already wide in 1940, had widened to a chasm. Output per worker in the machinery branch in 1944 was seven times that in light industry compared with 1.6:1 four years previously.[19] Part of the explanation for the divergence is to be found in changes in annual hours, which rose everywhere, but more in defence industry than in other sectors, so that the trend of productivity per hour worked was less spectacular in defence industry, although more dismal elsewhere. The greater part of the widening gap must be explained by reference to trends in defence industry in contrast to other sectors; this is done below. In 1945, as postwar reconversion got under way, the trend in the machinery sector was reversed, but recovery faltered in other sectors.

In table 4.11, I approach the question of defence industry employment directly. This table shows industrial employment of all employees, manual and nonmanual alike. Total industrial employment is simply a matter of adding up the subtotals of employment in the public sector, artisan industry, and NKVD establishments (as table 4.9). Numbers employed in defence industry are the specialised workforce only; they do not include numbers employed indirectly in the provision of goods and services consumed by the defence industry as intermediate products, the latter being dealt with in chapter 5. Defence industry employ-

Table 4.11. *Employment in industry, 1940–5 (all employees, millions and per cent)*

		1940	1941	1942	1943	1944	1945
1	Defence industry	1.751	1.879	2.743	2.879	2.884	2.062
2	Civilian industry	12.004	10.712	5.916	6.099	7.269	9.511
3	Industry, total	13.755	12.591	8.659	8.978	10.153	11.573
3.1	of which, % in defence industry	13%	15%	32%	32%	28%	18%

Sources: Row 1: table D.4, row 9. Row 2: row 3, less row 1. Row 3: table G.5, row 7. Row 3.1: row 1, divided by row 3.

ment is estimated independently as a by-product of the trend in the value added/gross output relativity (appendix D). Civilian employment is the residual.

Defence industry employment remained roughly level in 1941 (a result which is only surprising at first sight, given the wholesale dispersal of the defence industry workforce associated with the decommissioning of capacity in the war zone in the second half of the year); the inability to increase employment was compensated by the rapid growth in output per worker. At the peak, specialised employment in the production of military equipment probably stood at 2.9 million, twice the level of 1940; however, given the clear decline in output per worker in civilian industry, indirect labour requirements exceeded this number by a substantial margin.

Table 4.12 shows what is implied for productivity. In defence industry, value added per worker trebled, roughly one third of the increase being attributable to the rise in annual hours. This result is subjected to a variety of tests in appendix E, and is found to be robust. In civilian branches (which on this definition included civilian machinery) value added per worker fell by 15–20 per cent in 1942–4, then fell further in 1945 as annual hours fell back towards peacetime levels and the disruption of postwar reconversion took effect.

Defence industry convergence?

This chapter has shown that various biases present in official and unofficial methodologies distorted previous results in several different directions. In practice, official figures understated the wartime trend of defence production, and of industrial production as a whole,

Table 4.12. *Labour productivity in industry, 1940–5 (all employees and net value added at 1937 factor cost)*

	1940	1941	1942	1943	1944	1945
(A) Rubles						
1 Defence industry	6019	8939	14108	16616	18135	17788
2 Civilian industry	5376	5273	4412	4562	4483	3706
3 Industry, total	5458	5820	7484	8428	8361	6215
(B) % of 1940						
1 Defence industry	100%	149%	234%	276%	301%	296%
2 Civilian industry	100%	98%	82%	85%	83%	69%
3 Industry, total	100%	107%	137%	154%	153%	114%

Source: Net value added (table 4.8, rows 1.1, 4, and 4.1), divided by total employment (table 4.11, rows 1, 2, 3).

while overstating the trend of civilian production. Raymond Powell's subsequent independent estimate understated the industry trend by even more.

New, comprehensive industrial product series in physical units, weighted by prewar prices and adjusted factor costs, give us the possibility of estimating new series for industrial production by branch and in total. These new estimates cannot be guaranteed free of bias, but are certainly more reliable than the old ones. They show clearly the huge wartime increase in defence industry activity at the same as civilian industry collapsed.

The sudden onset of mechanised warfare meant a huge increase in the demand for weapons. Two main factors account for the increase in wartime supply. First, from given resources, Soviet defence industry made many more weapons than in peacetime. There was a sharp fall in the quantities of metals and metal fabricates, fuel and energy, and other material inputs per unit of output. There was similarly a sharp fall in the labour requirements of each unit of output, measured in hours of work. The capital costs of each unit have not been measured, but probably also fell with rising capacity utilisation. As a result, defence industry output per unit input rose.

Second, there was a great increase in the quantity of inputs allocated to defence industry. The workforce doubled; taking into account the increase in annual hours of more than one third, total labour inputs rose by two and a half times. The supply of materials increased correspondingly. The increase in the total volume of inputs, combined with the increase in output per unit input, accounts for the five-fold growth of output.

The contrast of performance with civilian industry could not be sharper. There, falling output was combined with a negative productivity trend which rising hours could only mitigate, and not reverse.

The productivity contrast demands fuller explanation. There are several hypotheses, but for the present it is not possible to discriminate between them. One possibility is that defence industry trends were essentially driven by *technology and scale*. The huge increase in the scale of output, the transition to flow production, and the economies associated with both of these may sufficiently explain the great increase in productivity. The productivity collapse in civilian branches may then be explained by converse factors: declining scale, and supply breakdowns which disrupted the flow.

Comparative experience lends some support to this hypothesis. Other countries shared the tendency to rising productivity in defence industry and falling productivity in at least some civilian branches, regardless of the nature of the political régime and social system; productivity fell everywhere in coal mining, for example, and for roughly the same reasons – the nature of the work, the pressure for quick results, and the falling age, experience, and skill composition of the workforce.[20]

Comparative experience also suggests a variant of the first hypothesis. This is that defence industries displayed *productivity convergence*, at least at a regional level, while civilian industries displayed divergence. Productivity convergence would mean that wartime productivity growth was inversely correlated with the prewar productivity level. Convergence might be explained in terms of battlefield competition, forcing the rival powers to adopt a common military–technical standard, a common concept of mass warfare, and a common strategy of attrition. An impressionistic ranking of the European defence industries by their prewar productivity levels would probably show Germany or Britain in first place, the Soviet Union third. If, as seems likely, productivity gains were greater in Soviet defence industry than in Britain or Germany, then one might speak of European convergence. Global convergence seems less likely, taking American and Japanese performance into account at opposite ends of the development spectrum.

The previous hypotheses emphasise trends specific to the defence sector. A further possibility is that what happened in defence industries was driven by the general economic environment. In the Soviet case, suppose that productivity growth was not the natural consequence of increased scale and flow technology, but a forced reaction to *labour shortage and supply failure*. As will be shown in chapter 5, other sectors of the economy, not only civilian industry, and especially agriculture, displayed low and falling productivity; they trapped labour, which otherwise would have been available for employment in defence industry. Defence industry *had* to make more with less; otherwise, the Soviet Union would have lost the war.

Comparative experience again casts light on this idea, and shows that it too may be reduced to a modified convergence hypothesis. In this case, convergence would imply that defence industry productivity growth in wartime was inversely correlated with the prewar productivity level and wartime productivity trend in nondefence sectors. The better the performance of civilian branches, the more resources could be released for defence industry utilisation, removing the pressure for productivity growth in war production. Again, an impressionistic ranking in terms of nondefence productivity levels and trends would place Britain ahead of Germany, and both ahead of the Soviet Union, mainly on account of agriculture. If defence industry productivity grew less in Britain than in Germany, and less in both than in the Soviet Union, one could again speak of European convergence. Again, global convergence seems less likely, taking into account the facts of high American and low Japanese prewar productivity levels in nondefence sectors.

Of course, labour shortage and supply failure could not explain productivity trends in Soviet defence industry on their own. If they were a sufficient explanation, the postwar Soviet economy would have revealed accelerating productivity growth. This returns our attention to factors in productivity specific to wartime defence industry. The factors of technology and scale seem the most likely, but clearly there is scope here for further research.

5 GNP and the defence burden

Gross national product

In World War II, once the powers of the Axis had failed to win the lightning victories upon which their success depended, the predominant factor was the scale of national resources deployed by each side. It was shown in chapter 1 that here the Allied powers vastly outweighed the Axis.[1] But the relative advantage of the Allies was much narrower on the eastern front than on the western front, or in the Mediterranean or Pacific theatres. One reason was that Germany, a rich, industrialised country with a large economy, committed the great bulk of her forces to the eastern front. There they confronted the Soviet Union, which was vast but poor. The other reason is that early German successes robbed the Soviet side of a substantial proportion of its prewar assets and output. The Soviet Union depended for its military success, therefore, more than the other Allies, upon the ability to mobilise a very high proportion of limited resources for combat.

In this chapter the book's main findings are presented: wartime GNP, employment and output per worker in different branches, the mobilisation of the workforce, the defence burden, the role of foreign supply. These findings are systematically compared with those of previous authorities (the official TsSU figures, and the later findings of Abram Bergson and Raymond Powell), together with the reasons for divergence (especially secrecy, statistical distortion, and index number problems). Present findings emphasise the severity of the Soviet defence burden, which was understated in previous estimates, including most official figures.

Present estimates of Soviet wartime GNP by sector of origin, at 1937 factor costs, are shown in tables 5.1 (in billion rubles) and 5.2 (index numbers, per cent of 1940). These figures begin from Moorsteen and Powell's benchmark estimate of net value added in each sector in 1937;

Table 5.1. *Gross national product by sector of origin, 1937 and 1940–5 (billion rubles at 1937 factor cost)*

	1937	1940	1941	1942	1943	1944	1945
1 Agriculture	63.0	69.9	44.1	27.4	30.5	45.1	47.3
2 Industry	65.4	75.1	73.3	64.8	75.7	84.9	71.9
2.1 defence	4.3	10.5	16.8	38.7	47.8	52.3	36.7
2.2 civilian	61.1	64.5	56.5	26.1	27.8	32.6	35.2
3 Construction	10.5	10.6	6.9	3.2	3.4	4.4	4.5
4 Transport, communications	16.8	19.3	17.8	10.2	11.8	13.7	14.9
5 Trade, catering	10.4	11.1	9.3	3.8	3.5	4.1	5.0
6 Civilian services	32.9	46.4	42.3	28.2	30.6	37.7	35.3
6.1 housing	2.1	2.4	2.4	2.0	2.0	2.0	2.1
6.2 finance	1.9	2.9	2.9	1.9	1.9	2.4	1.9
6.3 health	3.2	4.8	5.4	4.2	5.0	5.8	4.0
6.4 education	9.8	13.9	14.2	9.6	10.2	13.1	10.8
6.5 government	3.1	4.3	3.8	2.5	2.8	3.8	3.4
6.6 other	12.8	18.0	13.6	8.1	8.7	10.6	13.0
7 Military services	3.9	7.9	11.1	17.4	18.2	18.7	18.6
7.1 Army, Navy	3.4	6.8	9.9	16.2	17.0	17.5	17.3
7.2 NKVD troops	0.5	1.1	1.2	1.2	1.2	1.2	1.2
8 Net national product	202.9	240.3	204.7	155.1	173.6	208.6	197.4
9 Depreciation	9.4	13.6	14.0	11.7	11.8	11.7	11.7
10 Gross national product	212.3	253.9	218.7	166.8	185.4	220.3	209.1

Sources: The accounting framework and most 1937 values are taken from Moorsteen and Powell (1966), 622–3. Exceptions, and sources for other years, are noted below. Row 1: interpolated on table 5.2, row 1. Rows 2, 2.1, 2.2: table 4.8, rows 1.1, 4, 4.1. Rows 3–5: interpolated on table 5.2, corresponding rows. Row 6: the sum of rows 6.1–6.6. Rows 6.1–6.5: interpolated on table 5.2, corresponding rows. Row 6.6: for 1937, value added in housing, finance, and all services, from Moorsteen and Powell (1966), 622–3, less the combined sums of rows 6.1–6.5 and 7; for 1940, interpolated on the subtotal of rows 6.1–6.5. Figures for 1941–5 are interpolated on table I.11, row 6 (total employment in civilian services). Row 7: the sum of rows 7.1, 7.2. Row 7.1: for 1940, value added in military services, from Moorsteen and Powell (1966), 622–3. Figures for years after 1937 are interpolated on table I.11, row 8.1. Row 7.2: for 1940, the 1941-plan share of military services in outlays on government and security at 1937 factor cost (table F.5, col. 28, row 20e divided by row 23), multiplied by final outlays in 1940 on government and security from Bergson (table F.7, row 2.2). Years after 1940 are interpolated on table I.11, row 8.2; 1937 is interpolated on row 7.1 of this table. Row 8: the sum of rows 1, 2, 3, 4, 5, 6, 7. Row 9: interpolated on table 5.2, row 9. Row 10: the sum of rows 8, 9.

Table 5.2. *Gross national product by sector of origin, 1940–5 (1937 factor cost and per cent of 1937)*

	1940	1941	1942	1943	1944	1945
1 Agriculture	111%	70%	44%	48%	72%	75%
2 Industry	115%	112%	99%	116%	130%	110%
2.1 defence	246%	392%	903%	1116%	1221%	856%
2.2 civilian	106%	92%	43%	46%	53%	58%
3 Construction	101%	66%	31%	32%	42%	43%
4 Transport, communications	115%	106%	61%	70%	82%	89%
5 Trade, catering	107%	90%	36%	34%	39%	48%
6 Civilian services	141%	129%	86%	93%	115%	107%
6.1 housing	117%	115%	93%	95%	96%	98%
6.2 finance	153%	151%	98%	101%	127%	102%
6.3 health	151%	169%	131%	155%	182%	126%
6.4 education	142%	145%	97%	104%	133%	110%
6.5 government	138%	123%	80%	89%	122%	111%
6.6 other	141%	107%	64%	69%	83%	102%
7 Military services	200%	284%	454%	474%	489%	484%
7.1 Army, Navy	200%	290%	476%	499%	515%	510%
7.2 NKVD troops	200%	222%	226%	228%	225%	222%
8 Net national product	118%	101%	76%	86%	103%	97%
9 Depreciation	145%	149%	124%	126%	124%	124%
10 Gross national product	120%	103%	79%	87%	104%	99%

Sources: Row 1: table H.5, row 15.1 Rows 2, 2.1, 2.2, 6, and 6.6–10: calculated from table 5.1, corresponding rows. Row 3: calculated from Moorsteen and Powell (1966), 386. Rows 4, 5: for 1940, Moorsteen and Powell (1966), 622–3; for 1941–5, interpolated on index numbers, per cent of 1940, in IVOVSS, vol. 6 (1965), 45. Row 6.1: for 1940 and 1945, Moorsteen and Powell (1966), 622–3; for 1941–4, Powell (1968), 31. Rows 6.2 6.5: for 1940 and 1945, Moorsteen and Powell (1966), 622–3; for 1941–4, interpolated on table I.11, rows 6.1–6.4, multiplied by an index of annual hours based on hours worked in public-sector industry (table G.6, row 8), taking annual hours in 1937 at 1822 hours, calculated from Moorsteen and Powell (1966), 647.

I follow Moorsteen and Powell to 1940, except in the case of defence industry. For 1941 through to the end of the war, most series are revised or completely reconstructed. In addition to the rebuilding of industrial series discussed in chapter 4, agricultural production is also reevaluated (appendix H). Estimates of the supply of civilian and military services are interpolated on employment. Construction is from Moorsteen and

Powell. Only series for transport and internal trade remain based on official index numbers.

It is worth bearing in mind that the figures in these tables reproduce one traditional bias not previously mentioned. This is the relative neglect of the measurement of real value added in the services sector. In the present work, far more time and trouble has been devoted to measurement of the production of goods than of services. The information base of series representing industry and agriculture, in particular, is much more detailed and finely processed. The real output of service sectors, on the other hand, is measured crudely by labour inputs – in the present case, employment or hours, with the implied presumption that real value added per worker or per hour worked in these branches was fixed.

Underlying this traditional approach are hidden assumptions which are highly debatable, and probably wrong. One is that in modern economic systems it is more important to measure goods than services, because the production of goods is either more basic to survival, or more important for economic progress. But the ultimate object of GNP measurement is the output neither of goods nor of services, as such, but of utilities. A more pragmatic underpinning of the traditional approach is that it makes sense to give more attention to the measurement of goods because goods are easier to measure – surely a mistaken belief, if the travails and complexities of chapter 4 are any guide. From the point of view of measuring military power in wartime, also, it may appear that the production of goods such as bread, fuel, and machinery, is more important than services – a still stranger misconception, when it is remembered that, from the viewpoint of the defence sector, such goods are nothing more than intermediate products in the delivery of military services.[2]

Subject to these limitations, the figures in tables 5.1 and 5.2 complete the picture of wartime change in the structure of value added. With the output of defence industry rose the output of military services. Other sectors declined without exception, reflecting the way in which the brunt of the invasion and mobilisation processes was redistributed away from the defence sector to the branches serving civilian needs. Within the pattern of civilian decline, however, two tendencies could be distinguished. By comparison with 1940 output, some branches fell back by 30–50 per cent in 1942; these, including transport and most civilian services, followed the trend in overall GNP. Other branches, including agriculture, civilian industry, construction, and trade, declined by 60–70 per cent. All branches showed some sign of recovery

Table 5.3. *National income, 1941–45: alternative estimates (per cent of 1940)*

	1941	1942	1943	1944	1945
(A) Excluding net imports					
1 Harrison	86%	66%	73%	87%	82%
2 Powell	81%	57%	66%	80%	79%
3 Bergson	–	–	–	89%	–
4 TsSU (at 1926/27 prices)	92%	66%	74%	88%	83%
5 TsSU (at 1940 prices)	–	–	–	70%	–
(B) Including net imports					
6 Harrison	86%	69%	81%	96%	–
7 Bergson	–	–	–	100%	–
8 TsSU (at 1940 prices)	–	56%	66%	80%	77%

Sources: Row 1 (GNP at 1937 factor costs): table 5.1, row 10. Row 2 (GNP at 1937 factor costs): Powell (1968), 7, 32. Row 3 (GNP at 1937 factor costs): Bergson (1961), 210. Row 4 (NMP produced at 1926/27 prices): TsSU (1959), 28, 71. Row 5 (NMP produced at 1940 prices): table 2.9, row 3. Row 6 (total final demand at 1937 factor costs): 1941 as row 1, 1942–4 as table 5.8, row 3. Row 7 (total final demand at 1937 factor costs): Bergson (1961), 210. Row 8 (NMP utilised at 1940 prices): table 2.11, row 1.

in 1943, although the detail of agricultural production reveals that yields of grain and meat continued to fall, despite the gain of recaptured territory and population. None of these sectors had recovered to prewar levels by 1945.[3]

A comparison with previous estimates is shown in table 5.3 and figure 5.1. The domestic-sector-of-origin estimates (excluding real net imports), shown in part (A) of the table, agree that there was a heavy fall in real Soviet national income under the impact of invasion and territorial loss. By 1942, overall economic activity was down by one third or more compared with 1940. As late as 1944, there was still a shortfall of 10–20 per cent, or more if the outlying TsSU figure calculated at 1940 prices is given credence. They agree that, since the decline of the defence sector's GNP contribution in 1945 was more rapid than the continuing recovery of nondefence branches, 1945 was worse than 1944 in terms of total output, with the effect that the Soviet economy was far from recovered when the fighting was over, despite the fact that prewar frontiers had been restored.

Other figures in table 5.3, part (B), show national income measured on a resources-available basis, including net foreign resources. In the context of a GNP accountancy, we will call this concept 'total final

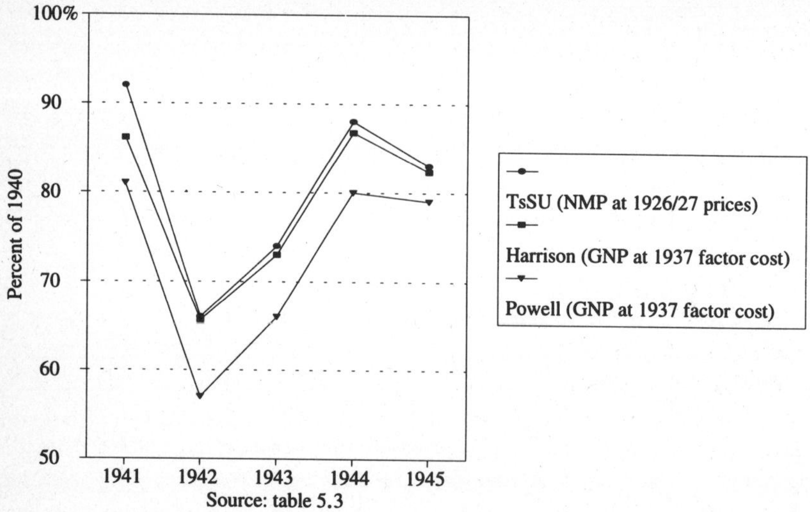

5.1 National income, 1941–5: alternative estimates

demand', since it represents the total value of all domestically produced and imported goods and services which are available for private and public consumption and investment outlays.[4] Here we begin to see the importance of foreign aid, which raised the Soviet budget constraint in 1944 by about one tenth of prewar GNP. The present estimate is supply-based, with an allowance for foreign supply. Bergson's and the TsSU series are expenditure-based.

There are big differences among the various figures. Present estimates (rows 1, 6) of the wartime movement in GNP are close to Bergson's (rows 3, 7) for 1944, if fractionally below (for detail see table 5.9, p. 107). On the other hand our estimates are well above Powell's (row 2) – not surprisingly, given the extent by which his industrial production index falls below ours (table 4.1, p. 59).

More surprising is the close match between present estimates and TsSU figures (row 4) for NMP produced at 'unchanged' 1926/27 prices. From the point of view of the alternative accountancies, the outstanding fact of wartime economic mobilisation was the huge growth in the role of military services, which contribute to GNP but not NMP. Given this fact, an index of wartime NMP at prewar prevailing prices should fall substantially below a GNP index at prewar factor cost.[5] Therefore, the closeness of the match between present real GNP index numbers and the official series for NMP at 1926/27 prices means that the latter should be judged extremely optimistic.

In contrast, TsSU numbers (rows 5, 8) for NMP utilised at 1940 prices do the expected thing, sagging below all the GNP estimates; but the shortfall is, if anything, too large, suggesting that this series may err on the side of pessimism.

The causes of discrepancy in the conflicting accounts are evidently varied, but without access to all the underlying computations it is impossible to be sure of them. In NMP figures the growth of military services was left out of account. In addition, at 'unchanged' 1926/27 prices the trend of industrial production was understated by TsSU; however, industry was also given an excessive weight relative to other sectors which fell by even more. This was probably the reason why, in the upshot, the NMP trend was overstated at 1926/27 prices.

Powell's procedure for calculating GNP took into account the growth of military services, but removed the excessive weight of industry, while retaining the understatement of the industry trend; it was probably this which led to his understatement of the overall trend in GNP.

The TsSU series for NMP produced and utilised at 1940 prices may have been biassed downwards. The underlying mechanism in the downward bias was most likely the same as for Powell: shifting from 'unchanged' 1926/27 prices to a later base year reduced the excessive weight of machinery products, without removing the mechanism causing the hidden deflation of the wartime trend of machinery production.[6] If TsSU at 1940 prices and Powell at 1937 factor cost had that much in common, then the rest of the shortfall below Powell can be explained by the NMP's exclusion of the growth of military services.

How much of the 34 per cent fall in GNP between 1940 and 1942 was due to the loss of territory? The territories touched by fighting had accounted in 1940 for 63 per cent of the public sector workforce, 58 per cent of the grain harvest, 42 per cent of railway freight traffic, 38 per cent of state and cooperative investment, and 33 per cent of industrial production at 1926/27 prices.[7] But these and other figures should not be subtracted mechanically from All-Union totals to find out what was left for the wartime economy since significant elements of both the human and physical resources of the occupied territories were evacuated and withdrawn to the interior in 1941–2. By these means the loss of territory, population, and immovable assets was partially offset. The economy of the interior regions experienced significant wartime expansion, especially in defence industry, metallurgy, and the fuel and electricity supply industries. However, the civilian machinebuilding, light industry and agriculture of the interior regions all declined.

Table 5.4. *The working population, by type of establishment, 1940–5 (millions and per cent of total)*

	1940	1941	1942	1943	1944	1945
(A) Millions						
1 Public sector (pre-1960)	31.2	27.3	18.4	19.4	23.6	27.3
2 Artisan industry	2.1	1.8	0.9	1.0	1.2	1.5
3 Collective farms	47.0	34.9	22.7	23.8	28.9	33.5
4 NKVD establishments	1.6	1.8	1.4	1.1	1.1	1.3
5 Armed forces	5.0	7.1	11.3	11.9	12.2	12.1
6 Working population	86.8	72.9	54.7	57.1	67.1	75.7
(B) Per cent of total						
1 Public sector (pre-1960)	36%	37%	34%	34%	35%	36%
2 Artisan industry	2%	2%	2%	2%	2%	2%
3 Collective farms	54%	48%	41%	42%	43%	44%
4 NKVD establishments	2%	2%	2%	2%	2%	2%
5 Armed forces	6%	10%	21%	21%	18%	16%
6 Total	100%	100%	100%	100%	100%	100%

Source: Table I.10, corresponding rows.

The working population

Soviet employment series for the whole economy are compiled by adding up numbers in the public sector, artisan industry, collective farms, NKVD enterprises, and the armed forces (see figure 5.2). Table 5.4 shows that in 1940 collective farmers were still the majority of the workforce; the socialised sector (collective farmers and public-sector employees, excluding artisan industry) made up 90 per cent of the workforce. The computations for other branches are less wearisome than for industry, and are shown in appendix I, with the main results reported in tables 5.4 to 5.6.

The special position of forced labourers is worthy of separate note. The figures used here support estimates of the population under direct NKVD control at the lower end of the scale, previously advocated by Timasheff, Jasny, and Wheatcroft; higher figures in the range from 5.5 million to 20 million espoused at various times by Conquest, Dallin and Nicolaevsky, Rosefielde, Swianiewicz, and Kravchenko are rejected.[8] Forced labour was more prevalent, however, than may appear from a cursory glance at table 5.4.

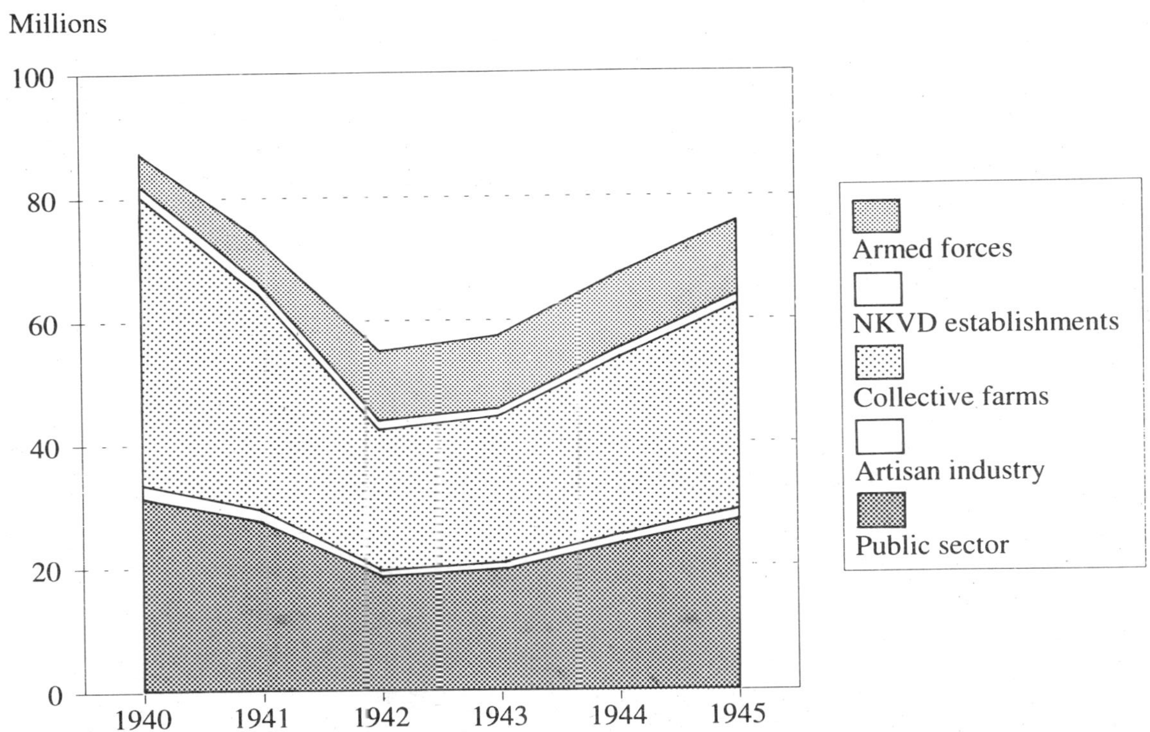

Source: table 5.4

5.2 The working population, by type of establishment, 1940–5

Table 5.5. *The working population, by branch of employment, 1940–5 (millions)*

		1940	1941	1942	1943	1944	1945
1	Agriculture	49.3	36.9	24.3	25.5	31.3	36.1
2	Industry	13.8	12.6	8.7	9.0	10.2	11.6
2.1	defence	1.8	1.9	2.7	2.9	2.9	2.1
2.2	civilian	12.0	10.7	5.9	6.1	7.3	9.5
3	Construction	2.4	2.3	1.5	1.5	1.9	2.2
4	Transport, communications	4.0	3.5	2.4	2.4	3.0	3.6
5	Trade, catering	3.3	2.8	1.7	1.7	2.1	2.5
6	Civilian services	9.1	7.7	4.8	5.1	6.5	7.7
7	Military services	5.0	7.1	11.3	11.9	12.2	12.1
7.1	Army, Navy	4.6	6.6	10.8	11.3	11.7	11.6
7.2	NKVD troops	0.5	0.5	0.5	0.5	0.5	0.5
8	Working population	86.8	72.9	54.7	57.1	67.1	75.7

Source: Table I.11, corresponding rows.

Table 5.6. *The working population by branch of employment, 1940–5 (per cent of total)*

		1940	1941	1942	1943	1944	1945
1	Agriculture	57%	51%	44%	45%	47%	48%
2	Industry	16%	17%	16%	16%	15%	15%
2.1	defence industry	2%	3%	5%	5%	4%	3%
2.2	civilian industry	14%	15%	11%	11%	11%	13%
3	Construction	3%	3%	3%	3%	3%	3%
4	Transport, communications	5%	5%	4%	4%	4%	5%
5	Trade, catering	4%	4%	3%	3%	3%	3%
6	Civilian services	11%	11%	9%	9%	10%	10%
7	Military services	6%	10%	21%	21%	18%	16%
8	Working population	100%	100%	100%	100%	100%	100%

Source: Table I.11, corresponding rows.

The population under NKVD control fell into two basic categories: prisoners held in camps and colonies, and deportees and exiles living in labour settlements. The distinction between camps and colonies was minor. Camps were holding institutions subordinated to the All-Union

GULAG (chief administration of corrective-labour camps of the NKVD) in Moscow. Camps held prisoners with longer sentences (more than three years), most of whom were engaged in forced labour on NKVD projects. In contrast most (but not all) colonies were administered by local NKVD organs. A higher proportion of their inmates tended to be subcontracted for work under civilian agencies.[9] 'Labour-settlers' (known before 1934 and after 1944 as 'special' settlers) were deportees exiled indefinitely to specified places of work and residence under NKVD jurisdiction and control. The civil rights of labour-settlers were less restricted than those of prisoners, but all may be classed as forced labourers.

The annual average of this population in 1941 is estimated in appendix I at just over 3 million, of whom 2 million were prisoners and 1 million lived in labour settlements. Of the 3 million, some were unfit for work, some were subcontracted to work as forced labourers in establishments subordinated to civilian production commissariats, and the remainder worked in NKVD establishments. Those in work represented up to 3.5 per cent of the total Soviet working population in 1941, being concentrated in basic industry (as noted in chapter 4) and construction, where they formed a significant part of the workforce. Subcontracted NKVD labourers are already counted in public-sector employment totals, so it is only those employed by NKVD establishments who are traditionally left out of account and must be added on.

Total Soviet employment declined in wartime, then recovered, approximately in proportion with the GNP series estimated above. The workforce fell by three eighths between 1940 and 1942, and was still one eighth below the prewar level at the end of the war. Within the total, as table 5.5 shows, the number of soldiers and specialised defence industry workers rose sharply, while all other sectors declined.

These figures do not tell the whole story. Indeed, when translated into percentage shares, they suggest unexpected stability. This is the message of table 5.6, in which the only notable shift to be reported is a large flow from agriculture (and civilian services, but less so) into military services (and defence industry, again to a lesser extent). This repeats the picture previously conveyed in table 5.4, where the workforce was disaggregated by type of establishment. The collective farm sector shrank in proportion to the growth of the armed forces, but there was little or no wartime change in the relative importance of other sectors – the public sector, artisan industry, and NKVD establishments.

The surface appearance of little structural change conceals large-scale reallocation of resources towards military needs, much of which took place *within* such branches as agriculture, construction, transport, and

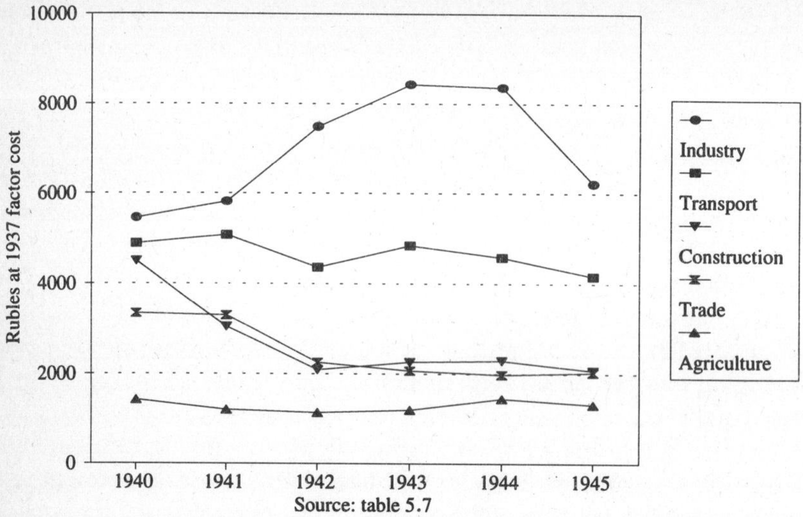

5.3 Net value added per worker in material production, 1940–5

trade. In order to trace the course of these reallocations, two further steps are necessary. First is to assess the overall resource requirement of the war; this requires evaluation of the defence budget as a whole in real terms, and of the defence burden on GNP. The second step is to translate this burden into the direct-plus-indirect requirements placed upon each branch, including the intermediate stages of producing defence goods and services. These two steps form the subject of the following sections of this chapter.

When employment is divided into GNP, we obtain value added per worker across the whole economy, and by sector. This is shown in table 5.7 and figure 5.3. This table is best read from the bottom, starting with net national product (net value added) per worker across the whole economy (row 8). Total value added rose a little in proportion to employment, but the average is not very meaningful; more important is the violent divergence of trends among different sectors of activity. Series for the service sectors, rows 6 (civilian) and 7 (military), are dominated by the assumption that labour input measured output (minor fluctuations in row 6 and 7 are explained by composition effects within each sector, and by increases in hours worked in some branches of civilian services). Substantive findings are confined to rows 1–5, which represent material production; here what is striking is the contrast

Table 5.7. *Net value added per worker, 1940–5 (rubles and 1937 factor cost)*

	1940	1941	1942	1943	1944	1945
1 Agriculture	1417	1194	1129	1193	1441	1311
2 Industry	5458	5820	7484	8428	8361	6215
2.1 defence	6019	8939	14108	16616	18135	17788
2.2 civilian	5376	5273	4412	4562	4483	3706
3 Construction	4503	3040	2085	2256	2286	2069
4 Transport, communications	4891	5077	4361	4849	4585	4160
5 Trade, catering	3336	3286	2248	2065	1976	2026
6 Civilian services	5079	5494	5863	5959	5826	4573
7 Military services	1579	1561	1537	1535	1534	1533
8 Net national product	2767	2809	2837	3039	3109	2608

Source: Net value added (table 5.1) divided by employment (table 5.5)

between the steady ascent of value added per worker in defence industry to the 1944 peak, and its decline everywhere else, not just in civilian industry but also in agriculture, construction, trade, and (to a limited extent) transport too.

Final demands and the defence burden

In moving from the economy's supply side to analysis of how resources were used, we must first take into account the contribution of the foreign sector. The evaluation of Soviet wartime net imports at 1937 factor cost is the subject of appendix J. In table 5.8, estimated net imports are added onto GNP to give annual series for 'total final demand', i.e. the value of domestically produced and imported goods and services available for final use in household and government consumption and investment. Foreign trade was absolutely negligible in the late 1930s – no more than one half of one per cent of national income by 1937, according to one authority;[10] there was a burst of commercial activity under the terms of the 1939 nonaggression pact with Germany, but still the magnitude was tiny in proportion to the whole economy. In wartime there was a great expansion of links with Britain and America, and a major increment to Soviet resources through Allied aid. By 1944, as table 5.8 shows, total Soviet final demand exceeded GNP by more than one tenth. (In real terms, however, the total of resources available was still much less than before the war.)

Table 5.8. *Gross national product by final use, 1940 and 1942–4 (billion rubles at 1937 factor cost and per cent)*

		1940	1942	1943	1944
1	Gross national product	253.9	166.8	185.4	220.3
2	Net imports	0.0	7.8	19.0	22.9
3	Total final demand	253.9	174.5	204.4	243.2
4	Fixed capital formation	39.9	10.1	9.4	18.4
5	Inventories	10.2	–10.7	8.1	1.9
6	Defence	43.9	101.4	113.2	117.2
7	Govt., security	10.1	5.4	6.0	7.9
8	Communal services	27.0	15.6	17.2	20.7
9	Household consumption	122.8	52.6	50.5	77.1
9.1	per worker	100%	68%	63%	81%
9.2	per head	100%	–	58%	–

Note: Total final demand (TFD) is defined as the value of domestically produced and imported goods and services available for household and government consumption and investment, and is equal to GNP plus imports less exports (net imports).

Sources: Row 1: table 5.1, row 10. Row 2: table J.1, row 18. Row 3: row 1, plus row 2. Row 4: for 1940, Bergson (1961), 128 (fixed investment includes livestock); for 1942–3, fixed investment is from Powell (1968), 21, and for 1944 from Moorsteen and Powell (1966), 358, with the addition of net investment in livestock from table H.5, row 14. Row 5: for 1940, Bergson (1961), 128; other years are from Powell (1968), 21 (1942–3), and Moorsteen and Powell (1966), 358 (1944). Row 6: table K.4, row 9. Rows 7, 8: for 1940 and 1944, Bergson (1961), 128; other years are interpolated on budget spending on sociocultural provisions and administration, from TsSU (1959), 457. Row 9: row 3, less the sum of rows 4–8. For row 9.1 I take row 9, divided by table 5–5, row 8. For row 9.2, row 9 is divided by annual average population as follows: Andreev, Darskii and Khar'kova (1990a), 41, give the Soviet population within contemporary frontiers on the first of 1940 and 1941 as 192,598,000 and 195,393,000 respectively. For 1943 I take the average of the figures given by Mitrofanova (1984), 347–8, as 130 million and 143 million for November 1942, and "the end of 1943" respectively. Figures in rubles are as follows:

	1940	1942	1943	1944
Per worker	1414	963	884	1149
Per head	633	–	370	–

How were the available resources used? The final-use side of wartime Soviet GNP has been examined in previous literature, but the analysis is to some extent scattered. Bergson directly estimated all the main components of final demand using 1937 ruble prices and adjusted factor costs, but only for 1940 and 1944. Filling in the intervening years is more complicated. From archival and other sources it is possible to arrive at quite detailed estimates of real wartime government outlays on defence in each year (appendix K); these are preferred to Bergson's. Real government nondefence outlays (i.e. on communal services, administration, and security) for the years not covered by Bergson can be interpolated on corresponding budget series. Annual series after 1940 for investment outlays (real gross fixed capital formation and inventory investment) can be taken from Powell.

Wartime consumption

The residual is real household consumption. There remains no satisfactory overview of Soviet living standards during World War II. A few stylised facts may be presented.[11] For the mass of people, wartime consumption was limited to housing, heating, basic clothing, and food. Food supplies were the critical factor determining survival, and during most of the war there was not enough food to go round. Half the population (mainly soldiers and public-sector employees) was covered by the official rationing system. Food rations were differentiated by economic role and status. The most important commodity was bread, which supplied 80–90 per cent of rationed calories and proteins. The calories and proteins supplied according to official ration norms were not guaranteed from central stocks, and in any case were insufficient to sustain life for more than a privileged minority of essential workers. They had to be supplemented by access to food supplies from sideline farming (both organised and individual), and from the unofficial sector. Even when other aspects of economic life were improving, food supplies per head of the population continued to deteriorate through 1943, because of harvest difficulties, and because the liberation of previously occupied territory increased demand faster than supply.

Less is known about the living standards of the rural population. Collective farmers lived off the meagre residual product of the collective farm and the product of their own sideline activities. The latter was particularly important, given the power of the state to command a prior share of collective farm output, and sideline activities tended to encroach upon the collective sphere during the war years, requiring a sharp postwar campaign of correction. Anecdotal evidence suggests pervasive hardship, and tends to confirm that World War II (in contrast to World War I) saw a loss of social privilege for food producers.[12] Food producers did not retain food surpluses, the Soviet economy did not disintegrate, and the burdens of war were forcibly spread across the population, urban and rural alike.

From the point of view of quantifying the aggregates, consumption is not literally a 'blank space', since Bergson went into it in some detail, producing figures for nominal and real retail consumption in official and kolkhoz markets, the consumption of military households, farm consumption in kind, and the consumption of housing and consumer services. An immediate problem lies in the fact that such estimates tend to be inconsistent with sector-of-origin GNP measures, the expenditure measures being consistently a little too large.

Were they of equal reliability, one would resolve the discrepancy by means of an averaged, 'compromise estimate'. In this case I believe that the sector-of-origin figures are relatively reliable. Of the final-use components, government defence and nondefence consumption, and investment outlays, can be gauged with a degree of confidence, but measures of household consumption cannot be trusted. In particular, there is no good independent measure of wartime farm consumption in kind, and there is some indication that the collection of data on farm food residuals was actively discouraged on the grounds that it would inevitably limit the discretion of government food procurement agencies.[13] Consumer transactions in the allegedly extensive black market in food also went unreported. Therefore, I measure real household consumption only as a residual, after deducting government and investment outlays. I believe there is not much more to be learnt from aggregate measures of the wartime trend in Soviet living standards on the basis of present knowledge; what little there is, is reported below. More useful information is yet to be obtained from local studies which can take into account qualitative factors and distributional trends.[14]

Comparison of the resulting figures with Bergson's is shown in table 5.9. Present estimates of nondefence consumption fall below Bergson's by 5 per cent in 1940 and 7 per cent in 1944. I do not want to claim much superiority for present estimates. Their main virtue lies in the fact that they are consistent. By comparison with Bergson's they are also cruder, being less detailed. I believe, however, that they are not seriously misleading.

Some confirmation of this can be found in the implications for the trend of wartime consumption. This trend is illustrated in table 5.8,

Table 5.9. *Gross national product by final use, 1940 and 1944: alternative estimates (billion rubles and 1937 factor costs)*

	1940: Present estimate (1)	Bergson (2)	Col. 1, % of col. 2 (3)	1944: Present estimate (4)	Bergson (5)	Col. 4, % of col. 5 (6)
1 Fixed capital formation	39.9	39.9	100%	18.4	24.5	75%
2 Inventories	10.2	10.2	100%	1.9	9.8	19%
3 Defence	43.9	45.2	97%	117.2	115.2	102%
4 Govt., security	10.1	10.1	100%	7.9	7.9	100%
5 Communal services	27.0	27.0	100%	20.7	20.7	100%
6 Household consumption	122.8	129.5	95%	77.1	82.9	93%
7 Total final demand	253.9	261.9	97%	243.2	261.0	93%

Sources: Cols 1, 4: table 5.8. Cols 2, 5: Bergson (1961), 128.

rows 9.1 and 9.2. The household consumption residual was large in 1940 at nearly half of total final demand, but was dramatically squeezed in 1942 as defence spending soared and overall resources declined. It fell still further in 1943, despite the beginnings of recovery of total final demand, because defence and investment outlays rose still faster. By this point, the household consumption share in overall resources had been reduced to less than one quarter. Consumption per worker was at its lowest point of the war, having fallen by more than one third compared with 1940; per head of the population in Soviet controlled territory it had fallen by two fifths (and 1940 itself was by no means the prewar peak). In 1944, however, nondefence consumption per worker recovered to a level about one fifth below 1940.

The 1944 position shown in table 5.8 is roughly confirmed in table 5.10, which shows figures for households' cash outlays on goods and services in legitimate transactions. Consumption in kind of various groups is excluded, notably that of farmers, soldiers, and forced labourers. The nearest appropriate population to divide into these figures for consumption per worker is therefore that of public-sector employees and artisan workers; but the match is not exact, since the cash outlays of collective farmers and soldiers are not excluded. When deflated to 1940 prices, the 1944 figures show private consumption per worker as one fifth below 1940, virtually the same as the figure which emerges from table 5.8.

Table 5.10. *Households' consumer spending in cash, at current and constant prices, 1940 and 1944*

	At current prices:		At 1940 prices:
	1940 (1)	1944 (2)	1944 (3)
(A) Billion rubles			
1 Official trade	184.3	146.3	81.3
1.1 goods	165.0	125.5	64.0
1.2 services	19.3	20.8	17.4
2 Kolkhoz market	28.0	204.9	44.0
3 Total	212.3	351.2	125.3
(B) Rubles			
4 Per worker in public sector and artisan establishments, total	6375	14148	5048
4.1 % of 1940	100%	222%	79%

Sources: Row 1: the sum of rows 1.1, 1.2. Rows 1.1, 1.2: for cols 1, 2, see GARF, f. 4372, op. 4, d. 1585, l. 980. These figures are taken from a 'Balance of money incomes and outlays of the population'; figures are inclusive of the cash incomes of wage-earners, soldiers, collective farms, and those in receipt of government benefits, but exclude 'cash turnover among groups of the population' (i.e. incomes derived from the kolkhoz market and retrading of official goods), military subsistence, and subsistence of the population under control of the NKVD. Farm consumption in kind is also by definition excluded. Col. 3 is deflated by index numbers of prices from table A.1, rows 7.1, 8. Row 2: as table A.5, rows 3, 6. Row 3: the sum of rows 1, 2. Row 4: row 3, divided by table 5.4, the sum of rows 1, 2. Row 4.1: calculated from row 4.

The defence burden

The other thing which emerges from the pattern of final demand is the defence burden. However, the concept of the defence burden is full of ambiguity. One kind of ambiguity is whether it should be measured at current or constant prices; this issue was considered in chapter 2.[15] Here I am concerned with the defence burden measured only in constant prewar prices, which convey the changes in relative magnitudes of war and nonwar uses of resources by comparison with the prewar period, and not with wartime opportunity costs.

The other source of amgibuity is how the defence burden was distributed between the domestic economy and the foreign sector; this arises in the context, common to all the countries participant in World War II, of major international transfers. The trouble here is to gauge the extent to which the defence burden was met from domestic resources, or was significantly alleviated by large-scale foreign supply. Here one might imagine two contrasting hypotheses. Both assume that domestic and foreign goods were substitutes in production and consumption. One alternative is to suppose that by 1942–3 the wartime requirements of human subsistence and capital replacement rigidly constrained the domestic resources available to the Soviet state for prosecution of the war. If so, then foreign supply enabled the Soviet war effort to take on a larger scale than would otherwise have been the case, and carried a major part of the Soviet defence burden. Correspondingly, a smaller part of the burden was borne out of domestic resources. Alternatively, suppose that the Soviet state was prepared to commit the necessary resources to the war effort, regardless of the cost to human subsistence and the capital stock. If so, then foreign supply reduced this cost, by releasing resources for consumption and investment; it carried the burdens of civilian maintenance, not of defence, which bore solely on domestic resources.

As will be argued more fully in chapter 6, there is no straightforward, value-free method of choosing between these hypotheses, and establishing the degree to which foreign supply added to resources for defence utilisation on one hand, or for civilian use on the other. It will be shown that the truth probably lay between these extremes. Here I confine myself to presenting alternative measures of the defence burden, and setting upper and lower bounds on the measure of the burden on the domestic economy; this is done in table 5.11.[16] A first step is to combine GNP with net imports, which provides a measure of the total of resources available (total final demand), regardless of their origin (rows 1–3) (see figure 5.4). After that, overall defence outlays may be compared with overall resources. This gives a measure of the general priority attached to the military effort by Soviet government, and is shown by dividing total final demand into total defence outlays (row 4.1). The defence burden in this most general sense rose from 17 per cent of total final demand in 1940 to 58 per cent in 1942. In 1943 it began to fall back as domestic recovery and the growth of the Allied aid programme increased overall supply more rapidly than the growth of defence outlays; by 1944, the defence share had fallen to less than one half.

Table 5.11. *Gross national product and the defence burden, 1940–4: alternative measures (billion rubles at 1937 factor cost and per cent)*

		Symbol	1940	1941	1942	1943	1944
1	Total final demand	$V + M$	253.9	219.0	174.5	204.4	243.2
2	Gross national product	V	253.9	218.7	166.8	185.4	220.3
3	Net imports	M	0.0	0.3	7.8	19.0	22.9
3.1	% of TFD	$M/(V + M)$	0%	0%	4%	9%	9%
3.2	% of GNP	M/V	0%	0%	5%	10%	10%
4	Defence outlays	D	43.9	61.8	101.4	113.2	117.2
4.1	% of TFD	$D/(V + M)$	17%	28%	58%	55%	48%
4.2	% of GNP	D/V	17%	28%	61%	61%	53%
5	Defence outlays, less net imports	$D - M$	43.9	61.5	93.7	94.1	94.3
5.1	% of GNP	$(D - M)/V$	17%	28%	56%	51%	43%

Sources: Row 1: row 2, plus row 3. Row 2: table 5.1, row 10. Row 3: table J.1, row 18. Rows 3.1, 3.2: row 3, divided by rows 1, 2. Row 4: table K.4, row 9. Rows 4.1, 4.2: row 4, divided by rows 1, 2. Row 5: row 4, less row 3. Row 5.1: row 5, divided by row 2.

What of the burden on domestic supply? The upper bound (row 4.2) is based on the assumption that, whatever their declared purpose, imports released resources solely for civilian use. National defence was the overriding priority of Soviet government ('All for the front!'), and the resources actually allocated to the war effort would still have been committed even if there had been no foreign economic assistance. Therefore, any increment to domestic resources made no difference to defence outlays, which were predetermined, and only made more civilian outlays possible. This concept of the defence burden is measured by the total direct-plus-indirect requirements of defence outlays, without any downward adjustment for their actual import content; it includes resources which were actually imported, but which are assumed to have released resources for civilian use, so I refer to it below as 'gross of imports'. On this measure the defence burden on the domestic economy rose from 17 per cent of GNP in the last prewar year to 61 per cent in 1942–3.

A lower bound on the defence burden is shown in row 5.1. Here it is assumed that, although national defence was the first priority of government, in practice the ability of government to devote resources to the war effort was constrained by civilian requirements which could not be overridden – for example, the need to avoid mass starvation and keep

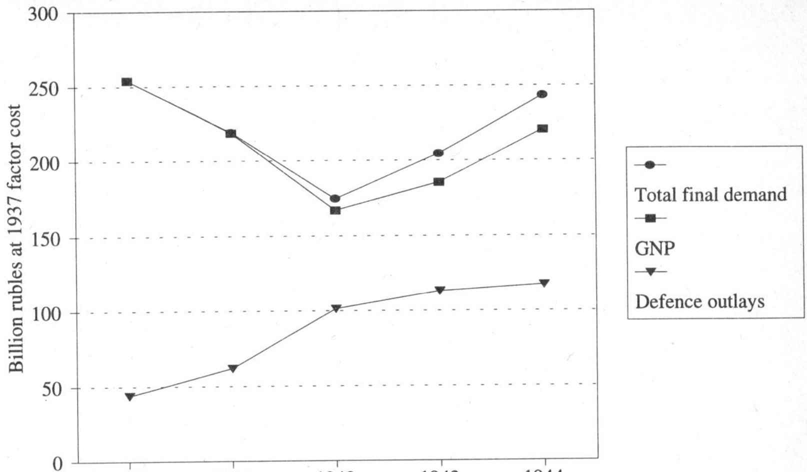

Source: table 5.11

5.4 Defence outlays and total final demand, 1940–5

most people alive, or to replace depreciating fixed assets and war damage to them in order to prevent the capital stock from collapsing too far. Therefore, additional resources accruing from foreign economic assistance, whatever their material form, contributed directly to raising defence outlays, or released domestic resources for defence use which otherwise would have been necessarily retained and used within the civilian sector. This concept of the defence burden is measured by the total direct-plus-indirect requirements of defence outlays *less* TOTAL net imports, and I refer to it below as 'net of imports'. The defence burden on the domestic economy, measured in row 5.1, peaked at 56 per cent of GNP in 1942, then fell sharply as the growing import of foreign goods took the strain.

The 'true' defence burden on the domestic economy lies between these measures. It cannot be established without more detailed modelling of the wartime priorities of Soviet government and the nongovernment constraints on high level decisions, which forms the business of chapter6. For present purposes it may be said of the period after 1942 that, given the improved military situation, the desperate conditions of the civilian economy, the activisation of planning for postwar reconstruction, and the accumulating human costs of malnourishment and overworking, resources would have had to be withdrawn from the defence sector in the absence of foreign aid, which now either contributed directly to defence uses, or released domestic resources for defence uses. Foreign aid permitted a degree of domestic relaxation; the burden on the domestic economy probably moved gradually towards the lower bound, 51 per cent in 1943 and less in 1944, as postponed civilian requirements and looming postwar needs moved up the agenda.

Direct-plus-indirect requirements

Given wartime final demand and an input/output table, it is possible to estimate the direct-plus-indirect requirements of Soviet final demand outlays during the war. The input/output table is the same one already used to estimate 1940 industry value added in chapter 4.[17] The derivation of the Leontief matrix follows the lines of appendix F. The 1941-plan Leontief multipliers applied above to 1940 are assumed to have persisted through each year of the war, with an exception being made for the defence industry. It was shown in chapter4 that the defence industry's ratio of intermediate inputs to gross output fell markedly during the war years. Incorporating assumptions consistent with this analysis yields a Leontief matrix which shifts through the war years towards falling technical coefficients and multipliers for the defence industry.[18]

Final demand, taken from table 5.8, is distributed among the processing sectors in the input/output table as follows. Defence outlays are disaggregated into final products from archival sources, and each final product is associated with a processing sector; for example, outlays on fuel are assumed to be supplied by the petroleum industry, while outlays on weapons and military equipment are matched with the defence industry, and outlays on soldiers' personal kit are divided equally between the textile and light industries. Since defence outlays amounted to more than half of Soviet GNP at the war's height, it follows that the distribution of more than half of national spending among processing sectors is reasonably accurately known.

For nondefence aggregates (household consumption, fixed investment and stockbuilding, government outlays on communal services, administration, and security), the 1941-plan composition of demands on processing sectors is applied to all subsequent years, with two exceptions. First, under government administration and security, outlays on weapons and personnel for the military formations of the NKVD are tied directly to numbers of NKVD troops, so that they are allowed to rise in wartime rather than falling with outlays on administration.

Second, under inventory investment, the RAND version of the input/output table for 1941-plan allowed nonferrous metallurgy to make a substantial contribution to gold stocks. There may well have been de-stocking of gold (as of other commodities) in 1942, but surely not for productive purposes. In wartime Soviet defence industry required copper, aluminium, and other nonferrous metals, but not gold. If gold was de-stocked, it was for monetary purposes. Therefore, I fix the allocation of nonferrous metals stockbuilding after 1941 arbitrarily at zero. Other elements of stockbuilding are increased in proportion.

The structure of industry

By means of the input/output table, we can examine the requirements of inter-industry balance under the pressure of the violent shift in final demands experienced in 1940–2. A whole-economy simulation is technically feasible, but of limited value given the difficulties of adequately representing construction, transport, and civilian services. The present discussion is restricted to evaluating change in the structure of the production industries.

The historical context is that, in 1941–2, Soviet military mobilisation and defence production soared, but the rest of the economy appeared to collapse. The statistical record converges with anecdote on the proposition that, by 1942, not only the consumer sector (agriculture and light industry) but the heavy industries (the energy sector, metallurgy, and engineering) and transport were in a critical state. In 1943 there was some stabilisation, but it was only relative; heavy industry began to recover, but, when the recovery of population on Soviet territory is taken into account, consumer supply worsened. By peacetime standards the economy remained in deep crisis through 1944.

An input/output exercise can throw some light on the historical process, although the light may be limited. By simulating the evolution of wartime supply, we can see whether the Soviet economy supplied the quantities of power, metal, and machinery which appear to have been warranted by wartime final demands. Any shortfalls which we find may suggest either failures of supply or failures of the model, and we are unlikely to be able to discriminate between the two. Modelling failure may arise from the crudeness of our initial hypotheses governing both final demand and intermediate supply interdependence. Supply failure imposed forced substitutions upon industrial users and household consumers (in the case of households, this could include forced intertemporal substitutions, i.e. not consuming in the present), but the

Table 5.12. *Large-scale industrial production, by branch of origin, implicit and realised, 1940 and 1942–4 (value added at 1937 factor cost)*

		1940	1942	1943	1944
(A) Gross value added, implicit, million rubles					
1	Electric power	1.9	1.2	1.3	1.4
2–4	Coal, peat, petroleum	13.8	5.4	10.4	10.3
5–5a	Iron, steel	3.7	2.0	2.3	2.2
6	Nonferrous metals	2.1	1.0	0.7	0.4
7	Fab. metal products	11.7	5.1	3.4	3.8
8	Defence industries	11.0	40.1	49.6	54.2
9	Chemicals	1.6	1.3	1.1	1.0
10	Construction materials	1.4	0.1	0.5	0.6
11–12	Timber, paper, and products	6.2	3.7	4.4	4.9
13–14	Textiles, light industry	11.8	4.9	7.6	7.0
15	Food processing	12.2	7.3	7.3	7.7
1–15	Industry, total	77.2	72.2	88.6	93.5
(B) Net value added, realised, million rubles					
1	Electric power	1.6	1.0	1.1	1.3
2–4	Coal, peat, petroleum	12.8	5.8	7.0	8.9
5–5a	Iron, steel	3.0	1.2	1.3	1.7
6	Nonferrous metals	1.8	1.5	1.6	1.8
7	Fab. metal products	10.6	2.3	2.7	3.7
8	Defence industries	10.5	38.7	47.8	52.3
9	Chemicals	1.4	0.8	1.0	1.1
10	Construction materials	1.2	0.2	0.2	0.3
11–12	Timber, paper, and products	5.7	2.9	3.2	3.3
13–14	Textiles, light industry	11.2	3.9	4.1	4.5
15	Food processing	11.7	5.2	4.4	4.5
1–15	Industry, total	71.7	63.5	74.4	83.6
(C) Elasticity over 1940, realised to implicit					
1	Electric power	–	94%	97%	114%
2–4	Coal, peat, petroleum	–	116%	73%	93%
5–5a	Iron, steel	–	77%	72%	95%
6	Nonferrous metals	–	176%	266%	567%
7	Fab. metal products	–	49%	88%	106%
8	Defence industries	–	100%	100%	100%
9	Chemicals	–	68%	98%	123%
10	Construction materials	–	212%	47%	64%
11–12	Timber, paper, and products	–	83%	79%	73%
13–14	Textiles, light industry	–	84%	56%	68%
15	Food processing	–	73%	62%	61%
1–15	Industry, total	–	95%	90%	96%

forced substitutions were successful in the sense that, as hindsight tells us, the Soviet economy was sufficiently balanced, *ex post*, to allow actual final outlays to be realised. Subject to these qualifications, there is still something to be learnt.

The changes in wartime output by branch of industry, gross value added implied by the 1941-plan input/output table, and net value added realised in practice, are both shown in table 5.12. *Implicit* in this table means 'implicit in final demands and Leontief multipliers'; *realised* means 'estimated from supply-side product series'. To show the degree of match between changes in outputs realised and implied I report the elasticities of realised to implicit net outputs; this normalises the scale discrepancies between implicit gross value added and realised net value added in 1940 which arise partly from the fact that one is net and the other gross of depreciation allowances, partly from unexplained differences affecting civilian industry.[19]

Given a good match between realised supply and implicit requirements, the elasticities would all be close to one; this is the case for defence industry (row 8), for example, where both sets of figures have a common basis. In other cases there are discrepancies. Some are of little significance, while others matter very much. The input/output table consistently fails to predict the wartime output of nonferrous metals (row 6), required in large quantities for weapons manufacture; according to the input/output table, in wartime the Soviet Union imported enough nonferrous metals and ferroalloys for output of nonferrous metal products to fall by more than half in 1942, and to continue falling throughout the war. Considerable efforts have been made to model accurately their inter-industry use, linking it partly to defence industry products, partly to iron and steel for the defence industry, but probably the model is still too crude.

Sources for table 5.12: (A) Gross value added, implicit: final demands (table 5.8), times Leontief multipliers for each year, less intermediate inputs, from tables D.5 and F.5. For the distribution of final demands among processing sectors, see the text. (B) Net value added, realised: as tables 4.8 and 5.1. (C) Elasticity, realised to implicit: for R (realised value added) and I (implicit value added) in year t, E (the proportional change in realised output over 1940, compared with the proportional change over the same period in output implicitly required) is given by:

$$E_t = \frac{R_t}{R_{1940}} \cdot \frac{I_{1940}}{I_t}$$

Realised value added in the construction materials industry (row 10) in 1942 also exceeded that implied by the input/output table by a factor of more than four times, but in this case both ruble sums were very small, because investment and construction had fallen to such low levels.

Conversely, shortfalls of civilian machinery (row 7), light industry products, and food products (rows 13–15) appear to have been substantial. These figures imply wartime success on the part of civilian machinery users in getting by without new machines, shouldering productive burdens by other means; households got by without consumer goods and food products, shouldering additional burdens of deprivation. But the figures do not convey any impression of the resulting pattern of capital depreciation, exhaustion of the workforce, and undernourishment of the population.

A main generalisation arising from table 5.12 is that the general extent of shortfalls and forced substitutions was if anything worse in 1943 than in 1942. According to the input/output table there was no absolute shortfall of fuel and power, for example, in 1942. In terms of the supply of basic materials (fuels and ferrous metals) 1943 witnessed worse shortages. Again, 1942 saw shortfalls of consumer manufactures and especially food products, but all these were worse in 1943. Only the supply of fabricated metal and chemical products improved, and for fabricated metal products the degree of shortage remained severe.

Of course these are only superficial inferences. By definition the Soviet economy was sufficiently balanced, *ex post*, to allow actual expenditures to be realised. Among the factors already mentioned which made this possible were the great decline in the intermediate requirements of the defence industry, and the more widespread forced substitutions of producers and consumers. But there were also others, including the release of commodities from accumulated stocks in 1942, and the increase in net imports in 1943 and 1944. To the extent that these processes were also forced by the collapse of overall Soviet supply, they represent further successful counter-measures to shortfalls which would otherwise have still more profound effects.

De-stocking and net imports

Table 5.13 throws a further sidelight on wartime mobilisation processes. It shows the extent to which wartime gross output requirements for industrial products were facilitated by net imports and, in 1942 only, by withdrawals from existing stocks ('de-stocking').

Table 5.13. *Implicit supply of gross industrial output required from de-stocking and net imports, 1942–4 (per cent of total)*

		From de-stocking	From net imports		
		1942	1942	1943	1944
1	Electric power	0%	0%	0%	0%
2–4	Coal, peat, petroleum	29%	1%	2%	3%
5–5a	Iron, steel	5%	5%	5%	7%
6	Nonferrous metals	0%	20%	38%	59%
7	Fab. metal products	0%	18%	41%	53%
8	Defence industries	0%	3%	6%	4%
9	Chemicals	2%	7%	24%	31%
10	Construction materials	63%	5%	13%	8%
11–12	Timber, paper, and products	5%	0%	0%	0%
13–14	Textiles, light industry	33%	1%	6%	10%
15	Food processing	7%	5%	16%	14%
1–15	Industry, total	7%	5%	10%	12%

Note: Implicit gross industrial requirements: $x_i + m_i - \Delta s_i$, where x is gross output implicit in the input/output table, m is net imports, and Δs is stockbuilding. "De-stocking" is negative stockbuilding.
Source: As table 5.12.

Table 5.13 emphasises that inter-industry balance in 1942 was bought to a large extent through the rundown of commodity stocks (e.g. of coal, steel, timber, and consumer goods), which could not be repeated in subsequent years. The bottom line of the table (row 1–15) should be interpreted as showing that, in 1942, 7 per cent of Soviet gross industrial requirements were met from de-stocking, compared with 5 per cent from net imports. De-stocking was particularly important for fuels, construction materials, and light industry products. On the other hand net imports supplied a significant share of overall requirements for nonferrous metals and fabricated products. In 1943 and 1944 stockbuilding turned positive (which diminished gross output available for other uses), but this was accompanied by a growing contribution of foreign sources to supply of nonferrous metals, fabricated metal goods, chemicals, construction materials, and processed foods.

The figures in table 5.13 should not be taken too literally, because the underlying estimates of overall stock changes, although not implausible, are very weakly founded. However, this table does give a general sense that in 1941–2 previously accumulated stocks were a significant factor in economic mobilisation, probably just as significant as foreign supply, but their role could not and did not persist beyond 1942.

The defence burden

Appendix K shows final defence outlays; appendix L also suggests the associated outputs contributed by the processing sectors in each year, together with the required numbers employed by each sector. Sector value added is converted to employment requirements using value added per worker in the main branches of the economy (from table 5.7).

Real defence outlays can be broken down into detailed branch requirements for gross output and value added, but the detailed figures are not of much significance in themselves and are confined to appendix L. More interesting are the employment implications, shown in table 5.14. The number of war workers sounds like an 'objective' measure of defence commitment, but is just as slippery a concept in reality as the defence burden, because some of the workers supplying Soviet wartime needs were in British and American factories; whether their labour supplied (or released) resources for defence use or civilian use in the Soviet economy cannot be known with certainty. Therefore the employment figures shown in table 5.14 use the same upper- and lower-bound methodology as in table 5.11.

First, table 5.14 shows that every Red Army soldier was supported by one or more war workers in the domestic economy (how many more depends on both the year and the concept). Second, among the war workers, specialised defence industry employment was just the tip of the iceberg; in 1942 there were at least 16–17 million war workers all told, of which only 2½ million were employed in defence industry. There were always more 'war workers' in agriculture than in defence industry, although this says as much about low agricultural productivity as about the importance of food.

These figures, translated in percentages (table 5.15), show that the defence share of employment (counting both direct and indirect requirements) was always somewhat smaller than the defence/GNP share; by 1942, on a lower-bound concept, defence claimed nearly 60 per cent of domestic output, but perhaps little more than 50 per cent of the workforce in and out of uniform – a result guaranteed by the low-productivity agricultural 'tail' of Soviet employment. When, as in table 5.15, the potential contribution of imports to relieving the pressure on Soviet labour resources for defence is fully taken into account, 1942 was

Table 5.14. *Employment in direct and indirect requirements of defence outlays, 1940 and 1942–4 (thousands)*

		1940	1942	1943	1944
(A) Gross of imports					
1	Electric power	94	244	253	255
2–4	Coal, peat, petroleum	612	1311	1407	1519
5–5a	Iron, steel	183	488	502	519
6	Nonferrous metals	115	328	345	346
7	Fab. metal products	363	808	751	854
8	Defence industries	1560	2806	3041	3005
9	Chemicals	112	292	301	297
10	Construction materials	27	47	38	42
11–12	Timber, paper, and products	242	651	679	679
13–14	Textiles, light industry	591	1157	917	935
15	Food processing	763	1343	1304	1149
1–15	Industry, total	4662	9476	9540	9602
16	Agriculture	3882	7276	6580	4900
17	Construction	475	968	515	628
18–19	Transport, comms	557	1094	1184	1285
20	Trade	192	548	615	620
20e	Military services	4550	10832	11346	11718
21	Defence sector total	14318	30193	29779	28752
21a	of which, war workers	68%	64%	62%	59%
(B) Net of imports					
1	Electric power	94	202	171	145
2–4	Coal, peat, petroleum	612	1177	1112	1127
5–5a	Iron, steel	183	345	291	207
6	Nonferrous metals	115	183	105	20
7	Fab. metal products	363	524	166	–217
8	Defence industries	1560	2696	2854	2869
9	Chemicals	112	243	155	112
10	Construction materials	27	33	11	8
11–12	Timber, paper, and products	242	598	579	560
13–14	Textiles, light industry	591	1112	664	569
15	Food processing	763	1189	789	662
1–15	Industry, total	4662	8302	6898	6061
16	Agriculture	3882	6577	4096	2808
17	Construction	475	968	515	628
18–19	Transport, comms	557	986	952	990
20	Trade	192	493	466	437
20e	Military services	4550	10832	11346	11718
21	Defence sector total	14318	28127	24206	22548
21a	of which, % war workers	68%	61%	53%	48%

Source: Table L.5.

Table 5.15. *Employment in direct and indirect requirements of defence outlays (net of imports), 1940 and 1942–4 (per cent of total employment)*

		1940	1942	1943	1944
1–15	Industry, total	34%	96%	77%	60%
16	Agriculture	8%	27%	16%	9%
17	Construction	20%	63%	35%	33%
18–19	Transport, comms	14%	42%	39%	33%
20	Trade	6%	29%	27%	21%
20e	Military services	91%	96%	96%	96%
21	Defence sector total	16%	51%	42%	34%

Source: Defence requirements (table L.5), divided by sector and total employment (table 5.5).

the year of maximum strain. If imports are credited fully against defence uses, all the increase in employment in 1943 was allocated to supply of civilian needs, and some existing war workers were also transferred to civilian work.

An input/output approach, however crude, has advantages over other methods. These are apparent from table 5.16, which compares present estimates with two conventional measures of workforce mobilisation. Part (A) of the table shows an application of the Gosplan figures cited above in tables 2.12 and 2.13. Percentages of gross output of industry, agriculture, construction, and transport utilised for 'war needs' are translated into employment shares and numbers of employees engaged in war work. To war workers are added soldiers and sailors. This calculation suggests that the percentage mobilisation of the workforce for 'war needs' rose from 15 per cent in 1940 to 45 per cent in 1942, remained at this level in 1943 according to preliminary figures, and was planned to fall back only slightly, to 42 per cent, in 1944. For 1940–2 these figures are presumed to understate the rate and rate of change of labour mobilisation, only the first- and second-order requirements of 'war needs' being counted; but the understatement is not large. The preliminary and plan figures for 1943–4 turn out to be seriously overstated, however.

Part (B) of the table contrasts with this the results of applying the British official statistical concept. This divided the workforce into four groups: the armed forces (not only the conventional fighting forces but also police and civil defence, so in Soviet translation it seems appropriate here to include the internal security forces of the NKVD), and a

Table 5.16. *Defence and nondefence employment, 1940 and 1942–4: alternative estimates (millions)*

	1940	1942	1943	1944
(A) Gosplan classification				
1 War workers	8.9	13.9	14.5	16.2
1.1 agriculture	4.2	5.7	6.2	7.2
1.2 industry	3.5	5.9	5.9	6.1
1.3 construction	0.3	0.4	0.3	0.3
1.4 transport	0.6	1.4	1.6	2.0
1.5 trade	0.2	0.5	0.5	0.6
2 Army, Navy	4.6	10.8	11.3	11.7
3 Defence sector total	13.4	24.8	25.9	28.0
3.1 % of working population	15%	45%	45%	42%
(B) British classification				
4 War workers	11.8	7.8	8.1	9.5
4.1 group I ('munitions')	5.0	3.8	4.0	4.4
4.2 group II ('essential')	6.9	4.0	4.1	5.1
5 Armed forces	5.0	11.3	11.9	12.2
6 Defence sector total	16.8	19.1	20.0	21.7
6.1 % of working population	19%	35%	35%	32%
(C) Input/output classification (net of imports)				
7 War workers	9.8	17.3	12.9	10.9
8 Army, Navy	4.6	10.8	11.3	11.7
9 Defence sector total	14.3	28.2	24.3	22.6
9.1 % of working population	16%	52%	42%	34%

Sources: Row 1: the sum of rows 1.1–1.5. Rows 1.1–1.5: total sector employment (table 5.6), multiplied by percentages of sector gross output allocated to 'war needs', calculated from table 2.13. Row 2: Army and Navy personnel (table 5.5, row 7.1). Row 3: the sum of rows 1, 2. Row 3.1: row 3, per cent of table 5.4, row 6. Row 4: the sum of rows 4.1, 4.2. War workers were classified in two industry groups (Hancock and Gowing (1949), 78). Group I (munitions and related industries) comprised 'metal manufacture, engineering, motors, aircraft and other vehicles, shipbuilding and ship-repairing, metal goods manufacture, chemicals, explosives, oils, etc.', while group II (essential industries) covered 'agriculture, mining, national and local government services, gas, water and electricity supply, transport and shipping'. This left 'food, drink and tobacco, textiles, clothing and other manufactures, building and civil engineering, distribution trades, commerce, banking and other services' in group III (inessential industries). Row 4.1: in Soviet terms, group I is taken to comprise MBMW, iron and steel, nonferrous metallurgy, and chemicals. For 1940, employment is as table 4.7, col. 3. For

Sources for table 5.16 (contd.)
subsequent years, MBMW employment is as table E.7, row 2; for other sectors, employment is interpolated on value added (table 4.8), divided by an index of value added per manual worker in 'other' basic industry (table 4.10, row 2.2). Row 4.2: for present purposes I exclude agriculture from group II, which therefore covers fuels and power, government administration, and transport. For nonindustrial sectors, employment is as table I.11. Employment in the fuel and power industries is calculated as metallurgy and chemicals in row 4.1. Row 5: Armed forces personnel, including NKVD troops (table 5.5, row 7.2). Row 6: the sum of rows 4, 5. Row 6.1: row 6, per cent of table 5.4, row 6. Row 7: the sum of table 5.14 (B), rows 1–20. Row 8: table 5.14 (B), row 20e. Row 9: the sum of rows 7, 8. Row 9.1: row 9, per cent of table 5.4, row 6.

sector-of-origin classification of industries into three groups. The latter comprised groups I (munitions and related industries), II (essential industries, including agriculture, mining, transport, utilities, and government services), and III (inessential industries). Here I apply this with one change, the exclusion of agriculture from group II. Unlike Britain, the Soviet Union was a poor country, largely self-sufficient in food, with a substantial agricultural productivity lag; its large agricultural workforce was bound to dominate any such calculations.[20] This methodology turns out to be the least effective in capturing the dimensions of wartime mobilisation. It shows a shift in the proportion of soldiers and war workers from 19 per cent in 1940 to no more than 35 per cent in 1942; but the 1940 figure is somewhat exaggerated, partly because much of the output of group I and II industries in 1940 was destined for civilian utilisation; the 1942 figure is understated, partly because by then the war effort was claiming increasing shares of output of light industry and agriculture.

The picture revealed in part (C) of the table is very different, and very striking. Here, all the direct-plus-indirect requirements of defence outlays are calculated in each year, giving maximum credit for the defence contribution of imports. It transpires that between 1940 and 1942 the defence share of employment rose from 16 to 52 per cent, the change representing more than one third of the total. The overall number of soldiers and war workers may have risen from 14.3 million in 1940 to 28.2 million in 1942, an increase of 13.9 million. At the same time the total workforce fell by 32.1 million, from 86.8 million to 54.7 million. Thus, the workforce supplying civilian needs fell by 13.9 + 32.1 = 46.0 million, from 72.5 to 26.5 million. One can hardly imagine a bigger shock.

These figures portray the course of Soviet labour mobilisation as a switchback ride of jolting violence, with 1942 as a very sharp peak of intensity, followed by a somewhat less sharp turn back to relaxation in 1943. Since the number of soldiers and munitions workers continued to grow, the relaxation was entirely due to a reduction in the demand for labour in domestic supply of dual-purpose products (e.g. communications equipment, vehicles, fuel, and food) and the indirect requirements of war production, as foreign supply increased. The turn is not, however, detectable on the basis of the conventional Soviet and British methodologies used in parts (A) and (B) of the table.

The test of war

It was argued at the beginning of this chapter that, in World War II, once the powers of the Axis had failed to win the lightning victories upon which their success depended, the predominant factor was the scale of national resources deployed by each side. In this the Allied powers greatly outweighed the Axis. But the relative advantage of the Allies was much narrower on the eastern front than on the western front, or in the Mediterranean or Pacific theatres. Not only was the Soviet Union a poor country relative to Germany, despite its larger population and territory. In addition, early German successes robbed the Soviet side of a substantial proportion of its prewar assets and output.

Table 5.17 and figure 5.5 show that the economic advantage of the Allies over the Axis was not only overwhelming at the outbreak of war, but grew steadily year by year until, by 1944, Allied GNP exceeded the GNP of the Axis powers by 4:1. But Hitler's invasion robbed the Soviet Union of its initial superiority over Germany in GNP, which was not restored until the German economy collapsed in 1945. This table strongly reinforces the proposition that the Soviet Union depended for its military success, more than the other Allies, upon the ability to mobilise a very high proportion of limited resources for combat.

The Soviet pattern of wartime economic mobilisation was in many ways remarkable. A deep penetration of Soviet territory cut off the assets under Soviet control from major facilities, stocks, and labour supplies. Resources and output fell sharply. Under intense military pressure, the authorities threw everything available into combat. It would have been normal at this point for the Soviet economy to have collapsed. Despite Stalin's five-year plans, the Soviet Union was still a poor country, and the experience of two world wars showed that, under prolonged attack, the economies of poor countries tended to disintegrate.

Table 5.17. *Gross domestic products of the great powers, 1939–45 (billion international dollars and 1985 prices)*

		1939	1940	1941	1942	1943	1944	1945
1	USA	788	851	1001	1190	1407	1522	1494
2	UK	215	237	258	265	271	260	249
3	USSR	308	345	297	227	252	300	284
4	subtotal	1311	1433	1557	1681	1929	2081	2026
5	Germany	271	273	290	294	300	308	216
6	Italy	114	115	114	112	102	83	65
7	Japan	135	139	141	141	143	136	68
8	subtotal	521	528	545	547	544	527	349
9	Allies/Axis	2.5	2.7	2.9	3.1	3.5	4.0	5.8
9.1	USSR/Germany	1.1	1.3	1.0	0.8	0.8	1.0	1.3

Sources: Rows 1, 2, 5, 6, 7: for 1940, see table 1.1; other years are interpolated on index numbers of GDP within constant frontiers from Maddison (1991), 212–15 Row 3: for 1940, see table 1.1. Other years are obtained as follows. In 1937–8 Soviet GNP/head was approximately as 1940, according to Davies, Harrison and Wheatcroft (1994), 269. Therefore, for 1939 I adopt the 1940 figure, adjusted pro rata for the smaller territory in 1939 compared with 1940 according to population figures within the old and new frontiers in Andreev, Darskii and Khar'kova (1990a), 41. For years after 1940 I refer to table 5.1, row 10. Row 4: the sum of rows 1–3. Row 8: the sum of rows 5–7. Row 9: row 4, divided by row 8. Row 9.1: row 3, divided by row 5.

The exact mechanism of disintegration of poor countries varied, but was typically already present in peacetime, in a low-productivity, poorly commercialised agriculture, and a general lack of resource diversity. The latter depended partly upon poverty, since poor economies relied heavily upon agriculture and could not afford a wide assortment of other activities, and partly upon smallness, since size promoted diversity. Mobilisation disrupted trade internally and externally; when industry was concentrated upon war production, there was nothing left to sell to peasants and foreigners in exchange for their food and oil. Imports and domestic food supplies disappeared from the urban economy. Poor countries also lacked the commercial and administrative infrastructure which modern governments could use to foster the objectives of wartime economic policy. Mobilisation was therefore either ineffective or else self-limiting, and tended if anything to accelerate economic collapse.

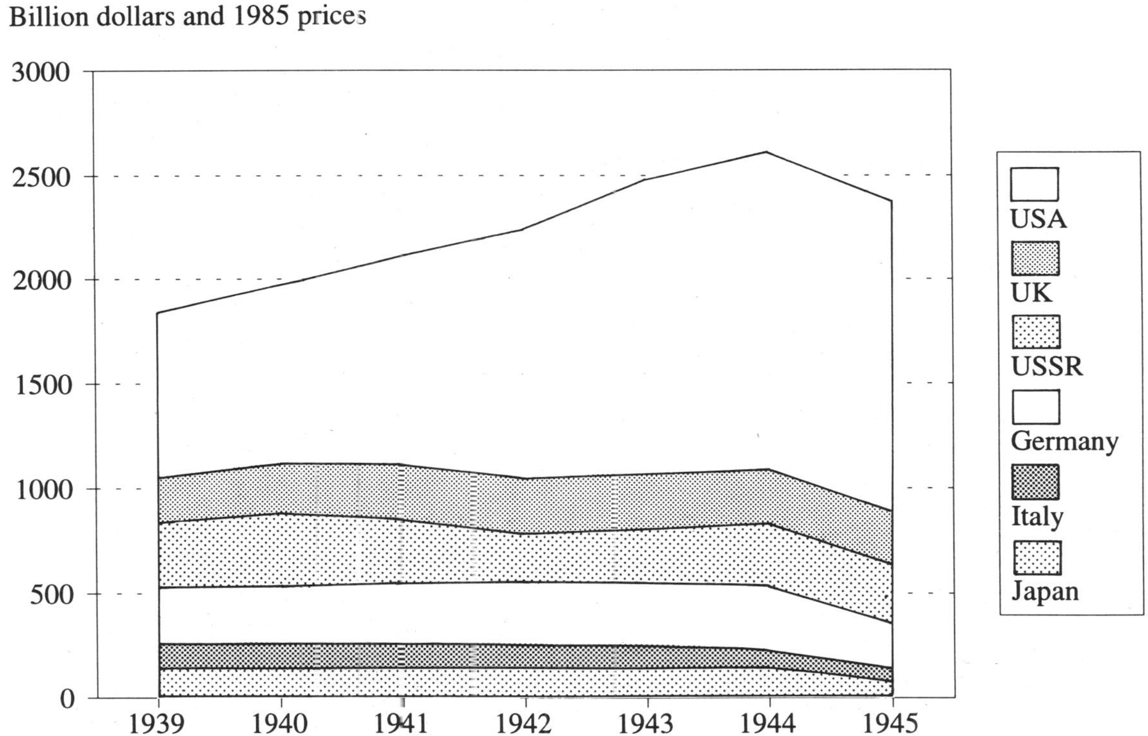

Source: table 5.17

5.5 Wartime GDPs of the great powers, 1939–45

Table 5.18. *The military burden: five great powers, 1939–44 (per cent of national income)*

	1939	1940	1941	1942	1943	1944
1 USA	2%	3%	14%	40%	53%	54%
2 UK	15%	44%	53%	52%	55%	53%
3 USSR	–	17%	28%	61%	61%	53%
4 Germany	32%	49%	56%	66%	71%	–
5 Italy	10%	21%	30%	31%	40%	–

Sources: Row 1 (per cent of NNP at current factor cost): Harrison (1988), 184. Row 2 (per cent of net national expenditure at current prices): Howlett (1994), 2. Row 3 (per cent of GNP at 1937 factor cost): table 5.11, row 4.2. Row 4 (per cent of NNP at current prices): Overy (1994), 312. Row 5 (per cent of GDP at current prices): Zamagni (1993), 255.

In World War I this happened first to Russia, then to Austria–Hungary, finally to Germany itself. In those cases it was the collapse of urban–rural trade which speeded economic decline. In World War II it happened to Italy first, then Japan – not because Japan was richer than Italy, but because that was the order of Allied attack. These economies suffered most from external disruption of supply.

But the Soviet economy, comparable with the Japanese in terms of income per head, did not collapse. Partly this was a matter of size; the Soviet Union was bigger than Japan in population and GNP, and far bigger in territory, and was already virtually self-sufficient before the war. But size alone does not sufficiently explain Soviet resilience, given the precedent of Russian disintegration and collapse in World War I.

The Soviet economy did not just 'not collapse'. Despite the loss of wealth and income, the authorities were able to mobilise half the work-force, and three fifths of national income, into the war effort. Table 5.18 shows that this degree of mobilisation was far more intense than the Italian mobilisation, was comparable with or greater than the mobilisation achieved in Britain and America, and was probably exceeded only in Germany.

The explanation for this success lay in the Soviet institutional capacity to manage shortages and distribute the defence burden. This meant the capacity to define priorities, to ration steel and power to the top priority users and deny these commodities to everyone else, to ration labour among the armed forces, defence industry, and the civilian economy when each sector required far more than was available, and to ration food among consumers when there was not enough food to keep everyone alive. This capacity made the difference between Russian defeat in World War I, and Soviet victory in World War II.

The distribution of the defence burden was not only a domestic matter. The domestic dimension was a matter of distributing the sacrifice between consumption and investment, and of sharing it among soldiers, workers, and farmers. But there was also an international dimension, provided by opportunities for redistribution of the burden among the Allied economies. Aid to Russia, one of the most controversial issues of postwar historical writing, is the subject of chapter 6.

6 The Alliance

Conventional wisdoms

There is a long history of studies of Allied economic relations with the USSR during World War II. This has been the most widely examined aspect of Soviet wartime economic experience in the west. Most of these studies, however, were written from the viewpoint of diplomacy and strategy, and they were commonly influenced by a desire to search retrospectively for historical roots of the Cold War which followed.[1]

Until quite recently, economic studies of wartime inter-Ally relations were much fewer, and little special reference was made to aid to the USSR.[2] This is surprising since Lend-Lease was nothing if not a resource transfer, and it was the economic significance of the transfer to the USSR which fuelled controversy for so many years. Without independent economic analysis the controversy was unlikely ever to be resolved; it could never rise above the claim of the recipient that the scale of the transfer in cash and percentage terms was small, and of the donors that such overall totals were immaterial since it was the physical form of Allied aid which represented the critical ingredient in Soviet victory.

Allied aid to the USSR raises a distinctively economic problem. The core of the problem is to understand what would have happened without the transfer of resources. Our ability to recast historical alternatives by the use of 'counterfactual hypotheses' is limited, and many historians rightly flinch from overt speculation. However, it is important to understand that, even after a certain amount of Cold War inflation of the American contribution in the late 1940s and early 1950s had been overcome, the western literature in this field remained dominated by very strong, usually unspoken assumptions about economic alternatives which economists would often prefer to question or qualify.

This chapter reviews the contribution of Allied aid, especially

Lend-Lease, to the Soviet war effort, and arrives at a new view. The economic origins of postwar diplomatic and doctrinal controversy are also explained. The role of Allied aid is shown to have been substantial, but its contribution was as much to Soviet investment and consumption outlays as to the common war effort. This was absolutely inevitable under the circumstances, and did not reflect any deliberate Soviet intention to misuse Allied resources (whether or not such intentions were formed). Contemporary expectations that the Soviet use of Allied resources should have been restricted to purely military purposes were naive, and displayed a misunderstanding of the nature of allocation processes common to all societies.

A feature common to most western studies of aid to Russia has been an additive, 'building-block' approach. At its simplest, the Soviet war effort was comprised of a number of building-blocks of military personnel and matériel, each of which was complementary to the effort as a whole at the given stage of the war; take away any one of these blocks, and the whole war effort was disabled. Some of these blocks were labelled as domestically sourced, some as originating in Great Britain and the United States. The main blocks of Red Army firepower and personnel, which sufficed to stave off defeat in 1941–2, were made at home. Added to these in 1943–5 were imported blocks of more technically sophisticated means of communication and mobility which made possible the great strategic offensives. This approach is additive in the further sense that it sees the allocation of domestic blocks to the war effort as predetermined independently of the availability of imported blocks, which were therefore simply added on to the war effort; if taken away, they could not have been replaced from domestic sources.

The timing and composition of aid are both seen as important to this analysis. The time factor was as follows. The inflow, slow at first, began the period of its peak rate in the second half of 1943. By then the Germans had already suffered three huge defeats on the eastern front, at Moscow, Stalingrad, and Kursk–Orel. The strategic offensive capacity of the Wehrmacht had in practice been eliminated. With the turn in the war's tide, a new phase was under way which determined the character of Allied victory and German defeat. But German troops were still deep inside Russia, and in the west Allied forces had only just won their first toehold on the continent of Europe in Sicily. The Battle of the Atlantic was still intense. The German war economy was intact, despite Allied bombing, and German war production was accelerating. Without a further rapid unravelling of the German position in the east it was easy to suppose that many years of fighting lay ahead. At the same time, the military feats of the Red Army had been purchased at huge cost in human life and equipment, while living and working conditions in the Russian interior were very poor and food supplies were even deteriorating.

The composition of Allied aid to Russia has been seen in this context as having made a disproportionate contribution. The Soviet Union produced its own firepower in World War II, but relied extensively on imported means of mobility. The particular material form which aid took reinforces this view. Imported firepower (mainly aircraft and tanks) was prominent in the first trickle of aid in 1941–2, but from 1943 onwards it was motor vehicles, high-grade fuels, communications equipment, industrial machinery, naval vessels, and concentrated and processed foodstuffs which predominated, all essential to the manoeuvrability and logistical supply of modern armies.

Thus, the Red Army's destruction of Germany's offensive power in 1941–2 was accomplished largely on the basis of Soviet domestic supply; but its technical ability to pursue the retreating Wehrmacht, to project Soviet military power into the heart of Europe, to meet up with the Allied ground forces advancing from the west, and end the war in Europe in May 1945, was based significantly upon western resources.[3]

Why did the Soviet Union need this western aid? The explanation implicit in this approach stressed critical gaps and shortfalls in the technological and organisation assets available to Soviet industry, usually in high-technology processes or the capacity to finish products where qualitative attributes were crucial. On the whole, in this view, the technical form of each block was its defining characteristic; there was little or no substitutability between high-grade and low-grade building blocks, and similarly between blocks of domestic and foreign resources. A lack of high-technology, high-quality equipment could not be counterbalanced by increasing the availability of low-grade goods and human services; since Soviet industry could not match the quality of flow products of American electrical and mechanical engineering and petrochemicals, foreign resources could not be replaced by domestic resources.[4]

While reporting dollar and ruble totals of the aid inflow, and calculating them in varying percentages of Soviet industrial production or national income at the time, western studies tended to attach little importance to such figures; in more than one expert view, 'United States aid to Russia played a much more vital war role than it would appear from the cold statistics'.[5] What did the cash value or percentage ratio matter, if the simple truth was that without Lend-Lease it could not have been done? The literature emphasised the 'disproportionate effects' attributable to Lend-Lease supplies,[6] which filled 'critical gaps', made good 'painful shortages',[7] and permitted 'real additions' to the available assortment of supply.[8] Western resources were simply indispensable to the Soviet war effort. In this spirit Khrushchev's reminiscences are often cited: 'Without Spam we wouldn't have been able to feed our army'; of American trucks, 'Just imagine how we would have advanced from Stalingrad to Berlin without them!'[9]

The additive, building-block approach, with its stress on the qualitative differences between Soviet and western products, captured an important aspect of reality – especially the way in which the military effectiveness of Soviet-produced defence assets was augmented as a result. However, the idea that there was no substitutability between domestic and imported means, or between products in military and civilian use, was excessively deterministic and led to unfortunate results. On one side the contribution of western aid to the Soviet war effort was exaggerated; the possibility that it released Soviet resources for nonwar uses, while admitted in theory, was not identified in practice. On the other side, where identifiable lend-leased goods were diverted to nonwar applications, this was judged illegitimate. Like some undeserving recipient of social security accused of going on holiday at the taxpayers' expense, the Russians were not supposed to have purposes of their own. Here the additive approach was very much in the spirit of the United States Lend-Lease Act, which intended aid commodities to be used only for the war, and to be additive to domestic resources already so committed. For the social scientist, however, it is behaviour which tests the law, not the law which tests behaviour.

In strictly converse fashion the official Soviet historiography remained dominated by a broad assumption that without Lend-Lease not much would have been different. Western analysts were accused of spreading the myth that the Red Army had won its victories only because of western means,[10] and that only American aid had 'saved Russia';[11] Lend-Lease was described, in relative terms, as 'highly insignificant'.[12]

The scale of assistance

During World War II all the great powers except for the United States benefited from a significant net import of resources. Both aid and trade contributed to the Soviet economy, but aid was more important.

As far as trade is concerned, between 1941 and 1944 the total Soviet deficit on the external merchandise account reached 4 billion

Table 6.1. *Allied aid, total and to the USSR, 1941–45*
(A) United States Lend-Lease ($ million)

To:	1941–2	1943	1944	1945	Total	(%)
1 British Empire	5839	9031	10766	4437	30073	69%
2 USSR	1396	2436	4074	2764	10670	24%
3 Other	–	–	–	–	2872	7%
4 Total	–	–	–	–	43615	100%

(B) United Kingdom reciprocal aid (£ million)

To:	To June 1943	July 1943 to June 1944	July 1944 to Sept. 1945	Total	(%)
1 USA	229.7	420.9	550.6	1201.2	63%
2 USSR	187.7	93.3	31.0	312.0	16%
3 Other	–	–	–	382.8	20%
4 Total	–	–	–	1896.0	100%

Source: Allen (1956), 529, 535.

foreign-trade rubles; this deficit represented the net value of resources which the rest of the world allowed the Soviet Union to acquire without immediate payment of equivalent export resources. This value was equal to $765 million at the official exchange rate then current; alternatively, it represented roughly two prewar years' imports, which sounds a lot until it is recalled that this represented perhaps only 1 or 2 per cent of prewar annual GNP.[13] Trade was particularly important in 1941–2, because the first agreements to ship munitions to Russia were essentially financed through barter, the Americans and British agreeing to accept Soviet raw materials in exchange.[14]

The trade deficit was dwarfed by the far larger volume of resources imported into the USSR without charge from the United States and Great Britain under mutual aid. Table 6.1 shows that US Lend-Lease to the USSR alone accounted for $10.67 billion, and British aid for a further £312 million ($1.26 billion), making nearly $12 billion in total.[15] This aid (despite the 'lend-lease' appellation of the American component) was transferred free of charge, or rather it was to be paid for in military and diplomatic rather than commercial terms.

Table 6.2. *United States Lend-Lease exports to the USSR, 1941–5 ($ million and per cent)*

						1945	
		1941	1942	1943	1944	Jan.– June	July– Dec.
1	Munitions, total	0.110	854.2	1442.6	1502.9	579.7	153.4
1.1	ordnance, ammunition	0.075	213.9	368.3	190.4	35.2	3.9
1.2	aircraft and parts	0.000	303.4	502.0	557.9	183.4	50.3
1.3	tanks and parts	0.035	176.8	74.7	166.4	54.6	0.0
1.4	motor vehicles and parts	0.000	149.1	406.0	503.3	265.7	87.0
1.5	watercraft	0.000	11.0	91.6	84.9	40.8	12.3
2	Petroleum products	–	–	–	40.5	31.2	8.2
3	Industrial products, materials	0.435	312.9	853.6	1306.9	509.3	95.0
4	Agricultural products	0.000	184.8	591.9	579.1	272.1	58.3
5	Total	0.545	1351.9	2888.1	3429.3	1392.4	314.9
6	of which, civilian or dual-purpose goods	0.435	657.8	1943.1	2514.7	1119.2	260.7
6.1	% of total	80%	49%	67%	73%	80%	83%

Source: United States President (1944), 31, (1945a), 15, (1945c), 8, except that row 6 is the sum of rows 1.4, 1.5, 2, 3, 4; row 6.1 is row 6, divided by row 5.

According to incomplete records, the bulk of Lend-Lease shipments – some 57 per cent by dollar value – arrived in the 18 months from July, 1943, to December 1944.[16] The timing and composition of aid are illustrated further in table 6.2. In 1942, when the flow was still restricted, weapons predominated, but from 1943 onwards the greater part of lend-leased items by dollar value consisted of civilian or dual-purpose products (industrial, transport, communications, and farm equipment, metals and metal products, chemical, fuel and food products).

In terms of overall resources of the western allies these large-sounding transfers amounted to less than one might suppose at first sight. Aid to Russia was not even a quarter of the total of economic assistance rendered by the British and Americans to each other and to others, as Soviet historians unfailingly pointed out.[17] It was still smaller as a fraction of the combined war expenditures of the United Kingdom and United States, which totalled approximately $295 billion from mid-1942 through mid-1945; compared with this, aid to the USSR amounted to no more than 4 per cent.[18]

By coincidence, 4 per cent has another significance. At the end of 1947, Voznesenskii wrote of the growth of Soviet imports in 1942–3, mainly from Britain and America, compared with the much lower level of 1940:

> a comparison between the amount of these allied deliveries of industrial goods to the U.S.S.R. and the volume of industrial production at the Soviet Socialist enterprises in the same period will show that these deliveries amounted to only about 4 per cent of the domestic production during the war economy period.[19]

(But whether 'the same period' meant 1942–3, or 'the war economy period' as a whole, was left irritatingly vague. In later writing, Russian and western, this figure would be extensively misquoted, and was most commonly rendered as the proportion of all Allied deliveries to the total wartime product of the entire Soviet economy, with 'only' as an additionally wounding qualifier – '*only* 4 per cent'.)[20]

Since 'only' 4 per cent did not sound like much at all (and certainly much less than $10,670,000,000), American responses were angry. Alexander Gerschenkron pointed out, correctly, that in 1942–3 Allied deliveries had not yet reached their peak, and that any comparison of nominal values would understate the value of imports relative to Soviet domestic production because of wartime overvaluation of the ruble, and because of double-counting of domestic output in the Soviet production accounts; he also signposted the future course of western historiography by adding: 'the tremendous contribution to the Russian war economy made by scarce commodities delivered under lend-lease cannot be significantly measured in terms of a global percentage.'[21]

For the record, it is worth stating that 'only 4 per cent', although probably not an outright lie, certainly presented a misleading view of the real volume of Allied aid to the USSR. Tables 5.8 and 5.11 showed present estimates of the volume of Allied aid compared with real Soviet wartime GNP and defence outlays. They showed that by 1943, Allied aid was contributing one tenth of overall resources available to the Soviet economy. This puts a very different complexion on the scale of assistance, of course, although a net import ratio to GNP of even 10 per cent was not out of line with the wartime experience of other European countries.[22]

The official Soviet accounting for Allied aid and trade remained secret throughout the period of existence of the Soviet state. Government archives now show that in spirit the Soviet finance ministry treated Allied aid in the same way as the Treasury treated Lend-Lease in the United Kingdom; that is, Lend-Lease goods acquired by the armed forces and industry were treated as expenditure items by the relevant spending departments; the resulting hole in the state budget was filled by treating Allied aid as revenue from a counterpart fund.

Soviet budgetary practice also displayed a special feature, by which foreign aid was made to work twice over. *The first revenue* was created equivalent to the ruble value of the dollar goods imported. *A second revenue* was then created *on the same goods* by additionally charging high import duties. The reason for the imposition of duties on lend-leased imports was to compensate for the overvaluation of the ruble; at the dollar price times the ruble/dollar exchange rate, foreign munitions were too cheap compared with equivalent domestic goods, so the foreign ministry levied a tariff to bring the price up to the domestic price level before the weapons were transferred to the defence ministry. Both the first and the second revenues contributed to the budgetary finance of war spending. Commercial trade, although on a much smaller scale, also contributed to budgetary finance through duties imposed on incoming goods and effectively paid by the departments which procured western commodities.

The rate at which tariffs were set was effectively arbitrary – arbitrary because 'domestic market prices are not applicable to the given commodities' (equipment and munitions). At the end of 1941 it was proposed to set the tariff on aid commodities at 100 per cent; thus the 5.5 billion rubles of foreign revenue arising from the current lines of US and British credit ($1 billion and £10 million respectively), would be doubled in terms of total revenues accruing to the budget.[23] In the upshot, a higher tariff was initially adopted. Thus, considering 1942 in prospect, the people's commissariat of foreign trade, Narkomvneshtorg, forecast revenues of 5.3 billion rubles ($1 billion) from Lend-Lease credits, plus import duties from associated imports estimated at 7.95 billion rubles – an average *ad valorem* tariff of 150 per cent.[24] In the 1942 outturn, this plan was nearly achieved: Narkomvneshtorg revenues were reported as loans (4.45 billion rubles) plus import duties (7.2 billion rubles, a levy of roughly 160 per cent), and virtually all of this was a net contribution to the budget.[25] (However, the high tariffs of 1942 would apparently prove temporary, as will be shown below.)

Table 6.3 shows a more detailed pattern. In 1942 and the first half of 1943 the cumulative total of budget revenues from Lend-Lease credits and import duties reached 20,830 million rubles, of which just over half (11,263 million rubles) constituted original dollar aid. The planned figures for the first quarter of 1942 illustrate the anticipated gains from aid (cruelly disappointed, at least to begin with), augmented by an import levy at 150 per cent. Not all import duties were raised on

Table 6.3. *Revenues to the state budget from foreign transactions, 1942–3 (million rubles)*

Quarter	I	II	III	IV
(A) Planned, 1942				
1 Lend-Lease	2000	2000	1500	950
2 Import duties	3000	2250	2500	2860
3 Total revenues	5000	4250	4000	3810
3.1 import duties, % of Lend-Lease	60%	53%	63%	75%
(B) Realised, 1942				
4 Lend-Lease	1	852	363	2567
5 Import duties	1405	3554	2095	1198
6 Total revenues	1407	4405	2458	3764
6.1 import duties, % of Lend-Lease	100%	81%	85%	32%
(C) Planned, 1943				
7 Lend-Lease	–	–	3900	–
8 Import duties	–	–	600	–
9 Total revenues	–	–	4500	–
9.1 import duties, % of Lend-Lease	–	–	13%	–
(D) Realised, 1943				
10 Lend-Lease	3380	4100	5420	–
11 Import duties	702	615	544	–
12 Total revenues	4082	4714	5964	–
12.1 import duties, % of Lend-Lease	17%	13%	9%	–

Source: RGAE, f. 7733, op. 28, d. 865, l. 9. 'Realised' figures for 1943 (third quarter) are anticipated. Percentages are calculated from the source.

lend-leased goods, of course. Particularly in 1942 the Lend-Lease operation encountered immense logistical difficulties, which constricted the inflow of aid; on the other hand, there was still some commercial importing for Narkomvneshtorg to tax. Levies on commercial imports undoubtedly confuse the picture shown in table 6.3. By 1943, however, two changes had taken effect: aid flows had reached a far larger scale than commercial trade, which was still shrinking; and the charges levied on imports, both actual and planned, had fallen to much more modest levels. While the trend suggested by the table is deceptive (because not all the import charges were levied on lend-leased goods, and this was especially the case in 1942), the actual decline in duties collected is so clear that a change of policy must be assumed; the planned figures also show clearly the intended downward trend.

One possibility is that the high import duties imposed on aid commodities in 1942 were determined under peacetime rules, which set higher, penal rates for unplanned imports compared with planned imports. Why else, at the end of 1942, did foreign trade minister A.I. Mikoian sign a decree exempting wartime imports (virtually all of which were 'unplanned') from these penal duties?[26]

A straightforward exchange-rate conversion of the $11.93 billion worth of Allied aid was 63 billion rubles. The tariffs levied on the aid ensured that its overall budget contribution substantially exceeded this sum, although certainly not by 150 per cent. The wartime total of budget revenues raised on it is given variously as 78 billion rubles for the period from mid-1941 to mid-1945,[27] and 82.7 billion rubles for the period up to the end of 1945.[28]

Table 6.4 shows the wartime outlays of the defence commissariat (for the Army and Air Force), including those sums specifically allocated to imports. According to table 6.4, when charged to the defence budget at current prices and taxes, imported items for Army use alone amounted to 31 billion rubles over 1942–5, and 10 per cent of all Army procurement at the peak in 1944; in that year imported products (part (B) of the table) accounted for one quarter by value of all the food and fuel consumed by the Army, and one eighth of Army equipment (part (A)). The figure of 31 billion dollars is an underestimate not only of the total import bill (since it excludes purchases of aided commodities charged against civilian agencies) but also of the import reliance of the army itself, since it does not account for the intermediate import content of Soviet final products shown in part (A).

Foreign transactions explained a large gap in the official wartime national accounts between NMP produced and utilised. As mentioned above, budgetary sources reported 'other sources of income' to the budget over 1942–5 from Lend-Lease (82.7 billion rubles) and, in addition, 'special revenues' (23.4 billion rubles, 1944–5), and reparations (2.3 billion rubles in 1945) – a total of 108.4 billion rubles.[29] In principle these figures should correspond to the excess of NMP utilised over NMP produced in the same period. Part (A) of table 6.5 shows Sukharevskii's preliminary national accounts from chapter 2; in 1942–5 (row 3), the material utilisation/production gap reached 96 billion rubles. But in this row no account is taken of insurable asset losses, which were a deduction from resources available for use. To find net imports at domestic prices, a sum attributable to losses (over four years, say 40 billion rubles) must be added to the gap, making a grand total of foreign receipts somewhere in the region of 140 billion rubles, which is rather

Table 6.4. *Budget outlays of the defence commissariat, total and supplied from imports, 1941–5 (billion rubles)*

	1941 July–Dec.	1942	1943	1944	1945 Jan.–June
(A) Total outlays					
1 Munitions	14.0	33.2	38.6	42.5	21.1
2 Maintenance					
2.1 pay	9.2	26.2	31.9	34.8	20.8
2.2 food	8.2	21.4	25.1	25.3	9.0
2.3 personal kit	5.4	9.7	8.0	9.6	4.2
2.4 fuel	1.2	2.6	3.0	3.6	2.1
2.5 transport	1.1	2.3	4.6	5.6	2.6
3 Construction	2.3	2.1	1.2	1.6	0.7
4 Other	2.8	5.7	5.4	6.5	3.1
5 Total	44.3	103.0	117.9	129.4	63.5
(B) Imports					
1 Munitions	–	2.3	2.6	5.0	2.3
2 Maintenance					
2.1 pay	–	–	–	–	–
2.2 food	–	0.0	4.2	6.2	3.7
2.3 personal kit	–	0.3	0.2	0.9	0.6
2.4 fuel	–	0.0	0.4	0.9	1.0
2.5 transport	–	–	–	–	–
3 Construction	–	–	–	–	–
4 Other	–	0.1	0.1	0.2	0.0
5 Total	–	2.7	7.5	13.2	7.6

Source: RGAE, f. 7733, op. 36, d. 1892, ll. 75 (imports), 83 (outlays). Navy items are excluded. Imported munitions and equipment include vehicles and parts. 'Other' imports are horses. For imports in 1945 the calendar year is covered, not the first half.

too high. But the impression gained from subsequent figures for 1940 and 1944–5 in part (B) of the table is that, on top of the normal revision of NMP estimates, Sukharevskii had probably overstated the likely revenues in 1945 from Lend-Lease (which was shut off abruptly in May) and postwar reparations. The evidence of the national accounts is therefore very approximately consistent, to within a few billions of rubles, with the budgetary data.

A final complication, to be mentioned only in passing, is Soviet reverse Lend-Lease. During the war the Soviet Union provided

Table 6.5. *Sources of net material product, 1940–5 (billion rubles and current prices)*

	1940	1942	1943	1944	1945	Total, 1942–5
(A) From Sukharevskii						
1 NMP produced	385	329	415	453	475	1672
2 Other sources	2	4	22	36	34	96
3 NMP utilised	387	333	437	489	509	1768
(B) From the 1946 TsSU 'Balance'						
4 NMP produced	386.2	–	–	489.6	441.4	–
5 Other sources	–7.4			33.6	26.0	–
5.1 losses	–11.5	–	–	–11.1	–10.5	–
5.2 foreign sources	4.1	–	–	44.7	36.5	–
6 NMP utilised	378.8	–	–	523.2	467.4	–

Sources: Rows 1-3: table 2.3, rows 3–5. An accompanying report (GARF, f. 3922/4372, op. 4, d. 115, ll. 40–2) states that the excess of products utilised over domestic supply in 1945 is partly covered by 'about 25 billion rubles' of imports, compared with 40 billion rubles of imports in 1944. Rows 4–6: table 2.9, rows 3–6 (cols 1–3); row 5 is the sum of rows 5.1 and 5.2, and all three rows are renamed for comparability with rows 1–3. Figures for 1945 are preliminary.

American transport ships and bomber aircraft with base and repair facilities and supplies, to a value officially reported at $2.2 billion.[30] Since there is no independent means of auditing this large sum, and since it was all spent on Soviet territory, I make no further allowance for it below.

Aid and overall resources

The character of Allied credits to the USSR is an issue which, unresolved at the time, continues to haunt the writing of World War II history. The issue has two aspects, one international and one domestic. Aid affected the inter-Ally allocation of resources. Was aid a unilateral subsidy from rich to poor; or was it, rather, one aspect of a broader wartime pooling of resources based on mutual specialisation and collaboration of equal partners? Aid also affected the domestic allocation of resources of the recipients. In the Soviet case, was aid essential to the

Soviet war effort, to what extent did it support the civilian economy, how much was diverted to postwar economic objectives? Such domestic implications of aid are difficult to analyse, and mutual incomprehension often added to inevitable suspicions.

In terms of the Soviet domestic economy, aid had two aspects. It was an addition to overall resources, and it came in particular material forms. The material form of aid was often that of high-technology, high-grade products, which undoubtedly augmented the effectiveness of Soviet fighting power. It would have been very difficult and costly for the Soviet economy to have matched the military–technical qualities of American vehicles, fuels, communications equipment, and food rations. Nonetheless, if the Soviet armed forces had been denied these western resources, they would have procured replacements. The replacements might well have been inferior in quantity and quality. But military units still had to manoeuvre, communicate, and feed and clothe their troops on the march. From given total resources, they would have relied more on horses, despatch riders, dried fish, and stale bread. They would have moved more slowly, with less efficient coordination, and they would have fought more hungrily. The same applies to the American machine tools, power generating equipment, and farm machinery imported to meet the needs of the productive economy. If aid had taken the form only of additional Soviet-technology, Soviet-grade products, the needs would still have been there, and would also have been met, but at higher cost and less well.

Aid was also an addition to overall resources. From this point of view its technical or military–technical form did not matter. What mattered was that aid gave the Soviet government the capacity to allocate more resources of all kinds towards all of its objectives, whether military or civilian, immediate or postwar. How did it, in fact, choose to do so?

The choices made by Soviet leaders in allocating resources between war and nonwar uses varied at different stages of the war. They were the outcome of a process of decision making which operated at two levels of abstraction. Their starting point was the extreme consequences of defeat for national and personal survival; defeat was to be avoided at all costs. At a higher level one may suppose, therefore, that Soviet leaders would have liked to maximise the resources for the war effort, subject to the maintenance of a minimum level of civilian and infrastructural economic activity. In practice, however, the location of the minimum was impossible to discover *ex ante*. This was for several reasons. For one thing, officials systematically repressed unofficial expression of civilian discontent, and mistrusted the signals of consumer and producer need officially transmitted upward through the administrative system from firms and households. For another, the degree of economic deprivation which could be tolerated by society depended on the period of time over which it had to be endured, and this could not be known in advance.

At a lower level of abstraction, therefore, in the first phase of the war, rather than risk immediate defeat for lack of sufficient mobilisation, the authorities followed a course of taking everything available for the war effort – 'All for the front!'. In the process the civilian economy collapsed, the minimum tolerance limits of society were breached, overworking and undernourishment became widespread, civilian mortality rose, and the infrastructure of war production was undermined. Postwar perspectives played no role in this first period, since the only priority was to stave off defeat and ensure the ability to continue fighting. During 1942 there took place a transition to a second phase in which the narrowly military mobilisation ceased to be all-important. The civilian economy rose in priority, and ceased to decline. From now on, defence outlays were allowed to rise only on the basis of newly available resources. This was also a period in which, with the prospect of eventual victory, postwar perspectives reasserted themselves, and were expressed in a series of plans for reconstruction of industry and the capital stock.[31]

In chapter 5 it was argued that the 'true' defence burden on the domestic economy fell between an upper and a lower bound. The upper bound was marked by the share of defence outlays in domestic output (GNP).[32] The burden would reach this upper bound on the assumption that the allocation of resources to defence was rigidly predetermined and did not depend upon Allied aid; in this case, defence preempted domestic supply, and it was the change in foreign aid which provided or released resources for civilian consumption and investment. The lower bound was found by deducting the share of net imports from the defence/GNP share.[33] The burden fell to the lower bound on the assumption that it was the requirements of civilian consumption and investment which constrained policy; in this case, the change in defence outlays depended upon the change in external resources, and it was the change in foreign aid which provided or released additional resources for defence.

Of course, no minuted decision tells us in what proportions Stalin's war cabinet proposed to allocate the incremental resources represented by aid, year by year, among competing civilian and defence uses. However, the actual allocation of resources in 1942–4 estimated in

Table 6.6. *The defence burden with and without foreign aid and trade, 1942–4 (billion rubles and 1937 factor costs)*

		1942 (1)	1943 (2)	1944 (3)	Total (4)	Gain (5)
(A) Actual						
1	Gross domestic product	166.8	185.4	220.3	572.5	0.0
2	Net imports	7.8	19.0	22.9	49.7	49.7
3	Total final demand	174.5	204.4	243.2	622.2	49.7
4	Defence outlays	101.4	113.2	117.2	331.8	11.9
5	Gross investment	–0.6	17.5	20.3	37.2	28.4
6	Nondefence consumption					
6.1	by government	21.1	23.2	28.6	72.9	2.8
6.2	by households	52.6	50.5	77.1	180.3	6.6
6.2a	surplus	4.3	0.0	17.8	22.1	6.6
6.2b	minimum	48.3	50.5	59.3	158.2	0.0
7	Total public outlays	121.9	153.9	166.1	441.9	43.1
8	Total surplus outlays	126.2	153.9	183.9	464.0	49.7
(B) Hypothetical						
9	Total final demand	166.8	185.4	220.3	572.5	–
10	Defence outlays	101.4	107.5	111.0	319.9	–
11	Gross investment	–4.0	5.3	7.7	8.9	–
12	Nondefence consumption					
12.1	by government	21.1	22.2	26.8	70.1	–
12.2	by households	48.3	50.5	74.8	173.7	–
12.2a	surplus	0.0	0.0	15.5	15.5	–
12.2b	minimum	48.3	50.5	59.3	158.2	–
13	Total public outlays	118.4	134.9	145.5	398.9	–
14	Total surplus outlays	118.4	134.9	161.0	414.3	–

Sources: Col. 4 is the sum of cols 1–3; col. 5 is the excess of actual over hypothetical values in col. 4 (row 3 less row 9, row 4 less row 10, etc.). Cols 1–3 are derived as follows: Rows 1–6.2: table 5.8. Row 6.2a: row 6.2, less row 6.2b. Row 6.2b: household consumption, per head of the working population, in rubles at 1937 factor cost, is taken from table 5.8 (note to row 9). The lowest figure of the series (that shown for 1943) is taken to represent an absolute minimum. The 1943 figure, multiplied by employment in each year (table 5.4, row 6), yields minimum total consumption. Row 7: row 3, less row 6.2. Row 8: row 3, less row 6.2b. Row 9: row 1 (assuming zero net imports). Rows 10, 11, 12.1 (1942 only): rows 10 and 12.1 are taken from rows 4, 6.1; row 11 is the residual when all other uses of resources have been deducted from row 9. Rows 10, 11, 12.1 (1943 only): the hypothetical 1942 figure, plus the

Sources for table 6.6 (contd.)
hypothetical increase in total public outlays (row 13) over 1942, multiplied by the respective shares of actual defence, investment, and government nondefence consumption (NDC) outlays in the actual increase in total nonconsumption over 1942, calculated from rows 4, 5, 6.1, 7, as follows:

Billion rubles	Increase	Share
Defence outlays	11.7	37%
Gross investment	18.1	57%
Government NDC	2.2	7%
Total public outlays	32.0	100%

Rows 10, 11, 12.1, 12.2a (1944 only): for 1944, the hypothetical 1943 figure, plus the hypothetical increase in total surplus outlays (row 14), multiplied by the shares of actual defence, investment, and surplus consumption outlays in the actual increase in total surplus outlays over 1943, calculated from rows 4, 5, 6.1, 6.2a, and 8, as follows:

Billion rubles	Increase	Share
Defence outlays	4.0	13%
Gross investment	2.8	9%
Nondefence consumption		
by government	5.4	18%
by households, surplus	17.8	59%
Total surplus outlays	30.0	100%

Row 12.2: the sum of rows 12.2a, 12.2b. Row 12.2a (1942 and 1943 only): set at zero by assumption (see text). Row 12.2b: as row 6.2b. Row 13: row 9, less row 12.2. Row 14: row 9, less row 12.2b.

chapter 5 is shown in table 6.6, part (A) (columns 1–3). Here are shown series for GNP, net imports, and total final demand at prewar constant factor costs. Total final demand is distributed among defence outlays, gross investment, and nondefence consumption by government and households. Real defence outlays (row 4) rose somewhat from year to year, and were 15.8 billion rubles higher in 1944 than in 1942, but the increase was much less than in total final demand (68.7 billion rubles, from row 3). Thus, civilian uses also benefited.

Civilian uses are shown as gross investment and nondefence consumption. Gross investment (row 5) collapsed with the outbreak of war, and was slightly negative in 1942, with small amounts of fixed capital formation more than offset by de-stocking; to set these figures in context, nearly 12 billion rubles of fixed investment were necessary just to replace annual depreciation of the fixed capital stock in Soviet hands.[34] Investment recovery after 1942 was guided first by requirements of the defence industry, but as the chances of victory improved the Soviet government also began rapidly to restore its peacetime industries, raising the priority of housebuilding and civilian capital construction.

Nondefence consumption was carried out by government and households. Government consumption (row 6.1), having fallen sharply at the outbreak of war, followed a gently rising trend from 1942 onwards. Aggregate household consumption (row 6.2), on the other hand, was lower in 1943 than in 1942, but recovered sharply (if incompletely) in 1944. Of crucial importance is what this pattern implied for consumption per head; lacking good wartime population figures, we make do with consumption per worker.[35] Consumption per worker reached the minimum point of the war in 1943; at this point, starvation-related deaths were already widespread. In the table I use this fact to calculate the annual breakdown of total household consumption between the amount required to maintain consumption per worker at the 1943 minimum and the amount surplus to this requirement in each year (rows 6.2a, 6.2b).

The last part of part (A) of the table presents two subtotals: total public outlays (row 7), i.e. all outlays other than by households, and total surplus outlays (row 8), i.e. all outlays above the amount required to maintain consumption per worker at the 1943 minimum; in 1943, when household surplus consumption was at zero, the two series coincide.

In part (B) of the table I suggest a simulation of what might have happened to the overall Soviet resource balance in the absence of aid. For this purpose, net imports must be set at zero; under the hypothesis of no foreign aid, total final demand (row 9) could not rise above GNP. I assume that in 1942 total defence and nondefence government consumption remained unchanged. Defence outlays (row 10) could not have been reduced given the desperate military plight, and the government would also have chosen not to reduce outlays on administration, welfare, and security (row 12.1). Therefore the loss of foreign aid would have first of all pushed household consumption down towards the floor (row 12.2), which would have been reached straight away, and would second have been reflected in further disinvestment (row 11).

For 1943 I assume that, since the authorities actually allowed consumption per worker to fall in 1943 to the assumed minimum, under the hypothetical case the authorities would have simply left it on the floor already reached in 1942, only permitting the aggregate to increase strictly in line with employment. Resources above this minimum (row 12.2) were available for total public outlays (row 13). A note to rows 10, 11, and 12.1 for 1943 shows how the authorities actually allocated the increase over 1942 in resources available among public outlays – first to investment, second to defence, third to government nondefence consumption. I assume that the additional resources hypothetically accruing from domestic output alone would then have been allocated among total public outlays in the given proportions.

For 1944, I assume that, with the emergency atmosphere lifting and the domestic economy in recovery, the authorities would have allowed some increase in consumption per worker above the floor. But household consumption still had to compete with other uses of total surplus outlays (row 14). A further note shows how the authorities actually allocated the increase over 1942 in resources available among total surplus outlays – first to household consumption, second to nondefence government consumption, third to defence, fourth to investment. I assume that the additional resources hypothetically accruing from domestic output alone would have been allocated among total surplus outlays in the given proportions.

The possible gain from foreign aid is shown in table 6.6 from columns 4 and 5. Column 4 shows the total of resources available and used under each set of circumstances, actual and hypothetical, and column 5 shows the difference made. Allied aid contributed roughly 50 billion rubles at 1937 factor cost, which averages out at 8 per cent of total resources available (row 3) over the three years. The largest proportion of it (nearly three fifths) was used to supply or release resources for additional investment (row 5). A quarter of it was reflected in higher defence outlays (row 4), and nearly all the remainder in higher household consumption in 1942 and 1944 (row 6.2). The implicit assumption underlying this rather uneven distribution of the consumption gain through time is that in 1942 household consumption was maintained some distance above the floor by a delay in mobilising resources out of the household sector (without foreign aid, the mobilisation would have been completed sooner); and that in 1944 household consumption was lifted above the floor by deliberate choice.

This analysis is undeniably crude. The numbers, though apparently precise, do no more than illustrate the argument. Moreover they rest on significant assumptions of the *ceteris paribus* kind. They presume that, in the absence of aid, the Soviet domestic product would have remained the same; in fact, one of the major determinants of Soviet wartime GNP was the loss and gain of territory, so anything detracting from the quantity and quality of the Soviet war effort would certainly have also reduced the total output of the domestic economy. Quality, as well as quantity: the military effectiveness of a billion rubles laid out on Soviet defence was surely higher if the package included lend-leased means of transport, communication, and soldiers' kit. The absence of aid also implied substantial cutbacks of civilian consumption and investment. Without aid, gross investment would have remained below replacement levels, resulting in a steady contraction of the capital stock available for use; this too would have forced Soviet GNP below actually achieved levels in 1942–4, with fewer resources then available for defence. Since there was a limit to the resources freed by cutting investment, living standards would also have been depressed below the levels actually experienced, which were already associated with widespread deaths from starvation. More starvation deaths amongst the working population would have forced an additional decline in domestic output.

These problems arise from the one-dimensional character of the counterfactual hypothesis employed, and define the numerical values shown as purely heuristic. But they do not modify the core proposition that the impact of western aid can only be understood in light of the overall objectives and constraints of the Soviet economy; aid did not simply add additional blocks of imported resources to a predetermined domestic allocation, but also influenced this allocation. Aid freed resources for civilian use, both for investment and consumption; however, it seems likely that the effect of these civilian uses was no more than to mitigate undernourishment of the population and depreciation of the capital stock. This was necessary and inevitable given the high degree of domestic economic mobilisation, the extreme deprivation of the civilian sector, and the consequent blurring of the distinction between front and rear.

The technical form of aid

The proposition illustrated in table 6.6 makes no concession to the view that the material form of lend-leased commodities was significant for the outcome of the aid process. Western aid consisted of equipment in a broad sense (including weapons, machinery, vehicles, ships, means of communications, materials, and fuels), some for military and some for civilian use, and processed foodstuffs intended only for military use. To understand its impact, consider the Soviet workforce divided among soldiers, industrial workers, and farmworkers. All of these were equipment users, but only industrial workers were equipment producers. Everyone was a food consumer, but only farmworkers produced food. Moreover, while in the long run the Soviet economy could theoretically be organised to produce any kind of food product or equipment, the innovation of some kinds of high-technology processes and high-grade products would certainly have been very expensive given the Soviet economy's skill, technology, and management deficits, and was not an option in the short run.

Probably, western *equipment for military use* unambiguously increased the Soviet capacity to devote resources to the war effort at all stages of the war, and was directly reflected in enlarged defence outlays. There was no immediately available domestic capacity for serial production of reliable motor vehicles, communications equipment, and so on. The replacement of high-grade imports would have required large quantities of domestically produced low-grade horsepower and equipment; this would always represent an inferior option. For example, railway transport could not solve the problem of dispersal of supplies across a front line of combat from the railhead. Domestic horse-drawn equipment and manpower could not create an offensive logistical capacity equivalent to motorised transport, partly because of slowness, partly because of the large supply multiplier attached to the requirements of horse and supply troops when advancing.[36] Imported American trucks, jeeps, field telephone systems, and portable radio sets were also complementary to Soviet equipment. Thus the import of western equipment for military use had a compound effect: it added to the quality of Soviet fighting power, made existing Soviet resources already committed to the war much more effective, and released at least some resources for civilian use.

It was important that aid resources arrived in a complementary package. High-quality imported vehicles without the high-grade imported fuels and fuel additives for their efficient operation, without the communication systems to enable coordination of highly mobile motorised infantry, without the ration packs to enable troops to subsist independently for days on the march, would have resulted in unused capacity and waste.

Other considerations probably applied to imported western munitions, which gained a poor reputation among Soviet fighting personnel. This poor reputation arose because western weapons were typically unsuited to combat conditions on the eastern front. British tanks were insufficiently rugged for climate, terrain, and the character of German opposition; British and American aircraft tended to be excessively sophisticated for ill-educated and untrained Soviet operators. Such weapons added little to Soviet fighting power, and for that reason were no substitute for Soviet-produced weaponry. (Having no civilian use, they were also no substitute for Soviet-produced civilian equipment or consumer goods.) Probably imported weapons were reflected in increased ruble outlays on the war, and did not release Soviet domestic resources from the war effort. But they did not make Soviet fighting power more effective.

A different range of effects can be attributed to imported *equipment for civilian use*. Industrial, power, and farm machinery imports released Soviet workers from equipment-making, and allowed their transfer to other equipment-using activities. 'Equipment-using' here has a broad sense – soldiers used military equipment, munitions workers used industrial equipment to make weapons, and agricultural workers used farm equipment to make food. In principle, therefore, imported equipment released resources in any of these directions. What decided the outcome was the policy context in which, from 1942 onwards, additional resources were shared out first to the equipment users in the defence sector, then to food producers whose task was to secure minimum consumption levels. To the extent that both military priorities and minimum food norms had been achieved (which may only have meant that no one of great significance was starving), however, Soviet workers could be retained in equipment-making to the benefit of civilian investment objectives, including for the postwar period.

In the first stages of the Lend-Lease operation, a relevant constraint was the rate at which resources could be released from equipment-making to equipment-using. Since overall labour resources were limited, it was possible in the short run to import too many machines. Western observers commented fretfully on the often neglectful attitude of Soviet handlers of western equipment, sometimes left to rot on sidings and in marshalling yards. But the underlying reason was probably not ungrateful or careless indifference; instead, there was a lack of absorptive capacity. It was rational to allow imported machinery to rust if there was no factory accommodation available in which to instal it, or workers to use it once installed. At this stage of the war, contrary to common perceptions, the Soviet economy needed overall resources more than it needed Lend-Lease dollars, which could not be utilised effectively under the circumstances.[37]

Imported *processed foodstuffs*, largely in tinned or concentrated forms, were intended solely for military use. This increment to food resources clearly released domestic food supplies for civilian use, and prevented overall nutritional standards from falling further. To the extent that minimum standards had been achieved, however, then farmworkers could be released for other equipment-using employment – military service, or equipment-making for industry and the military. Moreover, since agricultural work was of very low productivity by 1943–4, in ruble terms far below that of industrial workers, especially in engineering and munitions, the transfer of workers from farm to factory could significantly affect total output.[38] To the extent that military needs were satisfied, capital investment gained.

The importance of lend-leased equipment for the Soviet capital stock and postwar reconstruction has received some attention. Some light was shed on this topic when, in 1946, Voznesenskii reported the results of a Gosplan investigation into the cessation of Lend-Lease, undertaken in response to war cabinet instructions of the previous summer. He concluded that while, in many branches, domestic shortages of previously lend-leased commodities would be automatically compensated by a reduction in the requirements of war production, a number of persistent shortages would require special attention. The 'deficit' commodities, including iron and steel products, nonferrous metals, chemical and rubber products, paper, equipment, food products, and aircraft fuel, are listed in table 6.7, which illustrates the quantitative dependence of Soviet industry on imported supplies under each heading in 1944.

Dependence of the Soviet economy on external machinery supplies in this period has been emphasised recently by Khanin. He has suggested that between 1941 and 1950, two fifths of gross investment in the stock of Soviet metal-cutting machine tools was derived from imports comprising lend-leased supplies and postwar reparations.[39]

Aid and inter-Ally specialisation

By comparison, the inter-Ally dimension of wartime aid is easier to grasp. Was aid a subsidy from rich to poor, or an instance of resources shared among equal partners? Wartime governments naturally tended to emphasise the latter. It suited equally the Anglo–American desire to cement the USSR into a temporary union of strange bedfellows, and Soviet national feeling. Nor were the ideas of pooled resources and effective collaboration merely rhetoric. There was a real, practical logic at work, expressed in the division of labour among the Alliance partners. Within the alliance the wealthy, capital-abundant United States economy specialised relatively in the production of capital-intensive commodities such as weapons and machinery,

Table 6.7. *Commodities in short supply, 1946 (Lend-Lease deliveries, per cent of domestic output in physical units, in 1944)*

		%
1	Iron and steel	
1.1	rolled steel	8.1%
1.1a	ordinary	16.5%
1.1b	high-grade	3.9%
1.2	tubes (wire, solid-drawn, pipeline)	16.4%
1.3	metal fabricates	22.0%
2	Nonferrous metals	
2.1	lead	40.0%
2.2	tin	28.6%
2.3	cadmium	66.0%
2.4	wolfram concentrate	51.7%
2.5	molybdenum concentrate	81.3%
3	Chemicals	
3.1	caustic soda	32.0%
3.2	phenol	45.0%
3.3	dibutyl-phthalate	50.0%
3.4	methanol	33.5%
4	Rubber products	
4.1	conveyor belts	39.2%
4.2	transmission belts	48.5%
4.3	natural rubber	100.0%
5	Paper	50.0%
6	Equipment	
6.1	press-forging equipment	–
6.2	lifting equipment	–
6.3	excavating equipment	–
6.4	complex machine tools	–
7	Food products	
7.1	meat products	33.0%
7.2	animal fats	58.0%
8	Aircraft fuel	37.0%

Source: GARF, f. 3922/4372, op. 4, d. 7, ll. 173–8.

high-grade materials and fuels, and high-grade concentrated and long-life processed foods. The Soviet Union continued to produce a broad range of military and civilian goods and services but, relative to the Allies, specialised in the labour-intensive activity of fighting. The United Kingdom occupied an intermediate position, supplying weapons to Russia in the early stages of the war on the eastern front, but

Table 6.8. *Allied military losses and prewar GDP per head*

	Soldiers killed and died, per cent of prewar population (1)	GDP per head, 1940, international dollars and 1985 prices (2)
1 USA	0.2%	6440
2 UK	0.5%	4910
3 USSR	4.5%	1780

Sources: Col. 1: prewar populations from table 1.1, col. 1; military losses, rows 1, 2 from Urlanis (1971), 294, and row 3 from Krivosheev (1993), 130–1. Col. 2: table 1.1, col. 3.

meanwhile receiving food, fuel, and machinery from the United States; eventually, American supply reached a scale sufficient to release significant British labour resources for the invasion of Europe from the west.

In principle, to the extent that the pattern of specialisation followed a common Grand Strategy of the wartime Allies, each of the countries in receipt of American aid could have claimed a counterbalancing 'export' credit item based on the supply of military services to the Alliance as a whole, matching the import of American machinery and matériel. Alan Milward has suggested that 'in those cases where British tank crews had used American tanks it would make at least as much sense to charge the United States for the crew as the United Kingdom for the tank'.[40]

In practice, of course, no such crediting took place. It was not just an accident of peacetime accounting conventions that the result appeared to show Britain and the USSR as in receipt of a large subsidy. For one thing, any alternative would have involved the distasteful business of costing the expenditure of British and Russian human effort (on current account) and human lives (on capital account) in the same currency as machinery and fuel. It would have meant recognising that the Alliance had chosen to spend life most carelessly where it was cheapest. That this was indeed the outcome is suggested by table 6.8, which shows that the proportion of military losses in the prewar population was inversely proportional to prewar incomes per head.[41] Later, Soviet historians noted Truman's candid statement after the fact that Lend-Lease dollars were aimed at saving American lives: every Russian, British, or Australian soldier who went into battle equipped by means of American aid reduced the danger to young Americans.[42]

For another reason, despite the rhetoric of Allied collaboration and the pooling of resources, there was never any doubt as to the national subordination of military personnel. Even on the western front, the command structures of the British and American forces were merged only at the apex of command. In the east the coordination of Soviet with Allied military action was fragile in the extreme. Whether Soviet troops were to operate with lend-leased American equipment, but under Soviet command, or would themselves be lend-leased to some multinational UN force, would have been a matter of vital national interest, not of financial accounting.

In the end, therefore, it suited everyone to talk about mutual specialisation and the pooling of resources, but in practice to account for resource transfers as aid and trade favouring the poorer countries of the Alliance. Both British and Soviet accountants dealt with the resulting ambiguity (aid as pooled resource, or as subsidy) by means of a common device; they accepted Lend-Lease, used it to swell their own budget spending on defence, and hid the associated budget revenues.

Nonetheless, it seems that Allied aid to the USSR made possible the division of labour which won the war. Without it, everyone on the side of the Allies would have had a worse war. The Russians would have had to fight on their own resources, which were inadequate in quantity and quality, and would have fought less well, maybe only to a stalemate. The British and the Americans would have had to fight harder, because they would have had to take on a larger share of the killing of Germans and being killed by them; they would have had to choose either fighting with the same bitterness and intensity as the Russians, or accepting stalemate in the west. Perhaps, in 1942 and 1943, in place of combat for the few in the night skies over German cities, they would have had to choose combat for the many in the killing fields of Kent and Sussex; perhaps the required bitterness and intensity would have been supplied by an occupation régime on the south coast of England, with concentration camps on the Kent coast, and corpses hanging from telegraph poles in Wiltshire villages.

The aid relationship

Even now when the archives are becoming more accessible, there is no 'true story' waiting to be uncovered among dusty documents, which will tell the world just how Lend-Lease was spent in the Soviet Union. Identification of the resources released by aid remains a matter for theoretical reasoning and scholarly conjecture, and will not be found in any auditor's report.

It remains only a plausible suggestion that no more than a quarter of every Lend-Lease dollar was reflected in increased Soviet defence outlays. Different proportions could easily be justified with equal or greater plausibility. In any case, to the extent that the technical form of lend-leased goods for military use increased the military effectiveness of Soviet defence outlays as a whole, 25 cents in the dollar must understate the direct impact of Lend-Lease.

The other 75 cents went, under assumptions reviewed above, to underpinning the bare subsistence of the working population, and to investment in the maintenance of inventories and the fixed capital stock. Whatever the true proportions of its utilisation, aid must certainly have freed some resources for civilian use, both for investment and consumption; this was necessary and inevitable given the high degree of domestic economic mobilisation, the extreme deprivation of the civilian sector, and the consequent blurring of the distinction between front and rear. In the last stages of the war, continued Allied aid may have freed some resources for postwar reconstruction. But there is a strong possibility that civilian resources were already too constrained for aid to do much more than avert further deterioration in both the working population and the capital stock.

Aid to the USSR contributed to the mutual specialisation of the Allies according to the comparative advantage of each. This specialisation made sense in so far as it allowed everyone to do what they were good at. The western powers could specialise in the serial production of sophisticated weapons, and in using them to fight at a distance, while the Russians could get on with combat at close quarters. This pattern was nonetheless perceived as burdensome on each side, since the qualitative differences of role were not felt to be mutually compensating. The British, and still more the Americans, resented the Russians' economic dependence, their official presumptions of moral superiority, and lack of official gratitude. The Russians resented the way their richer partners used their wealth to help the Russians to kill and be killed.

Here were the roots of mutual suspicion – the potential use and abuse of aid by both donors and recipients for purposes which had less to do with winning the war than with civilian and postwar objectives. Was Lend-Lease used in the Allied interest, substituting young Russian lives for those of Britons and Americans? Was it exploited by the Russians for civilian as well as military purposes, to serve postwar as well as wartime objectives? The answer to both these questions is, realistically, 'yes'. But Allied aid was also, nonetheless, an effective 'Weapon for Victory', and there was no good alternative to it under the constraints of the time. Without it, everyone would have had a worse war. The western Allies would have had to kill and be killed in greater numbers. The Russians would have done less killing and more being killed. The tensions were simply inherent in the aid relationship, as the history of postwar development aid will amply testify.

7 War losses

Physical destruction

As a result of World War II, the Soviet Union suffered both current costs and capital losses. The current costs of the war effort are encapsulated in the idea of the defence burden or sacrifice borne by Soviet citizens in order to defend their country and punish the invader. In previous chapters we examined how this burden compared with national resources, and the extent to which it was alleviated by foreign aid. The distinctive feature of current costs is that they had to be met within the war period itself. No part of the immediate cost of the real resources used to defeat Germany could be postponed to the period after Germany's defeat, although the cost could to some extent be redistributed among the Allies. In contrast, the impact of capital losses, although it took effect immediately while the war was still in progress, persisted far into the postwar period.

Capital losses must be understood broadly. The Soviet Union entered World War II with stocks of physical, human, and other sorts of capital. Physical assets can be understood conventionally as the total value of structures, equipment, inventories, and farm stocks. Human assets are represented by the value embodied in the workforce through the process of rearing, education, and training. Neither physical nor human assets can be evaluated without difficulty. Just as important, but still more difficult to measure, is the intangible stock of accumulated scientific knowledge. In this chapter I find measures of the impact of the war upon Soviet physical and human capital, but I ignore the intangible stock of knowledge, because its prewar value, and the effects upon it of the war, raise issues far beyond the scope of the present work.

World War II saw huge destruction on the eastern front. The scale which destruction assumed is explained partly by the special nature of the war in Russia – on Germany's side, a war of extermination, on the

Russian side a war for national survival – the 'Great Patriotic War'. In addition to the factors of blind hatred and national feeling must be considered the rational calculation of ends and corresponding means, the technological possibilities of mechanised war, the scale of resources which each side was willing to commit to the struggle, the productive capacities of the Soviet and German economies, and German actions which aimed to destroy, exploit, or transfer to Germany the physical and human assets of the occupied territories; these are the rest of the explanation. They made the campaign on the eastern front the biggest theatre and the fiercest struggle of World War II, in fact the greatest land war of all time, accounting for two thirds of the global war dead.

Soviet losses in World War II are generally acknowledged to have been very heavy, but economic analysis of these losses has advanced little beyond stating the obvious.[1] While stating the obvious is justifiable, given the general ignorance of the subject in western public life, it is possible to do more. Stephen Broadberry and Peter Howlett have criticised traditional approaches to accounting for the economic costs of war, argued for a balance-sheet approach based on the evaluation of trends in both physical and human assets, and showed how one might be compiled for the United Kingdom in World War II.[2] In this chapter I make the attempt to draw up a similar balance sheet for the USSR.

Soviet historiography followed something like the traditional methodology of E.L. Bogart's influential study of World War I for the Carnegie Fund.[3] Bogart distinguished between direct and indirect costs. 'Direct costs' were the budgetary costs of the war effort, while 'indirect costs' comprised property losses, lost output, and the capitalised value of lost lives. The overall cost of the war was derived by simply summing the various direct and indirect costs, irrespective of their stock or flow character, over the war's period.

Soviet balance sheets tended to follow Bogart in spirit, departing from his approach only in matters of detail and terminology. Thus war-related budgetary costs were termed 'direct costs' by Bogart, and 'direct expenditures' by Voznesenskii and his successors. Bogart listed losses of fixed capital under 'indirect costs', but these became 'direct losses' in Soviet parlance. Lost income resulting from enemy occupation and the loss of life also came under Bogart's 'indirect costs' (the latter as the capitalised value of human life); in the Soviet version they became simply 'other costs and losses'.[4]

Table 7.1 shows the ruble values traditionally placed upon these various items, which totalled 2,569 billion rubles. Adding together all the various direct and indirect costs and losses, whether capital or

Table 7.1. *Material costs of World War II: official figures (billion prewar rubles)*

		(1)	(2)
1	Direct losses of physical assets on occupied territory	679	679.0
2	Direct budgetary and other costs	1890	1890.0
3	Direct budgetary costs, total	>600	582.4
3.1	wartime military outlays	551	–
3.2	servicemen's pensions, etc.	>50	–
4	Other costs of conversion, evacuation, air defence, and forgone material product of occupied territory	–	1307.6
5	Total costs and losses	2569	2569.0

Sources: Col. 1: traditional figures, obtained and further defined as follows. Row 1, 'the damage inflicted on the national economy of the USSR and private rural and urban residents', at 1941 prices, from ChGK (1945). Row 2, 'direct war expenditures and additional expenditures caused by the war as well as the losses in the national income of the population and Socialist enterprises', from Voznesensky (1948), 130. Rows 3 ('direct military outlays in connection with the Great Patriotic War'), 3.1 ('direct outlays on the maintenance of the Armed Forces'), 3.2 ('pensions and benefits of servicemen and their families'), from Tamarchenko (1967), 134. Row 4, 'war spending in connection with conversion of the national economy to wartime purposes, evacuation and reevacuation of enterprises, outlays on air defence, ... additional shortfalls and losses in connection with the impossibility of producing output in the regions subject to occupation, the diversion to the war of millions of people of the most productive age-groups, and the loss of people resulting from combat actions and the occupiers' annihilation of the part of the USSR's population'; this is the residual defined by Tamarchenko (1967), 135, after deducting row 3 from row 2. Row 5, 'the total damage borne by the national economy in the war years, together with military outlays and the temporary loss of incomes from industry and agriculture in the regions undergoing occupation' (i.e. the sum of rows 1, 2), from TsSU (1959), 53; see also Tamarchenko (1967), 131. Col. 2: alternative figures from IVMV, vol. 12 (1982), 149, for the separate components of direct budgetary and other costs (rows 3, 4); the same source confirms the traditional totals and other figures (rows 1, 2, 5) long sanctified by official use.

current, at fixed prices or nominal values, to make up this grand total, was another point of conformity of Soviet practice (at least, after Voznesenskii) with Bogart's precedent.

From the point of view of a national balance sheet of assets, the relevant figure is not 2,569 billion rubles, but only the 679 billion rubles' worth of war damage to the capital stock. The other 1,890 billion rubles represent a wartime flow of resources the opportunity cost of which was incurred within the war period; they are not relevant to an estimate of permanent losses arising from the war.[5] The 679 billion rubles of direct losses, although a relatively small part of the grand total, represented a large sum, and were later estimated at 'about 30 per cent of national wealth'.[6]

The figure of 679 billion rubles was originally calculated by a special state commission established at the end of the war to evaluate Soviet losses. Various aspects of the figure's composition were revealed – a breakdown by ownership, which showed the main loser to have been the state, although there was also great destruction of collective-farm and personal property; a territorial breakdown, which showed the main destruction as having occurred on the territory of the Russian and Ukrainian republics; and a list of physical assets (the residential accommodation of 25 million people, 31,850 industrial establishments, 239,000 electric motors, 175,000 machine tools, 65,000 kilometres of railway track, and so on).[7]

The commission's report cannot be verified on present information. Much depends on its intrinsic veracity. Here the problem is that the release of all such information in the 1940s was heavily influenced by two competing considerations: a desire to influence western policy on reparations and postwar reconstruction aid in the direction of generosity, and an offsetting desire to conceal the wounds inflicted on the country's economic and social fabric from the outside world. What little is known about other aspects of the commission's work does not inspire confidence. An uncritical account of its findings with regard to demographic losses, hitherto secret, was published recently by A.A. Sheviakov. Among many glaring inconsistencies it revealed a completely impossible total of up to 21 million civilian deaths from shooting and starvation, on occupied territory alone.[8]

As for the official figures on direct capital losses, the story which they tell is at least consistent. Moorsteen and Powell attempted an audit as follows.[9] First, they found that the official list of physical assets wholly or partly destroyed supported an overall loss in the range 'between 20 and 40 per cent of the prewar stock' (this was before the figure of 'about 30 per cent' had been officially adopted). Second, they cited Voznesenskii's claim that direct losses represented 'about two-thirds of the pre-war national wealth' of the occupied territories; since the prewar population of the occupied territories represented about 45 per cent of the USSR prewar population, this (i.e. 67% times 45%) could also be taken as support for a figure of 30 per cent.[10] Third, Voznesenskii had given prewar public-sector firms' fixed assets as 709 billion rubles, and the decline in the second half of 1941 as 215 billion rubles (both figures at 1945 prices), again a decline of 30 per cent.[11]

The commission's story was consistent, but may still be exaggerated, as the figures for war deaths have revealed. For present purposes I scale down the official figure of 679 billion rubles in line with Moorsteen and Powell, who proposed the figure of 25 per cent for Soviet losses of prewar fixed assets, in light of the possibility that official claims were somewhat overstated.[12]

Demographic losses

The war on the eastern front resulted in both heavy combat losses of military personnel, and widespread premature deaths amongst the civilian population. In the interior of the country, malnutrition was widespread. It was not confined to famous episodes such as the siege of Leningrad where hunger and hunger-related causes carried off 800,000 people, one third of the city's prewar population; across the breadth of Soviet-controlled territory, hunger was a daily fact for tens of millions, and undoubtedly carried off many less well remembered victims. Poor dietary conditions were also conducive to the spread of diseases, and the incidence of typhus, typhoid fever, and tuberculosis rose sharply in 1942, although determined measures checked their subsequent spread.[13]

Death rates for the population as a whole, but presumably excluding those arising from enemy action, are said to have risen from 18 per thousand in 1940 to 24 per thousand in 1942, falling to 9 per thousand in 1945. But even these figures are surely incomplete. Reports from Siberia, remote from the front line, also confirm a mortality peak in 1942, and a particularly sharp increase in mortality amongst the urban population (29 per thousand in 1942, compared with 21 per thousand in the countryside), despite the predominance of younger and older age groups in the village. After 1942 death rates fell, not because conditions were improving, but because the most vulnerable members of society had already been carried off.[14]

The demographic consequences of combat fatalities and civilian deprivation are now clear in outline, if not in detail. Succeeding generations of Soviet leaders put the total of premature deaths at 7 million

Table 7.2. *Population movements, mid-1941 to end-1945 (millions)*

	(1)	(2)
1 Total population, mid-1941	196.7	199.4
2 Emigrated by end-1945	2.7	2.7
3 Remained at end-1945	159.5	159.5
4 Died during war		
4.1 actual	34.5	37.2
4.2 normal	11.9	11.9
4.3 excess	22.6	25.3
5 Births, mid-1941 to end-1945	16.4	16.4
6 Survived to end-1945	11.0	11.0
7 Died during war		
7.1 actual	5.4	5.4
7.2 normal	4.1	4.1
7.3 excess	1.3	1.3
8 Total population, end-1945	170.5	170.5
8.1 born before mid-1941 (from row 3)	159.5	159.5
8.2 born since mid-1941 (from row 6)	11.0	11.0
9 Excess deaths since mid-1941	23.9	26.6
9.1 born before mid-1941 (from row 4.3)	22.6	25.3
9.2 born since mid-1941 (from row 7.3)	1.3	1.3
10 War losses (including emigration)	26.6	29.3

Sources: Andreev *et al.* (1990b), 26–7, except that alternative allowances are made for the Maksudov dilemma (namely, the whereabouts of 2.7m missing net emigrants) on lines suggested by Ellman and Maksudov (1994), 672–3. Col. 1: assuming that net emigration is concealed in war deaths as estimated by Andreev *et al.*, the total of excess deaths is reduced by 2.7m below the Andreev figure. Col. 2: assuming that the prewar population of the territories annexed in 1939–40, as estimated by Andreev *et al.*, has already been adjusted downward by the number of net emigrants, the true prewar population is shown as 2.7m higher than in the Andreev figures, while the Andreev estimate of war deaths is confirmed.

(Stalin), 20 million (Khrushchev), and 'more than 20 million' (Brezhnev).[15] More recently, an expert commission of Goskomstat reported the excess mortality of the war years as 26–27 million; its figures are shown in table 7.2. The mid-1941 population (within contemporary frontiers) is given as 196.7 million, and the population at the end of 1945 as 170.5 million; the point estimate for war deaths is 26.6 million.[16]

The Goskomstat figure of 26.6 million was admittedly subject to a substantial error margin ('26–27 million'). Moreover, in addition to the acknowledged hazards of measurement, this figure was blurred conceptually on the score of emigration. According to the estimate of S. Maksudov, there was a net wartime and postwar emigration of some 2.7 million prewar Soviet citizens (mainly ethnic Poles, Germans, and Jews). Whether these should be deducted from war deaths estimated by Goskomstat, or whether they have already been deducted from the Goskomstat figure for prewar population of the territories newly annexed in 1939–40, remains unclear. I refer to this below as the Maksudov dilemma.[17] Depending on the answer to the Maksudov dilemma there are two possible underlying figures for war deaths, the official 26.6 million, and 26.6–2.7 = 23.9 million.

Of course, 'only' 23.9 million would still be a very large number of premature deaths. If we accepted even the lower figure, and combined it with a conservative 7.8 million excess deaths of regular military personnel, then roughly speaking, the war carried off 2 in 9 Soviet soldiers, and 1 in 10 civilians (including partisans).[18] An equivalent figure for combined Anglo–American civil plus military losses would be 1 in more than 250.

Wartime losses of population exceeded war deaths by the extent of net emigration, since those who were expelled or took the opportunity to emigrate represented a loss of population and human capital to the Soviet Union just as surely as those who died prematurely (in distinction from the latter, however, they also formed a gain to the countries where they settled). The Maksudov dilemma therefore yields two possible underlying figures for total war losses of population, 26.6+2.7 = 29.3 million, and 26.6 million.

Combined losses

In table 7.3, I make a rudimentary comparison of overall Soviet wartime losses of physical with human capital. First, I take from table 7.1 the figure of 679 billion rubles' worth of assets destroyed on occupied territory. I also combine this with the statement that it represented 'about 30 per cent of national wealth' to derive a figure of 2,263 billion rubles' worth of prewar physical assets. But then I scale down the estimate of capital losses out of this sum from 30 to 25 per cent, giving a monetary value of 566 billion rubles of war damage to fixed assets.

The valuation of human capital losses is more complicated. In addition to the mystery and secrecy which traditionally shrouded the

Table 7.3. *Losses of physical and human assets during World War II (billion rubles at prewar prices and per cent)*

	(1)	(2)
(A) Loss of physical assets		
1 Prewar assets, total	2263	2263
2 War losses, billion rubles	566	566
3 % lost	25%	25%
(B) Loss of human assets		
4 Prewar assets, total	1489	1515
5 War losses, billion rubles	268	294
6 % lost	18%	19%
(C) Loss of combined assets		
7 Prewar assets, total	3753	3778
8 War losses, billion rubles	834	860
9 % lost	22%	23%

Sources: Cols 1 and 2 correspond to the same columns in table 7.2, and show the same alternative ways of accounting for the Maksudov dilemma. Row 1: according to Tamarchenko (1967), 134, and IVMV, vol. 12 (1982), 148, the sum of 679 billion rubles (table 7.1, row 1) represented about 30 per cent of national wealth, giving the latter as 2,263 billion rubles at prewar prices. Row 2: row 1, multiplied by row 3. Row 3: Moorsteen and Powell (1966), 75. Row 4: row 5, divided by row 6. Row 5: table M.3, row 6. Row 6: table M.3, row 4.1. Row 7: the sum of rows 1, 4. Row 8: the sum of rows 2, 5. Row 9: row 8, divided by row 7.

number of war deaths, Soviet historians were always philosophically disinclined to put a ruble value on the loss of life. Naturally, the loss of life cannot be reduced to its financial aspect, but it can hardly be denied that the financial aspect exists, and deserves analysis. 'The problem', Broadberry and Howlett point out, 'is that the capitalised value of human life overstates the social loss, since people consume as well as produce. In a national balance sheet framework, all that we require is the cost of rearing and training a worker, since this is what is lost to society by premature death.'[19]

The process of deriving rough estimates of the annual average prewar cost of rearing and training Soviet children is explained in appendix M. These costs work out at 589 and 562 rubles per year at 1940 prices respectively. If Soviet working-age citizens had been reared for 15 years and educated for 7 years, then each premature death deprived the Soviet economy of roughly 12,774 rubles. Depending on how we resolve the Maksudov dilemma, Soviet war losses included either 21 or 23 million citizens of working age, so that the overall loss of human capital works out at 268 or 294 billion rubles.

The figures of 21 or 23 million losses (premature deaths plus emigration) among people of working age, compared with the associated numbers in the prewar working-age population, imply that 18–19 per cent of Soviet human capital was lost or destroyed, approximately speaking. This was only three quarters or four fifths the rate of destruction of physical capital (18–19 per cent, compared with 25 per cent). In other words, despite a demographic catastrophe unmatched in the wartime experience of any other great power, the Soviet Union entered the postwar reconstruction period with a shortfall of physical relative to human capital.

Lastly, dividing 268 or 294 billion rubles' worth of human capital destroyed by 18–19 per cent suggests alternative figures for the total prewar stock of human capital close to 1,500 billion prewar rubles and straddling this sum on either side. By implication, the Soviet prewar ratio of human to physical capital was therefore roughly 66–67 per cent, somewhat below the 72 per cent ratio estimated for prewar Britain by Broadberry and Howlett, which was in turn less than the US ratio calculated by Kendrick.[20]

Summing prewar stocks and wartime losses gives a final estimate of 22–23 per cent for total Soviet losses from the combined prewar stocks of physical and human capital.

This evaluation of overall Soviet war losses remains incomplete in so far as it makes no allowance for wartime additions to stocks of assets, whether physical or human, tangible or intangible. For example, the physical capital stock of the defence industry was enlarged, and this investment proved to be of some value from the point of view of postwar needs. Human capital was enhanced in wartime by the rapid absorption of workers from agriculture into industry, and even the armed forces, where they received training and were subjected to learning-by-doing. Wartime additions to the intangible stock of scientific and technical knowledge should also be taken into account, although this is not done here. These may well represent a war-induced acceleration of prewar trends; if the war had not taken place, the pace of such additions to the stock of assets might well have been slower. It seems unlikely, however, that taking this into account would greatly change the overall picture.

A standard production-function approach suggests that the postwar shortfall of physical capital must have raised its marginal product relative to that of human capital, lowering the returns to human capital and labour, and reducing GNP per head. Suppose that real output (Q) in period t is determined by a Cobb–Douglas production function augmented for human capital in the spirit of recent work on global postwar economic development trends by Mankiw, Romer and Weill: there are three factors of production of roughly equal status, physical capital (K), human capital (H), and labour (L), combined on the basis of a given technological and organisational state (A), characterised by diminishing returns and constant returns to scale:[21]

$$Q_t = A_t \cdot K_t^{1/3} \cdot H_t^{1/3} \cdot L_t^{1/3}$$

If all the independent variables are index numbers set to one in the prewar period, then the impact on postwar GNP of war losses, considered in isolation under the assumption of given technology and organisation, can be evaluated by setting $K_{postwar} = 0.75$ (from table 7.3), and $H_{postwar} = L_{postwar} = 0.81$ (a compromise estimate); this suggests that, other things being equal, postwar Soviet GNP should have been lowered by 21 per cent; with a 19 per cent loss of working population, GNP per worker should have fallen by 2.5 per cent. Since there was little change in the dependency ratio between 1940 and 1950, 2.5 per cent may also stand for the expected GNP shortfall, per head of the total population.[22]

Standard economic theory suggests that this shortfall should not have persisted. The same is true of capital investment; during the war, the capital stock is damaged or depreciated, and the capital/labour ratio may even fall, but this makes postwar investments abnormally profitable, so that investment is encouraged and the capital stock grows more rapidly than before, precisely because it is starting from a lower postwar level. The increased return to physical capital should have spurred additional efforts to accumulate it, enabling a return to the prewar trajectory.[23] Here is a ready rationale for the postwar transfer of physical assets to the Soviet Union from occupied Germany, and the intense physical investment effort of the fourth five-year plan (1946–50). In the Soviet case, however, the negative effects of the war were much more persistent than the standard argument would have predicted.

Were war losses permanent?

The war constituted a profound supply-side shock to the Soviet economy. One fifth of the country's human assets, and one quarter of its physical assets, were lost. The evidence available, although somewhat heterogeneous in character, suggests that the supply-side shocks to the Soviet population, fixed capital, and GNP resulting from World War II were persistent in character, and that their effects on postwar levels of these variables were never made up, at least, not within any historically relevant timespan.

In other words, commentators may speak loosely of the Soviet Union requiring 5, 10, 20, or 30 years to recover from the war, but this must be understood as a simplification; the reality is that, although prewar levels of GNP, population, and so on were soon surpassed, the Soviet Union *never* returned to its prewar economic trajectory. This may be considered surprising since, for the reasons given above, a negative shock such as a war may normally be expected to be followed by accelerated growth. The fundamental Soviet economic variables do not, however, show this expected postwar acceleration.

First, as far as population is concerned, the USSR began 1946 with an overall demographic deficit arising from the war of approximately 35 million, combining excess war deaths and emigration with the wartime birth deficit.[24] Conventional demographic theory suggests that a postwar demographic deficit should be accompanied by accelerated population growth. For example, war accelerates the mortality of the very old and young, and also results in delayed marriages and births, and an increase in terminations of pregnancy; after the war, at least some of the marriages postponed in wartime are normally celebrated, and there may also be a baby boom, while the mortality of the very old and young diminishes; the population may be smaller than before, but its growth accelerates. Ellman and Maksudov point out that the war was not followed by the increase in fertility rates which might have been expected. On the contrary, fertility rates (which had been falling in the 1930s) continued to decline, and never regained their prewar levels. Therefore, depending on one's assumptions about postwar fertility rates in the absence of World War II, the postwar demographic deficit of 35–36 million (17 per cent of the expected end-1945 population) was either simply not made up, or continued to increase indefinitely throughout the postwar period.[25]

Second, the shock to the fixed capital stock also appears to have been permanent. On the basis of figures similar to those adopted here, and taking into account prewar and postwar investment and depreciation trends, Moorsteen and Powell found the net stock of fixed capital in 1950 to be approximately 51 per cent of an extrapolation of the prewar log-linear trend; alternatively, the war caused the capital stock to attain

Table 7.4. *Trends and breaks in Russian and Soviet economic growth, 1885–1985 (GNP per head, per cent change)*

1 Trend growth, 1885–1913, per year	1.7%
2 Drop in level, 1914	–26.9%
3 Trend growth, 1928–40, per year	3.6%
4 Drop in level, 1941	–10.7%
5 Trend growth, 1950–74, per year	3.6%
6 Trend growth, 1974–85, per year	0.5%

Source: Table N.6.

a given value some 6–7 years later than it would have done otherwise. They estimated the trend annual rates of growth of the capital stock in the 1930s and 1950s from log-linear regression against time, and found scant evidence of postwar acceleration (4.2 per cent, rising to 4.7 per cent), suggesting again that war losses were never made good, or made good only very slowly.[26]

Third, the wartime shock to Soviet GNP has been evaluated by Tony Syme, who tested GNP series estimated by Moorsteen and Powell (1928–50) and CIA (1950–87) for the presence of a stationary trend in the underlying mechanism generating the data, while allowing for endogenously detected breaks in the level and trend of GNP.[27] He found support for growth of GNP along a constant trend from 1928 through to 1973; the trend *annual growth rate* of GNP over this period, 5.2 per cent, was unaffected by the wartime experience, and persisted until the early 1970s. But allowance must be made for a sharp break of the GNP *level* associated with the war, involving a postwar shortfall of some 37 per cent below the extrapolated prewar trend, or nearly 7 years' lost growth. This setback was permanent, since it was not followed by acceleration allowing a postwar return to the level suggested by extrapolating the prewar trend path.

The development level of the Soviet economy, its productive potential and potential for satisfying consumer needs are better measured by GNP per head than by aggregate GNP. The behaviour of Russian and Soviet GNP per head over the whole period from 1885 to 1985 may be similarly investigated (the procedure is outlined in appendix N). The data can be read in different ways, but the most convincing hypothesis suggests a consistent story, summarised in table 7.4: from 1928 to 1974 GNP per head grew at a steady, relatively rapid rate of 3.6 per cent per year, but World War II inflicted a permanent penalty involving the loss of about 11 per cent of GNP per head, or three years' growth.

Several interesting comparisons suggest themselves. One is with the much smaller expected postwar shortfall of GNP per head (2.5 per cent) which was calculated above on the basis of estimated asset losses. In other words, the Soviet economy's capital losses are too small to explain the actual postwar GNP per head shortfall. Even if the higher, official figure for physical capital losses of 30 per cent were adopted, the expected shortfall of postwar GNP per head would still be only 4.7 per cent. In any case, standard economic theory suggests that this shortfall should have been only temporary, whereas in fact it proved to be permanent. The postwar shortfall of Soviet GNP per head is therefore essentially unexplained by wartime asset losses.

Another comparison may be made between the Russian and Soviet experience of two world wars. It appears that, in terms of demographic losses alone, the wars of 1914–21 and 1941–45 were equally devastating. Excess deaths in World War I and the Russian Civil War (including the postwar famine and emigration) amounted to roughly 18 million, or 12 per cent of the prewar population within interwar frontiers.[28] This figure may be compared with at least 26.6 million (again 12 per cent) lost from the prewar population in World War II. There is no means of comparing the capital losses of the two wars. But the loss of output per head attributable to the earlier episode appears much greater, with a 27 per cent shortfall below the extrapolated prewar trend in 1928, compared with the 11 per cent shortfall arising from World War II in 1950. Perhaps recovery from World War II was not complicated by revolutionary transformations of the kind which followed World War I. Another explanation may be that they global economic environment was also much calmer and more confident after World War II, in contrast with the unstable trading conditions of the interwar world economy, to which the Soviet economy of the 1920s was much more exposed.

On an international comparison, it appears that the Soviet Union was the only one of the victors to suffer a significant economic setback from World War II. Tests for trend breaks in GDP per head applied by Nick Crafts and Terry Mills suggest that, for most countries of the present-day OECD, the hypothesis of a negative wartime shock to growth is rejected. Only defeated Austria, Finland, France, Germany, and Japan display marked declines in trend GNP growth over 1940–50 compared with 1920–39. For several countries (neutral Switzerland, and victorious Australia, Canada, and the United States), 1940 initiated an acceleration phase.[29] From this point of view the effects of the war on the Soviet economy were far more consistent with the experience of the vanquished countries than with the experience of the victors, Britain or the United States.

Moreover, unlike others, the Soviet Union's wartime setback was not followed by postwar acceleration. Trend growth in all countries in Crafts and Mills' sample, victors and vanquished alike, was more rapid after 1950 than before 1940. This was not just a matter of postwar recovery since, with minor exceptions (Finland, Sweden, and Switzerland) postwar OECD trend growth rates remained more rapid after 1950 than before 1940 right up to 1989, long after any recovery effect had faded.[30] This was not the case for the USSR. Soviet economic growth was already rapid in the 1930s, of course, and postwar recovery brought a resumption of prewar trend growth, but at a lower level of GNP. There was not even the temporary acceleration and return to the extrapolated prewar trend which could have been expected on the basis of the increased marginal product of physical capital arising from its higher rate of wartime destruction compared to losses of other factors. The difference of levels between the postwar trend and extrapolated prewar trend was never made up.

This loss must be attributed to a permanent loss of economic efficiency which arose during the war. The factors contributing to economic efficiency in this sense are many – technology, economies of scale, the degree of utilisation of resources, the efficiency with which they are allocated. On present knowledge any comments can only be speculative. However, it is hard to avoid the suggestion that the postwar period was characterised by permanently increased allocative inefficiency associated with the wartime formation of a semi-autonomous defence-industry complex of the remote interior, more disintegrated from the civilian economy than before, and also a heavier postwar defence burden, more secrecy, and higher barriers to the free flow of information, technology transfer, and international trade.

A permanent loss of 6–8.5 per cent or even 11 per cent of GNP per head arising from World War II may not seem much, especially by comparison with the negative shock arising from World War I and its aftermath. Even 11 per cent represents only 3–4 years of postwar Soviet economic growth. But it is large in comparison with, say, the efficiency gains sometimes associated with increased postwar regional and global economic integration.[31] For example, the permanent GDP gain from completing the internal market of the European Community in 1992 was estimated at 4.8–6.4 per cent from summing the partial equilibrium effects, or 4.5 per cent on a general equilibrium basis.[32] By such standards, the permanent effects of the war on the level of Soviet GNP per head should be considered large. The size of the loss may be better appreciated by remembering that it would be incurred over several decades; even after discounting, the cumulative sum would be relatively large.

Over the postwar decades the general trend among the former allies and enemies was for the prewar inequalities of GNP per head to lessen. Among Britain, France, Germany, Italy, and Japan there was a clear pattern of convergence, and the gap between western European and north American productivity and living standards also lessened. But the Soviet economy did not join in the convergence process. The gains of a more liberalised world economy, with freer flows of capital, technology, and information, failed to accrue to the Soviet Union. Half a century after the war, the convergence of productivity and living standards in the former Soviet Union upon western European levels remains an unfinished task.

8 Conclusion

The attempt to rebuild the statistical record of the Soviet economy in World War II may have appeared foolhardy, but the effort leaves us with some important insights.

The reconstruction presented in this book proceeded from Soviet data of production, prices, outlays, and employment. It was argued that, despite their deficiencies, such data were not arbitrary fabrications; they are meaningful (although the meaning was rarely to be found on the surface), are capable of interpretation and, if interpreted correctly, provide a sufficient foundation for statistical aggregation and economic evaluation. Soviet GNP can be measured.

The process of rebuilding the Soviet wartime national accounts has confirmed how heavy was the blow inflicted by the German invasion of 1941. Between 1940 and 1942, Soviet GNP fell by one third. By the end of the war, despite the recapture of occupied territory, recovery was far from complete.

In order to defeat the invader, the Soviet Union had to mobilise a high proportion of its diminished resources. At the peak of intensity, which came already in 1942, nearly three fifths of its national product had been committed to the war effort. At this stage, insufficient resources were left available for subsistence or replacement of either the human or the physical capital stock; living standards collapsed, and people starved.

After the peak of intensity, the Soviet Union was able to continue to increase the volume of resources devoted to the war effort while at the same time relaxing the severity of domestic mobilisation. This was achieved partly from increased total output, partly from the rising volume of foreign aid. Foreign aid was one factor which enabled defence, investment, and consumption outlays to grow simultaneously, although the nondefence items remained far below peacetime standards.

Stalin proposed that World War II had provided 'an all-round test' of the Soviet Union's 'material and spiritual forces'.[1] In so far as this idea had a scientific kernel, the Soviet economy passed the test; in fact, judged by historical and comparative criteria, the Soviet success in World War II was very striking.

The Soviet Union was a low-income country with a large, low-productivity agrarian sector. It was a newly industrialising country, with a prewar decade of very rapid growth, but against the gain which this represented relative to other powers had to be set the losses of World War I and the Civil War, the forced collectivisation of agriculture at the end of the 1920s, the induced famine of 1932, and the sweeping prewar purges.

In both the world wars of the first half of the twentieth century, when poor countries of similar or even somewhat more advanced development level and economic structure were subjected to massive attack, even if their armies were initially militarily successful or at least did not immediately collapse, their economies soon disintegrated. This did not happen in the Soviet case.

Of course the Soviet Union had the advantages of size and a high degree of external self-sufficiency, but even a large economy soon lost any advantage if it could not be coordinated and mobilised from the centre. The examples of Russia itself, Austria–Hungary, and eventually even Germany in World War I, and of Japan and Italy in World War II, may all be given in evidence.

In Russia in World War I, the army took the products of the urban economy and the young men and horses of the rural economy. When the urban economy's products were mobilised for war, nothing was left to supply the village. Food production fell, and what was produced was retained in the village, while the urban population eventually went hungry or migrated to the countryside.

The Soviet economy did not disintegrate in World War II; the resources of both town and country were mobilised for war, despite the fact that there soon emerged an absolute shortage of products to keep everyone alive.

Our findings show that this mobilisation was far from well coordinated, did not proceed 'according to a single plan' (even if a single plan could be shown to have existed), and relied on foreign aid to an extent much greater than 'only 4 per cent'. But this is not surprising; if such traditional formulae of conservative Soviet historiography were validated, *that* would have been even more surprising. Nor does their refutation undermine the Soviet wartime economic achievement, judged by its real record.

'Brute force' was one of the evils (along with 'bad faith, injustice, oppression', etc.) enumerated by Neville Chamberlain in his radio broadcast of 3 September 1939, against which the people of Britain were to fight.[2] Eventually, however, brute force became the Allies' main weapon, and what was tested in World War II was the capacity of the Allies to apply it.[3] The powers of the Axis were finally crushed by superior economic resources, translated into overwhelming quantitative advantage of military might.

Brute force was applied, and not only to the enemy. In varying measure, each government had to apply it also to the population under its own control.

This necessity arose from two tendencies. One was the tendency of private individuals and working collectives, farmers and firms to judge their own chances of survival in defeat to be better than that of the state; any government had to close off this option by force. Another was the capacity of private agents to seek a 'free ride' or some other private advantage from the war effort of others. This avenue also had to be blocked.

The power of Stalin's régime to apply such force was by no means complete; the history of the Soviet war effort is threaded with accounts of speculation on alternative outcomes, collaboration with the enemy, and outright betrayal. In the end, however, these tendencies were not decisive. The Soviet economy was mobilised; despite severe burdens and heavy losses, it did not disintegrate.

When the war was over, the Soviet Union was left with its heavy losses. The Soviet economy was traumatised like the economies of defeated Germany, Italy, and Japan. However, the defeated countries all showed unexpected postwar economic resilience, and soon caught up with and overtook their own prewar trend paths. For the Soviet economy war losses were permanent. The Soviet economy was able to resume its prewar trend growth rate of GNP and GNP per head, but at a lower level than would otherwise have been attained. There was no postwar acceleration, so that wartime losses of income, capital stock, and population were never made good. Postwar recovery was rapid in absolute terms, but failed to return the economy to its prewar trajectory, or converge upon the income levels of European competitor nations.

In World War II the Soviet economy supplied the eastern front with tens of millions of soldiers and weapons. These soldiers and weapons destroyed Hitler's dream of a German empire in Europe. At the same time, they conserved the Soviet empire for the next 50 years. Whether their postwar maintenance became the burden which eventually undid the Soviet empire is a project for further investigation.

Appendix A: price deflators

Soviet prices were determined partly by the pressure of administrative determination of prices for officially rationed goods, partly by supply and demand in unregulated markets. In wartime the different markets displayed sharply divergent trends. Official prices of industrial and consumer goods and transport services rose (in some cases quite substantially), but the increases were strictly controlled. Weapon prices fell. In unofficial markets for consumer goods, upon which fell the entire burden of frustrated household demand for goods and services in short supply at official prices, the price level became hugely inflated.

Although wartime trends in official prices were closely regulated, and did not reflect market supply and demand, they were not arbitrary. Soviet price controllers continued to follow the cost-plus methodology established in peacetime, and went on trying to get official prices right, at least in terms of their own methodology.

Of the documents which express this striving, none is more evocative than correspondence of 1944 between Narkomugol (the commissariat of the coal industry), Gosplan, and NKVD. The deputy head of finance of Narkomugol explained that early in 1943 the NKVD had contracted to supply the coal industry with forced labourers, each at 35 per centof the going wage rate. But in March the government had effectively doubled the official wage rate for miners; this had triggered a corresponding increase in payments for subcontracted NKVD labourers, further raising the average cost of mined coal. But since the cost to society of maintaining and administering forced labourers was unaffected by miners' wages, and had not increased, it followed that NKVD was reaping a financial surplus at the expense of the coal industry and coal users. Kosiachenko (then deputy head of Gosplan) accordingly requested Beria (for NKVD) to review the agreement, and set 20 per centas a ceiling for a revised figure.[1]

Other examples discussed elsewhere in this book illustrate the point further. In appendix E, it will be shown how the authorities continually monitored the falling unit cost of munitions and pushed down weapon prices in proportion. In chapter 6 it was shown how the authorities responded to the problem of how to charge for weapons imported under the United States Lend-Lease programme; at the official exchange rate imported weapons were too cheap in comparison with the price level for domestically produced weapons, so the authorities levied a tariff on them to bring their prices up to the domestic level before transferring them to the army.

Price deflators are used for several purposes in this book. The most important uses are to deflate nominal wartime outlays to constant prewar prices, and (in conjunction with other information) to estimate trends in unit costs. Index numbers of prices are invariably calculated in the Paasche form, using weights of the current year, for analytical consistency with Laspeyres index numbers of output calculated using weights of a fixed base year (usually 1937 or 1940). This maintains the identity which holds that an index of nominal values is equivalent to a volume index of the Laspeyres type, calculated using prices of a fixed base year, multiplied by a price index of the Paasche type.[2]

Table A.1 shows the most important deflators used. Part (A) of the table deals with nonagricultural goods and services. Comparisons of 1940 over 1937 are mostly taken from the work of Bergson and his associates. After 1940, for nonmilitary, nonagricultural goods and services our main information pertains to 1944, with other years estimated by interpolation. The trend of munitions prices in years after 1940 is calculated from official sources, detail being given in tables A.2 and A.3; according to these calculations, by 1942 weapons prices were one third below the prewar level, and slipped by a further small margin during the remaining war years. Such figures match the statement of Voznesenskii, according to whom defence industry product prices in 1942 were 72 per cent of 1940.[3] Further information on this subject will be found in appendices B and E.

Consumer goods and services are the subject of part (B) of table A.1. Price trends in the official and kolkhoz market sectors of retail trade are calculated from estimates of values and volumes taken from Chapman for 1940 over 1937 (table A.4), and official documents for subsequent years (table A.5). Estimates of trends in the consumer services sector are based on Chapman, with interpolation between 1940 and 1944.

Our heavy reliance on interpolation for index numbers in the 1941–3 period may of course be questioned. But it is noteworthy that, in series

Table A.1. *Prevailing prices of goods and services, 1940–5 (per cent of 1937)*

	1940	1941	1942	1943	1944	1945
(A) Nonagricultural products and services						
1 Munitions	120%	101%	80%	73%	71%	69%
2 Munitions inputs	126%	130%	135%	139%	144%	–
3 Civilian machinery	106%	107%	108%	109%	110%	–
4 Basic industrial goods	121%	123%	124%	126%	128%	–
5 Construction,	113%	108%	106%	108%	114%	–
5.1 construction materials	108%	112%	116%	120%	124%	–
6 Railway freight	156%	165%	175%	185%	196%	–
(B) Consumer goods and services						
7 Retail trade	134%	212%	289%	480%	472%	358%
7.1 official markets	125%	144%	163%	188%	222%	245%
7.2 kolkhoz markets	200%	661%	1121%	2033%	1646%	932%
8 Consumer services	142%	149%	155%	163%	170%	–
(C) Average labour costs						
9.1 Annual earnings	130%	138%	145%	154%	162%	171%
9.2 Hourly earnings	116%	106%	102%	103%	110%	132%

Sources: Row 1: for 1940, see Bergson (1961), 367; subsequent years are interpolated on table A.2, row 3. Rows 2–4, 6: for 1940 and 1944, see Bergson (1961), 367–8; intervening years are interpolated geometrically. Row 5: row 5.1, combined with the public-sector hourly earnings index (row 9.2), with labour costs weighted at 70 per cent. Row 5.1: for 1940 and 1944, Bergson (1961), 350, with geometric interpolation of intervening years. Rows 7, 7.1, 7.2: for 1940, as table A.4, rows 4–6; 1942–5 are interpolated on table A.5, rows 7–9, and 1941 on 1942 and 1940. Row 8: for 1940 and 1944, Chapman (1963), 81, 350, with geometric interpolation of intervening years. Rows 9.1, 9.2: for 1937 and 1940, annual earnings are taken from Bergson (1961), 422, and hours from Moorsteen, Powell (1966), 647. For subsequent years, see table G.7, rows 1, 2.

where the gap may be filled from official sources, the trend of prices in the official sector appears to have been strictly monotonic (rows 1, 7.1).

Part (C) of table A.1 deals with trends in wage earnings. Here our information is extremely restricted. Figures are for manual workers in public-sector industry. Annual or monthly wage earnings are known for 1937, 1940, and 1944; this gives us the corresponding entries in row 9.1, which show substantial wage inflation in each benchmark year by comparison with the preceding one. Manual workers' annual hours also increased over each period, but the biggest increase was between 1940 and 1944. So the index of hourly earnings shows an increase in 1940 over 1937, followed by a slight fall over the period ending in 1944.

Table A.2. *Price indices for munitions, 1941–5, from NKO budget data (per cent of 1940)*

	1941	1942	1943	1944	1945
1 Army, air force	85%	65%	60%	59%	56%
2 Navy	85%	78%	72%	68%	65%
3 Total	85%	66%	61%	59%	57%

Sources: Row 1: table A.3, row 4. Row 2 (naval munitions): 1941 is as row 1; figures for the change of prices in each year after 1941 over the preceding year are chained together from Terpilovskii (1967), 354. Row 3 (total): the two subindices are weighted by current shares of the NKO (Army and air force) and NKVMF (navy) in overall munitions outlays, from table K.3, rows 1, 10, yielding a Paasche index of price change for munitions of all kinds.

Table A.3. *A Paasche index of ground and air munitions prices, 1940–5, from NKO budget data (million rubles and per cent)*

	1940	1941	1942	1943	1944	1945
(A) Million rubles						
1 EXP_t	14530	24221	33156	38649	42531	30335
2 SAV_t	–	4440	9691	3495	1066	1204
3 $EXP_t + SAV_t$	–	28661	42847	42144	43597	31540
(B) Per cent of 1940						
4 P_t	100%	85%	65%	60%	59%	56%

Source: Row 1: table K.3, row 1. Row 2: Terpilovskii (1967), 63, 80, 84, 86, 87. Row 3: the sum of rows 1, 2 gives munitions outlays in each year, as if in prices of the preceding year, i.e.:

$$EXP_t + SAV_t = \frac{EXP_t \cdot P_{t-1}}{P_t}$$

Row 4: the previous year (with 1940 = 100%), multiplied by row 1, divided by row 3, i.e.:

$$P_t = \frac{P_{t-1} \cdot EXP_t}{EXP_t + SAV_t}$$

The main problem concerns the intervening years which must be filled, once again, by geometric interpolation. But which series should be interpolated – annual earnings, or hourly earnings? If hourly earnings (which might be thought reasonable under most normal circum-

Table A.4. *Retail trade turnover and prices, 1937, 1940, and 1944, from Chapman*

	1937	1940	1944
(A) Retail turnover (billion rubles and current prices)			
1 Total trade	92.9	141.2	113.8
2 Official trade	76.9	115.0	77.8
3 Kolkhoz trade	16.0	26.2	36.0
(B) Price level (% of 1937)			
4 Total trade	100%	134%	203%
5 Official trade	100%	125%	143%
6 Kolkhoz trade	100%	200%	2200%

Sources: Rows 1–3, 5, 6: Chapman (1963), 104–5. Row 4: the average of rows 5, 6, weighted by shares in retail turnover at current prices.

Table A.5. *Retail trade turnover and prices, 1940 and 1942–5*

	1940	1942	1943	1944	1945
(A) Retail turnover (billion rubles and current prices)					
1 Total trade	203.5	160.2	262.9	324.2	294.8
2 Official trade	175.5	77.8	84.0	119.3	160.1
3 Kolkhoz trade	28.0	82.4	178.9	204.9	134.7
(B) Retail turnover (billion rubles and 1940 prices)					
4 Total trade	203.5	74.5	73.6	92.2	110.5
5 Official trade	175.5	59.8	56.0	67.3	81.6
6 Kolkhoz trade	28.0	14.7	17.6	24.9	28.9
(C) Price level (% of 1940)					
7 Total trade	100%	215%	357%	352%	267%
8 Official trade	100%	130%	150%	177%	196%
9 Kolkhoz trade	100%	561%	1016%	823%	466%

Sources: Rows 1–6: GARF, f. 4372, op. 4, d. 1585, l. 213. Rows 7–9: rows 1–3 divided by rows 4–6.

stances), then annual earnings should show a marked peak in 1943, when wartime hours were at a maximum. If annual earnings should be interpolated, then the hourly series should dip in the intervening years as hours soared. In table A.1 I have exercised judgement in favour of the latter. The dip in hourly earnings suggested in row 9.2 in 1942–3, should, I think, be interpreted not as a simple cut in the hourly earnings implicit in piece rate norms, but as a trend to unpaid overtime, suggested by memoirs and other historical writing. Correspondingly, I assume that the upward drift of annual earnings in the years between 1940 and 1945 was gradual; in the early years of the war there was of course extra upward pressure on wages from the demand-for-labour side, but there were also extra reasons to hold wages down for reasons of macroeconomic balance.

Appendix B: defence industry production

Data

The new data, derived from archival documents of the former Soviet government, cover the ground and air weapons supplied to the Soviet Army during World War II. They are broadly consistent with the much more aggregated figures published in the 1970s and early 1980s, but throw additional light on the volume of wartime munitions output in three main respects. First, individual models of weapon are identified in great detail, allowing much finer judgement of the changing assortment. Where previously we knew series only for 'bombers', or for 'medium and large calibre guns', we now have data by model and calibre. Second, the range of weapons covered is wider than before, extending in particular to the significant and hitherto neglected category of small arms ammunition. Third, the new data show the whole period from 1 January 1941, to 30 September 1945, in quarterly detail.

A summary of the new data appears in tables 4.2 (annual series) and B.1 (quarterly series), in the form of selected physical aggregates. Table 4.2 suggested that Soviet war production peaked in 1943 or 1944 (1942 in the case of small arms), at which point the increase over 1940 in physical units produced was two or three times (small arms and ammunition), four times (combat aircraft, and also artillery shells), or eight to ten times (guns and tanks). Table B.1 adds to this picture in two significant regards. First, the figures reveal the crisis which struck the defence industry in the fourth quarter of 1941, with sharp cutbacks in the output of aircraft, small arms, and ammunition for both small arms and guns. Recovery to the level of the third quarter of 1941, was immediate in the case of small arms output, but was delayed for shell supplies by one further quarter, by two further quarters for combat aircraft, and by six quarters for cartridges. The supply of armoured vehicles and guns, however, rose without interruption.

Table B.1. *Finished output of ground and air munitions, quarterly series, 1941–5 (units)*

		1941	1942	1943	1944	1945
(A) Combat aircraft						
	I	2089	3301	6372	8150	8209
	II	2089	4967	7369	8150	8209
	III	5535	6219	8050	8455	2241
	IV	2665	7194	8050	8455	2241
(B) Armoured vehicles						
	I	1047	4684	6134	6549	7562
	II	1366	6337	5982	7272	7860
	III	1981	7099	5761	7559	7168
	IV	2196	6599	6129	7603	–
(C) Guns						
	I	3741	23971	30471	30835	30455
	II	6060	29667	31470	30732	31378
	III	13815	38344	34231	29427	15269
	IV	16931	36110	34123	31391	–
(D) Shells (million)						
	I	11.5	19.0	37.0	44.5	46.4
	II	15.8	29.2	44.1	46.4	35.7
	III	29.7	41.0	46.5	47.3	5.7
	IV	26.2	44.1	47.4	45.8	–
(E) Small arms (thousand)						
	I	487	1111	1315	1016	617
	II	554	1328	1380	1055	536
	III	1041	1503	1279	1006	259
	IV	874	1416	1106	967	–
(F) Cartridges (million)						
	I	916	729	1147	1777	1814
	II	1038	999	1399	1746	1449
	III	1530	1188	1637	1937	375
	IV	852	1201	1772	1946	–

Sources: (A): as Harrison (1985), 251. (B)–(F): RTsKhIDNI, f. 71, op. 25, d. 7882, ll. 4–20.

Second, table B.1 shows that while output did generally peak in 1943 or 1944, it had typically reached a high level, equal to or within a few per centof peak output (the exception being small arms ammunition), by the end of 1942. This was already the edge of a high plateau of war production, the crossing of which would take until the middle of 1945 when the war in Europe was already over.

Table B.2. *Munitions prices, 1941–5 (thousand rubles per unit)*

	1941	1942	1943	1944	1945
(A) Aircraft					
1 Iak-1	208	102	–	–	–
2 Iak-7	–	–	110	–	–
3 Iak-9	–	–	115	–	–
4 Il-2	330	191	162	–	–
5 Il-4	800	468	380	380	380
6 Li-2	650	510	424	424	–
7 La-5	–	–	110	–	–
8 Pe-2	420	353	265	265	265
9 U-2	–	–	26	–	–
(B) Armoured vehicles					
10 KV	635	295	225	–	–
11 T-34	270	193	135	135	–
12 T-34-85	–	–	164	164	142
(C) Armament					
13 7.62 mm rifle	0.163	0.120	0.100	0.100	0.100
14 PPSh machine pistol	0.500	0.400	0.140	0.148	0.148
15 Machine guns					
15.1 7.62mm Degtiarev	–	0.535	–	–	–
15.2 7.62mm Maxim	–	2.800	–	–	–
16 Antitank rifles					
16.1 14.5mm Degtiarev	–	0.450	–	–	–
16.2 14.5mm Simonov	–	1.570	–	–	–
17 Antitank cannon					
17.1 45mm (1934)	–	5.0	–	–	–
17.2 45mm (1937)	–	10.5	–	–	–
18 Tank guns					
18.1 76mm F-34	27.0	10.0	–	–	–
18.2 76mm ZIS-5	25.7	12.5	–	–	–
18.3 76mm (1927)	32.4	16.5	–	–	–
19 Divisional cannon					
19.1 76mm USV	57	28	–	–	–
19.2 76mm ZIS-3	35	8	–	–	–
20 Howitzers					
20.1 122mm M-30	94	39	35	35	35
20.2 122mm	182	80	–	–	–
20.3 152mm	–	77	–	–	–
21 Mortars					
21.1 50mm (company)	2.6	1.6	–	–	–
21.2 82mm	7.3	3.1	–	–	–

Table B.2. *(contd.)*

	1941	1942	1943	1944	1945
21.3 120mm	13.0	6.0	–	–	–
22 Aircraft cannon					
22.1 20mm	12.5	4.1	–	–	–
22.2 23mm	25.0	9.0	–	–	–

Sources: Rows 1–9: Terpilovskii (1967), 84, 87; RGAE, f. 4372, op. 93, d. 720, l.72 (prices listed under 1 January 1942, and 1 March 1943, are assumed to have prevailed through 1941 and 1942 respectively; see further below), and d. 1044, l. 72. Rows 10–12: Terpilovskii (1967), 87; the same or similar figures can be found in RGAE, f. 4372, op. 93, d. 720, l. 72 (prices listed in archival documents for 1 January, 1942, and 1 March, 1943, are the same as those given by Terpilovskii as prevailing through 1941 and 1942 respectively), d. 1095, ll. 3–4, and d. 1110, l. 67. Rows 13–22.2: Terpilovskii (1967), 87; RGAE, f. 4372, op. 93, d. 720, l. 72 (prices listed under 1 January 1942, and 1 March 1943, are assumed to have prevailed through 1941 and 1942 respectively).

These tables do not reveal the underlying comprehensive detail of the new data by type and model of weapon. They include 15 types of fighter aircraft, assault aircraft (2 types), bombers (11), and other aircraft including training, transport, and reconnaissance (16), tanks (9) and self-propelled artillery (6), field guns (11), antitank guns (2) and tank guns (5), guns for self-propelled artillery (6), antiaircraft guns (6), aircraft guns, small arms (5), small arms ammunition (4), and other ammunition comprising separately artillery shells, bombs, mortar shells, aircraft shells, mines, and grenades, making 105 series in total. Other than aircraft, each series has 5 annual observations beginning in 1940, and 19 quarterly figures starting from January 1941. In some cases monthly figures through 1941 are also available. The aircraft series are more aggregated, with annual data only (1937–45) for individual aircraft models, and half-yearly data for the war years (quarterly from mid-1941 to mid-1943), for broad types only ('fighters', 'bombers', etc.), requiring some interpolation.

The main defect of the new data set, in common with the previous one, is the continued lack of adequate series for supply of naval munitions.

To supplement the new serial data, we also have a much wider sample of defence industry product prices gathered from various wartime years. These are shown in tables B.2 (ground and air munitions) and B.3 (warships). Their range is narrower than the product

Table B.3. *Warship prices, 1944 (million rubles)*

1	Torpedo boat	
1.1	duraluminum	0.655
1.2	steel	1.715
2	Sea launch	2.222
3	Patrol vessel	35.4
4	Submarine type K	23.4
5	Destroyer	21.6
6	Light cruiser	170.5

Source: RGAE, f. 4372, op. 93, d. 718, l. 52, and d. 1173, l. 10.

sample for which production is known; frustratingly, no prices appear to be accessible as yet for ammunition.

Reliability

How trustworthy are the available series for supply of defence industry products in physical units? In a well known intervention published in 1988, the historian B.V. Sokolov cast doubt on their accuracy. He used official series for the supply of combat aircraft and armoured fighting vehicles from domestic production, in combination with figures for estimated imports, and combat stocks at various times, to estimate Soviet losses of these items in each period of the war.[1] He then compared Soviet losses estimated in this way with German equipment losses on the eastern front. He found that Soviet losses far exceeded German losses over the same periods, regardless of whether Soviet forces were losing or winning the war, often by a factor of two or three to one, occasionally by more.

Accepting the contribution of Stalinist deformations (excessive centralisation, despotic authority, unthinking obedience, a low valuation of life) to excessive Soviet losses, Sokolov judged it impossible to explain all the excess by reference to such factors. He argued that Soviet losses estimated in this way are implausibly high, and concluded that the fault lies with the underlying supply series, which must be overstated. Reported output was inflated by defence industry leaders, whose lives depended on 100 per centplan fulfilment.[2] The contribution of industry to Soviet victory should be downgraded, he argued (and that of the Soviet military should presumably be upgraded correspondingly).

In my view there is nothing wrong with the supply figures, which should be accepted without correction. I maintain this view for three reasons. First, there was undoubted pressure on defence industry establishments to satisfy output quotas, but there was no obvious reticence of enterprises and ministries when plans failed, even in the most critical months of 1941–2. Plan failure was reported, not concealed.[3] Such reports are inconsistent with the view that industrial leaders inflated output returns to show 100 per centplan fulfilment because their lives depended on it.

Secondly, the Red Army knew exactly what it was receiving; the defence ministry maintained inspectors in every defence factory, who were responsible for controlling the quantity, quality, and assortment of military goods, and authorised to accept or reject deliveries. This system, already established before war broke out, made falsification of defence output figures virtually impossible.[4]

Third, Soviet figures on equipment losses are now exhaustively documented and verified by type of model of equipment, period, and combat operation, and have been shown to be approximately consistent with supply figures.[5] Soviet equipment losses were therefore as heavy as the supply figures imply.

Methods

The evaluation of this wide range of wartime products of the Soviet defence industry involves pricing of each physical product in rubles of a given year. Ruble values are then summed across broad product groupings (aircraft, armoured vehicles, and armament). Ammunition and naval munitions must be dealt with differently, however. A second summation can then take place across the product groupings. Below I deal first with the ground and air munitions procured by the Soviet Army, in two stages.

Ground and air munitions

Valuation in rubles. The weapon prices shown in table B.2 confirm that the war years saw an exceptionally sharp deflation, especially in 1942 compared with 1941. But it is worth noting that these prices display much greater volatility than was suggested by index numbers calculated from official measures of price change reported above.[6]

The prices shown in table B.2 have entries for many products and years (none of them from the prewar period), but there are also many gaps, and many products for which we have output data do not appear

Table B.4. *Regression output: testing for change in the structure of Soviet munitions prices, 1941–3*

Dependent variable:	*lp*(42)	*lp*(42)
1 Observations	21	8
2 Degrees of freedom	19	6
3 Regression output:		
3.1 constant	−0.6739	0.1303
3.2 SEE	0.3343	0.0825
3.3 *R*-squared	0.9805	0.9993
4 Independent variable:	*lp*(41)	*lp*(43)
4.1 X-coefficient	0.9989	1.0081
4.2 SE of coefficient	0.0323	0.0112
4.3 *t*-statistic	30.903	89.637

Sources: For data see table B.2 (all values are transformed into logarithms, so *lp(t)* is the logarithm of the price in rubles in period *t*). The PPSh (machine pistol) is excluded from the second regression (1942 on 1943), since its 1943 price was clearly set 'too low' (the error was corrected in 1944).

at all. The first decision was which year to use for a base period. Here 1942 was an obvious choice, since it had the most complete data with only five missing observations. It was important, however, to establish whether this was a sensitive decision, and whether it was legitimate to interpolate missing observations from data for other years.

Table B.4 reports the results of statistical testing of the structure of munitions prices for significant differences in 1941 and 1943 compared with 1942. Could relative prices of munitions in 1942 be 'predicted' retrospectively from comparable data for either 1941 or 1943? In each case the answer was 'yes', with the X-coefficient not significantly different from unity in a log-linear regression, and the regression model generally performing well despite a restricted number of observations. These findings also suggest that a decision to favour 1942 over other wartime years was not a sensitive choice, since there was no detectable change in the structure of munitions prices from year to year. On this basis I decided to value everything at the first stage as if in prevailing ruble prices of 1942.

The size of the constant terms reported in table B.4 compared with official measures of the fall in munitions prices may suggest a lag in the latter behind underlying trends – concealed deflation.[7] This issue is further reviewed in appendix E.

A second set of decisions was required to extend the price set of table B.2 to cover defence industry products for which no prices were available in any year. To justify this I invoke the principle (demonstrated many years ago by Peter Wiles) that 'it is better to guess a weight than to omit a growth series'.[8]

The methods used for interpolation are superior to guesswork, even if only by a little. In each case technical data were associated with weapons of which prices or costs were known in order to generalise a crude model for determining individual product prices. Most *aircraft* could be valued on the basis of known prices for comparable models, with comparability being established on the basis of the aircraft's military–technical function, engine number, and engine capacity. Lacking prices of more complex four-engined aircraft, I assumed that the price of bombers rose with the square of engine number. *Armoured vehicles* could be valued roughly on the basis of a linear relationship observed between rubles and tons (for P, the ruble price of the vehicle, and T, tons weight, $P = 6000 \cdot T$). For *armament*, the limited number of observations suggested a log-linear relationship between cost and calibre (for P, price, and C, calibre in millimetres, $\log(P) = 0.5+2 \cdot \log(C)$).

In the case of *ammunition*, no prices were known. Initially I added up physical units across two broad subgroups, large-calibre ammunition (artillery shells, bombs, mortar shells, aircraft shells, static mines, and grenades), and small-calibre cartridges. I take the typical shell (say, 76mm) as 10 times the calibre of the typical cartridge (say, 7.62mm), and therefore 10^3 times its mass. At the same time I assume that a law of two thirds, characterising throughput economies of scale, applied to shell production, such that the proportional increase in unit cost of a shell was only two thirds the proportional increase in its mass. Therefore, the unit cost of a shell was not $10^3 = 1{,}000$ times that of a cartridge, but only $1{,}000^{2/3} = 100$ times. I use this assumed relativity to add up shells and cartridges for the total volume of ammunition.

These steps led to the index numbers for output of the main branches of ground and air munitions shown in table B.5. As in my earlier estimate, real output is shown to have increased by far more than official index numbers allowed. In most series, however, I revise downward the wartime expansion of output from my previous estimate, with a small upward revaluation of the dynamic only in the case of armoured vehicles. In the case of aircraft and artillery some downward revision arises because some lines of prewar output, expensive in unit cost and limited in numbers produced (e.g. the DB-3 (Il-4) and SB bombers, and very large-calibre guns), were quickly discontinued when war broke out in

Table B.5. *Finished output of ground and air munitions, 1941–5: alternative estimates (per cent of 1940)*

	1941	1942	1943	1944	1945
(A) Harrison (1996)					
1 Aircraft	127%	196%	268%	287%	189%
2 Armoured vehicles	435%	1487%	1537%	1881%	–
3 Armament	161%	409%	426%	411%	–
3.1 guns	166%	431%	438%	487%	–
3.2 small arms	157%	387%	414%	338%	–
4 Ammunition	175%	368%	470%	458%	–
4.1 shells, etc.	195%	512%	639%	590%	–
4.2 cartridges	144%	137%	198%	246%	–
(B) Harrison (1990)					
5 Aircraft	145%	204%	270%	316%	–
6 Armoured vehicles	385%	1465%	1442%	1788%	–
7 Armament	233%	656%	670%	651%	–
8 Ammunition	278%	528%	861%	906%	–
(C) IVOVSS (1965)					
9 Aircraft industry	126%	178%	223%	239%	177%
10 Tank industry	112%	184%	234%	296%	276%
11 Armament industry	145%	191%	200%	206%	156%
12 Ammunition industry	152%	218%	264%	310%	171%

Sources: Rows 1–4.2: product series are from Kostyrchenko (1994), 235–7 (aircraft), and RTsKhIDNI, f. 71, op. 25, d. 7882, ll. 1–20 (other munitions). For methods of valuation, see text. Rows 5–8: calculated from Harrison (1990a), 582 (series based on 1941). Rows 9–12: IVOVSS, vol. 6 (1965), 52.

favour of smaller, cheaper weapons which were more readily mass-produced in large numbers. The number of units produced therefore grows more rapidly than constant-price ruble values. More striking downward reevaluations affect the picture of armament and ammunition through inclusion of substantial, slowly growing series for small arms and cartridges.

Summing across product groups. The second stage involves adding up the broad subgroups shown in table B.5. At this point we have to deal more generally with the problem of their representativeness.

For my 1990 estimate I reweighted the branch subindices of ground and air munitions by their shares in NKO outlays on munitions (using

Table B.6. *Finished output of ground and air munitions: representativeness of output series in physical units, 1941–4 (billion rubles at current prices and per cent)*

	1941	1942	1943	1944
(A) Defence commissariat outlays				
1 Air armament	8.5	9.3	12.3	11.5
2 AFV, other vehicles	3.7	7.0	7.8	10.8
2.1 AFV armament	–	–	4.5	5.5
2.2 vehicles, tractors	–	–	3.2	5.3
3 Artillery armament	10.1	14.8	16.6	18.6
4 Other armament	1.8	2.1	2.0	1.7
5 Total	24.2	33.2	38.6	42.5
(B) Production				
6 Aircraft	5.6	4.4	5.3	5.7
7 AFV	2.3	4.0	3.6	4.4
8 Armament	2.4	3.2	2.9	2.8
9 Ammunition	3.6	3.8	4.3	4.2
10 Total	13.9	15.4	16.1	17.0
(C) Production, % of outlays				
11 Aircraft	66%	48%	43%	49%
12 AFV	62%	57%	47%	41%
13 Armament, ammunition	59%	47%	43%	37%
14 Other	0%	0%	0%	0%
15 Total	57%	46%	42%	40%

Sources: Rows 1–5: defence commissariat outlays, as table K.3, row 1, are disaggregated using per cent shares in budget spending from Terpilovskii (1967), 67. Rows 6–10: product series, calculated initially as if in prevailing ruble prices of 1942 (as table B.5 (A)), are then converted to current prices on the basis of price regressions reported in table B.4, additionally assuming no price change between 1943 and 1944. Rows 11–15: representativeness of product series is measured by dividing (A) into (B) as follows: row 1 into row 6, row 2 into row 7, row 3 into the sum of rows 8 and 9, row 5 into row 10.

1941 and 1944 as alternative base years), so far as I could determine them. A breakdown of the NKO budget for weapons and equipment derived from official figures is reproduced here in table B.6, part (A). The main problem with these figures was and is that they are inherently difficult to interpret for our purposes. Where, for example, is large-calibre ammunition? It cannot be accommodated within 'other' armament, so must be grouped under artillery armament, or else distributed among air, armoured, and artillery armament as appropriate. Similarly, where are small arms and their ammunition? Taken together, they are again too substantial to fit within 'other' armament, but no other heading seems appropriate. How were outlays distributed between armoured and other vehicles in 1940–2? Lastly, to what extent were ruble outlays on each category raised above acquisition from domestic sources by foreign supply in each year? These unanswered questions all create awkwardness, none more so than the lack of an expenditure share for ammunition, when we are unable at present to value the supply of ammunition of any calibre directly in rubles of any year.

For present purposes I do not try to use the budget data to reweight the series already calculated in prevailing prices of 1942, but simply add them up directly. Various considerations point to this outcome. One, already explained, is that deriving appropriate weights from the budget series is inherently difficult. Another is that, with a far larger number of product series than before (105 in place of 15), the risks of accidental unrepresentativeness are much reduced. Finally, table B.6 shows that the ruble values already obtained look reasonably and uniformly representative anyway.

In table B.6, part (A) shows the budget series. Under part (B) the new data for 1941–4, valued at prevailing prices of 1942, are adjusted to current rubles using the regression-based coefficients for 1941/42 and 1943/42 reported in table B.4. (Ammunition products are valued applying a 60:40 ratio to armament in 1944, for reasons given below.) In part (C) they are divided by the nearest equivalent budget series which is continuously reported for the war years. The results are uniform enough in each year to provide some degree of comfort. 'Other' armament and equipment is not represented, of course, but appears to have accounted for a small and fairly constant share of total NKO spending on munitions. Representativeness of the product data appears to decline through the war years; this may be explained either by the steady growth of outlays on imported equipment in 1942–4, or by errors in the deflation procedure used in part (B).

To value ammunition supplies, an arbitrary rule is invoked. For purposes of my 1990 estimate I assumed (from German and American comparisons) that ammunition and armament should be weighted in the ratio of 60:40.[9] In principle I carry this rule over, but with one minor modification which has little impact on results. As can be seen from table B.5, there were significant year-to-year variations in the Soviet wartime relativity of armament and ammunition supplies, reflected in wartime reports of a 'shell famine' which began in the second half of

Table B.7. *Finished output of ground and air munitions, annual and quarterly, 1941–5: alternative estimates (per cent of 1940)*

	1940	1941	1942	1943	1944	1945
(A) Harrison (1996)						
Annual	100%	164%	355%	423%	449%	285%
I	–	112%	225%	390%	427%	438%
II	–	131%	335%	425%	450%	431%
III	–	243%	421%	437%	462%	221%
IV	–	169%	439%	439%	456%	144%
(B) Harrison (1990)	100%	204%	435%	541%	598%	–
(C) IVOVSS (1965)	100%	140%	186%	224%	251%	–

Sources: (A): see text; the last quarter of 1945 is filled in on the basis of a quarterly index of 'war production' through 1945 (per cent of the first quarter) in IVMV, vol. 11 (1980), 348. (B): calculated from Harrison (1990a), 585 (series based on 1941, excluding naval munitions). (C): IVOVSS, vol. 6 (1965), 45.

Table B.8. *Naval munitions outlays, nominal and real, 1940–5, from Terpilovskii (per cent of 1940)*

	1940	1941	1942	1943	1944	1945
(A) At current prices						
1 Planned outlays (% of 1940)	100%	102%	81%	82%	94%	110%
2 Realised outlays						
2.1 % of plan	100%	63%	92%	100%	94%	100%
2.2 % of 1940	100%	64%	74%	82%	88%	110%
(B) At 1940 prices						
3 Realised outlays (% of 1940)	100%	76%	96%	115%	129%	168%

Sources: Row 1: Terpilovskii (1967), 334. Row 2.1: Terpilovskii (1967), 337, gives figures for 1941–4; 1940 and 1945 are assumed equal to 100%. Row 2.2: row 1, multiplied by row 2.1 Row 3: row 2.2, divided by table A.2, row 2.

1941 and continued through 1942; after war broke out, ammunition supply lagged for a time behind armament. Therefore, I interpret the 60:40 rule as a norm or equilibrium relationship, and apply it to 1944 as a year by which 'normal' proportions of ammunition to armament had been achieved.

Table B.9. *Finished output of munitions, 1940–5: alternative estimates (billion rubles at 1937 prices)*

	1940	1941	1942	1943	1944	1945
(A) Harrison (1996)						
1 Ground, air munitions	14.7	24.0	52.1	62.0	65.8	41.7
1.1 for Red Army	12.1	21.2	49.2	59.1	62.9	38.9
1.2 for NKVD	2.6	2.8	2.9	2.9	2.9	2.8
2 Naval munitions	3.4	2.6	3.2	3.8	4.4	5.8
3 Munitions, total	18.0	26.6	55.3	65.8	70.2	47.5
3.1 per cent of 1940	100%	148%	307%	365%	389%	263%
(B) Harrison (1990a)						
4 Munitions, total (% of 1940)	100%	169%	337%	419%	464%	-

Sources: Row 1: for 1940, the sum of rows 1.1, 1.2. Other years: 1940, multiplied by index numbers as table B.7 (A). Row 1.1: for 1940: nominal outlays of the defence commissariat (table K.3, row 1), deflated to 1937 prices by table A.1, row 1. Other years: row 1, less row 1.2. Row 1.2: calculated as 1940 nondefence consumption (table 5.8, row 3), multiplied by the proportion of 1941-plan nondefence consumption allocated to the defence industries (table F.5, col. 28 and row 8). Other years: interpolated on numbers of NKVD troops (table I.8, row 2). Row 2: nominal outlays of the navy commissariat (table K.3, row 10), deflated to 1940 prices by table A.2, row 2, then to 1937 prices by table A.1, row 1 (for 1940). Row 3: the sum of rows 1, 2. Row 3.1: interpolated on row 3. Row 4: calculated from Harrison (1990a), 585 (series based on 1941).

In practice this is not a sensitive choice. Since the wartime supply of ammunition followed the combined supply of other munitions fairly closely, quite large variations in the relative weight of ammunition make little difference to the final result.

Summing across the product groups for ground and air munitions therefore appears to be the shortest route to a representative measure of real output. This summation yields the index numbers (per centof 1940) for annual supply of the army and air force in table B.7. Attaching the index to the 14.7 billion rubles thought to have been laid out on munitions for the Red Army and NKVD troops in 1940 provides the ruble values for ground and air munitions also shown in table B.9 (rows 1–1.2).

Quarterly data. Identical procedures yield index numbers for the quarterly output of ground and air munitions, shown in table B.7, with some qualifications.

For *aircraft*, the quarterly data are defective in two respects. First, they are available only for broad aircraft types ('fighters', 'bombers', etc.); detailed series by model and mark give only annual totals. I deal with this by distributing detailed series across quarters in the same proportions as the aircraft types to which they belong. Second, as is obvious from table B.1, we have only half-yearly totals for the first half of 1941 and from mid-1943 to the end of 1945. I assume that the output for each half year was evenly split between the two quarters; this must result in some smoothing of aggregate figures for the quarters concerned.

For *ground munitions* we have no detailed series for the last quarter of 1945. However, we know from official data that the level of 'war production' in the second and third quarters of 1945 stood at 92 and 51 per centof the first quarter respectively, which is matched pretty well in table B.7. According to the same source, the last quarter saw only 12 per centof the annual total of 'war production' for 1945, and I apply this figure, with the result shown in the table.

Naval munitions

There has been little substantial improvement in our access to data for the production of naval munitions. Series for annual completion of warships of the 'basic classes' have long been available, but the four such ships built in 1944 cannot have amounted to more than one fifth of the total acquisition of naval munitions in that year, even if all were valued as capital ships. Therefore, for the same reasons outlined in support of my previous estimate, I do not attempt to calculate the supply of naval munitions from the product side, but use a measure of NKVMF (navy commissariat) outlays on munitions deflated to constant prices of 1940, the derivation of which is shown in table B.8.

The main advantage of the present estimate is that we have obtained authoritative series for wartime expenditure on munitions at prevailing prices from finance ministry archives. When it comes to a ruble valuation, we find that NKVMF outlays on munitions were consistently larger than my 1990 estimate suggested – for example, 15 per centof total munitions outlays in the second half of 1941, not the 11.5 per cent which I previously proposed for 1941 as a whole.[10]

Total ground, air, and naval munitions

The index of final output of ground and air munitions shown in table B.7 is given a 1940 value (in prices of 1937) based on budget outlays of the NKO in that year, plus an allowance for NKVD outlays on equipment of internal troops. When the ruble value of ground and air munitions is combined with that of naval munitions, we obtain the series for total munitions output reported in table B.9 (rows 3, 3.1). For the reasons already given, the trend undershoots my previous estimate by a significant margin.

Appendix C: civilian industry production

The real volume of Soviet civilian industrial production in the years of World War II is estimated from output data for 113 products in physical units, and ruble prices from 1937 or closely adjacent years.

Our product data (table C.1) are taken primarily from the limited-circulation statistical handbook for the war period. An abridged version was published by Goskomstat in 1990; however, the 1959 original is the basis of much of the data utilised here; it is the only source for nonferrous metallurgy, and it doubles the product coverage of light industry compared with the 1990 abridgement.

The product data are comprehensive, and contain no interpolations. Their scope (113 civilian products, which together with 105 defence products make 218 series in total) is sufficient for a reliable measure. It is comparable with Nutter's 203-product index, which spanned 1928–58 with a break between 1940 and 1945[1] Present coverage exceeds that of the 104-product index used by Khanin for 1928–80; Khanin is said to have also calculated parallel indexes covering approximately 400 and 1,000 products respectively, finding almost no divergence between the three series.[2]

At the same time it is clear that not all branches are covered equally well; as well as products whose output has remained secret, such as gold, there are also many products not included in the quantity data presented here. This is particularly the case with branches such as machinebuilding and the light and food industries, where the product assortment was most varied. For example, in the case of light industry there is no mention of cutlery, crockery, and cooking utensils.

The price data (table C.2) were mostly assembled years ago by Naum Jasny, Richard Moorsteen, Janet Chapman, and, more recently, Eugène Zaleski; our choice of 1937 as the base year is designed to allow comparability of our results with theirs.[3] Despite their efforts, however, prices are now less abundant than quantity series, and gaps in the price data

Table C.1. *Civilian industry products, 1940–5*

		1940	1941	1942	1943	1944	1945
1	Iron, steel						
1.1	Crude steel, '000 tons	18317	17893	8070	8475	10887	12252
1.2	Pig iron, total, '000 tons	14902.3	13815.6	4779.1	5591.1	7296.4	8802.7
1.2a	conversion	11791.6	10744.2	3896.8	4177.1	5332.3	6499.4
1.2b	foundry	2605.9	2577.6	692.3	1176.1	1660.7	1942.1
1.2c	other	504.8	493.8	190	237.9	303.4	361.2
1.3	Tubular steel, total, '000 tons	966.1	780.3	280.9	370.4	482	571.4
1.4	Rolled metal, total, '000 tons	13113	12588	5415	5675	7278	8485
1.4a	roofing steel	182	185	48	44	60	108
1.4b	rails	1360	874	112	115	129	308
1.4c	wire	680	649	210	191	224	350
1.4d	other	10891	10880	5045	5325	6865	7719
1.5	Iron ore, '000 tons	29866	24687	9763	9320	1163	15864
1.6	Manganese ore, '000 tons	2557	2306	767	901	1005	1470
2	Nonferrous metals						
2.1	Copper, '000 tons	138.5	185.4	117.9	129.8	139.9	136
2.2	Aluminium, '000 tons	60.1	67.6	51.7	62.2	82.7	86.7
2.3	Lead, '000 tons	91.9	100.3	77	48.5	44.9	43.3
2.4	Zinc, '000 tons	92.3	100.1	53.5	37.6	51	48.5
2.5	Nickel, '000 tons	10.3	11.3	8.9	13.4	15.8	18.4
2.6	Tin, tons	1709	2424	3622	2874	2884	3789
3	Fuel industry						
3.01	Coke, '000 tons	21102	18483	6903	8220	11495	13649
3.02	Coal, '000 tons	165923	151428	75536	93141	121470	149333
3.02a	black	139974	124418	48951	54767	76283	99428
3.02b	brown	25949	27010	26585	38374	45187	49905
3.03	Peat, '000 tons	33229	27431	14738	21274	22993	22443
3.04	Shale, '000 standard tons	600	700	140	150	170	400
3.05	Firewood, '000 standard tons	34100	30000	22500	29300	28800	28400
3.06	Oil, '000 tons	31121	33038	21988	17984	18261	19436
3.07	Gas, million cu. m.	3219	3555	2071	1847	2422	3278
3.08	Petrol, total, '000 tons	4435	4306	2537	2782	3792	3159
3.09	Kerosene, '000 tons	5553	4497	1906	2742	3156	3231
3.10	Diesel fuel, '000 tons	629	936	209	478	535	518
3.11	Motor fuel, '000 tons	1459	1313	306	535	419	528
3.12	Fuel oil, '000 tons	9858	9211	5305	5236	7011	6051
4	Electric power, million kWh	48309	46698	29068	32288	39214	43257

Table C.1. *(contd.)*

		1940	1941	1942	1943	1944	1945
5	Chemical industry						
5.1	Soda ash, '000 tons	536.1	463.1	62.4	105.1	158	235.3
5.2	Caustic soda, 92%, '000 tons	190.4	198.4	84.2	105.6	122.2	128.2
5.3	Mineral fertilizer, '000 tons	3237.7	2674.4	364.4	539.3	775.6	1121.2
5.4	Synthetic ammonia, '000 tons	337.7	338.3	166.9	244.9	290.2	275
5.5	Nitric acid, conc, '000 tons	231.7	273.3	251.7	342.1	367.5	203.2
5.6	Sulphuric acid, '000 tons	1586.6	1465.2	646	766.3	892.9	780.7
5.7	Toluene, '000 tons	37.9	57.9	38.1	39.8	38.3	33.5
5.8	Synthetic dyestuffs, '000 tons	34.3	31.3	6.5	9.9	13.1	15.3
6	MBMW						
6.01	Lathes	58437	44510	22935	23281	34049	38419
6.01a	turret	2088	2109	806	1932	2764	2920
6.01b	automatic, semiautomatic	2039	2327	895	519	419	419
6.01c	milling	3701	3471	1102	761	1181	1353
6.01d	planing	2221	1149	0	69	527	633
6.01e	drilling	15251	6956	3423	3468	5228	7168
6.01f	other	33137	28498	16709	16532	23930	25926
6.02	Presses	4668	3119	2210	2423	2691	2871
6.03	Steam turbines	57	45	3	4	6	8
6.04	Hydraulic turbines	89	74	0	17	34	414
6.05	Steam boilers	1784	854	141	267	426	726
6.06	Diesel engines	1329	1016	142	100	105	452
6.07	Steam turbine generators	27	13	0	7	19	22
6.08	Hydraulic turbine generators	4	5	0	9	9	13
6.09	Electric motors >100kW	3067	2570	209	453	1797	3237
6.10	Electric motors <100kW, '000	259.5	184.2	12	27.4	73	110.7
6.11	Power transformers	3506	3004	960	1086	1559	1848
6.12	Telephone switchboards	0	0	0	0	0	0
6.13	Trunkline steam locomotives	914	708	9	43	32	8
6.14	Trunkline diesel locomotives	5	1	0	0	0	0
6.15	Trunkline electric locomotives	9	6	0	0	0	0
6.16	Trunkline freight cars	30880	33096	147	108	13	819
6.17	Trunkline passenger cars	1051	552	0	0	0	5
6.18	Tram cars	252	151	0	0	0	0
6.19	Automobiles	145390	124176	34976	49266	60549	74657

Table C.1. *(contd.)*

		1940	1941	1942	1943	1944	1945
6.19a	trucks, buses	139879	118704	32409	46720	55167	69662
6.19b	cars	5511	5472	2567	2546	5382	4995
6.20	Bearings, million	44.8	38	21.8	29.8	33.4	34.2
6.21	Tractors	31649	23827	3520	1063	3154	7728
6.21a	caterpillar	26530	23827	3520	1063	2889	6562
6.21b	wheeled	5119	0	0	0	265	1166
6.22	Tractor ploughs	38438	18527	1338	3056	3371	8474
6.23	Horse ploughs	34252	36495	1212	41736	35638	39230
6.24	Tractor ridge ploughs	12845	2865	0	0	0	0
6.25	Tractor harrows	3753	3329	0	0	0	0
6.26	Horse harrows	81072	391	0	3266	8541	21999
6.27	Tractor seed-drills	21426	13173	0	0	504	1578
6.28	Horse seed-drills	10927	15591	33	151	1648	3289
6.29	Tractor potato-planters	3570	1244	0	1	10	0
6.30	Tractor cultivators	32309	11601	2250	1030	120	929
6.31	Horse cultivators	13843	6647	0	950	3767	14496
6.32	Grain combines	12756	5755	0	0	184	323
6.33	Tractor mowers	3317	1600	0	0	0	0
6.34	Horse mowers	46378	19859	3608	6354	7799	11552
6.35	Tractor rakes	870	724	0	0	0	0
6.36	Horse rakes	43050	24564	0	27	866	4742
6.37	Tractor threshers	2231	182	0	0	113	799
6.38	Horse threshers	3830	3005	50	49	2695	8810
6.39	Grain cleaners	4314	1381	0	0	0	0
6.40	Silage cutters	1614	950	0	0	0	522
6.41	Excavators multibucket	52	34	3	3	1	2
6.42	Excavators single bucket	222	201	7	4	6	8
6.43	Scrapers, bulldozers	2222	931	117	268	210	35
6.44	Graders	693	412	112	110	138	98
6.45	Concrete mixers	1584	887	30	5	30	466
6.46	Cranes	454	350	1	26	62	57
6.47	Elevators	513	268	12	11	9	44
7	Timber, paper						
7.1	Commercial timber, million cu. m.	117.9	115.1	48.2	43.4	52.4	61.6
7.2	Firewood, million cu. m.	128.2	114.2	84.5	110	108.2	106.8
7.3	Sawn timber, million cu. m.	34.8	29.7	15.1	13.1	13.2	14.7
7.4	Plywood, '000 cu. m.	731.9	429.7	154.9	133.9	125.1	192.2
7.5	Matches, million boxes	10	8	1.7	2.1	1.9	2
7.6	Paper, '000 tons	812.4	729.8	165.7	204.9	193	321.1
7.7	Cardboard, '000 tons	150.8	133.8	25.2	35.4	39.5	55.9
8	Construction materials						

Table C.1. *(contd.)*

		1940	1941	1942	1943	1944	1945
8.1	Cement, '000 tons	5675	5514	1133	980	1490	1845
8.2	Building/technical lime, '000 tons	4470	3392	780	786	1427	1929
8.3	Builders' plaster, '000 tons	892	746	143	159	239	357
8.4	Bricks, million	7454.7	5574.7	1572.2	1316.6	1558	2026
8.5	Slates, million	205.6	144.8	16.8	38.3	67	83.6
8.6	Rolled roofing, '000 sq. m.	127148	108806	19945	21855	33320	71232
8.7	Tiles, million	173.3	94.3	21.7	9.7	21.6	29.6
8.8	Window glass, '000 sq. m.	44690	38487	6333	7184	13533	23309
9	Light industry						
9.01	Cotton textiles, million m.	3953.8	3824.1	1643.5	1634.7	1778.6	1616.5
9.02	Woollen materials, '000 m.	119678	93829	44976	48946	52405	53570
9.03	Linen materials, '000 m.	285452	245733	74155	84445	91081	106454
9.04	Silk materials, '000 m.	77304	66121	30089	36027	38424	36353
9.05	Socks, stockings, '000 prs	485441	405143	89607	87831	90473	91043
9.06	Leather footwear, '000 prs	211033	157687	52675	55804	67423	63115
9.07	Clocks and watches, '000	2796.3	1838	61.2	416.7	354.6	336.2
9.08	Radios and TVs, '000	160.8	100.9	0	0	0	13.9
9.09	Refrigerators	3457	1100	0	0	0	301
9.10	Sewing machines , '000	175.2	200.1	0	0	0	0
9.11	Cameras , '000	355.2	0	0	0	0	0.01
9.12	Bicycles , '000	255	142.4	0	0	0.7	23.8
10	Food industry						
10.01	Sugar, granulated, '000 tons	2165	523	114	117	245	465
10.02	Sugar, refined, '000 tons	628	638	14	28	25	54
10.03	Meat, excl. kolkhoz, '000 tons	1501	1172	723	614	543	663
10.04	Fish, '000 tons	1404	1281	962	1208	1235	1125
10.05	Butter, '000 tons	226	205	111	101	106	117
10.06	Vegetable oil, '000 tons	798	685	253	215	238	292
10.07	Margarine, '000 tons	121	112	46	26	30	28
10.08	Tinned goods, million tins	1113	926	485	546	557	558
10.09	Confectionery, '000 tons	790	643	190	163	134	212
10.10	Macaroni, '000 tons	324	292	237	238	207	243
10.11	Raw spirit, million dcl.	89.9	66.4	24	20.1	17.7	26.5
10.12	Vodka, million dcl.	92.5	64.8	22.3	18.2	28.1	44.3
10.13	Beer, million dcl.	121.3	97.3	29.8	31	32.9	40.5
10.14	Salt, million tons	4.4	3.3	1.4	2.6	3.2	2.9
10.15	Tea, '000 tons	24.5	20.4	14.1	18	20	17.5
10.16	Cigarettes, billion	100.4	74.3	3.5	6.2	7.4	25
10.17	Makhorka, million boxes	4.6	3.9	1.4	1.2	1.2	0.7

Table C.1. *(contd.)*

	1940	1941	1942	1943	1944	1945
10.18 Tobacco, '000 tons	26.1	15.9	40.5	33	39.6	31.9
10.19 Soap, '000 tons	700	591	243	195	250	229
10.20 Flour, million tons	29	24	16	13	13	15
10.21 Milled groats, million tons	1.7	1.5	0.9	0.8	0.9	1.1
10.22 Starch, '000 tons	107	72	16	10	22	22
10.23 Treacle, '000 tons	140	108	22	7	10	14

Source: TsSU (1959), 69–269.

Table C.2. *Civilian industry product prices, 1937 or near year*

		Unit	Rubles
1	Iron, steel		
1.1	Crude steel	1 ton	276.4
1.2	Pig iron		
1.2a	conversion	1 ton	110.5
1.2b	foundry	1 ton	176.8
1.2c	other	1 ton	139.8
1.3	Tubular steel	1 metre	6.04
1.4	Rolled metal		
1.4a	roofing steel	1 ton	589.2
1.4b	rails	1 ton	260.9
1.4c	wire	1 ton	608.0
1.4d	other	1 ton	453.8
1.5	Iron ore	–	–
1.6	Manganese ore	–	–
2	Nonferrous metals		
2.1	Copper	1 ton	2322
2.2	Aluminium	1 ton	3768
2.3	Lead	1 ton	748.6
2.4	Zinc	1 ton	1210
2.5	Nickel	–	–
2.6	Tin	1 ton	8551
3	Fuel industry		
3.01	Coke	1 ton	47.80
3.02	Coal		
3.02a	black	1 ton	36.25
3.02b	brown	1 ton	30.07

Table C.2. *(contd.)*

		Unit	Rubles
3.03	Peat	1 ton	28.00
3.04	Shale	–	–
3.05	Firewood	–	–
3.06	Oil	1	20.50
3.07	Gas	–	–
3.08	Petrol	1 ton	1000
3.09	Kerosene	1 ton	700.0
3.10	Diesel fuel	1 ton	450.0
3.11	Motor fuel	1 ton	141.9
3.12	Fuel oil	1 ton	48.10
4	Electric power	1 kWh	0.20
5	Chemical industry		
5.1	Soda ash	1 ton	122.0
5.2	Caustic soda, 92%	1 ton	355.0
5.3	Mineral fertiliser	–	–
5.4	Synthetic ammonia	–	–
5.5	Nitric acid, conc.	1 ton	525.0
5.6	Sulphuric acid	1 ton	145.6
5.7	Toluene	–	–
5.8	Synthetic dyestuffs	–	–
6	MBMW		
6.01	Lathes		
6.01a	turret	1	12500
6.01b	automatic, semiautomatic	1	45000
6.01c	milling	1	10703
6.01d	planing	1	6492
6.01e	drilling	1	9491
6.01f	other	1	14827
6.02	Presses	1	6060
6.03	Steam turbines	1	46629
6.04	Hydraulic turbines	1	136305
6.05	Steam boilers	1	1289
6.06	Diesel engines	1	399.0
6.07	Steam turbine generators	1	1931
6.08	Hydraulic turbine generators	1	1931
6.09	Electric motors >100kW	1	6708
6.10	Electric motors <100kW, '000	1	906.7
6.11	Power transformers	1	12164
6.12	Telephone switchboards	1	938.6
6.13	Trunkline steam locomotives	1	152316
6.14	Trunkline diesel locomotives	–	–
6.15	Trunkline electric locomotives	–	–

Table C.2. *(contd.)*

		Unit	Rubles
6.16	Trunkline freight cars	1	8807
6.17	Trunkline passenger cars	–	–
6.18	Tram cars	–	–
6.19	Automobiles		
6.19a	trucks, buses	1	11431
6.19b	cars	1	10839
6.20	Bearings, million	–	–
6.21	Tractors		
6.21a	caterpillar	1	13377
6.21b	wheeled	1	3825
6.22	Tractor ploughs	1	758.7
6.23	Horse ploughs	1	65.81
6.24	Tractor ridge ploughs	1	800.0
6.25	Tractor harrows	1	606.0
6.26	Horse harrows	1	40.00
6.27	Tractor seed-drills	1	909.0
6.28	Horse seed-drills	1	298.7
6.29	Tractor potato-planters	1	556.0
6.30	Tractor cultivators	–	–
6.31	Horse cultivators	–	–
6.32	Grain combines	1	6700
6.33	Tractor mowers	1	3000
6.34	Horse mowers	1	303.0
6.35	Tractor rakes	1	4000
6.36	Horse rakes	1	141.0
6.37	Tractor threshers	1	3232
6.38	Horse threshers	1	555.0
6.39	Grain cleaners	–	–
6.40	Silage cutters	1	1212
6.41	Excavators multibucket	1	101000
6.42	Excavators single bucket	1	146654
6.43	Scrapers, bulldozers	–	–
6.44	Graders	1	7200
6.45	Concrete mixers	1	3179
6.46	Cranes	1	74999
6.47	Elevators	1	4967
7	Timber, paper		
7.1	Commercial timber	1 cu. m.	26.00
7.2	Firewood	1 cu. m.	26.00
7.3	Sawn timber	1 cu. m.	26.00
7.4	Plywood	1 cu. m.	370.0
7.5	Matches	10 boxes	0.20

Table C.2. *(contd.)*

		Unit	Rubles
7.6	Paper	1 ton	460.7
7.7	Cardboard	1 ton	420.0
8	Construction materials		
8.1	Cement	1 ton	57.16
8.2	Building/technical lime	1 ton	37.00
8.3	Builders' plaster	1 ton	108.0
8.4	Bricks	1000	56.00
8.5	Slates	–	–
8.6	Rolled roofing	–	–
8.7	Tiles	–	–
8.8	Window glass	1 sq. m.	3.34
9	Light industry		
9.01	Cotton textiles	1 metre	8.24
9.02	Woollen materials	1 metre	54.30
9.03	Linen materials	1 metre	12.07
9.04	Silk materials	1 metre	56.46
9.05	Socks, stockings	1 pair	2.76
9.06	Leather footwear	1 pair	70.72
9.07	Clocks and watches	1	300.0
9.08	Radios and TVs	–	–
9.09	Refrigerators	–	–
9.10	Sewing machines	1	183.8
9.11	Cameras	1	792.5
9.12	Bicycles	1	250.0
10	Food industry		
10.01	Sugar, granulated	1 kg	3.98
10.02	Sugar, refined	1 kg	4.10
10.03	Meat, excl. kolkhoz	1 kg	17.19
10.04	Fish	–	–
10.05	Butter	1 kg	16.00
10.06	Vegetable oil	1 kg	13.50
10.07	Margarine	1 kg	10.05
10.08	Tinned goods	–	–
10.09	Confectionery	–	–
10.10	Macaroni	1 kg	3.92
10.11	Raw spirit	–	–
10.12	Vodka	1 litre	13.10
10.13	Beer	–	–
10.14	Salt	1 kg	0.12
10.15	Tea	100 gm	8.00
10.16	Cigarettes	25	1.90

Table C.2. *(contd.)*

	Unit	Rubles
10.17 Makhorka	1 box	0.77
10.18 Tobacco	100 gm	6.32
10.19 Soap	1 kg	3.10
10.20 Flour	1 kg	2.40
10.21 Milled groats	1 kg	2.16
10.22 Starch	1 kg	1.30
10.23 Treacle	–	–

Sources: Jasny (1951b), Jasny (1952), Kaplan *et al.* (1952), Moorsteen (1962), Chapman (1963), Zaleski (1980). The price recorded for each product is from as near to 1937 as possible, in most cases from the period 1936–7, but in a few cases from as far away as 1946. Some prices required further adjustment of units for compatibility with product series (for example, a price is given for firewood per cubic metre, whereas its output figure is expressed in tons).

are one constraint on our ability to make use of available product data. We have filled some gaps with prices from other years, or by informed guesswork, resorting again to Wiles' principle that 'it is better to guess a weight than to omit a growth series'.[4]

For present purposes civilian products are grouped under ten industrial branch headings:

- iron, steel
- nonferrous metals
- fuels
- electric power
- chemicals
- civilian machinebuilding and metalworking
- timber, paper
- construction materials
- light industry
- food industry

The gross value of output is calculated for each branch separately, in constant prices of 1937, from the listed series of product quantities and prices. These values are then expressed as index numbers, with 1940 as the base year, results being reported for each branch separately in table C.3. The process of combining them with defence industry product series into a measure of overall industrial production is dealt with in chapter 4.

Table C.3. *Civilian industry gross output, by branch, 1941–5 (1937 prices and per cent of 1940)*

	1941	1942	1943	1944	1945
1 Civilian MBMW	83%	21%	25%	35%	45%
2 Iron, steel	96%	41%	44%	57%	65%
3 Nonferrous metallurgy	121%	84%	86%	102%	103%
4 Fuels	91%	45%	55%	70%	72%
5 Power	97%	60%	67%	81%	90%
6 Chemicals, rubber	100%	54%	70%	79%	61%
7 Timber, paper	91%	50%	56%	58%	62%
8 Construction materials	83%	19%	17%	26%	35%
9 Light industry	87%	35%	37%	40%	38%
10 Food industry	78%	44%	37%	39%	46%

Source: Products (table C.1), multiplied by 1937 prices (table C.2).

Appendix D: from gross output to value added

Framework

Here I present a more formal analysis of bias 4 and bias 5 within a simplified model, and I examine their consequences for measuring industry's contribution to GNP. After that, I put forward a methodology for gauging the extent of divergence between trends in value added and gross output at the sector level, which can be executed for three broad industrial sectors (defence industry, basic industry, and light industry).

In chapter 4, the two biases were defined as distortions arising from the application of incorrect weights to gross output series for purposes of measuring sector GNP (value-added) contributions. Bias 4 is generated by gross output value weights, and bias 5 by value-added weights. Below, a true value added index is shown in equation (7), bias 4 is illustrated in equation (12), and bias 5 in equation (14).

The symbols used are listed as follows. A subscript j refers to the jth sector of industry. A subscript t refers to period t. A superscript asterisk indicates a Laspeyres index number based on period $t = 0$.[1]

α material input per unit gross output
D price/cost disturbance
δ share of price/cost disturbance in nominal gross output
H^* a 'hybrid' value-added index
L labour input, hours
λ labour input per unit gross output
M material input, units
m material input per unit labour input
μ the share of sector 1 in total industry value added
n price per unit material input
p price per unit output
σ share of value added in nominal gross output
V real value added at constant base-year prices

v ratio of real value added index to gross output index
w wage cost per unit labour input
X real gross output, units

The first part of the analysis proceeds under the assumption that everything is measured at fixed prices, with no inflation, hidden or otherwise. Define net output, V (for value added) as gross output, X, *less* intermediate purchases of materials. Industry comprises j branches (for present purposes, $j = 1, 2$). Of the two branches, sector 1 supplies only materials, and sector 2 supplies only fabricated goods. Industry as a whole buys nothing from outside, and sells only to itself or to final users. Assume that within industry each branch is integrated, so that there are no intra-branch transactions and no distinction between gross and finished output. The gross output of materials (sector 1) is identically equal to sector 1 value added, while the gross output of fabricated goods comprises the value added in both sectors:

$$X_{1t} = V_{1t} \quad (1)$$

$$X_{2t} = \sum_j V_{jt} \quad (2)$$

For industry as a whole, gross output double-counts the value added in sector 1:

$$\sum_j X_{jt} = X_{1t} + X_{2t}$$

$$= V_{1t} + \sum_j V_{jt} \quad (3)$$

$$\sum_j V_{jt} = V_{1t} + V_{2t} \quad (4)$$

Define V^*_t as an index number of industry value added in year t, expressed as a percentage of the base year ($t = 0$). The index of value added, V^*_t, can be reached in two ways. One is by a base-year weighted average of index numbers of value added in the two branches, with weights μ_t and $(1 - \mu_t)$ set to equal the shares of sector 1 and 2 in industry value added in the base year ($t = 0$), so that:

$$V^*_t = \sum_j V_{jt} / \sum_j V_{j0} \quad (5)$$

$$\mu_t = V_{1t} / \sum_j V_{jt} \quad (6)$$

Therefore, from equations (4), (5), and (6):

$$V^*_t = \mu_0 \cdot V^*_{1t} + (1 - \mu_0) \cdot V^*_{2t} \quad (7)$$

The other way is from final products, which consist here of the output of fabricated goods. Sector 1 has a lot of value added (equation (1)), and of gross output, but no final product. Sector 2 has a share in value added (equation (4)), but supplies 100 per centof final output; its final output embodies its own value added, plus the value added in sector 1. Going along the final-product route, therefore, we find industry value added will be adequately captured by X_{2t} alone, so that:

$$V^*_t = X^*_{2t} \tag{8}$$

If all we have is index numbers of gross output of the two branches (equations (1), (2)), and we try to combine them using gross output weights, we risk serious distortion (bias 4). The source of the problem is the double-counting of intermediate transactions; the X_{1t} sold by sector 1 to sector 2 are credited first in the gross output of the originating sector, then a second time in the gross output of the receiving sector. Industrywide gross output can be rewritten (from equations (3) and (6)) as:

$$\sum_j X_{jt} = (1+\mu_t)\cdot \sum_j V_{jt} \tag{9}$$

so that the index of gross output becomes:

$$X^*_t = \frac{(1+\mu_t)}{(1+\mu_0)}\cdot V^*_t \tag{10}$$

This shows that the gross output index will mirror the path of an index of value added only when the relative weights of the different branches in value added remain constant over time. If the weight of the sector producing less highly fabricated goods (here, μ_t) declines, for example, X^*_t will understate the trend of industry value added. Here is bias 4.

A condition for the relative weights of the different branches in value added to remain constant over time is for their output to follow a common path. When values added in different sectors follow divergent trends, the effect of a gross output index is to give excessive weight to the sectors producing less highly fabricated goods. Equation (9) can be rewritten (from equation (3)) as:

$$\sum_j X_{jt} = 2\cdot V_{1t} + V_{2t} \tag{11}$$

Therefore,

$$X^*_t = 2\cdot\frac{\mu_0}{(1+\mu_0)}\cdot V^*_{1t} + \frac{(1-\mu_0)}{(1+\mu_0)}\cdot V^*_{2t} \tag{12}$$

which shows, in comparison with equation (7), that the weight of sector 2 is too small for X^*_t to track V^*_t accurately.

Bias 5 can be considered against this background. Consider the hybrid measure, H_t, resulting from a procedure which weights sector gross outputs by base-year value added:

$$H^*_t = \mu_0 \cdot X^*_{1t} + (1 - \mu_0) \cdot X^*_{2t} \tag{13}$$

For sector 1 (equation (1)), gross output and value added coincide; for sector 2 (equation (2)) gross output is the same as total industry value added. So this equation can be rewritten in terms of index numbers of sector value added, from equation (7), as:

$$\begin{aligned} H^*_t &= \mu_0 \cdot V^*_{1t} + (1 - \mu_0) \cdot [\mu_0 \cdot V^*_{1t} + (1 - \mu_0) \cdot V^*_{2t}] \\ &= \mu_0 \cdot (2 - \mu_0) \cdot V^*_{1t} + (1 - \mu_0)^2 \cdot V^*_{2t} \end{aligned} \tag{14}$$

Compare the weights of V^*_{2t} in equations (14), (12), and (7). Since $(1 - \mu_0)^2 < (1 - \mu_0)/(1 + \mu_0) < 1 - \mu_0$, it follows that, when the structure of industry is changing, the result of weighting gross outputs by value added (equation (14)) is *even more distorting* than gross outputs combined using gross weights (equation (12)). The undervaluation of the trend in sector 2, which produces more highly fabricated goods (such as weapons), is increased, and bias 5 exceeds bias 4.

Application

The extent to which trends in value added diverged empirically from gross output trends in different sectors of Soviet industry can be gauged very roughly from trends in sector prices, costs, and sources of disturbance in price/cost ratios. To begin with, consider a branch of industry which produces a gross output X, using labour L and materials M:

$$X = f(L, M) \tag{15}$$

Output and materials are measured in physical units, and labour is measured in total hours. Unit input requirements are given by α_t (for materials) and λ_t (for labour):

$$M_t = \alpha_t \cdot X_t \tag{16}$$

$$L_t = \lambda_t \cdot X_t \tag{17}$$

Prices are formed on the basis of direct costs (w_t, the hourly wage, and

n_t, the price of materials), *plus* an aggregate disturbance factor D_t, which is measured in rubles; in this case total revenue is given by:

$$p_t \cdot X_t = w_t \cdot L_t + n_t \cdot M_t + D_t \tag{18}$$

$$D_t = \delta_t \cdot p_t \cdot X_t \tag{19}$$

Roughly speaking, we can think of D_t as a term which picks up the disturbing influence of turnover taxation and budget subsidies, as well as general noise in the price/cost relationship, while δ_t is the proportion of the price made up by these influences.

From the four equations (16)–(19) we find the price of output determined as follows:

$$p_t = \frac{w_t \cdot \lambda_t + n_t \cdot \alpha_t}{1-\delta_t} \tag{20}$$

Real value added in prices of the base year ($t = 0$) is reached as a result of double deflation, i.e. the deflation of outputs and inputs separately:

$$\begin{aligned} V_t &= p_0 \cdot V_t - n_0 \cdot M_t - \delta_0 \cdot p_0 \cdot X_t \\ &= X_t \cdot [p_0 \cdot (1-\delta_0) - n_0 \cdot \alpha_t] \end{aligned} \tag{21}$$

where α_t is given from equation (20) as:

$$\alpha_t = \frac{p_t \cdot (1-\delta_t) - w_t \cdot \lambda_t}{n_t} \tag{20a}$$

Substituting this expression back into equation (21) gives:

$$V_t = X_t \cdot [p_0 \cdot (1-\delta_0) - \frac{1}{n^*_t} \cdot (p_t \cdot \{1-\delta_t\} - w_t \cdot \lambda_t)] \tag{22}$$

In the base year (t=0), however, this expression is reduced to:

$$V_0 = w_0 \cdot \lambda_0 \cdot X_0 \tag{22a}$$

Therefore, V^*_t is given by dividing equation (22a) into (22):

$$V^*_t = X^*_t \cdot \frac{[p_0 \cdot (1-\delta_0) - \frac{1}{n^*_t} \cdot [p_t \cdot \{1-\delta_t\} - w_t \cdot \lambda_t]}{w_0 \cdot \lambda_0} \tag{23}$$

At this point it simplifies matters to introduce two further symbols. The ratio of an index of value added to an index of gross output, v_t, is the correction factor to be applied to index numbers of gross output to calculate the corresponding index of value added, and is given by:

$$v_t = V^*_t / X^*_t \tag{24}$$

Equation (23) can now be rewritten to show this correction factor:

$$v_t = \frac{[p_0 \cdot (1-\delta_0) - \frac{1}{n^*_t} \cdot [p_t \cdot \{1-\delta_t\} - w_t \cdot \lambda_t]}{w_0 \cdot \lambda_0} \tag{25}$$

I also introduce a symbol σ_t for the share of value added (proxied by wage costs) in nominal gross output:

$$\begin{aligned} \sigma_t &= w_t \cdot L_t / p_t \cdot X_t \\ &= w_t \cdot \lambda_t / p_t \end{aligned} \tag{26}$$

Basic and light industry

Substituting equation (26) into equation (25) gives the general expression used for estimating sector value added of both basic and light industry:

$$v_t = \frac{1-\delta_0}{\sigma_0} - \frac{1-\delta_t}{\sigma_0} \cdot \frac{p^*_t}{n^*_t} + \frac{w^*_t \cdot \lambda^*_t}{n^*_t} \tag{27}$$

In the case of basic industry, since the prices of outputs and inputs are treated as essentially the same, $p_t = n_t$, and equation (27) can be simplified to:

$$v_t = \frac{\delta_t - \delta_0}{\sigma_0} + \frac{w^*_t \cdot \lambda_t}{n^*_t} \tag{27a}$$

Equations 27 (light industry) and (27a) (basic industry) are estimated in table D.1, the derivation of δ_t for each sector being shown in table D.2. For each sector the 1941-plan input/output table is used to derive the 1940 share of value added in gross output.[2] For wartime trends in product prices I use various deflators already described; for material inputs I refer to an index of prices of basic industrial goods and assume that the transfer prices of farm products used in industry, and transport and other commercial costs, followed the same pattern.[3] In estimating the trend of hourly labour costs, I follow a procedure outlined below; hours worked in basic and light industry are obtained separately.[4]

Table D.1. *From gross output to value added: basic and light industry, 1940 and 1942–4*

	Symbol	1940	1942	1943	1944
(A) Basic industry					
1 Nominal value-added share	σ	53%	–	–	–
2 Product price index	p^*	100%	103%	104%	106%
3 Hourly wage index	w^*	100%	82%	85%	91%
4 Input price index	n^*	100%	103%	104%	106%
5 Unit labour requirement index	λ^*	100%	170%	154%	142%
6 Disturbance factor	δ	3%	4%	–4%	–8%
7 Real value-added index ratio	v	100%	137%	112%	101%
(B) Light industry					
1 Nominal value-added share	σ	28%	–	–	–
2 Product price index	p^*	100%	130%	150%	177%
3 Hourly wage index	w^*	100%	97%	97%	100%
4 Input price index	n^*	100%	103%	104%	106%
5 Unit labour requirement index	λ^*	100%	144%	173%	196%
6 Disturbance factor	δ	43%	48%	48%	50%
7 Real value-added index ratio	v	100%	103%	97%	87%

Sources: Row 1: calculated from table F.5. Rows 2, 3, 4: index numbers of prices of basic industrial products and consumer products (p), and of the hourly wage (w), are taken from table A.1. For both branches of industry, the price index of basic industrial products is taken as a proxy for input prices (n). Row 5: unit labour requirements are calculated as the reciprocal of index numbers of gross output per hour worked by manual employees. Gross output of basic and light industry at 1937 factor costs in 1940 is taken from table F.8, col. 1; for years after 1940, figures are interpolated on index numbers from table 4.8, with results as follows (billion rubles):

	1940	1942	1943	1944
Basic industry	58.7	29.3	33.2	40.0
Light industry	99.2	40.1	36.6	39.0

Hours worked in basic and light industry are taken from table G.6, rows 2–3. Row 6: the disturbance factor (δ), the proportional deviation of transfer prices from unit costs attributable to turnover taxes and budget subsidies is taken from table D.2, row 4.1. Row 7: the ratio of an index of value added to an index of gross output, when both are expressed as percentages of 1940, is calculated from rows 1–6 as shown in equations (27) and (27a).

Table D.2. *From gross output to net value added: disturbance factors in basic and light industry, 1940 and 1942–4 (billion rubles at current prices and per cent)*

	1940	1942	1943	1944
(A) Basic industry				
1 Nominal gross output,				
1.1 gross of turnover taxes	73.2	37.9	43.4	53.2
1.2 net of turnover taxes	70.8	36.3	41.8	51.1
2 Turnover tax	2.4	1.5	1.6	2.2
3 Subsidy from budget	0.0	0.0	–3.4	–6.5
4 Total disturbance	2.4	1.5	–1.8	–4.3
4.1 disturbance factor (%)	3%	4%	–4%	–8%
(B) Light industry				
1 Nominal gross output,				
1.1 gross of turnover taxes	218.7	124.5	132.2	171.1
1.2 net of turnover taxes	124.1	65.1	68.7	86.3
2 Turnover tax	94.6	59.3	63.4	84.8
3 Subsidy from budget	–	–	–	–
4 Total disturbance	94.6	59.3	63.4	84.8
4.1 disturbance factor (%)	43%	48%	48%	50%

Sources: Row 1: nominal gross output (including depreciation) is calculated at prevailing prices, gross of turnover taxes (row 1.1) as the same net of turnover taxes (row 1.2) plus turnover taxes (row 2). Nominal gross output net of turnover taxes (row 1.2) is calculated from the value of gross output at 1937 factor costs, multiplied by index numbers of product prices of basic and light industry based on 1937, from table A.1. Figures of real gross output of basic and light industry are given in the note to table D.1, row 5. Row 2: the total of turnover taxes, given by TsSU (1959), 457, is allocated in the same proportion as in table F.4, col. 3, as follows:

to basic industry	2.3%
to light industry	89.4%

Row 3: budget subsidies to industry, from Zverev (1958), 212, are allocated 100 per cent to basic industry. Row 4: the sum of rows 2, 3. Row 4.1: the ratio of row 4 to row 1.1.

Sources of disturbance in the price/cost relationship are estimated as follows. In the case of light industry I assume that the only disturbance arose from turnover taxation, which bore mainly on retail goods. In contrast, the basic industries bore little more than 2 per centof the turnover tax burden. On the other hand subsidies to industry became significant from 1943 onwards, and postwar evidence suggests that they were concentrated on the basic industries. The aim was to hold down product prices in lossmaking branches where unit costs had risen, stabilising defence industry costs.[5] As a result defence industry costs were held down, but the cost to the budget of subsidising heavy industry grew steadily through the closing years of the war and postwar reconversion, eventually requiring a major price reform which was implemented on 1 January 1949.[6]

Results for both basic and light industry are shown in table D.1 (row 7). In light industry labour costs rose, and the burden of turnover taxes rose, but material input prices were stabilised, and product prices also rose. In basic industry labour costs rose, while product prices were stabilised, but material input prices were held down by the same token. On the wartime evidence, value added in civilian branches may have been somewhat variable in relation to gross output; between 1940 and 1942 the ratio of value added to gross output appears to have risen, slightly in the case of light industry, substantially in basic industry, but in each case the increase was followed by correction. These are rather jagged fluctuations, not showing a clear trend in relation to 1940.

These findings do not show a persistent divergence of value added from gross output trends in either basic or light industry. Temporary divergence (e.g. in basic industry in 1942) may reflect movements in fundamentals, errors in data (e.g. interpolated price and cost series), or faults in methodology (e.g. the neglect of extra-budgetary finance). Thus, caution is indicated.

Defence industry

In the case of defence industry life is simpler in one respect – the price/cost relationship was constantly revised as costs changed, and was not disturbed by factors other than administrative noise. For present purposes this enables us to set $D_t = 0$.

But in another direction life is more complicated, because we do not have figures for direct labour requirements. Instead, I determine requirements by fixing the ratio between requirements for labour and materials, m, so that the quantity of materials required per hour worked is treated as a constant, for reasons developed below. So, in addition to equations (16) and (17) we have:

$$\alpha_t = m_t \cdot \lambda_t \qquad (28)$$

This gives a new variant for equation (20), written as:

$$p_t = w_t \cdot \lambda_t + n_t \cdot m_t \cdot \lambda_t \qquad (20b)$$

which can be rearranged to put the unknown λ_t on the left hand side:

$$\lambda_t = \frac{p_t}{w_t + n_t \cdot m_t} \tag{29}$$

We can now rewrite equation (21) above in terms of $m_t \cdot \lambda_t$, setting δ_t=0, then substituting equation (28), and next equation (29):

$$\begin{aligned} V_t &= X_t \cdot (p_0 - n_0 \cdot \alpha_t) \\ &= X_t \cdot (p_0 - n_0 \cdot m_t \cdot \lambda_t) \\ &= X_t \cdot \left[p_0 - \frac{(p_t \cdot n_0 \cdot m_t)}{(w_t + n_t \cdot m_t)} \right] \end{aligned} \tag{21a}$$

The index of defence industry value added can now be obtained by dividing V_0 into V_t, then simplifying the resulting expression by substituting equation (26) and rewriting it in terms of the ratio v_t between value added and gross output index numbers:

$$v_t = \frac{1}{\sigma_0} - \frac{p^*_t}{n^*_t} \cdot \frac{1 - \sigma_t}{\sigma_0} \tag{30}$$

The last difficulty is that we do not know σ_t for $t > 0$. The latter can be estimated, however, from trends in costs and technology), as:

$$\begin{aligned} \sigma_t &= w_t / (w_t + n_t \cdot m_t) \\ &= \frac{\sigma_0 \cdot w^*_t}{\sigma_0 \cdot w^*_t + (1 - \sigma_0) \cdot n^*_t \cdot m^*_t} \end{aligned} \tag{31}$$

Remembering that $m^*_t = 1$ by assumption, equation (30) can be determined by substituting (31) into it. Equations (29), (30), and (31) are estimated in table D.3, row 6 revealing sustained divergence of trends in gross output and value added.

On this basis, and the wartime final output of defence industry,[7] the other most important wartime indicators of defence industry performance (value added, productivity, and employment) can be obtained, the results being reported in table D.4. In table D.5 the implications are set out for year-by-year evolution of the inter-industry matrix of the input/output table of appendix F.

The years of World War II saw a dramatic decline in Soviet weapon prices. It is shown in appendix E that the unit variable cost of weapons also fell, and it is argued that price/cost proportionality was roughly

Table D.3. *From finished output to value added: defence industry, 1940–5*

		1940	1941	1942	1943	1944	1945
1 Nominal value-added share	σ	60.6%	57.8%	56.0%	55.5%	56.2%	60.6%
2 Product price index	p^*	100%	85%	66%	61%	59%	57%
3 Hourly wage index	w^*	100%	92%	88%	89%	95%	114%
4 Input price index	n^*	100%	103%	107%	111%	114%	114%
5 Input per hour worked index	m^*	100%	100%	100%	100%	100%	100%
6 Real value-added index ratio	v	100%	108%	120%	125%	128%	132%
7 Unit labour requirement index	λ^*	100%	88%	69%	62%	58%	50%

Sources: Row 1: for 1940, see table F.5; this is the share of value added in finished, not gross output (i.e. gross output, less intraindustry use). For other years, extrapolated to other years from equation (31). Row 2: table A.1, row 1. Row 3: table G.7, row 2.1a. Row 4: table A.1, row 2. Row 5: see text. Row 6: as equation (30). Row 7: as equation (29).

maintained. The reduction in the cost of a unit of output reflected a mixture of a fall in the requirement of inputs per unit of output, and in the cost of each unit of inputs. Since trends in wage costs and input prices are known, at least approximately, the fall in input requirements per unit of output can be calculated as a residual. Since wage costs fluctuated uncertainly, and input prices rose somewhat, the main burden of explaining the downward trend in weapon prices must fall upon real decline in input requirements.

What is not known is how the fall in input requirements was divided between labour and nonlabour inputs. Here one may imagine two extreme assumptions. First, assume that nonlabour requirements remained unchanged. In that case, the share of value added in real gross output in defence industry remained steady, but labour requirements must have shrunk to the point of insignificance, implying a fantastic rise in output per hour worked. Second, assume that labour requirements remained unchanged. In this alternative case, nonlabour input requirements must have fallen virtually to vanishing point in order to explain the extent of price reductions, while the share of value added in gross output tended towards 100 per cent. In other words, both extreme cases are implausible; reality must have fallen between them, with a sharp (but not infinite) reduction in nonlabour input requirements, balanced by a similarly sharp increase in output per worker. The share of value

Table D.4. *Output and productivity in defence industry, 1940–5 (rubles at 1937 factor cost and millions)*

	1940	1941	1942	1943	1944	1945
(A) Gross and finished output (billion rubles)						
1 Finished output	18.0	26.6	55.3	65.8	70.2	47.5
2 Intraindustry use	2.0	2.6	4.3	4.6	4.6	2.7
3 Gross output	20.1	29.2	59.6	70.4	74.8	50.2
3.1 rubles per worker	11460	15560	21729	24440	25918	24330
3.2 rubles per hour worked	5.44	6.13	7.59	8.41	9.04	10.26
(B) Value added (billion rubles)						
4 Finished output	18.0	26.6	55.3	65.8	70.2	47.5
5 Interindustry supply	7.1	9.2	15.1	16.1	15.9	9.4
6 Gross value added	10.9	17.4	40.2	49.6	54.3	38.1
7 Depreciation	0.4	0.6	1.5	1.8	2.0	1.4
8 Net value added	10.5	16.8	38.7	47.8	52.3	36.7
8.1 rubles per worker	6019	8939	14108	16616	18135	17788
8.2 rubles per hour worked	2.86	3.52	4.93	5.71	6.32	7.50
(C) Employment						
9 Employees, million	1.751	1.879	2.743	2.879	2.884	2.062
10 Hours worked, million	3688	4770	7855	8371	8271	4891

Sources: Rows 1, 4: table B.9, row 3. Row 2: for 1940, row 3, less row 1; extrapolated to other years on row 5. Row 3: for 1940, table F.8, row 8, col. 1; for other years, row 1, plus row 2. Row 3.1: row 3, divided by row 9. Row 3.2: row 3, divided by row 10. Row 5: for 1940, row 4, less row 6; for other years, extrapolated on the basis of row 1, multiplied by table D.3, row 5 times row 7. Row 6: for 1940, row 1, multiplied by table D.3, row 1 (also, table F.8, col. 2, row 8); extrapolated to other years on the basis of row 1, multiplied by table D.3, row 6 (also, row 4, less row 5 in this table). Row 7: for 1940, table F.8, col. 3, row 8; extrapolated to other years on row 6. Row 8: row 6, less row 7 (for 1940, also table F.8, cols 4, 5, row 8). Row 8.1: row 8, divided by row 9. Row 8.2: row 8, divided by row 10. Row 9: for 1940, public sector employment in MBMW (3,519,000, from table G.1, row 1, col. 2) is multiplied by the defence industry share in total MBMW value added (table 4.7, col. 1, rows 1.1 and 1.2). Employment in subsequent years is taken from hours worked (row 8) divided by hours worked per worker in MBMW, from table G.6, row 5. Row 10: for 1940, row 9, multiplied by hours worked per worker in MBMW, from table G.6, row 5. Hours worked in subsequent years are interpolated on row 1, multiplied by table D.3, row 7.

Table D.5. *Defence industry, 1940–5: sums of input/output coefficients*

	1940	1941	1942	1943	1944	1945
1 Technical coefficients	0.45	0.40	0.33	0.29	0.27	0.24
2 Leontief multipliers	2.00	1.88	1.70	1.62	1.58	1.51

Sources: Row 1: for 1940 table F.6, col. 1, row 8; for other years, table D.4, the sum of rows 2, 5, divided by table D.4, row 3. Row 2: calculated by inversion of the (**I**–**A**)-matrix appropriate to each year, as table F.6, col. 2.

added in gross output rose, but remained (of course) far below 100 per cent.

For present purposes I assume that output per unit of labour and nonlabour inputs in defence industry rose in the same proportion (or, which comes to the same thing) that nonlabour inputs per hour worked remained constant. This approach is also supported by various indications reviewed in appendix E, where it is shown that results in terms of the implied productivity and employment trends in Soviet defence industry are consistent with other evidence in official documents, as well as the evidence of comparative trends in the defence industry of other countries involved in the war.

The defence industry trends suggested by table D.3 were quite different from those observed in civilian branches. On the assumptions explained above, the large product price deflation, unaccompanied by subsidies, must be explained either by huge increases in output per hour worked, or by huge cuts in material input requirements, or more plausibly by some combination of the two. It is implied (row 7) that gross output per hour worked in defence industry nearly doubled, but value added per hour grew more rapidly, peaking at 2.2 times the 1940 level in 1944.

Appendix E: cross-checks on defence industry trends

How much did prices fall?

In my view most results in chapter 4 should not arouse controversy. The results for defence industry value added deserve close scrutiny, however, given what they imply for defence industry employment and productivity, and their influence on the evaluation of industry as a whole. The suggested 2.2-fold increase over 1940–4 in value added per hour worked in Soviet defence industry, and 3-fold increase in value added per worker, are certainly large enough to evoke surprise.[1] Are such figures plausible?

The reader should not underestimate the importance of this issue. Present estimates of defence industry value added, employment and productivity are based on a complex structure of data, assumptions, and reasoning. This may make for an appearance of fragility. Results are obtained which make a startling impression. Their plausibility may be questioned – yet, at the same time, they are very hard to undermine on the basis of contemporaneous data and comparative trends. If these estimates are badly wrong, however, then a wide range of basic data consistent with them must also be called into question. If average costs fell dramatically, and labour requirements did not fall, material costs must have fallen still more dramatically; or, if material costs did not fall, labour requirements must have fallen by still more. If average costs did not fall, the trend of defence industry production must have been greatly exaggerated, or the evidence of price change must be in some way or other highly misleading, or our understanding of the budgetary record, and the mechanics of the defence procurement process, must be fraught with misinterpretation. Something would be fundamentally wrong, and we would not be able to identify it. The reader could think of this issue as the critical litmus test. If there is a flaw here, at this point, it undermines the conceptual basis of this book.

Table E.1. *Ground and air munitions: alternative measures of price change, 1940–5 (per cent of 1940)*

	1940	1941	1942	1943	1944	1945
1 From NKO budget data	100%	85%	65%	60%	59%	56%
2 From regression equations	–	85%	43%	38%	–	–
3 From Narkomfin budget data	100%	95%	54%	51%	54%	65%

Sources: Row 1: table A.3, row 4. Row 2: as table B.4, setting 1941 equal to row 1. Row 3: the numerator is nominal NKO outlays (table K.3, row 1); the denominator is the real total availability of finished ground and air munitions to the army and air force (table B.9, row 1.1), plus the foreign supply of weapons (table J.1, row 8).

How much did prices actually fall? The index numbers used above are not the only possible interpretation of what happened to prices. There are at least two other versions; all three appear in table E.1. The figures preferred above (row 1) are based on official data of cost savings to the budget in each year arising from the deflation of weapon prices, which give rise to a chain Paasche (current-weighted) price index. They suggest that between 1940 and 1945 weapon prices were reduced continuously, but at a decreasing rate, falling below 60 per cent of 1940 in the closing stages of the war.

It would be consistent with what was stated about hidden inflation and deflation in chapter 3 if this understated the downward trend. If official price indices normally lagged behind the actual trend, then the same could be expected to apply to munitions. Consider the classic problem – the introduction of new or improved weapons. According to Terpilovskii, official calculations added up the budget saving to the defence commissariat from price cuts, say, in 1942 compared with 1941. The easy part was to compute the saving on weapons produced in the same model and mark in both years. More difficult to estimate would have been the saving on new or improved weapons which arose from the fact that, if hypothetically they *had* been produced in 1941, they would have cost more in 1941 than in 1942. Neglect of the latter would lead inevitably to understatement of the total saving, and to an insufficiently downward trend in the resulting price index.

Other rows of the table offer some support for this idea. In appendix B examples were given of the ruble prices of particular weapons and their behaviour year by year. For 1941 and 1943, it was possible to calculate the time trend relative to 1942.[2] The regression equations are used to generate an index of price change which is unweighted, but the same regressions suggested that the weights do not matter very much. The index is calculated in table E.1, row 2, with 1941 arbitrarily set to equal row 1 for purposes of comparison. It suggests that in two years weapon prices fell by 55 per cent – a much sharper deflation than according to row 1. But the sample sizes are very limited, with 21 observations for 1941–2 and 8 for 1942–3, compared with an assortment of military goods which must have run into hundreds or thousands of items. The time span is also very limited, with a lack of suitable data for 1940 and 1944–5.

A more comprehensive alternative series can be calculated from a direct comparison of final budget outlays on munitions, in current rubles, with the real supply of weapons available to satisfy final demand. To ensure that both supply and expenditure series are independent, I limit the comparison to ground and air munitions available from both domestic and foreign sources for use by the defence commissariat. The result is an implicit deflator (table E.1, row 3) which again suggests a sharper fall in weapon prices than the series based on official data, almost 50 per cent in 1943 compared with 1940; if row 1 is preferred, there were not, apparently, enough nominal rubles spent on defence in 1943 to buy the real volume of weapons available. But the same implicit deflator then shows a rise in 1944 and 1945, ending at roughly two thirds the level of 1940, which not only contradicts all the piecemeal evidence of prices of particular weapons, but makes row 1 appear *too low* by the end of the war.

How much did weapon prices fall? The upshot is that table E.1 supplies us with three answers, each of which appears defective. The official data (row 1) may understate the extent of the deflation. The time trend of actual weapon prices (row 2) suggests a more dramatic story, but is deficient in coverage. An implicit deflator is available (row 3) which tells a not impossible story for 1941–3, but which goes wrong in 1944–5.

For the purposes of estimating the trend in defence industry value added I prefer the first series. It shows a sharp, persistent deflation, roughly consistent with the behaviour of actual weapon prices. The trend may be understated, making this a somewhat conservative choice, but it will be shown below that this choice produces results for labour requirements, productivity, and employment which are fully consistent with other evidence, where the implications of a sharper deflation would be hard to sustain. Therefore, I do not see this as a weak choice.

Nonetheless, I do not regard the first series as necessarily an accurate deflator of budget outlays on munitions. Below, when I come to the estimation of real defence outlays (appendix K), I deflate other defence items (e.g. on transport or construction) in the usual way, but for real outlays on munitions I read in figures for the available supply. Logically, this is equivalent to deflating budget outlays by the implicit deflator (table E.1, row 3) which, as explained above, I do not believe, but I do not think of it this way. It is just a way of indicating that, whatever the trend of nominal outlays and prices, the available supply of weapons is known with reasonable certainty, and was sufficiently demanded, without going further into the possible discrepancies.

Average-cost pricing

However we measure it, the wartime decline in Soviet weapon prices may be interpreted in different ways. The argument of appendix D rests upon the hypothesis that this price deflation was not artificial, but reflected a roughly equivalent fall in the underlying unit cost of weapons, so that price/cost proportionality was maintained. This hypothesis is supported by a variety of considerations.

When war broke out, several factors stimulated a decline in defence industry costs – the transition to mass production, fuller utilisation of labour, the operation of fixed capacity with fewer interruptions, the simplification of products and processes, and the reaping of economies of specialisation among the enlarged number of defence producers. There were many countervailing factors – the costs of introducing new models and a larger assortment of weapons, of conversion of civilian producers to defence production, of air attack and evacuation, the breakdown of centralised supply, and the mobilisation of labour for combat duties – but these were insufficiently strong to offset the downward trend of average costs.[3]

Meanwhile, the budgetary cost of defence procurement was spiralling upward out of control. The defence chiefs' priority was to obtain weaponry, not to count cash. In March 1942 (this was in the relative calm of the interval between the failure of the German offensive launched against Moscow in September 1941, and the renewal of the German offensive on the southern front in April 1942), deputy prime minister A.I. Mikoian launched a reform of the weapon procurement process which institutionalised continuous review of average costs and prices. From now on, the prices of weapons were determined so as to secure '(1) full compensation of costs of production incurred by enterprises; (2) provision for profitability of all normally operating enterprises producing military products'. Prices were cut immediately, and continued to fall, though by smaller and smaller amounts, in each year of the war.[4]

If weapon prices had been cut drastically without any corresponding decline in costs, widespread subsidised losses in defence industry would have been the result. This was Jasny's clear expectation. He believed that the fall in weapon prices was entirely artificial; he expressed outright disbelief about the reductions in direct labour requirements in defence industry claimed officially by Voznesenskii (see table E.5 below), and on which these price reductions were supposed in part to have been based, and argued that the apparent fall in prices required a matching increase in budgetary subsidies.[5] But the scale of wartime subsidies to the whole of industry remained modest relative to defence industry output (6.5 billion rubles in 1944, compared with munitions outlays in the same year of more than 46 billion rubles at current prices).[6] Moreover, the postwar evidence is that these losses were chiefly attributable to below-cost pricing of basic industry products, especially coal and timber.[7]

Only two complaints about losses in wartime defence industry have come to light. In October 1943, armament minister D.F. Ustinov (later Brezhnev's minister of defence) reported to Mikoian that prices for armament had been set too low; in the first eight months of 1943, a loss of 169 million rubles had been incurred by his commissariat, mainly on cartridges, with a further planned loss of 20 million rubles in the last quarter.[8] But these losses would represent only 1 per cent of Army outlays (maybe 17 billion rubles) on 'artillery armament' in 1943.[9] And at the end of June 1944, the commissariat for mortar armament reported a loss of 13.7 million rubles – attributable not to the production of weapons, but to the growing share of lossmaking agricultural machinery in ministerial output.[10]

According to Voznesenskii, unit costs in the engineering industry (which included all the main branches of the defence industry) fell sharply after the outbreak of war, and continued to decline year by year; his figures are included in table E.2. The evidence contained in government archives confirms this trend and its applicability to the defence industry in particular. One official report claimed that unit costs in the defence industry in 1943 stood at 50.8 per cent of 1940 'taking into account the influence of price changes', or 45.2 per cent 'without account of the influence of price changes'.[11] (The prices to which reference was made are presumably input prices, which rose gradually during the war years.) The data shown in table E.2 give results year by year for three supply commissariats (responsible for aircraft, tanks, and ammunition

Table E.2. *Unit costs in defence industry, 1940–5 (annual change, per cent of previous year)*

	1940	1941	1942	1943	1944	1945
(A) From Voznesenskii						
1 MBMW	–	–24%	–17%	–9%	–	–
(B) From ministerial files						
2 Aircraft industry	–	29.3%	–20.5%	–8.0%	–7.3%	–5.4%
3 Tank industry	–	–	–33.1%	–17.9%	–12.6%	–2.2%
4 Ammunition industry	–6.2%	–	–23.4%	–16.8%	–6.4%	2.3%

Sources: (A): Voznesensky (1948), 108. (B): RTsKhIDNI, f. 71, op. 25, d. 7882, l. 20 (the tank and ammunition industries), d. 7883, l. 90 (the aircraft industry). Unit costs are 'sebestoimost' sravnimoi produktsii' (the cost of comparable products).

Table E.3. *Ground and air munitions, 1941–3: unit costs, fourth quarter (rubles)*

	1941	1942	1943
(A) Armoured vehicles			
1 T-34 (plant 112)	–	–	164600
2 T-34 (plant 183)	–	–	124600
(B) Armament			
3 122mm howitzer	66780	39550	–
4 37mm antiaircraft cannon	64420	16266	–
5 76mm divisional cannon	30397	16231	–
6 T-34 tank gun	23270	15307	–
7 45mm antitank cannon	18207	9938	–
8 14.5mm Degtiarev antitank rifle	1011	529	–
9 PPSh machine pistol	427	142	–
10 7.62mm self-loading rifle	344	337	–
11 7.62mm rifle	135	98	–

Sources: Rows 1, 2: RGAE, f. 4372, op. 93s, d. 1109, l. 4. Rows 3–11: RGAE, f.

respectively). Again, the picture of substantial decline in unit costs is confirmed, with the sharpest reductions concentrated in 1941–2.

More detailed evidence from official documents shows wartime trends in the unit costs of particular weapons. The figures reported in table E.3 confirm sharp reductions in the cost of most types of armament. It was claimed more generally that by 1944 the unit cost of mod-

Table E.4. *Regression output: testing the average-cost pricing hypothesis in defence industry, 1941–3*

Dependent variable	*l* (price)
1 Observations	14
2 Degrees of freedom	12
3 Regression output:	
3.1 constant	0.1837
3.2 SEE	0.1379
3.3 *R*-squared	0.9865
4 Independent variable:	*l(cost)*
4.1 X-coefficient	0.9675
4.2 SE of coefficient	0.0327
4.3 *t*-statistic	29.591

Sources: Prices are from table B.2, and unit costs from table E.3. Data from several years are pooled. All variables are transformed into logarithms. Where the number of observations of cost exceeds the number of price observations, the mean is taken.

ernised types of weapons had fallen below the prewar cost of older, now obsolete models by one third for a fighter-bomber, one half for a medium tank, and two thirds for a heavy tank.[12]

A crude test of the average-cost pricing hypothesis for defence industry is presented in table E.4. We have 14 observations from 1941–3 for weapons of which both the prevailing price and unit cost are known. These observations are pooled in order to regress logarithmic values of price on cost. The regression equation is strongly significant, with an X-coefficient very close to one. On the data available, therefore, the cost-price model is not refuted.

Labour requirements

If weapon prices shadowed unit costs during the war years, it remains to separate out the implications for labour and nonlabour costs respectively. To what extent did the composition of costs change as they fell? This question is very important to resolve. If labour costs were the main source of saving, there need not have been any tendency for real value added to grow faster than gross output – but labour productivity rose all the more. Only if material costs fell significantly should we encounter any divergence of trend between gross output and value added.

The argument of appendix D rested upon a decomposition of cost changes into nominal and real effects.[13] Real trends are harder to assess.

From direct indications in government documents, it is clear that real defence industry output per worker rose sharply. Official summary data on finished output per worker employed suggest rapid wartime increases in labour productivity. For example, an official index of finished output (*vyrabotka*) of the defence industry per worker employed in 1943 stood at 190 per cent of 1940 (with no indication of the prices used to value output in each year, but remember that prices of defence industry products fell).[14] According to information already published by Soviet historians, by 1944 total output per worker in the aircraft industry stood at 168 per cent of 1940; in the artillery industry it was twice the 1940 level, 'more than twice' 1940 in the tank industry, and 2.5 times 1940 in the ammunition industry.[15] Such reports are hard to evaluate, however; our confidence that we know what they mean is undermined by the same considerations which lead to lack of confidence in official measures of real output generally.

More detailed evidence of falling direct labour requirements per unit of defence industry output was published by Voznesenskii in 1947. His figures are included in table E.5, with more detailed documentation of labour requirements in the armament industry set beside them. These two sources contribute to a picture of sharply falling labour inputs, which is internally consistent in a broad sense if not always in detail.

Present productivity estimates imply that, in comparison with 1940, direct labour requirements per unit of weaponry had fallen by a third in 1943 and by 40 per cent by 1944. Table E.6 compares these figures with official estimates of the change in labour requirements from table E.5. An unweighted average of Voznesenskii's figures suggests that by 1943, for aircraft, tanks, and guns, labour requirements had fallen by rather more (to 57 per cent of 1940, compared with 71 per cent on present estimates); on the other hand, Voznesenskii's figures are selective, and were presumably selected for effect. The trend of labour requirements of a second sample of armament and ammunition items taken from official files tracks our present estimates much more closely.

Nonlabour costs

Direct labour probably accounted for no more than half of total defence industry costs, and maybe much less. The indicated reductions in labour requirements are generally insufficient to explain the full decline in unit costs already observed. Nonlabour costs must also have fallen per unit of output, and the fall must have been substantial. If unit

Table E.5. *Ground and air munitions: direct labour requirements in defence industry, 1941–5 (hours worked per unit of output)*

		1941	1942	1943	1944	1945
(A) From Voznesenskii						
1	Aircraft					
1.1	Pe-2 bomber	25300	–	13200	–	–
1.2	Il-4 bomber	20000	–	12500	–	–
1.3	Il-2 fighter-bomber	9500	–	5900	–	–
2	Armoured vehicles					
2.1	KV heavy tank	14600	–	7200	–	–
2.2	T-34 medium tank	8000	–	3700	–	–
3	Armament					
3.1	152mm howitzer	4500	–	2400	–	–
3.2	divisional gun	2200	–	600	–	–
3.3	76mm regimental gun	1200	–	800	–	–
3.4	large-calibre machine gun	642	–	329	–	–
3.5	rifle	12.0	–	9.0	–	–
4	Ammunition					
4.1	TT cartridge (per 1000)	13.0	–	10.8	–	–
(B) From armament ministry files						
5.01	160mm MT-VM mortar	–	8540	–	5960	3329
5.02	152mm howitzer (1937)	4370	–	–	3170	3128
5.03	85mm antiaircraft cannon	2588	2361	–	1943	1838
5.04	122mm howitzer (1938)	–	2174	–	1459	1405
5.05	57mm ZIS-2 antitank cannon	1535	–	–	310	595
5.06	76mm antiaircraft cannon platform	1368	1103	–	593	601
5.07	23mm Volkov-Iartsev cannon	786.4	480.2	–	373.5	331.3
5.08	Antiaircraft rangefinder	543.2	–	–	290	274
5.09	12.7mm BZT-44 cartridges (1000)	–	173.4	–	162.7	146.8
5.10	7.62 ShKAS wing-mounted AC m/gun	140.0	–	–	126.7	119.5
5.11	PP-1 gunsight (m/gun, AT cannon)	129.8	123.3	–	101.0	93.4
5.12	7.62mm Degtiarev infantry m/gun	99.6	–	–	47.6	–
5.13	OP2-L optical gunsight	97.5	–	–	51.8	54.4
5.14	7.62mm GB cartridge clips (1000)	13.6	13.7	–	13.2	12.0
5.15	7.62mm carbine (1938)	13.4	10.7	–	8.7	9.9
5.16	7.62mm TT cartridges (1000)	11.4	11.5	–	10.6	9.7

Sources: (A): Voznesensky (1948), 92. (B): RTsKhIDNI, f. 71, op. 25, d. 7882, l. 24.

Table E.6. *Ground and air munitions: direct labour requirements in defence industry, 1943–5: alternative figures (hours per unit and per cent of 1941)*

	1943	1944	1945
(A) Present estimate			
1 Per ruble gross output at 1937 factor cost	73%	68%	60%
(B) From Voznesenskii			
2 Aircraft			
2.1 Pe-2 bomber	52%	–	–
2.2 Il-4 bomber	63%	–	–
2.3 Il-2 fighter-bomber	62%	–	–
3 Armoured vehicles		–	–
3.1 KV heavy tank	49%	–	–
3.2 T-34 medium tank	46%	–	–
4 Armament		–	–
4.1 152mm howitzer	53%	–	–
4.2 divisional gun	27%	–	–
4.3 76mm regimental gun	67%	–	–
4.4 large-calibre machine gun	51%	–	–
4.5 rifle	75%	–	–
5 Ammunition		–	–
5.1 TT cartridge	83%	–	–
6 Arithmetic mean	57%	–	–
(C) From armament ministry files			
7.01 152mm howitzer (1937)		73%	72%
7.02 85mm antiaircraft cannon	–	75%	71%
7.03 57mm ZIS-2 antitank cannon	–	20%	39%
7.04 76mm antiaircraft cannon platform	–	43%	44%
7.05 23mm Volkov-Iartsev (VIa) cannon	–	47%	42%
7.06 Antiaircraft rangefinder	–	53%	50%
7.07 7.62 ShKAS wing-mounted AC m/gun	–	91%	85%
7.08 PP-1 gunsight (m/gun, AT cannon)	–	78%	72%
7.09 7.62mm Degtiarev infantry m/gun	–	48%	–
7.10 OP2-L optical gunsight	–	53%	56%
7.11 7.62mm GB cartridge clip	–	97%	88%
7.12 7.62mm carbine (1938)	–	65%	74%
7.13 7.62mm TT cartridge	–	93%	85%
8 Arithmetic mean	–	64%	60%

Sources: Row 1: calculated from table D.3, row 7. Rows 2–5, 7.01–7.13: the change in hours per unit of finished output, calculated from table E.5. Row 6: the arithmetic mean of rows 2–5. Row 8: the arithmetic mean of rows 7.01–7.13.

nonlabour costs had not fallen significantly, labour requirements would have had to fall even faster to permit the reported declines in unit total costs to have taken place.

Direct evidence on this score is rather fragmentary. Unit nonlabour costs measured under market-economy accounting rules could be expected to have fallen simply because of increased fixed capacity utilisation and a declining ratio of overheads to the volume of output, without any change in variable nonlabour costs. But overhead costs carried little weight under Soviet accounting rules. Therefore, we have to look to changes in nonlabour variable costs to help explain the full decline reported in unit costs of defence industry output.

Wartime reductions in the 'materials intensity' (*materialoemkost'*) of Soviet weapons are authoritatively claimed. Anecdotes testify to substantial wartime saving of materials per unit of some kinds of weapons. Examples are given such as steel for tanks, and aluminium for aircraft, but do not demonstrate that such savings were typical. There are also many reported examples of the substitution of cheaper for more expensive materials in the manufacture of armament and ammunition.

At a higher level of generality, defence industry norms for utilisation of metal are said to have fallen by about one third by 1944 compared with 1941.[16] The total materials consumption of defence industry in 1944 was given as 4.5 per cent below 1943,[17] at the same time as the real final output of munitions had risen by 7 per cent.[18] (But it would have been more useful to know what had happened in 1942 and 1943.) The proposition that falling materials costs contributed significantly to the general decline in unit costs is therefore supported rather weakly by direct evidence, and is pursued here partly by default, since the alternative would be to place too great a burden on rising output per worker and per hour worked to explain falling average costs and prices. Indirect support, however, is available from the evidence given below of contemporaneous trends in German military industry.

For the purposes of appendix D, I assumed that output per unit of labour and nonlabour inputs in defence industry fell in the same proportion, or (which comes to the same thing) that nonlabour inputs per hour worked remained constant. I maintain this rather strong assumption because the consequences of weakening it are still more implausible. A weaker form of the proposition would require us to believe that labour productivity in Soviet defence industry rose in wartime at a rate not just comparable with other countries' experience (as will be shown below), but to an absolutely unbelievable extent.

Employment

Cross-checks on defence industry employment are shown in table E.7. One test is supplied by the total of employment in MBMW. Defence industry formed a large component of MBMW. In the period 1942–4, when civilian activity in the machinery sector had fallen close to zero, defence industry and MBMW became almost synonymous. Therefore, wartime employment in MBMW forms an upper bound on defence industry employment. Present estimates of the MBMW workforce in wartime are reached entirely independently of defence industry figures. If our estimate of the level of wartime gain in defence industry productivity were much overstated, then a wartime defence industry labour requirement far in excess of the entire MBMW workforce would be implied. Table E.7, rows 1 and 2, suggests that in 1942–3 defence industry converged on the MBMW total, and at the same time did not significantly exceed it.

Further checks are supplied by employment data at the commissariat level. In June 1940, four commissariats of defence industry (row 3) employed 1.2 million industrial workers, well below the 1.8 million shown for defence industry in row 1; but the lower figure excludes those employees of civilian commissariats who by now were working on subcontracted defence orders in large numbers, and also those engaged in the manufacture of new weapons for which specialised commissariats had not yet been formed (e.g. medium and heavy tanks). By 1942 four commissariats of defence industry (row 4) – but a different four this time, omitting shipbuilding and including tankbuilding – employed 1.6 million industrial workers, rising to 1.7 million in 1943; no greater increase over 1940 is implied than in my own estimate. When all employees of these commissariats are counted, bringing in construction and service workers, greater numbers are of course suggested. A broader definition of the defence industry, comprising six commissariats (row 5), yields still larger figures, reaching 2.5 million to 3 million workers by the peak of the war effort, depending on whether employment status or ration entitlement is counted. The conceptual match with defence industry employment in row 5 is still very imperfect, since some nonindustrial workers are included, and some industrial workers engaged in sideline defence work under civilian agencies are excluded. The bottom line of table E.7, however, is that there is nothing here to undermine the defence industry employment series in row 1.

Table E.7. *Employment in defence industry, 1940–5: alternative figures (millions)*

	1940	1941	1942	1943	1944	1945
(A) Present estimates						
1 Defence industry	1.751	1.879	2.743	2.879	2.884	2.062
2 MBMW, total	3.519	3.231	2.579	2.831	3.048	3.235
2.1 manual	2.395	2.304	1.874	2.092	2.186	2.261
2.2 nonmanual	1.124	0.927	0.705	0.739	0.862	0.974
(B) Archival sources						
3 Defence industry narkomaty, industrial employees	1.206	–	–	–	–	–
4 Four defence industry narkomaty:						
4.1 industrial employees	–	–	1.574	1.696	–	–
4.2 all employees (I)	–	–	–	2.131	2.172	–
4.3 all employees (II)	–	–	–	–	2.594	2.508
5 Six defence industry narkomaty:						
5.1 all employees (I)	–	–	–	2.453	2.532	–
5.2 all employees (II)	–	–	–	–	3.025	2.964

Sources: Row 1: table D.4, row 9. Row 2: for 1940, table G.1, col. 2, row 1; for other years, row 2.1, plus row 2.2. Row 2.1: table G.5, row 5.1. Row 2.2: for 1940, row 2, less row 2.1; for other years, the total of nonmanual employees in industry (table G.5, row 6), multiplied by the 1940 share of MBMW in the total (table G.1, col. 2, rows 1, 12) Row 3: RGAE, f. 4372, op. 41, d. 553, l. 108. The figure shown is calculated from the source as the sum of manual and nonmanual employees and ITR (engineering and technical workers). The commissariats are not specified, but probably comprised the aircraft, armament, ammunition, and shipbuilding industries (i.e. the old defence industry commissariat, which was broken up in January 1939). The figure shown is for the month of June. Row 4: these were the commissariats for the aircraft and tank industries, armament, and ammunition. Row 4.1 is from RGAE, f. 4372, op. 44, d. 450, l. 11; the 1942 figure is for the fourth quarter, and the 1943 figure for June. Row 4.2 is from ibid., d. 1336, l. 74; figures are for September in each year. Row 4.3 is from RTsKhIDNI, f. 644, op. 1, d. 329, l. 6 (1944), and d. 457, ll. 31–2 (1945); numbers shown are based on ration entitlement, rather than employment status. The 1944 figure is for the fourth quarter, and the 1945 figure for the third quarter. Row 5: these were the commissariats for the aircraft, tank, and shipbuilding industries, armament and mortar armament, and ammunition (i.e. as row 4, but with shipbuilding and mortar armament as well). Otherwise, row 5.1 is as row 4.2, and row 5.2 is as row 4.3.

Cross-country comparisons

The plausibility of present results may be also be tested by comparative reference to trends in production and productivity in the military industries of other countries involved in World War II. These other countries also saw a trend to rationalisation and cost reduction in the manufacture of weapons. The main sources of rationalisation were standardisation of the assortment of weapons allowing longer production runs, the introduction of serial production allowing a greater division of tasks among relatively unskilled workers using special-purpose machinery, and rigid economy in the use of materials. Large increases in final output of weapons were associated with striking price and cost reductions and sharp increases in output per worker and labour productivity.

In the United States, for example, contract prices for the War Department, Army Air Force, and Ordinance fell by 25 to 40 per cent in three and a half years (January 1942–August 1945), despite a 50 per cent increase in weekly earnings in manufacturing industry.[19] Behind this lay a doubling of output per worker in munitions in just two years, 1942–4, with only a small increase in the length of the working week.[20]

In German military industry, output per worker doubled between 1941 and 1944, despite sharp deterioration in workforce skills, and growth in the contribution of forced labour of prisoners and deportees.[21] A striking feature of the German case was the simultaneous reduction of unit requirements of both labour and materials in the manufacture of aircraft and components. Between 1940 and 1944 the hours of labour, and the kilogrammes of raw materials, required in manufacture of the BMW 801 aeroengine both fell by just less than 50 per cent. The production of gun armament and shells also saw huge reductions in material coefficients.[22] The result was a downward trend of prices and costs very similar to the Soviet case.

Richard Overy points out that the productivity gain in the German military–industrial sector after 1941 was made possible by large reserves resulting from productivity decline and cost inflation, 1938–41.[23] It is possible that the same prewar trend underlay wartime productivity gains in Soviet defence industry. If so, it is also conceivable that we have exaggerated the prewar (and therefore also wartime) level of defence industry productivity by comparison with civilian sectors.[24] However, there is no evidence that I have understated the level of employment in Soviet defence industry. As was shown above, present employment estimates track other figures on wartime defence industry accurately. Their adjustment to reflect a lower estimate for the prewar benchmark level of defence industry productivity would result in wartime employment levels which are 'too high', in the sense that they would exceed the number of engineering workers shown to have been available for defence industry employment by other sources.

From such evidence it may be deduced that a calculation of the ratio of gross output to value added for the defence industries of other countries would also reveal trends generally comparable to the figures proposed above for the defence industry of the USSR.

Appendix F: an input/output table

In this appendix I use input/output analysis in order to throw light on the structure of value added and gross output in the prewar Soviet economy, and especially in the industrial sector.

Input/output techniques have been little used by economic historians of the former Soviet Union.[1] However, sufficient data exist to compile a rough input/output table for the Soviet economy immediately before World War II. The work of compilation was begun in 1952 by a group of economists assembled at the RAND Corporation of the United States Air Force for a 10-week project under the leadership of Norman M. Kaplan.[2] The basis of their work was the captured Soviet annual economic plan for 1941, and the table which they compiled was for the Soviet economy as it was projected in the plan, not in reality.[3] So long as Soviet planning proceeded 'from the achieved level', and without undue inconsistency, the 1941 plan provided a legitimate basis for deriving the underlying input/output coefficients which drove the Soviet economy in reality.

Any attempt to make practical use of the 1941-plan input/output table must begin with the character of the 1941 plan itself. The plan was an ambitious document typical of the Stalinist era. Table F.1 compares its features with the 1940 outturn along various dimensions. (However, the authors of the plan, which was dated 17 January 1941, would have had at their disposal only preliminary data for part of 1940.)

Part (A) of the table compares physical indicators of real output. However, their coverage is limited by the exclusion of defence industry products. The unweighted mean of the growth rates of physical products over 1940 was 19 per cent. Agricultural products were planned to grow more rapidly than this, while civilian machinery and consumer manufactures were planned to grow less rapidly; the exception was railway goods – just to maintain the existing supply of railway services, a major effort to make good the investment deficiency of the railways

Table F.1. *The Soviet economy, 1941-plan compared with 1940 results*

	1941-plan (1)	1940 (2)	Col. 1, % of col. 2 (3)
(A) Physical products			
1 Electricity, bn kWh	54.0	48.3	112%
2 Coal, mn tons	190.8	165.9	115%
3 Petroleum, mn tons	38.0	31.1	122%
4 Pig iron, mn tons	18.0	14.9	121%
5 Steel, mn tons			
5.1 crude steel	22.4	18.3	122%
5.2 high-grade rolled steel	3.9	3.2	122%
6 Metal-cutting machine tools, '000s	58.0	58.4	99%
7 Motor vehicles, '000s	140.0	145.4	96%
8 Tractors, '000s	28.0	31.6	88%
9 Railway locomotives, '000s	1.3	0.9	142%
10 Railway trucks, '000s	60.0	30.9	194%
11 Soda ash, '000 tons	673.0	536.1	126%
12 Cement, mn tons	8.0	5.7	140%
13 Sawn timber, mn cu. m.	285.1	246.1	116%
14 Field crops, mn tons			
14.1 grain	123.0	95.5	129%
14.2 cotton fibre	3.0	2.2	135%
14.3 sugar beet	24.2	18.0	134%
14.4 potatoes	97.4	75.9	128%
15 Meat, mn tons	4.0	4.7	84%
16 Fish catch, mn centners	16.6	14.0	118%
17 Animal fats, 000 tons	203.0	226.1	90%
18 Lump sugar, mn tons	2.7	2.2	122%
19 Conserves, bn cans (400 gm)	1.3	1.1	113%
20 Alcoholic spirit, mn dcl	98.8	89.9	110%
21 Cotton cloth, bn m.	4.3	4.0	110%
22 Leather footwear, mn prs	221.6	211.0	105%
23 Freight, bn ton/km			
23.1 rail freight	430.9	415.0	104%
23.2 river freight	46.3	36.1	128%
24 Unweighted mean	–	–	119%
(B) GNP (billion rubles and user prices)			
25 Household consumption	327.0	260.8	125%
26 Communal services	40.7	36.4	112%
27 Government, security	14.4	13.9	104%
28 Defence	70.9	56.5	125%

Table F.1. *(contd.)*

		1941-plan (1)	1940 (2)	Col. 1, % of col. 2 (3)
29	Gross investment	88.3	67.6	131%
30	Gross national product	541.3	435.2	124%

Sources: (A) Physical products, col. 1: TsSU (1959), 8–15 and ff.; col. 2: SNK-TsK (1941), 3–6 and ff. (B) GNP, col. 1: Bergson (1961), 46; col. 2: Kaplan *et al.* (1952), 131–42.

was clearly envisaged. Defence products, not illustrated in part (A), were doubtless also scheduled for rapid growth.

Part (B) of the table supports a similar evaluation based on the Kaplan team's estimate of 1941-plan GNP at current prices with the same concept for 1940 estimated later by Abram Bergson. In 1941 Soviet GNP was intended to grow by 24 per cent; investment was scheduled to expand by almost one third after the investment standstill of the rearmament years 1937–40; investment was to grow at the expense of communal and government nondefence consumption, which were to expand much more slowly.

On the basis of the 1941 plan, combined with various kinds of specialist knowledge and comparative data, Kaplan's team assembled an input/output table with a 20 × 20 inter-industry matrix, and 7 final demand columns. The table was compiled in haste. Its authors left unresolved several main problems. First, it covered only the production industries, agriculture, transport, and trade, reconciliation with a GNP concept of production and expenditure (including construction and services) being confined to an appendix. Even within this narrow concept, there were vast areas of conjecture; basic industries, agriculture, transport, and internal trade were covered in some detail, but the row allocations of industries supplying more fabricated products (machinery, chemicals, building materials, timber, paper, and consumer products of all kinds) had to be estimated freehand. Kaplan identified 'a rectangle within the input–output table which is considerably more conjectural than the rest of the table' (rows 7 through 16 in tables below).[4] 'Nothing except ignorance', he wrote, 'can be inferred from a naked cell.'[5] Foreign trade was entirely neglected.

Second, the reconciliation was never finished. Total final expenditures were left substantially in excess of output by large gaps on the output side; some 32 billion rubles of gross output (5 per cent of the total) remained unallocated. There were also unresolved discrepancies between the three GNP aggregates: final demand, value added on the output side (gross output, *less* intermediate inputs), and value added measured by factor incomes originating in the various branches.

In each of tables F.2 and F.3, the first column illustrates the discrepancies in the original RAND table which had to be overcome, and the second shows the results of revision. Table F.2 sets out the discrepancies on a branch-by-branch basis. It compares total identified outlays on primary factor inputs plus intermediate inputs with gross output values; it shows that total outlays amounted to percentages of gross output varying between 69 and 111 per cent (but mostly within a narrower range, say 85–105 per cent). Table F.3 deals with the GNP aggregates (at prevailing prices, not at factor cost). It shows that, in the Kaplan version, the sum of final demands exceeded gross value added by 113 billion rubles, mainly because of the complete omission of construction and services from the processing sectors. The coverage of factor incomes of households, economic organisations, and government originating in production (including budget revenues from profits and turnover taxation) was even more sketchy, and fell below aggregate final demand by 161 billion rubles.

To make practical use of the table required three separate processes: balancing, repricing, and further structural refinement. *Balancing* involved the correction of at least some of these discrepancies and omissions, and its impact is seen in tables F.2 and F.3 (column 2). I treated the 541 billion rubles of GNP generated by aggregate final demand as the anchor for estimating gross value added on the output side. I inserted rows and columns into the inter-industry matrix for construction and five service sectors, including defence services (table F.2). I credited these new branches with supply of final demand to the tune of some 80 billion rubles. I redistributed 32 billion rubles of gross output of existing branches left unallocated by the RAND group, largely (but not exclusively) to stockbuilding. These steps almost entirely closed the gap between final demand and value added on the output side, leaving both at 541 billion rubles (table F.3).

In the process I identified a further 50 billion rubles of factor incomes, but decided not to try to find the rest. Factor incomes worth 110 billion rubles more on top of this were required to match GNP on the output and demand sides. It would have been necessary to find them in order

Table F.2. *Identified outlays on intermediate goods and services and factor services in the 1941-plan input/output table (per cent of gross output at prevailing prices)*

		Kaplan (1)	Revised (2)
1	Electric power	80%	80%
2	Coal	89%	89%
3	Peat	86%	86%
4	Petroleum	77%	77%
5	Iron, steel	103%	103%
6	Nonferrous metals	103%	103%
7	Fabricated metal products	93%	93%
8	Defence industries	88%	88%
9	Chemicals	111%	111%
10	Construction materials	110%	110%
11	Timber, wood products	87%	87%
12	Paper, paper products	79%	79%
13	Textiles	88%	88%
14	Light industry	101%	101%
15	Food processing	101%	101%
16	Other industries	–	0%
17	Agriculture	97%	97%
17a	Construction	–	50%
18	Transport	105%	105%
19	Communications	69%	69%
20	Trade	93%	93%
20a	Communal services	–	53%
20b	Personal services	–	0%
20c	Housing services	–	100%
20d	Government services	–	122%
20e	Military services	–	80%

Sources: Col. 1: Kaplan *et al.* (1952), 7. Col. 2: see text.

to model the household sector, but my main interest was limited to the inter-industry matrix. I made only a cursory attempt, for example, to find the factor incomes associated with the new processing sectors.

As well as being balanced, the RAND table had to be *repriced* in order to convert it to a usable basis. The original exercise had been carried out in the prevailing prices (including turnover taxes) anticipated in 1940 to prevail in 1941, whereas the main thrust of the SNIP project under Bergson was to evaluate Soviet GNP in constant factor costs of various

Table F.3. *Gross national product in the 1941-plan input/output table (billion rubles and prevailing prices)*

	Kaplan (1)	Revised (2)
1 GNP (expenditure)	541.3	540.9
2 GNP (output)	428.7	540.9
3 GNP (income)	380.5	429.1

Sources: Col. 1: Kaplan *et al.* (1952), 7. Col. 2: see text. GNP (expenditure) is measured by the sum of final demands, GNP (output) is measured by the sum of gross output, less intermediate inputs, and GNP (income) is measured by the sum of incomes reported as accruing to households, government, and economic organisations.

base years, among which 1937 was closest, but far from identical, to 1940 or 1941.

There was also the question of whether value added should be counted gross or net of depreciation. As far as the latter is concerned, the lack of information about depreciation outside industry and transport left little choice but to keep the input/output table on a gross basis; but it was important to know the rate and distribution of depreciation costs among the industrial processing sectors, and these are shown in table F.4, columns 1–2.

Prevailing prices of 1941-plan were then transformed into factor costs of 1937 in two stages. First, I removed the effects of turnover taxation (table F.4, columns 3–4) from output and input values, assuming that tax revenues anticipated in 1941 were levied exclusively on final demand, with the exception of taxes on electricity supply and chemicals.[6] Second, I carried out a double deflation of outputs and inputs to 1937 factor costs, using various deflators (table F.4, column 5) and assuming that (except for agriculture) 1941-plan prices were the same as those prevailing in 1940.[7]

The last stage involved *further structural refinement*. After some experimentation I inserted a further row and column for a sub-branch of the iron and steel industry supplying the defence industry, with the sole function of adding nonferrous metals to iron and steel products, in order to capture the defence-related use of ferroalloys and other nonferrous metal products.

Accounting for foreign trade also involved structural refinement. Foreign trade is not mentioned in the published version of the 1941-plan, nor did it feature in the work of Kaplan's team. There was foreign

Table F.4. *The 1941-plan input/output table: depreciation, indirect taxation, and price deflators (million rubles at prevailing prices and per cent)*

		Depreciation		Turnover tax		
			% of gross value added		% of gross value added	Deflator, 1941-plan, % of 1937
		(1)	(2)	(3)	(4)	(5)
1	Electric power	375	11.6%	399	12.3%	121%
2	Coal	209	4.4%	35	0.7%	121%
3	Peat	–	–	–	–	121%
4	Petroleum	492	3.6%	305	2.2%	121%
5	Iron, steel	743	13.4%	166	3.0%	121%
6	Nonferrous metals	238	8.7%	96	3.5%	121%
7	Fab. metal products	517	3.6%	1083	7.5%	106%
8	Defence industries	800	3.8%	–	–	120%
9	Chemicals	245	8.4%	981	33.6%	121%
10	Con. materials	127	7.3%	99	5.7%	108%
11	Timber, wood products	145	1.5%	460	4.7%	121%
12	Paper, paper products	90	8.7%	83	8.1%	121%
13	Textiles	315	1.2%	13581	51.9%	134%
14	Light industry	124	1.3%	5193	53.7%	134%
15	Food processing	536	0.6%	81688	86.0%	134%
16	Other industries	344	0.9%	2739	7.4%	134%
17	Agriculture	–	–	–	–	152%
17a	Construction	–	–	–	–	113%
18	Transport	2969	13.7%	–	–	156%
19	Communications	100	2.6%	–	–	116%
20	Trade	–	–	8581	41.3%	116%
20a	Communal services	–	–	–	–	116%
20b	Personal services	–	–	–	–	116%
20c	Housing services	–	–	–	–	116%
20d	Government services	–	–	–	–	116%
20e	Military services	–	–	–	–	116%

Sources: Col. 1: Kaplan *et al.* (1952), 145. Col. 3: Kaplan *et al.* (1952), 127. Cols 2, 4: cols 1, 3, divided by gross value added at prevailing prices (as table F.2, col. 2.). Col. 5: it being assumed with one exception (row 7) that 1941-plan prices were based on 1940 prevailing prices, 1940/37 price and (for service sectors) hourly wage cost ratios are taken as follows: rows 1–6, 9, 11–12 from table A.1, row 4; row 7 from table A.1, row 3; row 8 from table A.1, row 1; row 10 from table A.1, row 5.1; rows 13–16 from table A.1, row 7; row 17 from table A.1, row 7, multiplied by 113% being the estimate of Kaplan *et al.* (1952), 78, of the ratio of 1941-plan prices for agricultural products to 1940 prices; row 17a from table A.1, row 5; row 18 from table A.1, row 6; rows 19–20e from table A.1, row 82.

U	F	−M	X
V			
X			

trade, of course, but it was quantitatively slight – under 1 per cent of GNP in 1940.[8] Therefore, for 1941-plan I make no adjustment. In 1942–5, however, foreign resources were of great importance for the Soviet war effort, and must be taken accurately into account. I insert a fresh column for net imports in the final demand sector of the table. The import vector contains zeros for 1940, but significant values for other years (see appendix J). This implicitly treats all imported commodities as competitive with home products; they were not required in fixed proportions to output, but as substitutes for domestic sources of supply.

In principle we could gain further information about the appropriate balance and structure of the 1941-plan input/output table from resources not available to the Kaplan project. Chief among these are the 1959 input/output table,[9] and wartime Gosplan documents previously described which supposedly supplement the defence corner of the inter-industry matrix.[10] In practice, the latter are too fragmentary to be of direct value. The 1959 input/output table, while much more comprehensive, shows substantial discrepancies with 1941-plan; some of these stem from changes in classification of transactions both on and off the diagonal of the inter-industry matrix, while others must be the result of two decades of changing prices and technologies.

The revised input/output table for the 1941-plan, now with a 27 × 27 inter-industry matrix, calculated in factor costs of 1937, is shown in table F.5. Its general outline is shown above, where **U** is the matrix of intermediate, inter-industry utilisation, **F** is total final demand, **M** is net imports, **X** is gross outputs (so that $\mathbf{X} = \mathbf{U} + \mathbf{F} - \mathbf{M}$) and **V** is value added (so that $\mathbf{X} = \mathbf{U} + \mathbf{V}$).

Following standard procedures, the revised input/output table can be used to derive the technical coefficients (the direct intermediate input requirements per ruble of gross output of each branch), and the Leontief multipliers which show direct-plus-indirect input requirements per

Table F.5. The 1941-plan input/output table (million rubles and 1937 factor costs)

To:		Electric power 1	Coal 2	Peat 3	Petroleum 4	Iron, steel (civilian) 5	(military) 5a
From:							
1	Electric power	513	206	45	138	529	0
2	Coal	583	230	0	117	1072	0
3	Peat	417	0	60	0	0	0
4	Petroleum	613	14	14	1755	279	0
5	Iron, steel (civ.)	7	0	0	0	7931	2005
5a	Iron, steel (mil.)	0	0	0	0	0	0
6	Nonferrous metals	0	0	0	0	45	409
7	Fab. metal products	0	0	0	0	72	0
8	Defence industries	0	0	0	0	33	0
9	Chemicals	0	28	0	0	61	0
10	Con. materials	0	0	0	0	206	0
11	Timber, wood products	9	126	0	4	308	0
12	Paper, paper products	0	0	0	0	0	0
13	Textiles	0	0	0	0	0	0
14	Light industry	0	0	0	0	0	0
15	Food processing	0	0	0	0	0	0
16	Other industries	0	0	0	0	0	0
17	Agriculture	0	0	0	0	0	0
17a	Construction	0	0	0	0	0	0
18	Transport	224	112	20	216	1015	0
19	Communications	19	28	5	70	69	0
20	Trade	29	25	3	36	153	0
20a	Communal services	0	0	0	0	0	0
20b	Personal services	0	0	0	0	0	0
20c	Housing services	0	0	0	0	0	0
20d	Government services	0	0	0	0	0	0
20e	Military services	0	0	0	0	0	0
20f	Intermediate inputs	2413	768	148	2336	11775	2414
23	Gross value added	2461	3933	686	11199	4753	0
23a	Total outlays	4874	4701	834	13535	16528	2414

Table F.5. *(contd.)*

To:	Non-ferrous metals 6	Fab. metal prods 7	Defence industries 8	Chemicals 9	Constr. materials 10	Timber, wood prods 11
From:						
1 Electric power	414	282	500	461	93	49
2 Coal	96	155	223	81	83	8
3 Peat	0	0	8	0	17	0
4 Petroleum	19	49	91	21	8	57
5 Iron, steel (civ.)	6	4729	0	83	2	0
5a Iron, steel (mil.)	0	0	2414	0	0	0
6 Nonferrous metals	3711	661	997	201	0	0
7 Fab. metal products	0	2170	943	0	0	0
8 Defence industries	0	0	3358	0	0	0
9 Chemicals	70	279	1851	1747	70	1
10 Con. materials	29	236	0	59	294	0
11 Timber, wood products	106	251	1688	94	468	1596
12 Paper, paper products	0	0	331	0	165	0
13 Textiles	0	920	1154	911	37	923
14 Light industry	0	0	0	0	0	0
15 Food processing	0	0	0	968	0	0
16 Other industries	0	0	0	0	0	0
17 Agriculture	0	0	0	0	0	0
17a Construction	0	0	0	0	0	0
18 Transport	211	831	1008	156	174	254
19 Communications	37	93	174	42	14	32
20 Trade	80	181	516	92	25	29
20a Communal services	0	0	0	0	0	0
20b Personal services	0	0	0	0	0	0
20c Housing services	0	0	0	0	0	0
20d Government services	0	0	0	0	0	0
20e Military services	0	0	0	0	0	0
20f Intermediate inputs	4778	10836	15256	4915	1450	2949
23 Gross value added	2283	14266	18328	2073	1731	7957
23a Total outlays	7061	25103	33583	6988	3181	10906

Table F.5 *(contd.)*

To:	Paper, paper products 12	Textiles 13	Light industry 14	Food processing 15	Other industries 16	Agriculture 17
From:						
1 Electric power	73	187	47	95	0	50
2 Coal	0	40	19	2210	0	3
3 Peat	2	76	18	45	0	49
4 Petroleum	0	84	51	351	0	3868
5 Iron, steel (civ.)	0	0	7	6	0	0
5a Iron, steel (mil.)	0	0	0	0	0	0
6 Nonferrous metals	0	0	0	0	0	0
7 Fab. metal products	0	0	0	0	0	0
8 Defence industries	0	0	0	0	0	0
9 Chemicals	87	559	24	707	0	489
10 Con. materials	0	0	0	0	0	0
11 Timber, wood products	318	77	44	291	0	22
12 Paper, paper products	173	0	0	0	0	0
13 Textiles	0	6267	11181	0	0	0
14 Light industry	0	0	913	0	0	0
15 Food processing	0	0	968	18236	0	0
16 Other industries	0	0	0	0	0	0
17 Agriculture	0	5599	0	12186	0	45977
17a Construction	0	0	0	0	0	0
18 Transport	32	474	162	1933	0	1142
19 Communications	7	198	123	579	0	29
20 Trade	10	352	257	661	0	82
20a Communal services	0	0	0	0	0	0
20b Personal services	0	0	0	0	0	0
20c Housing services	0	0	0	0	0	0
20d Government services	0	0	0	0	0	0
20e Military services	0	0	0	0	0	0
20f Intermediate inputs	702	13915	13815	35312	0	51713
23 Gross value added	807	10067	3291	11506	25502	86417
23a Total outlays	1509	23982	17106	46816	25502	138130

Table F.5 *(contd).*

To:	Construction 17a	Transport 18	Communications 19	Trade 20	Services: communal 20a	Services: personal 20b
From:						
1 Electric power	0	252	3	22	0	0
2 Coal	0	1206	0	2	0	0
3 Peat	0	0	0	0	0	0
4 Petroleum	0	2271	24	0	0	0
5 Iron, steel (civ.)	0	439	0	0	0	0
5a Iron, steel (mil.)	0	0	0	0	0	0
6 Nonferrous metals	0	83	74	0	0	0
7 Fab. metal products	0	0	0	0	0	0
8 Defence industries	0	0	0	0	0	0
9 Chemicals	0	259	0	0	0	0
10 Con. materials	2120	0	0	0	0	0
11 Timber, wood products	731	433	0	3	0	0
12 Paper, paper products	0	0	0	165	0	0
13 Textiles	0	0	0	0	0	0
14 Light industry	0	0	0	0	0	0
15 Food processing	0	90	0	0	0	0
16 Other industries	0	0	0	0	0	0
17 Agriculture	0	0	0	0	0	0
17a Construction	0	0	0	0	0	0
18 Transport	1036	940	17	1935	0	0
19 Communications	177	328	17	529	0	0
20 Trade	12	122	23	6	0	0
20a Communal services	0	0	0	0	0	0
20b Personal services	0	0	0	0	0	0
20c Housing services	0	0	0	0	0	0
20d Government services	0	0	0	0	0	0
20e Military services	0	0	0	0	0	0
20f Intermediate inputs	4077	6422	158	2663	0	0
23 Gross value added	31812	12733	3389	11247	33174	11859
23a Total outlays	35889	19155	3547	13910	33174	11859

Table F.5 *(contd).*

To:		Services (contd.): housing 20c	government 20d	military 20e	Total inter-mediate demand	Total final demand 25
From:						
1	Electric power	0	0	0	3958	917
2	Coal	0	0	0	4138	563
3	Peat	0	0	0	692	142
4	Petroleum	0	0	0	9570	3965
5	Iron, steel (civ.)	0	0	0	15215	1313
5a	Iron, steel (mil.)	0	0	0	2414	0
6	Nonferrous metals	0	0	0	6181	880
7	Fab. metal products	0	0	0	3185	21918
8	Defence industries	0	0	0	3392	30192
9	Chemicals	0	0	0	6234	755
10	Con. materials	0	0	0	2945	235
11	Timber, wood products	0	0	0	6569	4336
12	Paper, paper products	0	0	0	834	675
13	Textiles	0	0	0	21394	2588
14	Light industry	0	0	0	913	16193
15	Food processing	0	0	0	20262	26555
16	Other industries	0	0	0	0	25502
17	Agriculture	0	0	0	63762	74368
17a	Construction	0	0	0	0	35889
18	Transport	0	0	0	11891	72641
19	Communications	0	0	0	2572	976
20	Trade	0	0	0	2695	11215
20a	Communal services	0	0	0	0	33174
20b	Personal services	0	0	0	0	11859
20c	Housing services	0	0	0	0	7444
20d	Government services	0	0	0	0	7315
20e	Military services	0	0	0	0	6492
20f	Intermediate inputs	0	0	0		
23	Gross value added	7444	7315	6492	188814	332724
23a	Total outlays	7444	7315	6492		

Table F.5 *(contd.)*

To:	Consumption:			Capital formation			
	household 26	communal 27	Govt, security 28	total 28a	gross construction 29	producer durables 30	inventories etc. 31
From:							
1 Electric power	845	36	36	0	0	0	0
2 Coal	266	0	0	296	0	0	296
3 Peat	94	0	0	48	0	0	48
4 Petroleum	1445	0	0	1028	0	0	1028
5 Iron, steel (civ.)	0	0	0	1313	1041	0	272
5a Iron, steel (mil.)	0	0	0	0	0	0	0
6 Nonferrous metals	0	0	0	880	16	0	864
7 Fab. metal products	3852	0	0	18066	0	18066	0
8 Defence industries	0	0	3019	0	0	0	0
9 Chemicals	210	0	0	545	489	0	56
10 Con. materials	0	0	0	235	0	0	235
11 Timber, wood products	980	0	0	2976	2976	0	0
12 Paper, paper products	263	75	150	150	0	0	150
13 Textiles	1822	15	0	600	0	0	600
14 Light industry	10895	0	0	1693	0	0	1693
15 Food processing	23260	0	128	1131	0	0	1131
16 Other industries	13785	1378	0	4825	0	0	0
17 Agriculture	74368	0	0	0	0	0	0
17a Construction	0	0	0	33240	33240	0	0
18 Transport	4678	84	11	1099	785	314	0
19 Communications	976	0	0	0	0	0	0
20 Trade	11215	0	0	0	0	0	0
20a Communal services	0	33174	0	0	0	0	0
20b Personal services	11859	0	0	0	0	0	0
20c Housing services	7444	0	0	0	0	0	0
20d Government services	0	0	7315	0	0	0	0
20e Military services	0	0	1298	0	0	0	0
20f Intermediate inputs							
23 Gross value added	168255	34762	11956	68127	38548	18380	6373
23a Total outlays							

Table F.5 *(contd.)*

	Defence 32	Gross output 33	Total intermed. inputs 33a	Gross value added 33b
From:				
1 Electric power	0	4874	2413	2461
2 Coal	0	4701	768	3933
3 Peat	0	834	148	686
4 Petroleum	1492	13535	2336	11199
5 Iron, steel (civ.)	0	16528	11775	4753
5a Iron, steel (mil.)	0	2414	2414	0
6 Nonferrous metals	0	7061	4778	2283
7 Fab. metal products	0	25103	10836	14266
8 Defence industries	27173	33583	15256	18328
9 Chemicals	0	6988	4915	2073
10 Con. materials	0	3181	1450	1731
11 Timber, wood products	380	10906	2949	7957
12 Paper, paper products	38	1509	702	807
13 Textiles	152	23982	13915	10067
14 Light industry	3605	17106	13815	3291
15 Food processing	2036	46816	35312	11505
16 Other industries	5514	25502	0	25502
17 Agriculture	0	138130	51713	86417
17a Construction	2649	35889	4077	31812
18 Transport	1392	19155	6422	12733
19 Communications	0	3547	158	3389
20 Trade	0	13910	2663	11247
20a Communal services	0	33174	0	33174
20b Personal services	0	11859	0	11859
20c Housing services	0	7444	0	7444
20d Government services	0	7315	0	7315
20e Military services	5194	6492	0	6492
20f Intermediate inputs			188814	
23 Gross value added	49624			332724
23a Total outlays		521538		

Source: For the original, see Kaplan *et al.* (1952), 7. Revisions are described in the text. Labels and row and column numbering are mainly as in the original; additions are identified by letter postscripts (e.g. row 20a).

Table F.6. *The revised 1941-plan input/output table (rubles and 1937 factor cost): sums of coefficients*

		Technical coefficients (1)	Leontief multipliers (2)
1	Electric power	0.50	1.67
2	Coal	0.16	1.24
3	Peat	0.18	1.25
4	Petroleum	0.17	1.22
5	Iron, steel (civilian)	0.71	2.58
5a	Iron, steel (military)	1.00	3.58
6	Nonferrous metals	0.68	2.61
7	Fab. metal products	0.43	1.95
8	Defence industries	0.45	2.00
9	Chemicals	0.70	2.60
10	Con. materials	0.46	1.74
11	Timber, wood products	0.27	1.44
12	Paper, paper products	0.47	1.79
13	Textiles	0.58	2.05
14	Light industry	0.81	2.69
15	Food processing	0.75	2.58
16	Other industries	0.00	1.00
17	Agriculture	0.37	1.59
17a	Construction	0.11	1.18
18	Transport	0.34	1.49
19	Communications	0.04	1.08
20	Trade	0.19	1.27
20a	Communal services	0.00	1.00
20b	Personal services	0.00	1.00
20c	Housing services	0.00	1.00
20d	Government services	0.00	1.00
20e	Military services	0.00	1.00

Source: Calculated from table F.5; for explanation, see text. The military branch of ferrous metallurgy (row 5a) is modelled as a subsector of the iron and steel industry which does not add value but only nonferrous metals to iron and steel used by the defence industries (row 8).

ruble of final demand for the products of each branch. The column sums of technical coefficients and Leontief multipliers, shown in table F.6, capture different aspects of production interdependence. The sums of technical coefficients show the proportions of gross output accounted for by the value of intermediate inputs. Thus the gross output of sectors producing defence products, fabricated metal products, metals, chemi-

Table F.7. *Gross national product by final use, 1928–44, from Bergson (billion rubles and 1937 factor cost)*

		1928	1937	1940	1944
1	Household consumption	105.7	113.2	129.5	82.9
1.1	retail purchases (households)	55.1	66.1	73.2	36.5
1.1a	in official sector	–	57.7	66.4	35.7
1.1b	in kolkhoz sector	–	8.4	6.8	0.8
1.2	housing; services	10.2	17.2	18.9	13.1
1.3	farm consumption in kind	39.8	28.0	33.6	20.2
1.4	military subsistence	0.6	1.9	3.8	13.1
2	Government consumption	10.6	46.5	82.3	143.8
2.1	communal services	6.1	22.6	27.0	20.7
2.2	govt. admin., security	2.8	6.9	10.1	7.9
2.3	defence (budget)	1.7	17.0	45.2	115.2
3	Gross investment	16.6	55.9	50.1	34.3
3.1	fixed	11.0	35.6	39.9	24.5
3.2	other	5.6	20.3	10.2	9.8
4	Gross national product	132.9	215.6	261.9	261.0

Source: Bergson (1961), 128.

cals, textiles, light industry products, and food products, was dominated by the value of inputs, with relatively little value added within the branch itself. On the other hand sectors extracting primary resources such as fuels, as well as sectors supplying services of various kinds, were mostly engaged in adding value. Two sectors, 'other industries' (row 16) and construction (row 17a), are given low technical coefficients from ignorance. In the case of construction I was able to identify intermediate inputs to account for only 13 per cent of industry gross output, compared with one half in the 1959 input/output table.[11]

Table F.6 also shows the column sums of Leontief multipliers for each sector. These show the ruble value of increased total output required by a 1-ruble increase in final demand for the products of each branch. For the services-only branches (as for 'other industries'), indirect requirements are set at zero, so the multiplier equals one. For branches supplying physical products and themselves requiring intermediate supplies of goods and services, the multiplier exceeds one; the products generating the most far-reaching supply implications are metals, chemicals, consumer manufactures, and food products. The interdependence of 'other industries' and construction is certainly understated by a large margin.

Bergson estimated final demands at factor costs of 1937 for a number of benchmark years before and during World War II, including 1940; his main results are shown in table F.7. I distinguish six categories of end use: household consumption outlays, government outlays on administration and security, government outlays on communal services, defence outlays, fixed investment, and stockbuilding. Final demand aggregates for 1940 are taken from this table, except for defence items. Within each category of end use, requirements must be distributed among the processing sectors supplying final demand. Defence outlays are disaggregated from budget sources and deflated by me.[12] For non-defence items the 1941-plan composition of demands on processing sectors is applied to 1940, except that, under government administration and security, NKVD outlays on military equipment and personnel are estimated separately.[13] Combined with estimated final demands in 1940, the Leontief multipliers give each sector's gross output and the value added by each sector implied for that year, as shown in tables F.8 (industry) and F.9 (the economy as a whole).

Figures for industry value added have immediate practical significance. In previous work I used employment weights (including an allowance for the role of forced labourers) to combine index numbers of net output in the different branches of industry, assuming by default that net output per worker was uniform across industry. The unadjusted results of the input/output table (column 1) suggest that employment-based weights were quite unreliable as a guide to the value-added contributions of different branches of industry.[14]

The unadjusted figures for 1940 gross value added reported in table F.8 (column 2) can be adjusted for purposes of recalculating the index of wartime industrial production, which requires index numbers of branch output to be multiplied by the weight of each branch in 1940 industrial net value added. The unadjusted total for gross value added of civilian industry (79.3 billion rubles) far exceeds the 64.5 billion rubles of net value added obtained from Bergson via Moorsteen and Powell.[15] The excess is attributable partly to the inclusion of capital depreciation, but mostly to the 11.6 billion rubles of value added by 'other industries' (row 16); the latter is a purely statistical result of the absence of information about intermediate inputs to set against the gross output of this sector in the input/output table. In the employment statistics 'other industries' carry a much smaller weight.[16] In subsequent columns of the table, the various divergences are corrected. Across columns 2–4, gross value added is converted to a basis net of capital consumption. In column 5, the total of civilian industry value

Table F.8. *Gross output and value added in industry, by branch of origin, 1940 (million rubles at 1937 factor cost and per cent)*

		Gross output (1)	Gross value added (2)	Depre-ciation (3)	Net value added, unadj. (4)	Net value added, adj. (5)
1	Electric power	3894	1966	227	1739	1633
2–4	Coal, peat, petroleum	17003	14103	512	13591	12769
5–5a	Iron, steel	14317	3703	495	3207	3013
6	Nonferrous metals	6533	2112	183	1930	1813
7–8	MBMW	40735	22697	832	21865	21180
7	fab. metal products	20670	11747	420	11327	10642
8	defence industries	20065	10950	412	10538	10538
9	Chemicals	5489	1629	137	1492	1401
10	Construction materials	2561	1394	102	1292	1214
11–12	Timber, paper, products	8886	6244	135	6110	5740
13–14	Textiles, light industry	36448	12111	148	11962	11239
15	Food processing	51117	12561	71	12490	11735
16	Other industries	11680	11680	109	11572	3338
1–16	Industry, total	198664	90200	2951	87249	75075
17	of which, civilian	178599	79250	2538	76712	64537

Sources: Cols. 1, 2: final demand aggregates for 1940, from table F.7, distributed among processing sectors in the same proportions as for 1941-plan (table F.5), are multiplied into the Leontief matrix (as table F.6) for gross outputs (col. 1), from which intermediate inputs are deducted for gross value added (col. 2). Col. 3: table F.4, col. 2, gives allowances for capital consumption by branch of industry for 1941-plan, in prevailing plan prices, converted to percentages of gross value added. These are used to calculate depreciation in 1937 prices from col. 1. Col. 4: col. 2, less col. 3. Col. 5: first, the figure for defence industry value added in col. 4 (row 8) is carried across, leaving 77.1 billion rubles of civilian industry value added in col. 4. Second, the col. 2 figure for gross value added in 'other industries' (row 16), inflated by inability to account for intermediate supply of this branch, is adjusted downward, being fixed in the same ratio to net value added in the textile, light, and food industries (rows 13–15) as the corresponding employment ratio (it being assumed that net value added per worker in these branches was comparable). According to the note attached to table G.1, row 11, employment in 1940 under 'other industry', including the printing industry but excluding nonferrous metallurgy, may be set at roughly 642,000, compared with 4,421,000 employees of the light and food industry (including artisan industry). This fixes the ratio of the figure in row 16 to the sum of rows 13–15,

Table F.9. *Gross national product, by sector of origin, 1940 and 1941-plan (billion rubles and 1937 factor cost)*

		Gross value added from the input/output table: 1941-plan (1)	1940 (2)	Net value added: 1940 (3)	Col. 2, % of col. 3: 1940 (4)
1–7, 9–15	Civilian industries, excl. 'other industries'	77.0	67.6	61.2	110%
8	Defence industries	18.3	11.0	10.5	104%
16	Other industries	25.5	11.7	3.3	350%
17	Agriculture	86.4	71.1	69.9	102%
17a	Construction	31.8	22.8	10.6	215%
18–19	Transport, communications	16.1	13.0	19.3	67%
20	Trade	11.2	8.8	11.1	80%
20a–d	Civilian services	59.8	46.8	46.4	101%
20e	Military services	6.5	7.9	7.9	100%
20f	Depreciation	–	–	13.6	–
21	Gross national product	332.7	260.6	253.9	103%
21a	excl. rows 16, 17a	275.4	226.1	240.0	94%

Sources: Col. 1, gross value added from table F.5, col. 33b. Col. 2: calculated as table F.8, col. 2. Col. 3: rows 1–16, as table F.8, col. 5; rows 17–20, as Moorsteen and Powell (1966), 622–3. Col. 4: col. 2, divided by col. 3.

added is constrained within Moorsteen and Powell's figure, while the 'other industries' share of net value added is constrained within a figure consistent with numbers known to have been employed, relative to the workforce in other light (textile, light, and food) industries. This gives a more realistic picture of the composition of industrial production in 1940.

Unresolved difficulties associated with the revised input/output table are illustrated in table F.9. This table shows gross value added

(Sources to table F.8)
and reduces the col. 4 subtotal for civilian industry to 69.0 billion rubles. Last, all the figures for civilian industry are scaled to fit the row 17 total of 64.5 billion rubles of net value added in civilian industry derived from Moorsteen and Powell (1966), 622–3.

required on the basis of 1941-plan final demands and revised 1941-plan Leontief multipliers, both in total and distributed across the whole economy (column 1). For comparison, the same is also shown on the basis of Bergson's 1940 final demands (except defence outlays, estimated by us) (column 2). The latter estimates for 1940 based on the input/output table can then be compared with 1940 net value added by sector of origin (mainly from Moorsteen and Powell) (column 3).

Discrepancies between the two routes to value added in 1940 are computed (column 4). Excluding 'other industries' and construction, there is a 6 per cent discrepancy in aggregate (row 21a); this is mostly the excess of Bergson's estimate of GNP by end-use over Moorsteen and Powell's sector-of-origin figure. The comparison of figures for individual branches is also distorted by the inclusion or exclusion of depreciation. Taking both of these factors into account, the two sets of estimates of values added appear roughly consistent for agriculture and industry. However, the input/output table appears to understate transport, communications, and trade requirements. 'Other industries' and construction, on the other hand, appear grossly overrepresented by the input/output table, the reason in both cases being the failure to find sufficient intermediate inputs to set against gross output for measuring value added.

Appendix G: industrial employment

Official figures for prewar and wartime industrial employment are shown in tables G.1 to G.3. Table G.1 deals with 1940. It shows the employment of 'industrial-production personnel' (*promyshlenno-proizvodstvennyi personal*, or PPP for short) in the public sector. PPP comprised both manual and nonmanual employees (*rabochie i sluzhashchie*), inclusive of engineering and technical personnel (*ITR*), apprentices and 'junior service personnel' (*mladshii obsluzhivaiushchii personal*), and security staff (*rabotniki okhrany*). Those providing training or other services to the workforce were not included in PPP. This is, however, the most inclusive of the available concepts.

In 1960 the statistical classification of the public sector changed, and figures for 1940 are available in both definitions, shown in columns 1 and 2 of table G.1. The most important change affected the numbers engaged in artisan industry (the *arteli promyslovoi kooperatsii*, or *promko-operatsiia* for short), which were excluded from the public sector before 1960. Most of these were engaged in light industry of various kinds. The inclusion of artisan industry appears to explain fully the increase in the PPP total arising from the 1960 reclassification.

Within the PPP total, the 1960 reclassification saw other small changes, too, for example, the reallocation of industrial workers employed on building sites. It should also be mentioned that the post-1960 classification was less detailed, at least in the published version (for example, the printing industry disappeared), and with a larger unclassified residual, into which disappeared such sensitive information as numbers engaged in nonferrous metallurgy.

Wartime employment is known from published sources only on the basis of the narrow, pre-1960 definition of the public sector. Such figures are presented in table G.2. The original data comprise a PPP total (row 1), and subtotals for manual employees (row 5) broken down into MBMW, the iron and steel industry, and the light and food industries.

Table G.1. *Employment in public-sector industry, 1940 (millions and per cent)*

	Pre-1960 classification		Post-1960 classification	
	(1)	%	(2)	%
1 MBMW	3.148	28.7%	3.519	26.9%
2 Metallurgy	0.494	4.5%	–	–
2.1 iron, steel	–	–	0.526	4.0%
3 Fuels	0.702	6.4%	0.808	6.2%
4 Electric power	0.110	1.0%	0.164	1.3%
5 Chemicals				
5.1 chemicals, rubber	0.340	3.1%	–	–
5.2 chemicals, petrochemicals	–	–	0.414	3.2%
6 Timber	1.810	16.5%	1.990	15.2%
7 Construction materials	0.373	3.4%	0.368	2.8%
8 Printing	0.110	1.0%	–	–
9 Light industry	2.237	20.4%	2.853	21.8%
10 Food industry	1.272	11.6%	1.568	12.0%
11 Other industry	0.373	3.4%	0.869	6.6%
12 Industry, total	10.967	100.0%	13.079	100.0%

Note: The most important difference between industry totals in cols. 1 and 2 is the exclusion of employment in artisan industry (see table G.3) from the former and its inclusion in the latter.

Sources: Col. 1: the industry total (row 12), in millions, and percentages (rows 1–10) are given in TsSU (1956), 43–4. Other figures are calculated by me. Row 11 is row 12, less the sum of rows 1–10. Col. 2: industry and sector totals, rows 1–10 and 12, are given in TsSU (1966), 140. Other figures are calculated by me. Row 11 is row 12, less the sum of rows 1–10. Row 11 is a residual calculated from figures in each source. In the case of the pre-1960 classification, we are told that industrial workers employed on building sites were included in the total, but not in the subtotals, and there were 600,000 of them in 1960, suggesting that these account for most of the 1940 residual. In the case of the post-1960 classification, the residual included employees in nonferrous metallurgy and printing, and may be further decomposed roughly as follows (millions):

Nonferrous metallurgy	0.227
Printing	0.110
Not specified	0.533
Other industry, total	0.869

The figure for the printing industry is from col. 1, row 8; that for nonferrous metallurgy shows employment under Narkomtsvetmet for the second quarter of 1940, from RGAE, f. 4372, op. 41, d. 553, l. 108; it therefore includes nonindustrial employees of the commissariat, and omits employees of other commissariats engaged in sideline nonferrous metallurgy.

Table G.2. *Employment in public-sector industry, excluding artisan industry, 1940–5 (pre-1960 classification and millions)*

	1940	1941	1942	1943	1944	1945
(A) All employees						
1 Industry, total	10.967	10.035	7.171	7.492	8.465	9.508
(B) Manual employees						
2 MBMW	2.395	2.304	1.874	2.092	2.186	2.261
3 Basic industry, total	3.398	3.394	2.179	2.221	2.566	3.129
3.1 iron, steel	0.332	0.286	0.166	0.193	0.244	0.298
3.2 other basic industry	3.066	3.108	2.013	2.028	2.322	2.831
4 Light industry, total	2.497	2.129	1.438	1.418	1.660	1.799
4.1 light industry	1.468	1.312	0.872	0.858	1.001	1.076
4.2 food industry	1.029	0.817	0.566	0.560	0.659	0.723
5 Industry, total	8.290	7.827	5.491	5.731	6.412	7.189

Source: Row 1: TsSU (1959), 414. Rows 2, 3.1, 4.1, 4.2, 5: TsSU (1959), 82. Row 3: row 5, less the sum of rows 2, 4. Row 3.2: row 3, less row 3.1. This assumes, in line with figures for 1940 shown in table G.1, that all employees not elsewhere specified were employed in basic industry other than iron and steel (i.e. rows 3–8 in table G.1, plus nonferrous metallurgy). Row 4: the sum of rows 4.1, 4.2.

Table G.3. *Employment in artisan industry (arteli promyslovoi kooperatsii), 1940–5 (millions)*

	1940	1941	1942	1943	1944	1945
1 *Promkooperatsiia*	2.112	1.801	0.900	1.000	1.200	1.500

Sources: 1940: the difference between public-sector employment totals on the post-1960 and pre-1960 classifications, from table G.1, row 12, cols. 1, 2. 1941: interpolated on table G.2, row 4. 1942–5: GARF, f. 3922/4372, op. 4, d. 115, ll. 10–15; this source also gives 2,200,000 for 1940.

There remains a large unclassified residual in all years, which I attribute to 'other basic' industry.

From these starting points we may set ourselves the goal of accounting for the industrial employment of both manual workers, and of all employees. As far as manual employment is concerned, table G.2 is deficient by omission of workers in artisan industry and in NKVD enterprises. Annual averages for employment in artisan industry are reported from archival sources or interpolated in table G.3, and are

Table G.4. *Employment in NKVD industrial establishments, by branch, 1940–5 (millions)*

	1940	1941	1942	1943	1944	1945
1 Nonferrous metals	0.270	0.302	0.235	0.194	0.195	0.226
2 Fuels	0.115	0.128	0.100	0.083	0.083	0.096
3 Timber	0.176	0.196	0.153	0.126	0.127	0.147
4 Construction materials	0.115	0.128	0.100	0.083	0.083	0.096
5 Industry, total	0.676	0.756	0.588	0.486	0.488	0.565

Source: Table I.3, rows 2–2.4.

attributed to employment in light industry. The role of GULAG as a supplier of labour is a little more complicated. I presume that forced labourers subcontracted to civilian narkomaty by GULAG are already counted in official public-sector totals. But those engaged in industrial production in NKVD establishments were not so counted, and must be added on to the number employed in 'other basic' industry (mining for gold and coal, logging, brickmaking and so on). Table G.4 shows a rough estimate of their numbers, the origin of which is reserved for appendix I.

Table G.5 summarises our knowledge or estimates of wartime employment in Soviet industry. Part (A) deals with all employees, and shows how totals for the public sector, artisan industry, and NKVD establishments may be summed for an aggregate figure in each year. Part (B) shows how the same may be done for manual employees alone, giving rise to a rudimentary sector classification: MBMW, basic industry (comprising the iron and steel industry, and 'other basic' industry), and light industry (comprising separately the light and food industries). It shows how the number of nonmanual employees may be derived in each year by subtracting manual employment from the PPP aggregate. And it shows how PPP employment in civilian branches may be derived by subtracting our estimate of defence industry employment (appendix D) from the industry total.

Hours of work of manual workers in industry can be established on almost the same sector classification as manual employment (only separate figures for the iron and steel industry are lacking). Table G.6 shows how figures for the length of the working day, and days worked, can be combined to give annual hours in industry as a whole in each year, and in MBMW, the light industry, and the food industry separately; the same for basic industry is then derived as a residual.

Table G.5. *Employment in Soviet industry, by type of establishment, type of employee, and branch of activity, 1940–5 (millions)*

		1940	1941	1942	1943	1944	1945
(A) By type of establishment							
1	Public sector (pre-1960)	10.967	10.035	7.171	7.492	8.465	9.508
2	Artisan industry	2.112	1.801	0.900	1.000	1.200	1.500
3	NKVD	0.676	0.756	0.588	0.486	0.488	0.565
4	Industry, total	13.755	12.591	8.659	8.978	10.153	11.573
(B) By type of employee and branch of activity							
5	Manual employees	11.078	10.383	6.979	7.217	8.100	9.254
5.1	MBMW	2.395	2.304	1.874	2.092	2.186	2.261
5.2	basic industry	4.074	4.150	2.767	2.707	3.054	3.694
5.2a	iron, steel	0.332	0.286	0.166	0.193	0.244	0.298
5.2b	other basic	3.742	3.864	2.601	2.514	2.810	3.396
5.3	light industry	4.609	3.930	2.338	2.418	2.860	3.299
6	Nonmanual employees	2.677	2.208	1.680	1.761	2.053	2.319
7	Industry, total	13.755	12.591	8.659	8.978	10.153	11.573
7.1	defence industry	1.751	1.879	2.743	2.879	2.884	2.062
7.2	civilian industry	12.004	10.712	5.916	6.099	7.269	9.511

Sources: Row 1: table G.2, row 1. Row 2: table G.3, row 1. Row 3: table G.4, row 5. Row 4: the sum of rows 1–3. Row 5: the sum of rows 5.1, 5.2, and 5.3. Rows 5.1 and 5.2a: table G.2, rows 2, 3.1. Row 5.2: the sum of rows 5.2a and 5.2b. Row 5.2b: table G.2, row 3.2, plus table G.4, row 5. Row 5.3: table G.2, row 4, plus row 2. Row 6: row 4, less row 5. Row 7: as row 4. Row 7.1: table D.4, row 9. Row 7.2: row 7, less row 7.1.

Table G.7 deals with trends in wage earnings. As explained in appendix A, our information is extremely restricted. Annual or monthly wage earnings of manual workers in public-sector industry are known for 1940 and 1944, the intervening years being filled by interpolation (row 1). Hourly earnings (row 2) are calculated by dividing annual hours into annual earnings, the resulting series showing a dip between 1941 and 1944, interpreted here not as a cut in hourly wage rates, but as an increase in unpaid overtime.

This table also makes an attempt to provide some sectoral differentiation to hourly earnings behaviour, but the attempt is very crude. Index numbers of annual hours in MBMW, basic industry, and light industry respectively are divided into index numbers of industrywide annual earnings (row 1.1) in order to suggest the trend of hourly earnings not just in industry as a whole (row 2.1) but also by sector (rows 2.1a

Table G.6. *Hours worked in public-sector industry, 1940–5 (pre-1960 classification and manual employees)*

	1940	1941	1942	1943	1944	1945
(A) Total hours, millions						
1 MBMW	5045	5849	5366	6082	6269	5363
2 Basic industry	6976	7831	5589	5968	6791	7511
3 Light industry	5024	4820	3319	3472	4148	4195
3.1 light industry	–	2899	1962	2115	2561	2529
3.2 food industry	–	1921	1357	1357	1587	1667
4 Industry, total	17044	18500	14275	15522	17207	17070
4.1 of which, non-MBMW	11999	12652	8909	9439	10939	11707
(B) Hours per worker						
5 MBMW	2106	2538	2863	2908	2868	2372
6 Basic industry	2053	2307	2565	2687	2647	2401
7 Light industry	2012	2264	2308	2448	2499	2332
7.1 light industry	–	2210	2250	2465	2558	2350
7.2 food industry	–	2352	2397	2423	2408	2305
8 Industry, total	2056	2364	2600	2708	2684	2374
8.1 of which, non-MBMW	2036	2291	2463	2594	2588	2376
(C) Days per worker						
9 MBMW	269.7	290.8	298.3	297.9	298.4	277.1
10 Basic industry	–	–	–	–	–	–
11 Light industry	–	–	–	–	–	–
11.1 light industry	267.7	274.5	261.4	276.0	283.3	271.4
11.2 food industry	273.2	288.2	288.5	286.4	286.0	279.8
12 Industry, total	269.8	284.1	286.3	291.5	293.0	280.0
(D) Hours per day						
13 MBMW	7.81	8.73	9.60	9.76	9.61	8.56
14 Basic industry	–	–	–	–	–	–
15 Light industry	–	–	–	–	–	–
15.1 light industry	–	8.05	8.61	8.93	9.03	8.66
15.2 food industry	–	8.16	8.31	8.46	8.42	8.24
16 Industry, total	7.62	8.32	9.08	9.29	9.16	8.48

Sources: Rows 1, 3.1, 3.2, 4: rows 5, 7.1, 7.2, 8, multiplied respectively by table G.2, rows 2, 4.1, 4.2, 5. Row 2: row 4.1, less row 3. Row 3: the sum of rows 3.1, 3.2, except for 1940 which is row 7, multiplied by table G.2, row 4. Row 4.1: row 4, less row 1. Rows 5, 7.1, 7.2, 8: rows 9, 11.1, 11.2, 12, multiplied respectively by rows 13, 15.1, 15.2, 16. Row 6: row 2, divided by table G.2, row 3. Row 7: row 11, multiplied by row 15, except for 1940 which is obtained by interpolation on row 8.1. Row 8.1: row 4.1, divided by table G.2 (row 5, less row 2). Rows 9–16: TsSU (1959), 86–9

Table G.7. *Wage earnings in public-sector industry, 1940–5 (rubles and per cent of 1940)*

	1940	1941	1942	1943	1944	1945
(A) Per year						
1 Wage earnings (rubles)	3960	4183	4419	4667	4930	5208
1.1 % of 1940	100%	106%	112%	118%	125%	132%
(B) Per hour						
2 Wage earnings (rubles)	1.93	1.77	1.70	1.72	1.84	2.19
2.1 % of 1940	100%	92%	88%	89%	95%	114%
2.1a MBMW	100%	88%	82%	85%	91%	117%
2.1b basic industry	100%	94%	89%	90%	97%	112%
2.1c light industry	100%	94%	97%	97%	100%	113%

Sources: Row 1: for 1940 and 1945, Mitrofanova (1971), 498; other years are obtained by geometric interpolation. Row 1.1: based on row 1. Row 2: row 1, divided by table G.6, row 8. Row 2.1: based on row 2. Rows 2.1a–2.1c: average annual earnings being assumed to grow in each case at the same rate as in industry as a whole, row 1.1 is divided by an index of hours worked based on table G.6, rows 5–7.

through 2.1c). Not surprisingly, since hours worked rose most in defence industry, less so in basic industry, and least in light industry, hourly earnings are shown as having fallen most in defence industry, and so on. This does not imply that the level of hourly earnings in defence industry fell below the level in other sectors, since only the trend, not the level is suggested; of course, the level was higher in defence industry, and remained higher throughout the war. If there was some convergence of levels, however, it would not be surprising or without parallel in other countries' experience.

Appendix H: agricultural production

Agricultural production is estimated mainly from product series in physical units, valued in rubles at 1937 prices, plus an allowance for net investment in livestock, but several minor complications arise on the way.

The product series are shown in table H.1. Official data are used except in the case of vegetables, for which entries under 1941–4 are missing. Table H.2 shows how the gap is filled; the area sown to vegetables is known from official data, and the trend of vegetable yields between 1940 and 1945 is interpolated on potato yields.

Net investment in livestock is estimated in table H.3 from figures for stocks on 1 January of each year, but assumptions must be made about the division of stock losses in the early years of the war between capital losses and disinvestment, since the latter, but not the former, is subtracted from agriculture's GNP contribution. A distinction is made between trends in the occupied and unoccupied regions. I count the decline in stocks in the occupied regions, *less* evacuated stocks, as a capital loss; I also assume that all net investment took place in the unoccupied regions, and that this net investment can be measured by stock increases *less* a contribution attributable to evacuated stocks which diminished through time.

Products (table H.1), *plus* net investment (table H.3), multiplied by 1937 prices (table H.4), give real gross output at 1937 prices (table H.5).

The remaining noteworthy feature of the procedure not yet described is an extra allowance for unrecorded output of potatoes and vegetables (table H.5, row 13), which begins in 1942, peaks in 1943–4, and tails off in 1945. The logic of this allowance stems from government legislation at the outbreak of war which extended the right to an allotment for private cultivation from the peasantry to the whole population. City allotment farming became widespread and clearly made a substantial contribution to the subsistence of the urban population. I assume that

Table H.1. *Agricultural products, 1940–5 (units)*

	1940	1941	1942	1943	1944	1945
1 Grains, million tons	95.5	55.9	29.7	29.4	49.1	47.2
2 Potatoes, million tons	75.9	26.4	23.8	34.9	54.9	58.1
3 Vegetables, million tons	13.7	5.5	4.3	6.7	10.2	10.3
4 Sunflower seeds, '000 tons	2636	909	283	784	1042	843
5 Sugar beets, mn tons	18.0	1.9	2.1	1.3	4.1	5.5
6 Raw cotton, '000 tons	2237	2478	1329	726	1131	1161
7 Flax fibre, '000 tons	349	133	210	156	167	150
8 Wool, '000 tons	161	161	125	100	103	111
9 Milk, million tons	33.6	25.5	15.8	16.4	22.0	26.4
10 Meat (live weight), '000 tons	7502	7044	3405	3288	3632	4690
11 Eggs, billion	12.2	9.3	4.5	3.5	3.6	4.9

Sources: Rows 1, 2, 4–7: TsSU (1959), 275, 291. Row 3: table H.2, row 1. Rows 8–11: IVOVSS, vol. 6 (1965), 319.

Table H.2. *Vegetable harvests, 1940–5*

	1940	1941	1942	1943	1944	1945
(A) Vegetables						
1 Harvest, million tons	13.7	5.5	4.3	6.7	10.2	10.3
2 Sown area, million ha.	1.5	1.0	0.8	1.2	1.7	1.8
3 Yield, tons/ha.	9.1	5.5	5.4	5.6	6.0	5.7
3.1 % of 1940	100%	61%	59%	61%	65%	63%
(B) Potatoes						
4 Sown area, million ha.	7.7	4.3	3.9	5.4	7.7	8.3
5 Yield, tons/ha.	9.9	6.1	6.1	6.5	7.1	7.0
5.1 % of 1940	100%	62%	62%	66%	72%	71%

Sources: Row 1: for 1940 and 1945, see IVOVSS, 6 (1965), 67; for intervening years, row 2 multiplied by row 3. Row 2: TsSU (1959), 302. Row 3: for 1940 and 1945, row 1 divided by row 2; for intervening years, interpolated on row 3.1. Row 3.1: for 1940 and 1945, based on row 3; for other years, based on row 5.1, corrected pro rata for the difference between rows 3.1 and 5.1 in 1945. Row 4: TsSU (1959), 302. Row 5: table H.1, row 2, divided by row 4 of this table. Row 5.1: based on row 5.

Table H.3. Net investment in livestock, 1941–5 (million head)

		1941	1942	1943	1944	1945	1946
(A) All-Union herds, 1 January							
1	Large horned stock	51.5	31.4	28.4	33.9	44.2	47.4
1.1	cows	27.8	15.0	13.8	16.5	21.6	22.7
1.2	other large horned stock	23.7	16.4	14.6	17.4	22.6	24.7
3	Pigs	27.5	8.2	6.0	5.6	8.8	10.5
4	Sheep, goats	91.6	70.6	61.8	63.3	70.2	69.9
5	Horses	21.0	10.0	8.1	7.7	9.9	10.7
(B) Herds in rear regions, 1 January							
6	Large horned stock	28.0	26.3	26.5	25.8	26.4	27.0
6.1	cows	12.9	12.6	12.7	12.1	12.1	12.3
6.2	other large horned stock	15.1	13.7	13.8	13.7	14.3	14.7
8	Pigs	7.9	6.5	5.8	4.1	3.8	3.8
9	Sheep, goats	60.9	58.6	59.1	55.5	56.0	54.0
10	Horses	9.8	8.5	7.6	6.3	5.7	5.8
(C) Evacuated from frontline to rear regions, 1941–2							
11	Large horned stock	–	–	2.390	–	–	–
11.1	cows	–	–	0.914	–	–	–
11.2	other large horned stock	–	–	1.476	–	–	–
13	Pigs	–	–	0.186	–	–	–
14	Sheep, goats	–	–	5.082	–	–	–
15	Horses	–	–	0.818	–	–	–
(D) Herds in rear regions, less evacuated stock, 1 January							
16	Large horned stock	28.0	24.5	24.1	23.4	25.2	27.0
16.1	cows	12.9	11.9	11.8	11.2	11.6	12.3
16.2	other large horned stock	15.1	12.6	12.3	12.2	13.6	14.7
18	Pigs	7.9	6.4	5.6	3.9	3.7	3.8
19	Sheep, goats	60.9	54.8	54.0	50.4	53.5	54.0
20	Horses	9.8	7.9	6.8	5.5	5.3	5.8
(E) Net investment							
21	Large horned stock						
21.1	cows	–1.0	–0.1	–0.6	0.5	0.7	–
21.2	other large horned stock	–2.5	–0.3	–0.1	1.3	1.1	–
23	Pigs	–1.5	–0.7	–1.7	–0.2	0.1	–
24	Sheep, goats	–6.1	–0.8	–3.6	3.0	0.5	–
25	Horses	–1.9	–1.1	–1.3	–0.2	0.5	–

Sources: Rows 1–10: TsSU (1959), 325. Rows 11–15: TsSU (1959), 281. Rows 16–20: the table assumes that three quarters of the livestock herds shown as having been evacuated during 1941–2 were present in livestock herds of the rear regions on the first of 1942; 100 per cent on the first of 1943 and 1944; 50

Table H.4. *Prevailing prices of agricultural products and livestock, 1937 (rubles)*

(A) Per ton	
1 Grains, tons	225
2 Potatoes, tons	210
3 Vegetables, tons	340
4 Sunflower seeds, tons	550
5 Sugar beets, tons	44
6 Raw cotton, tons	1650
7 Flax fibre, tons	1050
8 Wool, tons	7500
9 Milk, tons	570
10 Meat (live weight), tons	2080
(B) Per thousand	
11 Eggs	320
(C) Per head	
12 Cows	390
13 Other large horned stock	195
14 Pigs	140
15 Sheep, goats	48
16 Horses	390

Source: Rows 1–10: Bergson (1961), 324; Moorsteen and Powell (1966), 621. Rows 11–16: Moorsteen and Powell (1966), 107; prices are for average weight of 1932.

(Sources to table H.3)
per cent on the first of 1945, and nil by the first of 1946 (in other words, it is assumed that evacuated stock died or was returned to the western regions in the course of 1944–5). Rows 21–25: the change over each year in rows 16–20; that is, it is assumed that all net investment took place in the rear regions (in particular, all disinvestment in the occupied territories is treated as a capital loss). Net investment in the rear regions is then measured by deducting the gain in evacuated stock from the change in total stocks.

Table H.5. *Agricultural gross output, 1940–5 (billion rubles and 1937 prices)*

		1940	1941	1942	1943	1944	1945
1	Grains	21.5	12.6	6.7	6.6	11.1	10.6
2	Potatoes	15.9	5.5	5.0	7.3	11.5	12.2
3	Vegetables	4.7	1.9	1.5	2.3	3.5	3.5
4	Sunflower seeds	1.4	0.5	0.2	0.4	0.6	0.5
5	Sugar beets	0.8	0.1	0.1	0.1	0.2	0.2
6	Raw cotton	3.7	4.1	2.2	1.2	1.9	1.9
7	Flax fibre	0.4	0.1	0.2	0.2	0.2	0.2
8	Wool	1.2	1.2	0.9	0.8	0.8	0.8
9	Milk	19.2	14.5	9.0	9.3	12.6	15.1
10	Meat (live weight)	15.6	14.7	7.1	6.8	7.6	9.8
11	Eggs	3.9	3.0	1.4	1.1	1.1	1.6
12	Subtotal	88.3	58.2	34.3	36.1	50.9	56.3
13	Unrecorded output of potatoes, vegetables	0.0	0.0	1.3	3.8	6.0	3.1
14	Net investment in livestock	0.6	–2.1	–0.7	–1.2	0.5	0.7
15	Total	88.9	56.1	34.9	38.8	57.3	60.2
15.1	% of 1937	111%	70%	44%	48%	72%	75%

Sources: Rows 1–11: current yields (table H.1) valued at 1937 prices (table H.4, rows 1–11). Row 12: the sum of rows 1–11. Row 13: fixed at 20 per cent of the sum of rows 2, 3, in 1942 and 1945, 40 per cent in 1943–4. Row 14: net investment (table H.3, rows 21–25) valued at 1937 prices (table H.4, rows 12–16). Row 15: the sum of rows 12, 13, 14. Row 15.1: for 1940, Moorsteen and Powell (1966), 622–3; other years interpolated on row 15.

most of this activity took the form of own consumption of potatoes and vegetables, that the output (of potatoes) and area sown (to vegetables) went unregistered, and that an allowance is therefore necessary.

Appendix I: the workforce

The working population is built up from numbers employed in the public-sector and artisan industry, collective farms, NKVD establishments, and armed forces personnel.

Table I.1 shows official figures for public-sector employment by branch in each year of the war. The public sector is defined narrowly on the pre-1960 concept, excluding artisan industry. Thus, to find total civil employment, a number of excluded categories must be added. To industrial employment must be added numbers in artisan industry (table G.3). Public-sector agricultural employment was limited to state farms (*sovkhozy*) and establishments supplying machinery services (*MTS*), so to agricultural employment must be added collective farmers (table I.2). In addition, missing from all the public-sector employment figures are forced labourers in NKVD establishments (tables I.3 to I.7).

The population of forced labourers available to the NKVD may be thought of as originating in two categories, prisoners held in camps and colonies, and 'labour-settlers' (these groups were discussed in more detail in chapter 5). From the point of view of labour utilisation, this population was again divided into two parts. One part, sometimes referred to as the NKVD 'special contingent' (*spetskontingent NKVD*) was subcontracted to civilian agencies, and is already counted within the public-sector workforce totals shown in table I.1. The second part was retained to work within NKVD establishments ranging from state farms in agriculture and factories, mines, and timber camps in basic industry, to construction sites and transport operations including canals and railways (table I.3); these must be estimated from basic data by a complicated process (tables I.4 to I.7, which are built upon each other in reverse order).

Population totals for the population under NKVD control on the first day of each year (table I.6) are used to generate annual averages (table I.5), except for 1941 when it is clear that June saw a sharp peak in the

Table I.1. *Employment in the public sector, excluding artisan industry, 1940–5 (pre-1960 classification and millions)*

	1940	1941	1942	1943	1944	1945
1 Agriculture	2.290	1.904	1.554	1.743	2.310	2.532
1.1 sovkhozy	1.760	1.476	1.291	1.474	1.972	2.147
1.2 MTS	0.530	0.428	0.263	0.269	0.338	0.385
2 Industry	10.967	10.035	7.171	7.492	8.465	9.508
3 Construction	1.563	1.387	0.857	0.921	1.344	1.515
4 Transport, comms	3.903	3.447	2.306	2.396	2.958	3.537
4.1 transport	3.425	3.034	2.032	2.107	2.597	3.111
4.2 communications	0.478	0.413	0.274	0.289	0.361	0.426
5 Trade, catering	3.323	2.834	1.677	1.718	2.076	2.462
6 Civilian services	9.146	7.696	4.807	5.132	6.470	7.709
6.1 finance	0.262	0.224	0.133	0.131	0.166	0.197
6.2 health	1.507	1.402	0.965	1.125	1.336	1.419
6.3 education	2.930	2.648	1.606	1.634	2.128	2.551
6.4 government	1.825	1.440	0.924	0.970	1.301	1.645
6.5 other	2.622	1.982	1.179	1.272	1.539	1.897
7 Total	31.192	27.303	18.372	19.402	23.623	27.263

Source: TsSU (1959), 414.

Table I.2. *The collective farm working population, 1940–5 (millions)*

	1940	1941	1942	1943	1944	1945
(A) End of year						
1 Able bodied	35.4	16.4	15.1	16.6	22.0	23.9
2 Youths	7.1	4.0	4.7	5.3	6.4	6.1
3 Retired, unfit	4.4	2.5	2.8	3.2	4.5	4.3
4 Total	47.0	22.9	22.5	25.0	32.8	34.2
(B) Annual average						
5 Total	47.0	34.9	22.7	23.8	28.9	33.5

Sources: Row 1: Arutiunian (1970), 398. Row 2: Uchastie (1962), 26–7, except 1945 from Arutiunian (1970), 324. Row 3: Uchastie (1962), 26–7, except 1942 and 1945, interpolated on the number of youths (row 2). Row 4: the sum of rows 1–3. Row 5: the average of the figures for 31 December of the given year and the preceding year, except 1940 for which the figure of the given year alone is taken.

Table I.3. *Employment in NKVD establishments, 1940–5 (millions)*

	1940	1941	1942	1943	1944	1945
1 Agriculture	0.051	0.057	0.044	0.036	0.037	0.042
2 Industry	0.676	0.756	0.588	0.486	0.488	0.565
2.1 nonferrous metals	0.270	0.302	0.235	0.194	0.195	0.226
2.2 fuels	0.115	0.128	0.100	0.083	0.083	0.096
2.3 timber	0.176	0.196	0.153	0.126	0.127	0.147
2.4 construction materials	0.115	0.128	0.100	0.083	0.083	0.096
3 Construction	0.792	0.886	0.689	0.569	0.572	0.662
4 Transport	0.051	0.057	0.044	0.036	0.037	0.042
5 Total	1.570	1.755	1.365	1.128	1.133	1.312

Sources: Rows 1–4: row 5, multiplied by table I.4, corresponding rows. Row 5: table I.5, row 4.

Table I.4. *Employment in NKVD establishments, by branch, 1941-plan, from Jasny*

	Millions	%
1 Agriculture	0.075	3%
2 Industry	1.000	43%
2.1 nonferrous metals	0.400	17%
2.2 fuels	0.170	7%
2.3 timber	0.260	11%
2.4 construction materials	0.170	7%
3 Construction	1.172	50%
4 Transport	0.075	3%
5 Total	2.322	100%

Source: Jasny (1951c), 412–15.

NKVD-controlled population; in 1941, therefore, the average for the year exceeded the population totals for the first day of both 1941 and 1942, and must be calculated by a special procedure (table I.7). From the total population, now on an annual average basis (table I.5, row 1), those subcontracted to civilian agencies (row 2), and those unfit for work (row 3), must be deducted, treating GULAG prisoners and labour-settlers separately; at the end, a residual is left (row 4) for employment directly by the NKVD. The latter population is assumed to have been distributed among branches of the economy in the proportions shown in table

Table I.5. *Employment in NKVD establishments, 1940–5 (millions)*

	1940	1941	1942	1943	1944	1945
1 Total available	2.759	3.055	2.449	2.029	1.982	2.303
1.1 GULAG prisoners	1.795	2.077	1.631	1.332	1.320	1.509
1.2 labour-settlers	0.964	0.978	0.818	0.697	0.661	0.794
2 Subcontracted	0.704	0.758	0.616	0.515	0.498	0.585
2.1 GULAG prisoners	0.306	0.354	0.278	0.227	0.225	0.257
2.2 labour-settlers	0.398	0.404	0.338	0.288	0.273	0.328
3 Unfit for work	0.485	0.542	0.467	0.386	0.350	0.405
4 Retained by NKVD	1.570	1.755	1.365	1.128	1.133	1.312

Sources: Rows 1, 1.1, 1.2: for each year except 1941, the annual average is calculated from table I.6, rows 1–3 as the mean of the values on the first of the given year and the first of the year following. For 1941, see table I.7, col. 6. Row 2: the sum of rows 2.1, 2.2. Row 2.1: the figure for 1944 is from Zemskov (1991), 25, being 17 per cent of the annual average shown in row 1.1; other years are interpolated on the latter row. Row 2.2: according to Zemskov (1992), 16, the figure for the second half of 1941 was 387,070, which is 41 per cent of the average figure for the number of labour-settlers in the same period, estimated as 936,547 in table I.7, row 2, col. 5. This percentage is applied to row 1.2. Row 3: according to Zemskov (1991), 23, of the GULAG population, 23.6 per cent were unfit for work in 1941, rising to 25.5 per cent in 1942. These percentages are applied to the total potentially available for forced labour in NKVD establishments (row 1, less row 2), as follows: the 1941 percentage is applied to this total in 1940, 1941, and 1944–5, and the 1942 percentage to the total for 1942–3. Row 4: row 1, less the sum of rows 2 and 3.

Table I.6. *Forced labourers, 1 January 1940–6 (millions)*

	1940	1941	1942	1943	1944	1945	1946
1 GULAG prisoners	1.660	1.930	1.777	1.484	1.180	1.461	1.557
1.1 in camps	1.344	1.501	1.416	0.984	0.664	0.716	0.601
1.2 in colonies	0.316	0.429	0.361	0.500	0.516	0.745	0.956
2 Labour-settlers	0.998	0.930	0.912	0.724	0.670	0.653	0.936
3 Total	2.658	2.860	2.689	2.209	1.850	2.113	2.493

Sources: Rows 1, 1.1, 1.2: Bacon (1994), 24. Row 2: Bacon (1994), 30; the 1946 figure is actually for 1 December, 1945. Row 3: the sum of rows 1 and 2.

Table I.7. *Forced labourers, 1941 (millions)*

				1941:		
	1941 1 Jan. (1)	1941 1 Jul. (2)	1942 1 Jan. (3)	first half (4)	second half (5)	annual average (6)
1 GULAG prisoners	1.930	2.300	1.777	2.115	2.039	2.077
2 Labour-settlers	0.930	–	0.912	1.019	0.937	0.978
3 Total	2.860	–	2.689	3.134	2.975	3.055

Sources: Cols 1, 3: table I.6, rows 1, 2, 3. Col. 2: Bacon (1992a), 1077. Col. 4: row 1 is the average of cols 1, 2. Row 2 is interpolated on row 1. Row 3 is the sum of rows 1 and 2. Col. 5: row 1 is the average of cols 2, 3. Row 2 is a figure for 1 October from Zemskov (1992), 17. Row 3 is the sum of rows 1, 2. Col. 6: the average of cols 4, 5.

Table I.8. *Military personnel, 1940–5 (millions)*

	1940	1941	1942	1943	1944	1945
1 Army, navy	4.550	6.600	10.832	11.346	11.718	11.600
1.1 army	4.200	6.200	10.305	10.841	11.235	–
1.2 navy	0.350	0.400	0.526	0.505	0.483	–
2 NKVD troops	0.450	0.500	0.508	0.513	0.507	0.500
3 Total	5.000	7.100	11.340	11.858	12.225	12.100

Sources: Row 1: the sum of rows 1.1 and 1.2, except for 1945 which is taken from Sokolov (1968), 215. Row 1.1: the 1940 figure is obtained as follows. Khrushchev gave the size of the army and navy at the beginning of 1941 as 4,200,000 in *Pravda* (15 Jan., 1960). However, this figure seems on the low side, since the size of the Army was set at 3,990,993 in May 1940, according to *Izv. TsK KPSS*, 2 (1990), 180–1. According to Samsonov (1985), 24, the ground forces alone totalled 4,261,000 (79% of 5,373,000) at the beginning of 1941. Here, Khrushchev's figure is applied to the Army as an annual average for 1940. For 1941 I average an estimate of 5,000,000 for the first half with the September figure given in table I.9, row 1. For each year subsequent to 1941, I take the average of figures for the given year shown in table I.9, row 1. Rows 1.2, 2: figures shown for 1940 and 1941 are interpolated freehand on the basis of figures for 1942–4; the latter are averages of figures for the given year shown in table I.9, rows 2, 3. According to Samsonov (1985), 24, the Navy accounted for 312,000 service personnel in May 1940 (5.8% of 5,373,000). Row 3: the sum of rows 1 and 2.

Table I.9. *Armed forces' ration strength, 1941–4 (millions)*

	1941 (Sept.)	1942 (March)	1942 (May)	1942 (June)	1942 (July)	1942 (Aug.)
1. Army, total	7.400	10.529	10.900	10.200	9.977	10.072
1.1 regular rations	–	9.598	9.950	9.350	9.205	9.322
1.2 reduced rations	–	0.931	0.950	0.850	0.772	0.750
2. Navy, total	–	–	0.493	0.510	0.510	0.523
2.1 regular rations	–	–	0.526	–	0.540	0.540
2.2 reduced rations	–	–	0.019	–	0.019	0.019
3. NKVD	–	–	0.545	0.550	0.559	0.559
3.1 regular rations	–	–	–	–	–	0.519
3.2 reduced rations	–	–	–	–	–	0.004

	1942 (Oct.)	1943 (Feb.)	1943 (Apr.)	1943 (June)	1943 (July)	1944 (Mar.)
1. Army, total	10.154	10.445	10.552	11.119	11.247	11.235
1.1 regular rations	9.254	9.455	9.486	10.300	10.547	9.980
1.2 reduced rations	0.900	0.990	1.066	0.819	0.700	1.255
2. Navy, total	0.500	0.512	0.521	0.476	0.479	0.479
2.1 regular rations	0.465	0.450	0.400	0.400	0.410	0.410
2.2 reduced rations	0.015	0.016	0.016	0.016	0.017	0.017
3. NKVD	0.480	0.466	0.416	0.416	0.427	0.427
3.1 regular rations	0.496	0.506	0.516	0.471	0.473	0.473
3.2 reduced rations	0.004	0.006	0.005	0.005	0.006	0.006

Source: RTsKhIDNI, f. 644, op. 1, d. 9, l. 50; d. 23, ll. 127–9; d. 33, ll. 48–50; d. 39, ll. 74–8; d. 41, ll. 163–5; d. 50, ll. 71–4; d. 61, ll. 88–91; d. 73, ll. 119–22; d. 85, ll. 95–6; d. 100, ll. 117–18; d. 125, ll. 35–6; d. 138, ll. 205–6; d. 218, ll. 101–4.

I.4, derived from Jasny's original study of the 1941-plan, which has stood the test of time with remarkable endurance. Results appear in table I.3.

Those employed in the public sector, artisan industry, collective farms, and NKVD establishments are designated the 'employed population'. For the 'working population' the number of military personnel must be added. Military personnel fell under the jurisdiction of three commissariats: NKO (the defence commissariat, responsible for the Red Army, including the air force), NKVMF (the navy commissariat), and NKVD (internal affairs, responsible for internal troops). All are counted as supplying military services, but only the army and navy are consid-

Table I.10. *The working population by type of establishment, 1940–5 (millions)*

	1940	1941	1942	1943	1944	1945
1 Public sector (pre-1960)	31.192	27.303	18.372	19.402	23.623	27.263
2 Artisan industry	2.112	1.801	0.900	1.000	1.200	1.500
3 Collective farms	46.976	34.932	22.679	23.754	28.928	33.516
4 NKVD establishments	1.570	1.755	1.365	1.128	1.133	1.312
5 Armed forces	5.000	7.100	11.340	11.858	12.225	12.100
6 Total	86.850	72.891	54.656	57.142	67.109	75.691

Sources: Row 1: table I.1, row 7. Row 2: table G.3, row 1. Row 3: table I.2, row 5. Row 4: table I.3, row 5. Row 5: table I.8, row 3. Row 5: the sum of rows 1–5.

Table I.11. *The working population, by branch of activity, 1940–5 (millions)*

	1940	1941	1942	1943	1944	1945
1 Agriculture	49.317	36.893	24.277	25.534	31.275	36.090
2 Industry	13.755	12.591	8.659	8.978	10.153	11.573
2.1 defence industry	1.751	1.879	2.743	2.879	2.884	2.062
2.2 civilian industry	12.004	10.712	5.916	6.099	7.269	9.511
3 Construction	2.355	2.273	1.546	1.490	1.916	2.177
4 Transport, communications	3.954	3.504	2.350	2.432	2.995	3.579
5 Trade, catering	3.323	2.834	1.677	1.718	2.076	2.462
6 Civilian services	9.146	7.696	4.807	5.132	6.470	7.709
6.1 finance	0.262	0.224	0.133	0.131	0.166	0.197
6.2 health	1.507	1.402	0.965	1.125	1.336	1.419
6.3 education	2.930	2.648	1.606	1.634	2.128	2.551
6.4 government	1.825	1.440	0.924	0.970	1.301	1.645
6.5 other	2.622	1.982	1.179	1.272	1.539	1.897
7 Employed population	81.850	65.791	43.316	45.284	54.885	63.591
8 Military services	5.000	7.100	11.340	11.858	12.225	12.100
8.1 Army, Navy	4.550	6.600	10.832	11.346	11.718	11.600
8.2 NKVD	0.450	0.500	0.508	0.513	0.507	0.500
9 Working population	86.850	72.891	54.656	57.142	67.109	75.691

Sources: Row 1: table I.1, row 1, plus table I.2, row 5, plus table I.3, row 1. Rows 2, 2.1, 2.2: table G.5, rows 7, 7.1, 7.2. Rows 3, 4: table I.1, plus table I.3, corresponding rows. Rows 5, 6, 6.1–6.5: table I.1, corresponding rows. Row 7: sum of rows 1, 2, 3, 4, 5, 6. Rows 8, 8.1, 8.2: table I.8, rows 1–3. Row 9: sum of rows 7, 8.

ered part of the defence sector when it comes to calculating the defence burden. Estimated annual averages for numbers of military personnel under the various headings are shown in table I.8; these figures in turn are derived (sometimes on a rather freehand basis) from figures for ration entitlement fixed by the GKO on various dates (table I.9). This ration entitlement was determined first in September 1941, rather frequently through 1942 and 1943, then for the last time in March 1944.

Finally, comprehensive totals and subtotals by branch of activity and form of employment are reported in tables I.10 and I.11.

Appendix J: foreign trade and aid

The real external balance of the Soviet economy (table J.1) is built up from figures for the dollar balance of aid and trade, consisting of Soviet merchandise exports to the United States (table J.4), US merchandise exports to the Soviet Union (table J.3) and an allowance for non-US trade and aid (table J.2). In the process it is taken for granted (a) that Soviet trade before 1941 was economically negligible, however significant it was from a diplomatic point of view, and (b) that trade in invisibles was negligible throughout.

The United States Department of Commerce is the main source for this appendix, the main amendments and additions being as follows. First, the US figures (tables J.3 and J.4) deal with goods entering and leaving US ports. In the second half of 1941 and 1942, so far as is known, just over one quarter was lost to sinkings on the North Atlantic convoys; the value of goods leaving Soviet ports must therefore have been greater than suggested by US receipts, and the value arriving was less than that of cargoes on shipment leaving the United States; a correction factor is applied correspondingly.

Second, an allowance is made for non-US (mainly British) trade and aid, following roughly the trend of nominal UK transfers. The trend of UK transfers was quite different from that of transfers from the United States, almost half being concentrated in 1942 whereas the bulk of US transfers arrived between mid-1943 and the end of 1944. The effect of allowing for the divergent trend of non-US trade is therefore a modest boost to the contribution of the foreign sector in 1942 compared with later years.

Third, values at prevailing dollar prices must be converted to Soviet factor costs of 1937. As notes to table J.1 report, a first attempt on this was made by Bergson. For vehicles, industrial goods, and other civilian machinery I adopt his purchasing power parities without amendment, and with minor adjustments for consumer goods and foodstuffs. For

Table J.1. *Net imports arriving, by processing branch, 1941–4 (million rubles and 1937 factor costs)*

		1941	1942	1943	1944
1	Electric power	0	0	0	0
2	Coal	0	0	1	0
3	Peat	0	0	0	0
4	Petroleum	86	82	248	388
5	Iron, steel (civilian)	5	595	613	671
5a	Iron, steel (military)	0	9	10	81
6	Nonferrous metals	42	777	1275	1715
7	Fab. metal products	254	1962	4195	7636
8	Defence industries	72	2132	4123	3205
9	Chemicals	15	339	1174	1559
10	Con. materials	7	39	91	77
11	Timber, wood products	0	0	–7	–3
12	Paper, paper products	50	9	19	36
13	Textiles	15	151	1090	1470
14	Light industry	–232	–57	307	584
15	Food processing	–17	1586	5500	4996
16	Other industries	7	136	305	419
17	Agriculture	0	4	67	55
18	Total	255	7765	19012	22889

Source: Net imports arriving from the United States, in dollars and by commodity (table J.2, rows 1–11.2) are matched against rows (processing sectors) in table F.5. Non-US goods (table J.2, row 13) are matched to processing sectors in the same proportions as US goods. Dollar totals are converted to 1937 ruble prices as follows (ruble/dollar ratios):

Military goods	2.81
Vehicles, basic industrial goods	8.96
Other machinery	5.40
Consumer goods, foodstuffs	9.27

These derive ultimately from Bergson (1961), 99–100n, directly so in the case of vehicles, industrial goods, and other machinery. For consumer goods and foodstuffs I take Bergson's valuation at 1937 prevailing prices including trade margins and 'extra processing costs', and then convert from prevailing prices to factor costs on the basis of the ratio of household purchases in the official sector in 1937 at prevailing prices to the same at factor cost in Bergson (1961), 130. For Soviet munitions, a wide range of ruble prices of Soviet weapons is given in tables B.2 and B.3, and it is argued in appendix E that Soviet wartime prices were cost-related. Unit values of some lines of imported United States weaponry can be calculated directly from United States Department of Commerce (1945). Although the degree of detail concerning weapon characteristics is rather inadequate, rough comparisons under plausible

Table J.2. *Net imports arriving, by origin and commodity, 1941–4 (million dollars)*

		1941	1942	1943	1944
(A) US trade					
1	Animal products, edible	–0.5	101.2	430.3	428.2
2	Animal products, inedible	–23.5	–7.7	–4.3	10.9
3	Veg. products, beverages	0.2	18.1	92.4	75.2
4	Veg. products, inedible	–2.7	13.8	97.4	108.9
4.1	rubber and mfrs	0.5	10.0	57.5	54.9
4.2	tobacco	–0.8	–0.0	–0.6	–0.7
4.3	hops	–1.6	0.0	0.0	0.0
4.4	oils	–0.8	3.5	34.0	48.6
4.5	seeds	0.0	0.3	6.4	5.5
4.6	other	0.0	0.1	0.1	0.5
5	Textiles and mfrs	1.6	11.4	103.6	148.2
6	Wood and paper	–0.0	0.7	1.2	3.5
6.1	wood and products	0.0	0.0	–0.7	–0.3
6.2	paper and products	–0.0	0.7	1.9	3.8
6.3	other	–0.0	0.0	0.0	0.0
7	Nonmetallic minerals	10.4	9.9	34.4	50.0
7.1	coal	0.0	0.0	0.1	0.0
7.2	petroleum	9.6	6.4	24.4	40.5
7.3	construction materials	0.7	3.0	9.0	8.1
7.4	precious stones	–0.0	0.0	0.0	–0.2
7.5	other	0.1	0.4	1.0	1.7
8	Metals and mfrs	7.7	132.4	254.4	334.3
8.1	iron, steel	0.6	46.3	60.2	70.0
8.2	ferroalloys	0.0	0.7	1.0	8.4
8.3	nonferrous metals	4.7	60.4	125.3	178.8
8.4	metal products	2.4	25.0	67.9	77.1
9	Machinery, vehicles	58.3	544.7	1492.5	1912.5
9.1	military	21.0	371.4	918.9	876.6
9.2	nonmilitary	37.2	173.3	573.6	1035.8
9.2a	machinery	26.0	90.0	508.5	720.3
9.2b	vehicles, parts	11.3	83.3	65.1	315.5

(Sources for table J.1 contd.)
assumptions suggest 1944 purchasing power parities ranging from a few kopecks to 4 rubles per dollar, with a central tendency of approximately 2 rubles to the dollar. Therefore I take 2 rubles as the dollar parity for munitions in 1944, and adjust it to 2.8 rubles at 1937 prices on the basis that weapon prices rose by 20 per cent, 1937–40, then fell by 41 per cent, 1940–4 (table A.1, row 1).

Table J.2. *(contd.)*

		1941	1942	1943	1944
10	Chemicals and products	1.2	30.2	123.7	148.9
10.1	military	0.0	13.9	65.7	41.3
10.2	nonmilitary	1.2	16.3	58.0	107.6
11	Miscellaneous	5.3	152.7	334.5	186.7
11.1	military	4.5	143.0	306.5	146.5
11.2	nonmilitary	0.7	9.7	28.0	40.2
(B) Total trade					
12	US trade	58.0	1007.4	2960.1	3407.3
13	Non-US trade	0.0	438.0	400.0	240.0
14	Total	58.0	1445.4	3360.1	3647.3

Sources: Rows 1–11.2: table J.3, less table J.4, corresponding rows; but these figures are of US origin, so adjustment must be made for war losses due to sinkings en route in both directions in 1941–2 in order to find the net inflow of resources into the Soviet economy. For 1942 the value of goods leaving American ports for the Soviet Union are adjusted downward by 27 per cent (from Harrison (1985), 258), and figures for Soviet goods arriving at American ports are adjusted upward correspondingly, to allow for sinkings. For 1941 half the correction is applied, and for other years losses by sinking were negligible. Row 12: the sum of rows 1–11.2. Row 13: non-US goods: annual totals are estimated in terms of UK reciprocal aid from sterling values for varying periods given by Allen (1956), 535, converted freehand to calendar years and wartime dollars as follows: 1942 –$600 million, 1943 – $400 million, 1944 – $240 million, then adjusted for sinkings en route by subtracting 27 per cent from the 1942 figure (as the note to rows 1–11.2). Row 14: the sum of rows 12, 13.

Table J.3. *US exports to the USSR, 1941–4 (million dollars)*

		1941	1942	1943	1944
1	Animal products, edible	0.4	140.5	431.1	429.5
2	Animal products, inedible	4.2	22.0	15.4	47.3
3	Veg. products, beverages	0.2	24.8	92.4	75.2
4	Veg. products, inedible	1.5	21.6	98.0	110.3
4.1	rubber and mfrs	0.6	13.8	57.5	54.9
4.2	tobacco	0.0	0.0	0.0	0.0
4.3	hops	0.0	0.0	0.0	0.0
4.4	oils	0.9	7.3	34.1	49.3
4.5	seeds	0.0	0.4	6.4	5.5
4.6	other	0.0	0.1	0.1	0.5
5	Textiles and mfrs	2.0	15.6	104.0	149.0
6	Wood and paper	0.0	1.2	2.2	4.2
6.1	wood and products	0.0	0.0	0.0	0.1
6.2	paper and products	0.0	1.1	2.1	4.1
6.3	other	0.0	0.0	0.0	0.0
7	Nonmetallic minerals	12.0	14.4	34.8	50.6
7.1	coal	0.0	0.0	0.1	0.0
7.2	petroleum	11.1	8.8	24.4	40.5
7.3	construction materials	0.9	5.0	9.3	8.4
7.4	precious stones	0.0	0.0	0.0	0.0
7.5	other	0.1	0.6	1.0	1.7
8	Metals and mfrs	9.7	185.6	260.1	342.3
8.1	iron, steel	0.7	63.4	60.2	70.0
8.2	ferroalloys	0.0	1.0	1.0	8.4
8.3	nonferrous metals	6.3	87.0	131.1	186.8
8.4	metal products	2.7	34.2	67.9	77.1
9	Machinery, vehicles	67.4	746.1	1492.5	1912.5
9.1	military	24.3	508.7	918.9	876.6
9.2	nonmilitary	43.1	237.4	573.6	1035.8
9.2a	machinery	30.0	123.3	508.5	720.3
9.2b	vehicles, parts	13.0	114.1	65.1	315.5
10	Chemicals and products	1.7	41.9	124.9	149.3
10.1	military	0.0	19.1	65.7	41.3
10.2	nonmilitary	1.7	22.8	59.1	108.0
11	Miscellaneous	6.2	209.3	334.6	186.9
11.1	military	5.2	195.9	306.5	146.5
11.2	nonmilitary	1.0	13.4	28.1	40.4
12	Total	105.3	1422.9	2990.0	3457.0
12.1	of which, military goods	29.5	723.7	1291.1	1064.4

Source: United States Department of Commerce (1945), 5–8.

Table J.4. *Soviet exports to the United States, 1941–4 (million dollars)*

		1941	1942	1943	1944
1	Animal products, edible	0.7	1.1	0.8	1.2
2	Animal products, inedible	23.8	18.7	19.7	36.4
3	Veg. products, beverages	0.0	0.0	0.0	0.0
4	Veg. products, inedible	3.5	1.5	0.7	1.4
4.1	rubber and mfrs	0.0	0.0	0.0	0.0
4.2	tobacco	0.7	0.0	0.6	0.7
4.3	hops	1.4	0.0	0.0	0.0
4.4	oils	1.4	1.5	0.1	0.7
4.5	seeds	0.0	0.0	0.0	0.0
4.6	other	0.0	0.0	0.0	0.0
5	Textiles and mfrs	0.1	0.0	0.3	0.9
6	Wood and paper	0.0	0.1	1.0	0.7
6.1	wood and products	0.0	0.0	0.8	0.4
6.2	paper and products	0.0	0.1	0.2	0.3
6.3	other	0.0	0.0	0.0	0.0
7	Nonmetallic minerals	0.0	0.5	0.4	0.6
7.1	coal	0.0	0.0	0.0	0.0
7.2	petroleum	0.0	0.0	0.0	0.0
7.3	construction materials	0.0	0.5	0.4	0.3
7.4	precious stones	0.0	0.0	0.0	0.2
7.5	other	0.0	0.0	0.0	0.0
8	Metals and mfrs	0.6	2.4	5.7	8.0
8.1	iron, steel	0.0	0.0	0.0	0.0
8.2	ferroalloys	0.0	0.0	0.0	0.0
8.3	nonferrous metals	0.6	2.4	5.7	8.0
8.4	metal products	0.0	0.0	0.0	0.0
9	Machinery, vehicles	0.0	0.0	0.0	0.0
9.1	military	0.0	0.0	0.0	0.0
9.2	nonmilitary	0.0	0.0	0.0	0.0
9.2a	machinery	0.0	0.0	0.0	0.0
9.2b	vehicles, parts	0.0	0.0	0.0	0.0
10	Chemicals and products	0.3	0.3	1.1	0.4
10.1	military	0.0	0.0	0.0	0.0
10.2	nonmilitary	0.3	0.3	1.1	0.4
11	Miscellaneous	0.1	0.1	0.1	0.2
11.1	military	0.0	0.0	0.0	0.0
11.2	nonmilitary	0.1	0.1	0.1	0.2
12	Total	29.1	24.7	29.9	49.7

Source: United States Department of Commerce (1945), 9–10.

military machinery, unlike Bergson's, present estimates are based on direct comparison of unit values of Soviet and US weaponry, which leads me to adopt a much lower parity of 2.8 rubles to the dollar, compared with Bergson's 6 rubles; corresponding to this emerges a reduced valuation of American weaponry relative to other US goods and relative to Soviet weaponry.

Fourth, the commodity classification of US trade is matched to the processing sectors used in the input/output table described in appendix F, the classification of non-US trade being presumed to follow similar proportions year by year.

Appendix K: defence outlays

This appendix deals with the estimation of real defence outlays and their composition. The starting point is shown in tables K.1 and K.2, which deal with nominal outlays of the defence and navy commissariats; here we have two alternative and more or less consistent versions which are incomplete in different ways. Table K.1 shows the Terpilovskii figures, which cover an extended run of years (for some

Table K.1. *Defence outlays, 1940–5, from Terpilovskii (billion rubles and current prices)*

	1940	1941	1942	1943	1944	1945
(A) Defence commissariat						
1 Munitions	14.5	24.2	34.0	39.6	44.3	0.0
2 Pay	8.2	13.6	25.1	30.5	33.0	44.8
3 Other wages	0.5	0.7	1.1	1.7	2.1	2.4
4 Transport	1.3	1.7	2.2	4.5	5.5	4.9
5 Not specified	21.9	32.1	38.4	40.5	42.9	65.8
of which (% of 1940)						
5.1 construction	100%	110%	90%	51%	67%	76%
5.2 repairs	100%	228%	223%	281%	317%	410%
6 Total	46.4	72.3	100.9	116.7	127.8	117.8
(B) Navy commissariat						
7 Total	10.4	10.7	7.5	8.3	10.0	10.4
Defence as a whole						
8 Total	56.8	83.0	108.4	125.0	137.8	128.2

Sources: Rows 1–3: row 6, multiplied by the respective shares of these items in total defence commissariat outlays in each year, from Terpilovskii (1967), 66, 214–15. Row 4: Terpilovskii (1967), 157. Row 5: row 6, less the sum of rows 1–4. Row 5.1: Terpilovskii (1967), 116. Row 5.2: Terpilovskii (1967), 105. Row 6: Terpilovskii (1967), 57, 66. Row 7: row 8, less row 6. Row 8: Terpilovskii (1967), 29.

series, all the way back to 1938); but the decomposition of total outlays is not exhaustive. For the defence commissariat (the Red Army, including the air force), the breakdown is relatively detailed, but outlays on some items (construction and repairs) are given only as index numbers, and outlays on food, fuel, and personal kit of servicemen are left entirely undefined. Navy outlays are given only as a grand total; from Terpilovskii's other indications, however, it is just about possible to guess an index of outlays on naval munitions.[1]

In contrast to the teasing reticence of Terpilovskii, table K.2 reveals the full detail of defence outlays and their composition for the three years and two half-years of World War II. Rough consistency between the two tables is apparent, but there are minor discrepancies; table K.2 has the great virtue of a relatively complete accounting for both Army and Navy outlays under comparable headings, but 1940, the first half of 1941, and the second half of 1945 remain unaccounted for.

I combine both sets of primary data as far as may be considered plausible in table K.3.

The currency of table K.3 is still nominal outlays at prevailing prices. Given appropriate deflators, it would be a simple matter to convert each row to constant prices of 1937, and this is the procedure followed in table K.4 for rows 3 to 8. But for munitions (row 1) there are three alternative, conflicting deflators.[2] For present purposes I substitute figures for the total supply of munitions (at 1937 prices) from domestic and foreign sources, not allocated to NKVD, and therefore available for use by the defence and navy commissariats.

For military personnel (row 2) there is no separate wage deflator other than the average public-sector wage; again it seems more reliable to substitute figures for real value added in military services supplied by the army and navy.

Table K.2. *Outlays of the defence and navy commissariats, July 1941–June, 1945 (million rubles and current prices)*

	1941 second half	1942	1943	1944	1945 first half
(A) Defence commissariat					
1. Munitions	14028	33156	38649	42531	21088
2. Maintenance					
2.1 pay	9248	26154	31936	34784	20751
2.2 food	8232	21373	25064	25297	9021
2.3 personal kit	5411	9724	8020	9559	4198
2.4 fuel	1209	2553	2965	3576	2080
2.5 transport	1112	2290	4613	5645	2574
3. Construction	2286	2108	1197	1558	696
4. Other	2813	5691	5425	6491	3107
5. Total	44339	103049	117869	129442	63514
(B) Navy commissariat					
1. Munitions	2156	3008	3221	3611	1740
2. Maintenance					
2.1 pay	1048	1996	2070	2328	1288
2.2 food	692	1242	1131	1306	665
2.3 personal kit	330	491	423	539	357
2.4 fuel	266	409	440	439	247
2.5 transport	52	96	167	229	129
3. Construction	326	307	222	293	181
4. Other	288	388	384	485	287
5. Total	5158	7937	8057	9231	4894

Source: RGAE, f. 7733, op. 36, d. 1892, l. 86. 'Munitions' are *zakazy vooruzheniia i boevoi tekhniki*; 'maintenance' is *soderzhanie armii* or *soderzhanie flota*, and 'pay' is *denezhnoe soderzhanie*; 'personal kit' (for which thanks to Peter Wiles) is *veshchevoe soderzhanie*.

Table K.3. *Estimated defence outlays, 1940–5 (billion rubles and current prices)*

	1940	1941	1942	1943	1944	1945
(A) Defence commissariat						
1 Munitions	14.5	24.2	33.2	38.6	42.5	30.3
2 Pay	8.7	14.3	26.2	31.9	34.8	47.1
3 Food	10.6	16.0	21.4	25.1	25.3	18.9
4 Clothing, etc.	4.8	7.3	9.7	8.0	9.6	7.2
5 Fuel	1.3	1.9	2.6	3.0	3.6	2.7
6 Transport	1.3	1.7	2.3	4.6	5.6	4.9
7 Construction	2.3	2.6	2.1	1.2	1.6	1.8
8 Repairs, other	2.8	4.3	5.7	5.4	6.5	4.9
9 Total	46.4	72.3	103.0	117.9	129.4	117.8
(B) Navy commissariat						
10 Munitions	4.0	2.6	3.0	3.2	3.6	4.5
11 Pay	2.6	3.3	2.0	2.1	2.3	2.4
12 Food	1.6	2.0	1.2	1.1	1.3	1.4
13 Clothing, etc.	0.6	0.8	0.5	0.4	0.5	0.6
14 Fuel	0.5	0.7	0.4	0.4	0.4	0.5
15 Transport	0.1	0.2	0.1	0.2	0.2	0.2
16 Construction	0.4	0.5	0.3	0.2	0.3	0.3
17 Repairs, other	0.5	0.6	0.4	0.4	0.5	0.5
18 Total	10.4	10.7	7.9	8.1	9.2	10.4

Sources: For 1942–4, see table K.2; other years, as follows. Row 1: table K.1, row 1. Row 2: table K.1, row 2 plus row 3. Rows 3–5: row 9, multiplied by the ratio of each row to row 9 in 1942 (for 1940–1), or 1944 (for 1945). Row 6: table K.1, row 4. Rows 7, 8: table K.1, row 5.1 or 5.2 (index numbers), calibrated by 1942 value (for 1940–1) or 1944 value (for 1945). Row 9: table K.1, row 6. Row 10: index numbers from table B.8, row 2.2, calibrated by 1942 value (for 1940–1) or 1944 value (for 1945). Rows 11–17: row 18, multiplied by the ratio of each row to row 18 in 1942 (for 1940–1), or 1944 (for 1945). Row 18: table K.1, row 7.

Table K.4. *Estimated defence outlays, 1940–4 (billion rubles and 1937 prices)*

	1940	1941	1942	1943	1944
1 Munitions	15.5	23.8	54.5	67.0	70.5
1.1 domestic supply	15.5	23.8	52.4	62.8	67.3
1.2 foreign supply	0.0	0.1	2.1	4.1	3.2
2 Pay	6.8	9.9	16.2	17.0	17.5
3 Food	9.8	12.6	13.9	14.0	12.0
4 Clothing, etc.	4.4	5.6	6.3	4.5	4.6
5 Fuel	1.5	2.1	2.4	2.7	3.1
6 Transport	0.9	1.1	1.4	2.6	3.0
7 Construction	2.4	2.9	2.3	1.3	1.6
8 Repairs, other	2.6	3.8	4.5	4.2	4.8
9 Total	43.9	61.8	101.4	113.2	117.2

Sources: Row 1: the sum of rows 1.1, 1.2. Row 1.1: table B.9 (row 1.1, plus row 2). Row 1.2: table J.1, row 8. Row 2: table 5.1, row 7.1. Rows 3–8: table K.3, the sums of rows 3 and 12, 4 and 13, etc., deflated as follows: rows 3, 4 by prices in official retail trade (table A.1, row 7.1), row 5 by prices of basic industrial goods (table A.1, row 4), row 6 by railway freight charges (table A.1, row 6), row 7 by construction charges (table A.1, row 5), row 8 by munitions input prices (table A.1, row 2). Row 9: the sum of rows 1–8.

Appendix L: defence requirements

This appendix sets out the stages of computing the direct-plus-indirect requirements of defence outlays reported in chapter 5. Each table is divided into two. Columns on the left show outlays as in the budget ('gross of imports'); those on the right show outlays after deduction of net imports. Note that it is the *total* of net imports which is subtracted, not just imports of final products designated for defence use.[1]

Table L.1 shows how defence outlays are allocated among the 27 processing sectors, gross and net of imports. Taking into account the net import of nonmilitary final and intermediate products in 1942–4, a row-by-row survey of outlays net of imports reveals many negative cells (column totals remain large and positive, of course); negative entries just mean that net imports were large enough to satisfy all direct defence needs and contribute to direct nondefence requirements as well. Table L.2 shows the associated direct-plus-indirect requirements for gross outputs. Table L.3 converts the latter into percentages of available gross output, including output available from de-stocking in 1942, or *less* output required for stock recovery in 1943–4.

Table L.4 converts gross outputs into value added for defence use by sector of origin, and table L.5 applies coefficients of value added per worker to find out the labour requirements of defence outlays in each sector and year.

Table L.1. *Defence outlays on final products, by processing sector, 1940 and 1942–4 (million rubles at 1937 factor cost)*

		Gross of imports				Net of imports			
		1940	1942	1943	1944	1940	1942	1943	1944
1	Electric power	0	0	0	0	0	0	0	0
2	Coal	0	0	0	0	0	0	–1	0
3	Peat	0	0	0	0	0	0	0	0
4	Petroleum	1481	2380	2698	3137	1481	2298	2450	2749
5	Iron, steel (military)	0	0	0	0	0	–595	–613	–671
5a	Iron, steel (civilian)	0	0	0	0	0	–9	–10	–81
6	Nonferrous metals	0	0	0	0	0	–777	–1275	–1715
7	Fab. metal products	2637	4513	4171	4845	2637	2552	–25	–2791
8	Defence industries	15482	54531	66972	70526	15482	52398	62849	67321
9	Chemicals	0	0	0	0	0	–339	–1174	–1559
10	Con. materials	0	0	0	0	0	–39	–91	–77
11	Timber, wood products	0	0	0	0	0	–0	7	3
12	Paper, paper products	0	0	0	0	0	–9	–19	–36
13	Textiles	2182	3140	2252	2279	2182	2990	1161	808
14	Light industry	2182	3140	2252	2279	2182	3197	1945	1695
15	Food processing	9760	13906	13971	12006	9760	12320	8470	7010
16	Other industries	0	0	0	0	0	136	–305	–419
17	Agriculture	0	0	0	0	0	–4	–67	–55
17a	Construction	2416	2276	1310	1619	2416	2276	1310	1619
18	Transport	930	1364	2582	2997	930	1364	2582	2997
19	Communications	0	0	0	0	0	0	0	0
20	Trade	0	0	0	0	0	0	0	0
20a	Communal services	0	0	0	0	0	0	0	0
20b	Personal services	0	0	0	0	0	0	0	0
20c	Housing services	0	0	0	0	0	0	0	0
20d	Government services	0	0	0	0	0	0	0	0
20e	Military services	6800	16188	16956	17512	6800	16188	16956	17512
21	Defence total	43870	101441	113162	117200	43870	93676	94150	94310
21a	% of GNP	17%	61%	61%	53%	17%	56%	51%	43%

Sources: Real defence outlays, gross of imports, as table K.4; outlays net of imports are calculated by subtracting figures for total net imports in table J.1, rows 1–17.

Table L.2. *Gross output for defence use, 1940 and 1942–4 (million rubles at 1937 factor cost)*

		Gross of imports				Net of imports			
		1940	1942	1943	1944	1940	1942	1943	1944
1	Electric power	997	2133	2285	2265	997	1767	1545	1291
2	Coal	904	1814	1996	2003	904	1497	1394	1206
3	Peat	144	281	288	283	144	241	197	166
4	Petroleum	2918	4877	5454	5925	2918	4520	4526	4718
5	Iron, steel (military)	3422	7492	7960	8087	3422	5297	4618	3227
5a	Iron, steel (civilian)	1237	3034	3339	3254	1237	2906	3123	3025
6	Nonferrous metals	1906	4474	4869	4797	1906	2498	1486	277
7	Fab. metal products	3432	6274	6031	6734	3432	4065	1335	–1711
8	Defence industries	17210	58767	71632	75070	17210	56465	67216	71648
9	Chemicals	2034	4346	4632	4490	2034	3607	2389	1685
10	Con. materials	268	377	322	350	268	265	91	64
11	Timber, wood products	1625	3560	3841	3772	1625	3266	3264	3104
12	Paper, paper products	218	512	556	544	218	475	484	458
13	Textiles	6514	10643	8875	8885	6514	10139	6280	5257
14	Light industry	2305	3317	2379	2407	2305	3377	2054	1790
15	Food processing	16688	24117	24211	20965	16688	21352	14653	12076
16	Other industries	0	0	0	0	0	–136	–305	–419
17	Agriculture	8791	13134	12552	11289	8791	11873	7814	6470
17a	Construction	2416	2276	1310	1619	2416	2276	1310	1619
18	Transport	3304	5781	7194	7476	3304	5220	5897	5894
19	Communications	551	969	1003	965	551	868	729	652
20	Trade	793	1522	1572	1514	793	1371	1190	1067
20a	Communal services	0	0	0	0	0	0	0	0
20b	Personal services	0	0	0	0	0	0	0	0
20c	Housing services	0	0	0	0	0	0	0	0
20d	Government services	0	0	0	0	0	0	0	0
20e	Military services	6800	16188	16956	17512	6800	16188	16956	17512
21	Defence total	84475	175889	189257	190207	84475	159399	148246	141077

Source: Defence outlays (table L.1), multiplied by the Leontief matrix for each year, as tables F.6 and D.5.

Table L.3. *Defence requirements, including direct-plus-indirect requirements of de-stocking, 1940 and 1942–4 (per cent of available output)*

		Gross of imports				Net of imports			
		1940	1942	1943	1944	1940	1942	1943	1944
1	Electric power	29%	70%	72%	62%	29%	65%	63%	48%
2	Coal	28%	68%	71%	61%	28%	64%	63%	48%
3	Peat	25%	62%	64%	53%	25%	59%	55%	40%
4	Petroleum	30%	63%	67%	59%	30%	62%	63%	53%
5	Iron, steel (military)	29%	74%	76%	66%	29%	67%	65%	43%
5a	Iron, steel (civilian)	86%	95%	96%	96%	86%	95%	96%	96%
6	Nonferrous metals	54%	87%	89%	84%	54%	80%	71%	24%
7	Fab. metal products	17%	56%	57%	45%	17%	45%	22%	–26%
8	Defence industries	86%	95%	96%	96%	86%	95%	96%	96%
9	Chemicals	41%	79%	81%	73%	41%	75%	68%	50%
10	Con. materials	13%	44%	42%	29%	13%	35%	17%	7%
11	Timber, wood products	22%	66%	69%	56%	22%	64%	66%	52%
12	Paper, paper products	24%	66%	67%	56%	24%	64%	64%	52%
13	Textiles	36%	69%	66%	56%	36%	68%	58%	43%
14	Light industry	22%	48%	41%	31%	22%	48%	37%	25%
15	Food processing	36%	66%	67%	53%	36%	63%	55%	40%
16	Other industries	0%	0%	0%	0%	0%	–3%	–7%	–6%
17	Agriculture	8%	24%	24%	16%	8%	22%	16%	10%
17a	Construction	9%	28%	19%	13%	9%	28%	19%	13%
18	Transport	23%	58%	64%	54%	23%	55%	59%	48%
19	Communications	20%	52%	54%	43%	20%	50%	46%	33%
20	Trade	8%	27%	29%	20%	8%	25%	24%	15%
20a	Communal services	0%	0%	0%	0%	0%	0%	0%	0%
20b	Personal services	0%	0%	0%	0%	0%	0%	0%	0%
20c	Housing services	0%	0%	0%	0%	0%	0%	0%	0%
20d	Government services	0%	0%	0%	0%	0%	0%	0%	0%
20e	Military services	86%	93%	93%	93%	86%	93%	93%	93%
21	Defence total	22%	58%	61%	51%	22%	56%	55%	43%

Source: Gross output for defence use (table L.2), divided by gross output available (calculated as direct-plus-indirect requirements of total final demand, less demand for stockbuilding ($f_i - \Delta s_i$), multiplied by the Leontief matrix for each year.

Table L.4. *Value added for defence use by processing sector, 1940 and 1942–4 (million rubles and 1937 factor cost)*

		Gross of imports				Net of imports			
		1940	1942	1943	1944	1940	1942	1943	1944
1	Electric power	503	1077	1153	1143	503	892	780	652
2	Coal	757	1518	1670	1676	757	1253	1166	1009
3	Peat	118	231	237	233	118	198	162	137
4	Petroleum	2415	4035	4513	4902	2415	3740	3745	3904
5	Iron, steel (military)	984	2155	2289	2326	984	1523	1328	928
5a	Iron, steel (civilian)	0	0	0	0	0	0	0	0
6	Nonferrous metals	616	1447	1574	1551	616	808	481	90
7	Fab. metal products	1950	3566	3428	3827	1950	2310	759	–973
8	Defence industries	9392	39592	50534	54505	9392	38041	47418	52021
9	Chemicals	603	1289	1374	1332	603	1070	709	500
10	Con. materials	146	205	175	190	146	144	50	35
11	Timber, wood products	1186	2597	2802	2753	1186	2383	2382	2265
12	Paper, paper products	116	274	297	291	116	254	259	245
13	Textiles	2734	4468	3726	3730	2734	4256	2636	2207
14	Light industry	443	638	458	463	443	650	395	344
15	Food processing	4101	5926	5950	5152	4101	5247	3601	2968
16	Other industries	0	0	0	0	0	–136	–305	–419
17	Agriculture	5500	8217	7853	7063	5500	7428	4889	4048
17a	Construction	2141	2018	1161	1435	2141	2018	1161	1435
18	Transport	2196	3843	4782	4970	2196	3470	3920	3918
19	Communications	526	926	958	922	526	829	697	623
20	Trade	641	1231	1271	1224	641	1108	962	863
20a	Communal services	0	0	0	0	0	0	0	0
20b	Personal services	0	0	0	0	0	0	0	0
20c	Housing services	0	0	0	0	0	0	0	0
20d	Government services	0	0	0	0	0	0	0	0
20e	Military services	6800	16188	16956	17512	6800	16188	16956	17512
21	Defence total	43870	101441	113162	117200	43870	93676	94150	94310
21a	% of GNP	17%	61%	61%	53%	17%	56%	51%	43%

Source: Gross outputs for defence use (table L.2), less intermediate inputs (calculated as gross outputs multiplied by sums of technical coefficients, as tables F.6 and D.5).

Table L.5. *Employment in supply of defence uses, 1940 and 1942–4 (thousands)*

		Gross of imports				Net of imports			
		1940	1942	1943	1944	1940	1942	1943	1944
1	Electric power	94	244	253	255	94	202	171	145
2	Coal	141	344	366	374	141	284	256	225
3	Peat	22	52	52	52	22	45	36	31
4	Petroleum	449	915	989	1094	449	848	821	871
5	Iron, steel (military)	183	488	502	519	183	345	291	207
5a	Iron, steel (civilian)	0	0	0	0	0	0	0	0
6	Nonferrous metals	115	328	345	346	115	183	105	20
7	Fab. metal products	363	808	751	854	363	524	166	–217
8	Defence industries	1560	2806	3041	3005	1560	2696	2854	2869
9	Chemicals	112	292	301	297	112	243	155	112
10	Con. materials	27	47	38	42	27	33	11	8
11	Timber, wood products	221	589	614	614	221	540	522	505
12	Paper, paper products	22	62	65	65	22	58	57	55
13	Textiles	509	1013	817	832	509	965	578	492
14	Light industry	82	145	100	103	82	147	87	77
15	Food processing	763	1343	1304	1149	763	1189	789	662
16	Other industries	0	0	0	0	0	–31	–67	–93
17	Agriculture	3882	7276	6580	4900	3882	6577	4096	2808
17a	Construction	475	968	515	628	475	968	515	628
18	Transport	449	881	986	1084	449	796	808	855
19	Communications	108	212	198	201	108	190	144	136
20	Trade	192	548	615	620	192	493	466	437
20a	Communal services	0	0	0	0	0	0	0	0
20b	Personal services	0	0	0	0	0	0	0	0
20c	Housing services	0	0	0	0	0	0	0	0
20d	Government services	0	0	0	0	0	0	0	0
20e	Military services	4550	10832	11346	11718	4550	10832	11346	11718
21	Defence total	14318	30193	29779	28752	14318	28127	24206	22548
21a	% of total employment	16%	55%	52%	43%	16%	51%	42%	34%

Sources: Value added for defence use (table L.4), divided by value added per worker, from table 5.7.

Appendix M: human capital costs

The social cost of premature death or emigration of persons of working age is calculated as the loss to society of what was invested in rearing and educating them prior to entry into the workforce. Tables M.1 and M.2 deal with average rearing and education costs in 1940, at 1940 ruble prices. In table M.1, total household consumption is compared with the population of adults and children. It is assumed that adult consumption per head was three times a child's, since children lacked either individual purchasing power or control over family resources. This suggests a figure of 589 rubles as the annual average rearing cost of a child in 1940 which, multiplied by 15 years of preparation for entry into the workforce, leads to 8,839 rubles for the total rearing cost of a member of the workforce in 1940.

Table M.2 deals with education costs in a similar way. In 1940, 22.5 billion rubles were spent on educating 40 million persons at all levels of the state education system. The average education costs per person were therefore 562 rubles. It is assumed that seven years was the average educational experience of a person of working age in 1940; some (for example, university graduates) had more, of course, but many (especially those of rural origin or of the older generation) had less. The average cost multiplied by seven years suggests a figure of 3,935 rubles for the total education cost of a member of the workforce in 1940.

The total sum invested by society in each member of the 1940 working population was therefore 12,774 rubles.

In table M.3 the number of premature war deaths among people of working age is given as either 19 or 21 million (dependent upon alternative resolutions of the Maksudov dilemma). In addition, there was net wartime and postwar emigration of roughly 2.7 million people, among whom I assume 2 million were of working age, making 21 or 23 million people in total. These, multiplied by the average sum invested by society in each person, put the total cost of premature war deaths at either 268 or 294 billion rubles at 1940 prices.

Table M.1. *Rearing costs, 1940*

1	Household consumption, 1940, billion rubles	260.8
2	Total population, 1940, million	192.6
2.1	adults	125.0
2.2	children (0–14 years)	67.6
3	Adult:child differential	3
4	Annual cost per child, rubles	589
5	Years of rearing	15
6	Total rearing cost per person, rubles	8839

Sources: Row 1: Bergson (1961), 46. Rows 2, 2.1, 2.2: Andreev *et al.* (1990a), 46. Row 3: see text. Row 4: row 1, divided by the population (row 2) in child-units (the sum of rows 2.1 multiplied by row 3, and row 2.2). Row 5: see text. Row 6: row 4, multiplied by row 5.

Table M.2. *Education costs, 1940*

1	Education budget, 1940, billion rubles	22.5
2	Numbers in education, 1940, million	40.0
3	Annual cost per person, rubles	562
4	Years of education	7
5	Total education cost per person, rubles	3935

Sources: Row 1: Plotnikov (1955), 264. Row 2: TsSU (1977), 7 (numbers in pre-school, primary, secondary, higher, and vocational education). Row 3: row 1, divided by row 2. Row 4: see text. Row 5: row 3, multiplied by row 4.

Table M.3. *The cost of wartime demographic losses, 1941–5*

	(1)	(2)
(A) Population aged 15–64 years		
1 Prewar population, million	116.6	118.6
2 Premature deaths, million	19.0	21.0
3 Net emigration, million	2.0	2.0
4 Wartime demographic loss, million	21.0	23.0
4.1 % of prewar population	18.0%	19.4%
(B) Rubles at 1940 prices		
5 Cost per person in 1940, rubles	12774	12774
6 Total cost of war losses, billion rubles	268	294

Sources: Row 1: Andreev *et al.* (1990a), 46; there are two variants, depending on how we resolve the Maksudov dilemma. Col. 1 shows the unadjusted prewar population figure reported by Andreev *et al.*, combined with a figure for war deaths adjusted downward by estimated net wartime and postwar emigration of 2 million. Col. 2 shows a prewar population figure adjusted upward to include 2 million wartime and postwar emigrants of working age, and an unadjusted figure for war deaths. Rows 2, 3: the number of excess wartime deaths among persons of working age is estimated as follows. Andreev *et al.* (1990b), 26–7, supply two benchmarks. An upper limit is the 25.3 million war deaths amongst the population born before mid-1941 (but this includes many who were too old or too young to enter the working population). A lower limit is the 16.7 million war deaths among those born between 1901 and 1931 (but this figure excludes those aged 45–64, who were also part of the working population). A simple, if crude expedient would be therefore to take the midpoint of the range, i.e. 21 million, for war deaths amongst the working-age population. But where are the 2.7 million net emigrants? Col. 1 assumes that they are concealed within war deaths as estimated by Andreev *et al.* I assume that 2m emigrants were of working age, reducing the 21 million war deaths amongst the working-age population to 19 million. Col. 2 assumes that the prewar population reported by Andreev *et al.* has been adjusted downward to eliminate net wartime and postwar emigration, and makes no adjustment to the 21 million. These correspond to the assumptions generating cols 1 and 2 in table 7.2. Row 4: the sum of rows 2, 3. Row 4.1: row 4, divided by row 1. Row 5: table M.1, row 6, plus table M.2, row 5. Row 6: row 5, multiplied by row 4.

Appendix N: the trend in GNP

One route to an assessment of the long-run impact of the war on Soviet GNP per head is via econometric estimation of the long-run trend, if one can be found to exist; the war period can then be examined for signs of disturbance in the trend.

Index numbers of Russian and Soviet real GNP can be assembled from the work of Paul Gregory (net national product at 1913 prices, 1885–1913 and 1928), Moorsteen and Powell (GNP at 1937 factor cost, 1928–40 and 1950), and the CIA Office of Soviet Analysis (GNP at 1982 factor cost, 1950–85). Comparable population series are likewise taken from Gregory for the period before 1913, from recent Goskomstat revisions of the interwar population, and from official postwar figures. Tables N.1 to N.3 show the underlying data, and table N.4 shows the associated long-run index (see also figures N.1 and N.2).

Assembled in this way, the series embodies three major difficulties. First is the two substantial gaps, the first covering the period of World War I, the Civil War, and postwar recovery under the New Economic Policy, and the second covering World War II and postwar recovery. The reader will recall from chapter 5 that although for the second war period we have real GNP, we have no good annual population figures; we have annual GNP per worker, but this has little meaning, given the violent and anomalous structural changes of the war years.

The second major difficulty lies in the transition across each gap from one set of weights to another; this by itself may create the appearance of a trend break. The danger may be greater for the transition from 1937 weights to 1982 weights than for the less dramatic differences between the weights of 1913 and 1937.

The third difficulty is that the sources themselves are not beyond question; unusually, the question mark becomes larger the more recent the period. The estimates of Moorsteen and Powell and of the CIA have been strongly challenged by the independent real product growth esti-

Table N.1. *Population and net national product of the Russian Empire and the USSR, 1885–1913 and 1928 (millions and rubles at 1913 prices)*

Year	Population, millions	NNP, million rubles	NNP, rubles per head
1885	109	7904	72.5
1886	111	7732	69.7
1887	113	9210	81.5
1888	115	9012	78.4
1889	117	8527	72.9
1890	118	8572	72.6
1891	119	7917	66.5
1892	120	8739	72.8
1893	122	10069	82.5
1894	123	11533	93.8
1895	124	10766	86.8
1896	125	11950	95.6
1897	126	11842	94.0
1898	128	12356	96.5
1899	130	13312	102.4
1900	133	13327	100.2
1901	135	13869	102.7
1902	137	15293	111.6
1903	139	14438	103.9
1904	141	16196	114.9
1905	144	14646	101.7
1906	146	14184	97.2
1907	149	13915	93.4
1908	153	15452	101.0
1909	157	16623	105.9
1910	161	18194	113.0
1911	164	17126	104.4
1912	168	18953	112.8
1913	171	20266	118.5
1928	–	–	114.4

Sources: For 1885–1913, NNP and population are taken from Gregory (1982), 56–7. Income per head in 1928 is taken as 96.5 per cent of 1913, from Harrison (1994a), 42 and 333n.

Table N.2. *Population and gross national product, 1928–40 and 1950 (thousands and rubles at 1937 factor cost)*

Year	Population, thousands	GNP, billion rubles	GNP, rubles per head
1928	153155	123.7	808
1929	156060	127.0	814
1930	158637	134.5	848
1931	160846	137.2	853
1932	162377	135.7	836
1933	159850	141.3	884
1934	157482	155.2	986
1935	159151	178.6	1122
1936	161317	192.8	1195
1937	163996	212.3	1295
1938	167009	216.3	1295
1939	176460	229.5	1301
1940	189894	250.5	1319
1950	180050	304.3	1690

Sources: GNP is from Moorsteen and Powell (1962), 622–3; mid-year population is calculated from January totals given by Andreev *et al.* (1990a), 41, calculating the population on the first day of 1940 as equal to the first-day-of-1939 figure, plus 20 per thousand (the net reproduction rate in 1939), plus 12.5 million dwelling in eastern Poland, from Moorsteen and Powell (1966), 71.

Table N.3. *Population and gross national product, 1950–85 (thousands and rubles at 1982 factor cost)*

Year	Population, thousands	GNP, billion rubles	GNP, rubles per head
1950	180050	184.3	1024
1951	183200	185.3	1011
1952	186400	197.4	1059
1953	189500	206.0	1087
1954	192700	216.0	1121
1955	196150	234.4	1195
1956	199650	257.0	1287
1957	203150	262.4	1292
1958	206850	282.3	1365
1959	210600	296.1	1406
1960	214350	305.7	1426
1961	218150	323.1	1481
1962	221750	331.8	1496
1963	225100	324.2	1440
1964	228150	366.4	1606
1965	230900	387.0	1676
1966	233500	405.7	1737
1967	236000	423.8	1796
1968	238350	449.0	1884
1969	240600	455.6	1894
1970	242800	491.6	2025
1971	245100	505.1	2061
1972	247500	508.3	2054
1973	249800	551.7	2209
1974	252100	567.2	2250
1975	254450	569.1	2237
1976	256750	596.4	2323
1977	259000	610.2	2356
1978	261250	626.2	2397
1979	263450	623.0	2365
1980	265550	624.7	2352
1981	267700	630.6	2356
1982	270000	646.7	2395
1983	272500	667.3	2449
1984	275050	676.9	2461
1985	277550	682.9	2460

Sources: GNP is from CIA (1990b), table A.1; mid-year population is calculated from January totals given by TsSU (various years).

Table N.4. *Gross national product per head, 1885–1985 (per cent of 1913)*

1885	61.2%	1938	154.7%
1886	58.8%	1939	155.4%
1887	68.8%	1940	157.6%
1888	66.1%		
1889	61.5%	1950	202%
1890	61.3%	1951	200%
1891	56.1%	1952	209%
1892	61.4%	1953	214%
1893	69.6%	1954	221%
1894	79.1%	1955	236%
1895	73.3%	1956	254%
1896	80.7%	1957	255%
1897	79.3%	1958	269%
1898	81.5%	1959	277%
1899	86.4%	1960	281%
1900	84.5%	1961	292%
1901	86.7%	1962	295%
1902	94.2%	1963	284%
1903	87.6%	1964	317%
1904	96.9%	1965	331%
1905	85.8%	1966	343%
1906	82.0%	1967	354%
1907	78.8%	1968	372%
1908	85.2%	1969	374%
1909	89.3%	1970	399%
1910	95.4%	1971	407%
1911	88.1%	1972	405%
1912	95.2%	1973	436%
1913	100.0%	1974	444%
		1975	441%
1928	96.5%	1976	458%
1929	97.2%	1977	465%
1930	101.3%	1978	473%
1931	101.9%	1979	467%
1932	99.8%	1980	464%
1933	105.6%	1981	465%
1934	117.7%	1982	473%
1935	134.1%	1983	483%
1936	142.8%	1984	485%
1937	154.7%	1985	485%

Source: Tables N.1–N.3.

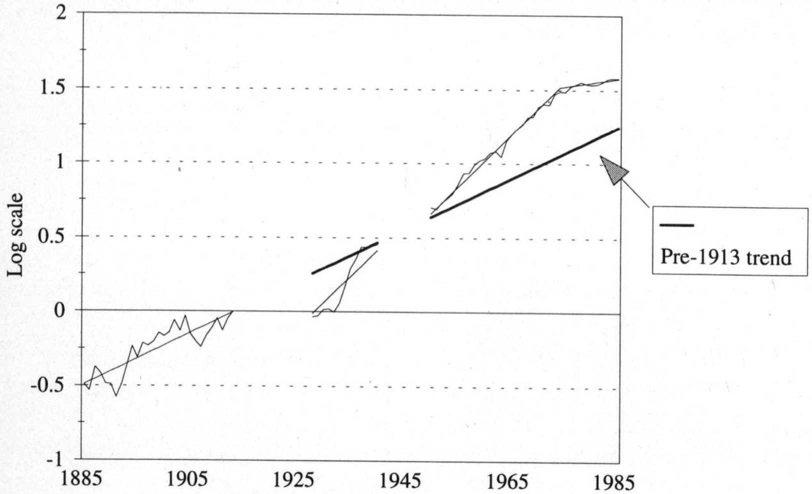

Source: tables N.4 and N.6

N.1 GNP per head, 1885–1985: the pre-1913 trend

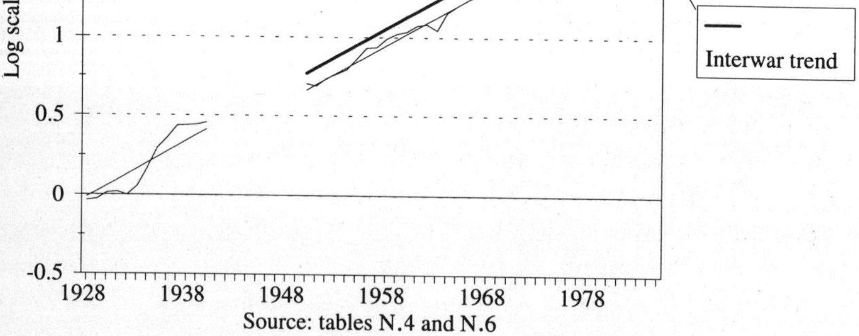

Source: tables N.4 and N.6

N.2 GNP per head, 1928–85: the interwar trend

mates of Khanin. For present purposes I prefer the American estimates. As I have indicated in chapter 3 and elsewhere, I regard the interwar growth estimates of Moorsteen and Powell as basically sound. As for postwar growth estimates of the CIA, they do not give any different long-run evaluation from Khanin, but they do give a different estimate of the phasing of Soviet growth, with less growth in the 1950s than Khanin allows, and more in the 1960s.[1] However, Khanin estimated real product growth only for benchmark years, which give an insufficient number and continuity of observations for estimation of the trend. Therefore there is no real alternative to CIA figures for present purposes, but below I will speculate on what difference an annual series calculated on Khanin's methodology might make.

Subsequent tables show the process of estimating the long-run trend in GNP per head. GNP per head is transformed into its natural logarithm, and X-coefficients may be interpreted as growth rates. The independent variables are as follows:

lgnp (–1) GNP per head (per cent of 1913), lagged one period
year the calendar year

dummy variables which allow for a permanent change in the level ('crash') of GNP per head, and a permanent change in its trend rate of growth:

crash (*T*) break of level: 0 (*year* < *T*), 1 (*year* ≥ *T*), *T* = (1914, 1941)
trend (*T*) break of trend: 0 (*year* ≤ *T*), *year–T* (*year* > *T*), *T* = (1928, 1950, 1974)

The year 1974 is chosen endogenously, by finding a local maximum in the early 1970s for the *t*-statistic of the coefficient of *trend*(*T*). This is a point of consistency with estimates of a break in trend growth rates of many of the market economies in the OECD in the late 1960s and early 1970s.[2]

Probably, if Khanin's postwar estimates were observed annually, with faster growth earlier in the postwar years, they would suggest an earlier, sharper postwar break.

The first question is whether the long-run series established on this basis shows stationarity of trend or difference. Difference stationarity would imply the absence of a long-run trend component in the series, since the disturbance (difference) in each annual observation compared with the previous year would persist indefinitely. Growth takes the form of a random walk driven by exogenous shocks of the same frequency as the period of observation, but no trend. Difference station-

Table N.5. *Regression output: testing for a unit root in gross national product per head, 1885–1985*

Observations	77						
Degrees of freedom	69						
Regression output:							
constant	−16.9148						
SEE	0.0507						
R-squared	0.9956						
	lgnp(−1)	*year*	*crash*(14)	*crash*(41)	*trend*(28)	*trend*(50)	*trend*(74)
X-coefficients	0.4911	0.0088	−0.1837	−0.1750	0.0184	−0.0110	−0.0130
SE of coefficient	0.0929	0.0020	0.0551	0.0705	0.0048	0.0041	0.0047
t-statistic	5.2878	4.4238	−3.3344	−2.4824	3.8159	−2.6776	−2.7442

Sources: Table N.4 and text.

arity is also sometimes referred to as the 'unit-root hypothesis', since it implies that the independent variable regressed against itself with a one-period lag will show a coefficient (root) not significantly different from unity.[3]

The long-run GNP series of many countries display difference-stationarity; however, the unit root usually disappears once a segmented trend is allowed for, with periodic, but infrequent, large exogenous shocks giving rise to permanent breaks of trend and/or level.[4] In the present case, with major discontinuities in the series, we cannot look directly for a unit root. However, table N.5 shows that, when wartime breaks of both trend and level are allowed, together with a break of trend in 1974, the coefficient of GNP per head lagged one period is significant, but significantly less than one. On this evidence, the hypothesis of a stationary, but segmented trend may be preferred.

What happened in the second war period is best approached from two extremes. In the early period (1885–1913), the evidence suggests a stationary trend of approximately 1.7 per cent annual growth. In the most recent period (1974–85), growth was no more than one half a per cent per year. The period from 1928 to 1974, however, is made more difficult to assess by the gaps in data and violence of fluctuations. There are several alternative hypotheses, and statistical techniques do not help us to choose between them. On this point I tend to go along with Lewis Evans who, in analysing Canadian output series, argued recently that by itself econometric testing of single growth series cannot help us either to define retrospectively what *was* a large, exogenous shock, or to discriminate between the unit-root hypothesis with no trend, a seg-

Table N.6. *Regression output: gross national output per head, 1885–1985, with trend and level breaks in 1913, a level break in 1940, and a trend break in 1974*

Observations		78			
Degrees of freedom		72			
Regression output:					
constant		−33.2160			
SEE		0.0639			
R-squared		0.9928			
	year	*crash*(14)	*crash*(41)	*trend*(28)	*trend*(74)
X-coefficients	0.0174	−0.2693	−0.1068	0.0182	−0.0303
SE of coefficient	0.0014	0.0472	0.0488	0.0021	0.0049
t-statistic	12.2317	−5.7006	−2.1870	8.7952	−6.1696

Sources: Table N.4 and text.

mented trend with infrequent, large, permanent shocks, and small permanent shocks which are relatively frequent, but less frequent than the period of observation. These require independent historical understanding and structural modelling of the growth process.[5]

My preferred hypothesis is to consider the years 1928–74 as a single period characterised by continuity of the underlying data-generating mechanism (the 'command-administrative economy', before it began to disintegrate), and by a uniform trend; but to qualify this hypothesis by testing for two breaks of level in GNP. The first test is applied to 1928 compared with the pre-1913 trend, the break of level being associated with World War I, the Civil War, and the famines of 1922 and 1932 (the latter came after 1928, of course, but because of it the level of GNP in 1929–32 was certainly lowered); the second break of level is associated with World War II. This model is estimated in table N.6; it suggests a permanent 27 per cent drop in the level of GNP per head arising from the wars and revolutionary transformations which began in 1914; and a trend growth rate of GNP per head of 3.6 per cent from 1928 through to 1974, qualified by a further permanent drop in the level of GNP per head after World War II of roughly 11 per cent.

Alternative hypotheses may also be tested; they give results which are statistically just as 'good', but they appear less plausible in terms of our underlying knowledge of the period. They can be classified as more and less optimistic in their interpretation of the trend in interwar Soviet growth. An optimistic interpretation would regard the interwar period as characterised by its own trend (5.0 per cent annual growth), segmented off from the periods before and afterwards. If this trend were extrapolated from 1940 to 1950, we would be led to attribute to World War II not only a far larger drop in the level of GNP per head, but also a sharp deceleration to slower postwar growth. This hypothesis may be criticised, however, for assuming that the rapid growth of the early five-year plans could have been sustained indefinitely, given continuity of the underlying mechanism generating the growth series – surely an implausible scenario.

A more pessimistic interpretation of the trend in interwar growth could be built upon the fact that, when the trend in pre-revolutionary GNP per head is extrapolated beyond 1913, it passes through or close to the observed GNP per head in both 1940 and 1950. It might be concluded that this was no accident – that the interwar five-year plans did no more than recover the trajectory established before 1913, and interrupted by war and revolution, and that the fourth (postwar) five-year plan did the same after World War II. In this case World War II resulted in no permanent loss of GNP per head, and after 1950 growth was more rapid than before.

This hypothesis, however, may likewise be criticised for lack of realism; it seems quite wrong to rule out *a priori* the possibility of permanent shocks arising from such huge economic traumas as those suffered by the citizens of the Russian Empire and the Soviet Union in the world wars of this century. It is also too deterministic. Few other major economies either continued along or returned to their pre-1913 trajectories during the 1930s; some (for example, Britain, Canada, and the United States) remained persistently below, while others (for example, Germany and Japan) rapidly surpassed it.[6] If World War I, being a lesser shock to most other countries' economies, broke *their* trend, why not also that of pre-revolutionary Russia?

A somewhat different, but equally pessimistic interpretation of the trend in interwar growth is that of Barbara Katz. In her work the Soviet production function was characterised by a constant elasticity of substitution (CES) between capital and labour, with the elasticity significantly less than one.[7] She applied a CES interpretation to the interwar years, finding support for diminishing returns to scale in the post-1937 period of economic slowdown and so-called 'gigantomania' (enthusiasm for very large-scale industrial projects). Katz's finding could imply that World War II temporarily saved the Soviet economy from secular crisis by destroying physical capital more rapidly than labour, and postponing the renewed onset of diminishing returns. I take this opportunity to note that the present finding of a stationary long-run trend in postwar Soviet GNP per head when fixed capital per worker was rising also refutes the CES hypothesis; transferred to the interwar period, our results suggest, contrary to Katz, that the post-1937 slowdown was a fluctuation about the trend, not a downturn of the trend itself.

My preferred conclusion therefore remains the one illustrated in table N.6: World War II resulted in a permanent loss of about one tenth of Soviet GNP per head, but there was no change in its trend rate of growth associated with the war. Soviet GNP per head growth before World War II was relatively rapid by interwar standards. After the war it continued at the same rate, but at a lower level (and the rate itself was no longer so rapid by the higher postwar standards of market-economy growth) through the postwar period until the early 1970s. This finding may be regarded as reasonably conservative (certainly in contrast to the 'optimistic' interpretation of interwar growth outlined above).

Again we can consider the likely implications of replacing Moorsteen and Powell's series by Khanin's lower interwar growth estimates, as if the latter had been observed annually. Lower interwar growth of GNP per head would imply raising the level of the starting point in 1928, and the level of the whole interwar trend, relative to the postwar trend. The estimated permanent loss of GNP per head associated with World War II would therefore be increased above the figure of one tenth proposed above.

Notes

Preface

1 Zinich (1994), part 1, 3.
2 Illarionov (1995).

Guide to national accounts

1 UNSO (1971).
2 UNSO (1953), UNSO (1968), EC-IMF-OECD-UN-WB (1993).

Note on index number relativity

1 This note is adapted from Wheatcroft and Davies (1994a), 31.

Introduction

1 Kornai (1992), 13.
2 Hanson (1988), 153, 162.
3 Khanin (1991), 114.
4 Khanin (1993), 92. This may seem a hard judgement of a school whose leader, Bergson, is said to have sold his trousers in a Moscow street for the sake of scholarship (to buy a handbook of official commodity prices), according to personal correspondence from Janet Chapman (15 May 1994).
5 Gregory (1994), 9–11.

1 The research agenda

1 The comparison between Russia in World War I and the Soviet Union in World War II has been pursued further by Gatrell and Harrison (1993).
2 These 'words of the pre-revolutionary poet' Nekrasov were cited by Stalin (1940), 365, in his speech of 1931, 'The tasks of business executives'.
3 Nove (1972), 286.
4 This subject was illustrated from the literature of the war by Fussell (1989), 164–80.

5 Gregory (1994), 12.
6 Bialer (1970), 42–4.
7 Stalin (1945), 100, speaking on the anniversary of the revolution, 6 November, 1943.
8 Kosiachenko (1944), 5–7.
9 Stalin (1945), 96-7, 106.
10 Voznesensky (1948), 61.
11 Cited by Rybakovskii (1989), 96.
12 Tamarchenko (1967), 134.

2 An inside view

1 Sukharevskii (1945a), (1945b).
2 Voznesenskii (1947).
3 These figures are introduced below in tables 2.8 and 2.12.
4 GARF, f. 3922/4372, op. 4, d. 115, ll. 35–9.
5 For explanation of material product system aggregates and their components, see the Guide to national account (p. xxvi).
6 Cf Bergson (1961), 23–4.
7 These are the words of Wiles (1987), 60. Wiles also details the history of the deceptions which followed Stalin's death. Davies (1993), 580, provides new evidence of budgetary deception in the early 1930s.
8 UNSO (1971), 59–60. For a brief overview, see above the 'Guide to national accounts'.
9 UNSO (1971), 20. For further discussion see Wiles (1987), 62.
10 Davies (1958), 250.
11 RGAE, f. 7733, op. 36, d. 1892, l. 63.
12 GARF, f. 3922/4372, op. 4, d. 115, ll. 50–3.
13 See table A.1 (rows 1, 7).
14 See table 5.11.
15 Voznesensky (1948), 56. 'Servicemen' was the official translation of the gender-neutral term *voennosluzhashchie*; women served as well as men.
16 For 'the means of waging war', see Kravchenko (1970), 125, 228; for 'armament', IVMV, vol. 6 (1976), 340.
17 Rather similar figures were published in 1971 by the veteran economic planner Gennadii Sorokin (1971), 105–6. They too showed Soviet national income produced, and the main utilisation categories, in 1940 and 1944, in constant prices of 1940. In keeping with the spirit of the times, however, there was no mention of defence; however, as Eugène Zaleski (1980), 352, was first to point out, Sorokin's figures could be used to derive a plausible defence-related expenditure series. Total consumption in each year, less material consumption of civilian households, could be attributed to the armed forces. Less obviously, total allocations to reserves, less the figure given for reserves 'used for accumulation', could perhaps be interpreted as allocations to military stockbuilding. Zaleski's accurate guesswork is vindicated by the greater detail and more explicit row titles of table 2.9. In one respect, however, the figures cited by Sorokin were highly misleading. His

figure for NMP produced in 1944 was only 239.3 billion rubles in 1940 prices – no more than 62 per cent of 1940, despite the fact that by the end of 1944 Soviet prewar frontiers had been roughly restored. Sorokin's figure understated NMP produced in 1944 at prewar prices, in comparison to the figures in table 2.9 (row 3), by roughly 30 billion rubles (more than one tenth). Sorokin's figure of 239.3 billion rubles also suggested an unbelievable gap between NMP produced, less losses, and NMP utilised, of 72 billion rubles (nearly one quarter of NMP utilised), all supposedly attributable to net imports. The equivalent figure from table 2.9 (row 5) is 45.6 billion rubles (15 per cent of NMP utilised at prewar prices), a far more credible sum, though still possibly overstated.

18 The level of national income suggested for 1944 (70 per cent of 1940 for NMP produced, and 80 per cent for NMP utilised) is also implausibly low. For a comparison with other estimates, see table 5.3.

19 See table K.3.

20 Compare GARF, f. 3922/4372, op. 4, d. 115, ll. 19–22 and 503.

21 Both quotations are from Cairncross (1991), 12. The first is cited by Cairncross from Ely Devons.

22 Bacon (1993).

3 Measuring Soviet GNP

1 Clark (1939).

2 Jasny (1949), Jasny (1951a), Hodgman (1954), Jasny (1961), Nutter (1962).

3 Bergson (1961), Moorsteen (1962), Chapman (1963), Moorsteen and Powell (1966); the latter is supplemented by Becker, Moorsteen and Powell (1968), and Powell (1968). For the intermediate stages, see Bergson (1953), Hoeffding (1954), Bergson and Heymann (1954), Hoeffding and Nimitz (1959), and Bergson and Hoeffding (1960).

4 According to Laurie Kurtzweg of CIA,

> classified work on the subject began in the early 1950s ... Because of changes in the availability of data, our present approach to estimating growth differs from that used by Bergson and his associates in two major ways. First, we primarily use data on changes in quantities of output weighted by base-year values, rather than data on changes in current values of output deflated by price indexes. Second, our estimates of the growth of total GNP are determined as a weighted average of growth rates estimated for industry and the other sectors in which GNP is produced. in contrast, in the Bergson-RAND approach, total GNP growth was a weighted average of estimates of the growth of purchases for consumption and other uses of GNP. (CIA (1990b), 2).

The methodology which Kurtzweg describes was also pursued by Moorsteen and Powell (1966), 619–41 (appendix P).

5 Personal communication (4 November, 1990).

6 Personal communication (29 January, 1991). According to R.W. Davies, however,

> It was different in the CIA. A girl who was working in defence expenditure visited us in Birmingham in about 1952–3 and when I said it was impossible to produce a precise

figure responded that they were under great pressure to come up with something definite (personal communication, May 1994).

7 See further the 'Guide to national accounts'.
8 E.g. Wheatcroft and Davies (1985).
9 UNSO (1971).
10 Bergson (1961), 26.
11 Higgs (1992), 46–8.
12 EC-IMF-OECD-UN-WB (1993), 14.
13 Cited by Higgs (1992), 47.
14 On this point Higgs (1992), 48–9, was on firmer ground.
15 Bergson (1953), 42–54. For more recent accounts of the adjusted factor cost standard, see Rosefielde (1981), 7–8; Pitzer (1990), 2–5.
16 Bergson (1953), 55–8.
17 Bergson (1953), 80.
18 Bergson (1944); Bergson (1953), 66.
19 Some wartime illustrations of these principles at work in price formation are given in appendix A.
20 Bergson (1953), 65n.
21 This argument was put to me by Philip Hanson (personal communication, 21 March 1994).
22 Voznesenskii (1947).
23 SNK-TsK (1941).
24 Bergson (1953), 7–9n. As Bergson recognised, the line between methodological deficiency and fabrication was sometimes finely drawn, especially when the deficient methodology was adopted deliberately for purposes of distortion. The high-level exaggeration of harvest yields in the 1930s, which involved an unacknowledged shift from barn yield to 'biological' yield in harvest measurement, is a case in point (see Wheatcroft and Davies (1994a), 30, 116). The important point, however, is that even here the distortion could be corrected once the methodology was understood. The same applies to the postwar concealment of the true defence budget; the published one was not freely invented, but was processed through a distorting methodology. In this connection, Igor Birman wrote:

> in the first place we need not a number, but the methodology; knowing the methodology, . . . we can calculate the number without needing to resort to lie detectors and other detective accessories (Birman (1991), 11).

For a rare example of free invention, the published defence budget in 1931–3, recently uncovered and in this connection deeply disturbing, see Davies (1993), 580.

25 Khanin (1991), 14–28.
26 Wiles (1962), 224.
27 Nove (1972), 381.
28 Khanin (1991), 107–8.
29 Hodgman (1954), 9–11.
30 Jasny (1951b), 110–16.
31 Hodgman (1954), 11.

32 Hodgman (1954), Nutter (1962).
33 Powell (1957).
34 Hodgman (1954), Nutter (1962), Moorsteen (1962).
35 Davies (1994), 140.
36 Gerschenkron (1951). See further the Note on index number relativity (p. xxxiii).
37 Jasny divided the nominal value of output by a Laspeyres price index based on 1926/27, so he called his figures real output in 'real', as opposed to distorted official 1926/27 prices. But the result of dividing nominal output by a Laspeyres price index is a Paasche index of volume (see the Note on index number relativity), so his figure for real output in 1937, for example, compared to 1928 was actually based on current (i.e. 1937) weights. See further Bergson (1961), 199.
38 Hanson (1988), 154.
39 Wiles (1962), 230, 245. Peter Wiles played a prominent role; the ideas which first appeared in Wiles (1955), (1956), were further developed in Wiles (1962), 222–52, and thereafter Wiles (1964).
40 Nove (1972), 381–8.
41 Khanin (1993), 51–93; this should not be taken to imply that Jasny did get it right.
42 Bergson (1950), part I, 210.
43 Jasny (1951b), 148.
44 Bergson (1953), 10n.

4 Industry

1 See table A.1, row 1.
2 Hodgman (1954), Kaplan, Moorsteen (1960), Nutter (1962), Moorsteen, Powell (1966).
3 Powell (1968), 6.
4 Powell (1968), 32.
5 See further the Note on index number relativity (p. xxxiii).
6 RGAE, f. 4372, op. 93, d. 718, l. 52; d. 720, l. 72; d. 1044, l. 72; d. 1095, ll. 3–4; d. 1110, l. 67; d. 1173, l. 10; also, Terpilovskii (1967), 84, 87. For more detail and discussion see chapter 5.
7 This work was originally carried out by Edwin Bacon, and the results are reproduced here with only two minor amendments – revision of the price of oil, and inclusion of a price for sawn timber. See Bacon and Harrison (1993).
8 Jasny (1951b); Jasny (1952); Moorsteen (1962); Chapman (1963); Zaleski (1980).
9 Nutter (1962), appendix B.
10 Khanin (1991), 118; Ericson (1988), 25.
11 Wiles (1962), 225–6.
12 Tupper (1981), 9–10.
13 GARF, f. 3922/4372, op. 4, d. 313, ll. 165–9.
14 IVOVSS, vol. 6 (1965), 45. This figure probably also formed the basis for

Voznesenskii's statement in 1947 that

> war production in the eastern and central areas of the USSR alone increased during the Patriotic War two and a half times over in comparison with the 1940 production level for the whole of the USSR' (Voznesensky (1948), 63).

15 Nutter (1962), 622, 633, estimated amortisation charges at 2.3 per cent of Soviet gross industrial production in 1955 and 2.4 per cent of the same in 1959.
16 Bergson (1953), 58–9.
17 Revenues to the state budget from enterprise profits in the public sector as a whole varied little in the war years, averaging 19.4 billion rubles annually over 1941–5 compared with 21.7 billion rubles in 1940, but falling markedly below this level in the two years of transition and conversion 1941 and 1945 (from TsSU (1959), 457).
18 Denison (1967), 59.
19 This divergence was previously noted by Malafeev (1964), 224–8.
20 Compare Zelkin (1969), 74–107, with accounts of the coal industry in wartime Britain (Court (1951), 107–24) and Japan (Cohen (1949), 167).

5 GNP and the defence burden

1 See table 1.1.
2 This inverts the proposition of Higgs (1992), 46–8, that wartime military services are an intermediate product in the supply of utility. But Higgs's argument does not alter the spirit of the point in the text, which concerns traditional neglect of measurement of the real output of services. Higgs's argument was discussed in more detail at the close of chapter 3, pp. 43–4.
3 See table H.5.
4 See the Guide to national accounts, (p. xxvi).
5 As long as the growth of military services was financed by an increase in indirect (turnover) taxes, nominal GNP and NMP, respectively at *current* factor costs and prevailing prices, could be expected to track each other. It is true that the material product accountancy considered final services to be 'non-productive', and the factor incomes generated in producing final services to be 'secondary' incomes redistributed out of the primary incomes generated in the production of goods. However, the primary incomes of society include the indirect tax revenues to government which in this case pay for the final services concerned (see further the Guide to national accounts). In fact, the wartime collapse of the retail market brought a temporary shift in budget revenues from indirect taxes to direct taxes and monetary finance; turnover taxes financed 61 per cent of budget spending and 27 per cent of NMP utilised in 1940, but only 36 per cent and 18 per cent respectively in 1944 (budgetary series from TsSU (1959), 457, and nominal NMP from table 2.9). But the divergence considered in the text arises between movements in wartime *real* GNP and NMP, and stems from a different mechanism, which operates only when both are calculated at *prewar* factor costs or prices.

6 See table 2.9 and accompanying discussion above.
7 TsSU (1959), 8–15, 34–7, 78. According to TsSU (1959), 1–2, these were the districts or republics of Pskov, Tula (but not the city of Tula), Kaluga, Kursk, Orel, Briansk, Smolensk, Velikie Luki, Rostov, Stavropol', Kabardinia, the Ukraine (including the Crimea), Belorussia, Lithuana, Moldavia, Latvia, Estonia, and parts of Leningrad (but not the city of Leningrad), Novgorod, Moscow (but not the city of Moscow), Voronezh, Kalinin, Grozno, Stalingrad, Astrakhan, Krasnodar, Northern Ossetia, and Karelia.
8 For a tabular summary of previous estimates, see Bacon (1994), 10.
9 Bacon (1994), 26.
10 For estimated peacetime trade ratios in time series see Gregory and Stuart (1990), 325.
11 See Moskoff (1990); Barber and Harrison (1991), 77–93.
12 Standard accounts are those of Arutiunian (1970), Nove (1985).
13 Arutiunian (1970), 200–2.
14 I state this without any desire to undervalue the contributions of previous investigators who laboured under the restrictions of what was allowed to be known under the old régime, including the classic works of Cherniavskii (1964) and Liubimov (1968), and the excellent Moskoff (1990). Much new material on wartime living standards in town and country is to be found in Zinich (1994).
15 See table 2.7.
16 For a precedent see Harrison (1988), 183–5.
17 See table 4.7, col. 1.
18 See table D.5.
19 See table F.9, rows 1–7, 9–15.
20 A similar reason, the widespread employment of low-productivity 'unpaid family helpers' in German agriculture, prompted Kaldor (1946), 38–42, to make the same decision in comparing labour mobilisation for World War II in Britain and Germany.

6 The Alliance

1 Dawson (1959), Jones (1969), Herring (1973), Martel (1979), Beaumont (1980), Titley (1991).
2 Thus Allen (1956), 518–556, made incidental reference to aid to the USSR in a broader study of transatlantic transfers. For brief evaluations of the importance of Lend-Lease within studies of other topics in Soviet economic analysis, see Bergson (1961), 99–100n, Nutter (1962), 214, Linz (1980), 25–33, Millar (1980), 116, Harrison (1985), 149–50, Linz (1985), 25–27, Moskoff (1990), 119–22, Barber and Harrison (1991), 33–34, 189–90. For special attention devoted to this neglected field see only Munting (1984a), Munting (1984b), van Tuyll (1989).
3 Munting (1984a), 495; Barber and Harrison (1991), 190.
4 This hypothesis is supported by the suggestion that the wide range of goods requested by the Soviet authorities for import under Lend-Lease arrange-

ments reflected a Soviet intention to copy across a wide range of western technology (van Tuyll (1989), 26).

5 Jones (1969), 238.

6 Herring (1973), 286: 'In some cases, raw materials or machinery *helped to expand Russian productivity*' (emphasis added here and below). Van Tuyll (1989), 72–3: 'American shipments of specialized chemicals, metals, and industrial machinery may have had a disproportionate effect on Soviet production'.

7 Herring (1973), 286:

> Arms, industrial equipment, raw materials, and food *filled critical gaps* in Russian output and allowed Soviet industry to concentrate on production of items for which it was best suited. Railroad and automotive equipment facilitated the delivery of all types of supplies to the battle fronts.

Jones (1969), 224:

> The total tonnage of oil products lend-leased to Russia represented only a fraction of her total petroleum consumption, but again this is a misleading fact. Although north-route convoys suffered severe attacks and frequent suspensions, a substantial amount of petroleum arrived in Murmansk, which was close to the northern front, thus *relieving painful shortages* caused by the interruption of Soviet rail communications with the Caucasus region. Also a little additive goes a long way, and many Russian aircraft flew on gasoline that was power-boosted in this manner; the hundreds of thousands of American-built trucks also consumed Soviet gasoline to which blending agents had been added. Once again, *comparison between Lend-Lease shipments and Russian production serves no useful purpose*.

Listing vehicles, railway and communications equipment, industrial machinery, and concentrated foods, Beaumont (1980), 212–13, found that

> certain categories of western supplies were vital to the Soviet war effort . . . . Other western supplies were not provided in such spectacular quantity but they were nonetheless significant in the Soviet war effort. Either they were *highly sophisticated and technically specialized or they filled important gaps* in Russian production . . . Other critical shortages in the Soviet economy were filled by aluminium and copper

8 Van Tuyll (1989), 72–3:

> Using gross percentage figures to evaluate Lend-Lease does not allow a clear view of whether Lend-Lease merely provided additional increments to materiel the soviets were already manufacturing, or which aid items were shipped *which they could or did not make*. Thus American shipments of specialized chemicals, metals, and industrial machinery may have had a disproportionate effect on Soviet production.

Moskoff (1990), 122, on food products imported under Lend-Lease: 'the meats and oils were *a real addition to* the diets of those who received them.'

9 Khrushchev (1971), 199.

10 IVOVSS, vol. 6 (1965), 48.

11 ISE, vol. 5 (1978), 545.

12 IVMV, vol. 12 (1982), 187. Munting (1984a), 495, concurs, describing the impact of allied deliveries as 'minor', relying in part on an official Soviet figure of 4 per cent which, if accepted, would probably support such an assessment; see also Millar (1980), 123n. The meaning of the 4 per cent is discussed further below.

13 Calculated from Minvneshtorg (1967), 60, applying the official exchange rate of 5.30 rubles per $1. For estimated peacetime trade ratios in time series see Gregory, Stuart (1990), 325.
14 Jones (1969), 52.
15 Figures are taken or calculated from Allen (1956), 529, 535, using current prices, and applying the official exchange rate of $4.03 per £1.
16 United States President (1944), 58, (1945b), 49.
17 ISE, vol. 5 (1978), 586, IVMV, vol. 12 (1982), 186.
18 See table 6.1 and, for war expenditures of the United States (in dollars) and United Kingdom (in sterling), Allen (1956), 542 (I assume that US war spending in the first half of 1942 amounted to 40 per cent of the annual total; calculations are again based on current prices and exchange rates).
19 Voznesensky (1948), 61.
20 Tamarchenko (1967), 54: 'The relative weight of [Allied] deliveries compared with domestic output in the period of the war amounted to *only 4 per cent*'. ISE, vol. 5 (1978), 546:

> Overall Anglo-American deliveries in comparison with the volume of domestic output amounted in the war-economy period to a total of only 4 per cent

More circumspectly, IVMV, vol. 12 (1982), 187:

> . . . Lend-Lease deliveries to the USSR were *highly insignificant – about 4 per cent* of the output of industrial products in the USSR' (emphasis added).

21 Gerschenkron (1948), 656.
22 Harrison (1988), 189.
23 RGAE, f. 7733, op. 27, d. 714, l. 11.
24 RGAE, f. 7733, op. 27, d. 714, l. 10. The forecast additionally listed commodities imported against foreign currency reserves, put at 1.7 billion rubles, making a total expected revenue for Narkomvneshtorg of 14.95 billion rubles.
25 RGAE, f. 7733, op. 27, d. 196, ll. 1–3.
26 RGAE, f. 7733, op. 27, d. 723, ll. 41–42.
27 RGAE, f. 7733, op. 36, d. 1847, ll. 1–2.
28 RGAE, f. 7733, op. 36, d. 1847, l. 53.
29 RGAE, f. 7733, op. 36, d. 1847, l. 53. What were the 'special revenues', which began to be collected only in 1944? They were bracketed with Lend-Lease and reparations as though they too were derived from foreign transactions – perhaps the seizure of assets in German territories under Soviet occupation prior to the creation of channels for the formal payment of reparations.
30 ISE, vol. 5 (1978), 540.
31 Harrison (1985), 192–97.
32 See table 5.11, row 4.2.
33 See table 5.11, row 5.1.
34 Calculated from Moorsteen and Powell (1966), 622–23.
35 For an attempt to compare the two concepts, see table 5.8, rows 9.1, 9.2.
36 On the increase in speed of movement with motorisation of the Red Army when advancing, see Jones (1969), 233–34; on the railway burden of supplying the food and fodder requirements of horse troops, see van Creveld

(1977), 111–13.

37 A classic treatment of this problem is the 'two-gap' model devised by Chenery, Strout (1966).

38 See table 5.7, rows 1, 2.1. This argument is couched in terms of real output at prewar prices, however. If the great wartime increase in food and consumer prices relative to prices of weapons (table A.1, rows 1, 7) reflected changes in social opportunity costs, then the argument might fall.

39 Khanin (1991), 265.

40 Milward (1977), 351; see also Howlett (1994).

41 The relative expenditure of human life was only partly endogenous to national decision making, as this assumes. Moreover, the rule did not apply on the side of the Axis. Italy and Japan were both poorer than Germany, but Germany (4.5 million soldiers killed and died) suffered more heavily in proportion to prewar population than either Japan (2 million) or Italy (400,000). For military losses, see Urlanis (1971), 294; for prewar populations, see table 1.1, col. 1.

42 Cited in IVMV, vol. 12 (1982), 186.

7 War losses

1 Exceptions to this rule include Millar and Linz (1978), and Linz (1980). Millar and Linz sought to evaluate Soviet non-human war losses in terms of the number of years of wage incomes and household consumption which they represented. Approaching the subject from various angles, they found a range of 3.2 to 7 years' lost earnings. Subsequently, Linz supported various estimates of years' lost earnings in a higher range.

2 Broadberry, Howlett (1994).

3 Bogart (1920); for a similar comparison between Bogart and the British official figures, see Broadberry and Howlett (1994).

4 See for examples Voznesenskii (1948), 126–7; Tamarchenko (1967), 128–9.

5 Both Millar and Linz (1978), and Linz (1980) used a figure of 1,840 billion rubles (184 billion rubles at the post-1961 rate) for Soviet material losses. This figure was obtained from table 7.1, column 1, as 'direct budgetary and other costs' (1,890 billion rubles), less servicemen's pensions, etc (50 or so billion rubles). It was therefore much greater than – but at the same time excluded – the only category of losses which concerns us here, the direct loss of fixed assets (679 billion rubles).

6 So far as I can tell, the first to make this calculation was Tamarchenko (1967), 134; it was afterwards echoed in authoritative works such as ISE, vol. 5 (1978), 559 ('almost 30 per cent of national wealth'), and IVMV, vol. 12 (1982), 148 ('about 30 per cent of national wealth').

7 ChGK (1945).

8 Sheviakov (1991), Sheviakov (1992). These and other figures reported below are reviewed by Ellman and Maksudov (1994).

9 Moorsteen and Powell (1966), 72–7.

10 The two thirds and the 45 per cent are from Voznesenskii (1948), 126, 129.

11 Voznesenskii (1948), 55. The decline was said to persist through 1942, with

wartime fixed capital formation offsetting further asset losses. Moorsteen and Powell insisted that 215 billion rubles overstates the permanent losses of public-sector firms' fixed assets, since a proportion would be recovered with the subsequent liberation of territory. However only a part of national assets is accounted for; 'inventories, livestock, and all losses by establishments other than enterprises' are not included. Given the agricultural specialisation of the occupied territory, losses by public sector firms located there may be expected to have been less significant than those of affected households and collective farms. Here I have in mind that the occupied territories accounted for only 33 per cent of prewar industrial production by gross output value at 1926/27 prices, and 38 per cent of public sector employment, but 45 per cent of the population; only 29 per cent of sheep and goat herds, but 45 per cent of large horned stock (and 50 per cent of cattle herds), 68 per cent of pig herds, and 57 per cent of farm tractor stocks (all figures from TsSU (1959), 46–7). Thus, the loss of household and kolkhoz assets may well have been steeper than losses of the public sector.

12 Moorsteen and Powell (1966), 75. The exact figure did not matter much to them. Their purpose was to calculate long-run series for the size of the capital stock from series for gross investment, depreciation, and exogenous shocks. The operation of given series for investment growth and given rates of depreciation combined to ensure that the influence on the capital stock series of widely differing assumptions about the size of shocks was negligible after a decade or so (ibid., 75–7).

13 On wartime civilian morbidity and mortality see further Zinich (1994), part 2, 84–108.

14 For detail, see Barber and Harrison (1991), 86–9.

15 Rybakovskii (1989), 96. Rybakovskii's own estimate (27–28 million) was little more than the new Goskomstat figures which were soon to appear.

16 Andreev, Darskii and Khar'kova (1990b), 26–7.

17 Ellman and Maksudov (1994), 672–3.

18 From armed forces records Krivosheev (1993), 130–1, 139, gives 8.7 million wartime military deaths from all causes, killed and died in combat, in accidents, and from illness, or failed to return from captivity, and a grand total of 34.5 million already in uniform at the outbreak of war or mobilised in the course of the war. But according to Maksudov (1993), 119, we should subtract from the 8.7 million up to 400,000 normal deaths, and half a million prisoners of war who either remained in Germany or returned to Soviet-controlled territory without passing through official filters. On other aspects of military losses, see further Bacon (1993). This leaves 7.8 million (8.7 million – 0.4 million – 0.5 million) excess military deaths. Civilian losses (23.9 million – 7.8 million = 16.1 million) and population (196.7 million – 34.5 million = 162.2 million) are in each case the residual left after deducting the military component from totals reported in table 7.2.

19 Broadberry and Howlett (1994), 6.

20 Broadberry and Howlett (1994), 9.

21 Mankiw, Romer and Weill (1992). By implication, other recent models of the

aggregate production function are excluded, for example those based on constant or increasing returns to fixed capital or machinery investment, e.g. Romer (1986), Lucas (1988), Rebelo (1991). As noted in appendix N, the finding of a stationary long-run trend in Soviet GNP per head when fixed capital per worker was rising also tends to refute the constant-elasticity-of-substitution (CES) hypothesis.

22 By means of premature death and emigration, the war removed a much higher proportion of the prewar working population (at least 18 per cent, from table 7.3) than of the prewar population as a whole (at least 13.5 per cent, from table 7.2). This would suggest a sharp rise in the postwar dependency ratio, but the rise disappears when the wartime birth deficit, which reduced the number of postwar dependants, is taken into account. In 1940 the annual average working population of 86,850 thousands (table I.10) represented 45.7 per cent of an annual average (not mid-year) population of 189,894 thousands (table N.2). For the working population in 1950, Bergson (1961), 443 gives 81.5 millions, 45.3 per cent of the mid-year 180,050,000 population (table N.3). Thus the dependency ratio barely changed.

23 Broadberry, Howlett (1994), 11, stress that postwar acceleration does not denote any beneficial effect of wartime destruction. They comment on the British figures:

> a setback to the national balance sheet such as that caused by wartime destruction is likely to be followed by relatively rapid reconstruction growth as a devastated country reinvests. However, this does not mean that the devastated country has benefited from defeat. Rather, it has been necessary to devote extra resources simply to get back to previously attained levels of productivity.

24 Higher figures of up to 50 million have also been adduced for the postwar demographic deficit; see for examples Erickson (1994), 257–8. Inexact readings of such accounts sometimes generate confusion, with estimates of the demographic deficit being reported as numbers of war deaths (e.g. *The Guardian*, 30 April, 1994). Ellman and Maksudov (1994) present a fuller review of the alternative estimates.

25 Ellman and Maksudov (1994), 674.

26 Moorsteen and Powell (1966), 243. Growth trends were estimated by imposing log-linear regression lines on annual series for 1928–40 and 1950–61; for regression equations and charts, see Moorsteen and Powell (1966), 238n, 240. Extrapolating the prewar growth rate from 1940, and the postwar growth rate from 1950, the prewar path would have been regained in 140 years.

27 See appendix to Harrison (1994d).

28 Wheatcroft and Davies (1994b), 63.

29 Crafts and Mills (1995), table 7.

30 According to Crafts and Mills (1995), Germany too was an exception. Their estimates of trend growth in German GDP per head are 3.30 per cent (1920–39), 0.71 per cent (1940–50), 13.89 per cent (1951–5), and 3.12 per cent (1956–1989). But this means that by 1956 the level of German GDP per head was roughly 30 per cent *above* the extrapolated prewar trend.

31 See for examples Richardson (1989).
32 Emerson *et al.* (1988), 203, 208. The partial effects included lifting the cost of trade and production barriers, and the gains from greater economies of scale and increased competition. The general effects included gains from the abolition of frontier controls, the opening up of public procurement, the liberalisation of financial services, and increased competition.

8 Conclusion

1 Stalin (1945), 100, speaking on the anniversary of the revolution, 6 November 1943.
2 Cited by Mowat (1956), 649–50.
3 *Brute force* is the title of the revealing study by Ellis (1990).

Appendix A: price deflators

1 RGAE, f. 4372, op. 44, d. 371, ll. 79–80, 84.
2 See further the Note on index number relativity, (p. xxxiii).
3 Voznesensky (1948), 102.

Appendix B: defence industry production

1 Sokolov (1988), 123. Define C_t as the level of combat stocks at the end of period t, and assume that there are no other stocks held in the rear or in reserve; the number of units produced during each period is given by Q_t, imported units by F_t, and the number of losses by L_t. Then:

$$L_t = Q_t + F_t - (C_t - C_{t-1})$$

The main difficulties of this methodology are hidden assumptions about initial reserves and rear formations, and the change in their level in each period, and about noncombat losses. However, any bias should diminish with the length of the accounting period (in other words, resulting discrepancies should be smoothed out over four years of fighting). In the long run, both imports and changes in combat and reserve stocks were small relative to output, so that domestic output should dominate (in the accounting sense) the determination of losses. The relative importance of combat and noncombat losses, however, would remain undetermined. According to figures published subsequently by Krivosheev (1993), 366, Soviet combat losses amounted to less than half of the wartime total in the case of aircraft, though not for other types of equipment.

2 Sokolov (1988), 125:

> Inflated reports [*pripiski*] – a defect inherent in our national economy as in the prewar, so in the postwar period, were apparent also in wartime when obligations were often handed down to enterprises subject to shortage of resources for their fulfilment and without taking account of real possibilities. The arbitrary administrative principle was triumphant, and on the fulfilment of these often unbalanced plans hung the fate, in the literal sense of the word, of enterprise leaders. Under such circumstances inflated reports were an inevitable evil.

3 Underfulfilment of quarterly and monthly plans for shell production by wide margins was reported period by period in the second half of 1941. By December 1941 the reported output of aircraft was down to two-fifths of ministerial targets, and that of aircraft engines was down to one-quarter. IVMV, vol. 4 (1975), 150–151.
4 Military inspection could be so strict, on occasion, as to delay the delivery of finished output and accentuate wartime shortages of weapons. Kovalev (1988), 22–3, reported the case of a plant where delays in military inspection of ammunition cases in the early months of the war aggravated the already severe shell famine.
5 Krivosheev (1993), 341–84.
6 See table A.3.
7 Again the relevant comparison is with table A.3.
8 Wiles (1962), 225–6.
9 Harrison (1990), appendix E.
10 Harrison (1993a), table D.3.

Appendix C: civilian industry production

1 Nutter (1962), appendix B.
2 Khanin (1991), 118; Ericson (1988), 25.
3 Jasny (1951b); Jasny (1952); Moorsteen (1962); Chapman (1963); Zaleski (1980).
4 Wiles (1962), 225–6.

Appendix D: from gross output to value added

1 See the Note on index number relativity (p. xxxiii).
2 See table F.8.
3 See table A.1.
4 See table G.6.
5 Malafeev (1964), 226.
6 This came on 1 January, 1949; see Nove (1972), 305–6.
7 See table B.9, row 3.

Appendix E: cross-checks for defence industry

1 See table D.4, rows 8.1, 8.2.
2 See table B.4.
3 Terpilovskii (1967), 76–7.
4 Terpilovskii (1967), 77–8. The quotation is from p. 76.
5 Jasny (1951b), 107.
6 Budget subsidies to industry are given by Zverev (1958), 212–13; outlays on munitions from the Army and Navy budgets are as table K.3.
7 Enabling basic industry product prices to catch up with wartime and postwar cost inflation was the main business of the price reform enacted on 1 January, 1949 (for index numbers of product prices, see TsSU (1968), 227).
8 RGAE, f. 4372, op. 93, d. 1103, l. 4.

9 See table B.6, row 3.
10 RGAE, f. 4372, op. 44, d. 360, l. 55. Gradual reversion of the mortar armament commissariat to its peacetime specialisation in 1944 was a forerunner of more widespread reconversion of defence industry.
11 GARF, f. 4372, op. 3, d. 1265, l. 50.
12 RGAE, f. 4372, op. 44, d. 372, l. 60 (for the second figure a wartime medium tank is compared with a prewar heavy tank, but medium must have been intended in both cases).
13 The nominal trends in unit prices of labour and nonlabour inputs were evaluated in table D.3, rows 3–4.
14 GARF, f. 4372, op. 3, d. 1265, l. 50.
15 ISE, vol. 5 (1978), p. 230.
16 Gladkov (1970), 61.
17 RGAE, f. 4372, op. 44, d. 372, l. 61.
18 See table 4.3.
19 The data are reported by Bergson (1961), 373–4.
20 According to charts published in United States War Production Board (1945), 10, 'productivity' (whether per worker or per hour worked is not specified) in munitions industries in 1944 stood at approximately two and one half times the 1942 level, while average hours worked in durable goods manufacturing rose over the same two years from roughly 45 to 47 hours.
21 Overy (1994), 367.
22 Overy (1994), 359–60, 367–72.
23 Overy (1994), 367.
24 See table 4.12, row 1.

Appendix F: an input/output table

1 A recent exception is Holland Hunter's ambitious multi-sector growth model of the interwar Soviet economy, designed to evaluate Stalinist peacetime economic development policies and processes. Built into Hunter's model were two input/output tables, one for 1928 and one for 1959, each with 12 processing sectors, the transition between them being the core technological development process. See Hunter, Szyrmer (1992).
2 Kaplan *et al.* (1952), 1. The joint authors included James H. Blackman, Hans Heymann, David Redding, and Nicholas W. Rodin; in addition, Abram Bergson, Marvin Hoffenburg, Joseph A. Kershaw, Wassily Leontief, and G. Warren Nutter acted as consultants to the project. Their long term goal was to contribute to building an input/output table for the postwar Soviet economy. Compilation of an input/output table for the prewar period was seen as an essential intermediate step.
3 SNK-TsK (1941).
4 Kaplan *et al.* (1952), 4.
5 Kaplan *et al.* (1952), 5.
6 On the postwar incidence of turnover taxes, see Nove (1965), 105, 139.
7 For agricultural prices in 1941-plan compared with 1940, see Kaplan *et al.* (1952), 77–80.

8 At current prices and exchange rates, Soviet imports and exports in 1940 amounted to 2,455 million rubles and 2,297 million rubles respectively, compared with GNP at prevailing prices of 435 billion rubles. See Minvneshtorg (1966), 9, and, for GNP, Bergson (1961), 46.
9 TsSU (1961), 103–51.
10 See table 2.13.
11 Kaser (1970), table 1.
12 See table K.4.
13 See tables 5.1, row 7.2, and B.9, row 1.2.
14 For a comparison of employment with value added after adjustment, see table 4.7.
15 Moorsteen and Powell (1966), 622–3.
16 See table G.1.

Appendix K: defence outlays

1 See table B.8.
2 See table E.1. In appendix E I try to discriminate among them, but it is not obvious which is preferable here.

Appendix L: Defence requirements

1 For argument and figures, see tables 5.8 and 6.4 and accompanying discussion.

Appendix N: the trend in GDP

1 See Harrison (1993c), 144–6. The more important criticism of the CIA figures is that they overstated the level of Soviet GNP in the 1980s relative to the United States, a charge which has no bearing on the subject discussed here. For alternative estimates of Soviet GNP per head ranging from 12–21 to 57 per cent of the United States in the 1980s, see Marer (1985), 86, IMEMO (1987), 150, Summers and Heston (1988), Åslund (1990), 43, CIA (1990a), 38, Martynov (1990), 15, Ehrlich (1991), 880, Rosefielde (1991), 606, Summers and Heston (1993).
2 For examples see Crafts and Mills (1995), table 4.
3 Granger (1986).
4 This was the original contribution of Perron (1989). For a recent application of relevance to the present study, see Crafts and Mills (1995).
5 Evans (1995). This was a response to Inwood and Stengos (1991); see also the latter authors' reply, Inwood and Stengos (1995).
6 This may be inferred from Crafts and Mills (1995), table 7.
7 Katz (1975). This model was first proposed in a Soviet context by Weitzman (1970); the CES literature has been reviewed recently by Ofer (1987), 1817–19.

Bibliography

Allen, R.G.D. (1956), 'Mutual aid between the US and the British Empire, 1941–1945', appendix 3 Sayers, R.S. *Financial policy, 1939–1945*, London, 518–56

Andreev, E., Darskii, L. and Khar'kova, T. (1990a), 'Opyt otsenki chislennosti naseleniia SSSR 1926–1941 gg.', *Vestnik statistiki*, no. 7, 34–46

(1990b), 'Otsenka liudskikh poter' v period Velikoi Otechestvennoi voiny', *Vestnik statistiki*, no. 10, 25–7

Arutiunian, Iu.V. (1970), *Sovetskoe krest'ianstvo v gody Velikoi Otechestvennoi voiny*, 2nd edn, Moscow

Åslund, A. (1990), 'How small is Soviet national income?', in Rowen, H.S. and Wolf, C., eds, *The impoverished superpower: perestroika and the Soviet military burden*, San Francisco, CA, 13–62

Bacon, E.T. (1992a), 'Glasnost' and the Gulag: new information on forced labour around World War Two', *Soviet Studies*, vol. 44(6), 1069–86

(1992b), 'L'importance du travail forcé dans l'Union soviétique de Staline', *Revue d'études comparatives Est–Ouest*, no. 2–3, 229–49

(1993a), 'Soviet military losses in World War II', *Journal of Slavic Military Studies*, vol. 6(4), 613–33

(1993b), 'Historiography of the Gulag', paper to Russian Academy of Sciences Conference on 'The Fortunes of History in the Twentieth Century', Moscow

(1994), *The Gulag at war: Stalin's forced labour system in the light of the archives*, London and Basingstoke

Bacon, E.T. and Harrison, M. (1993), 'The real output of Soviet civilian industry, 1940–1945', University of Warwick, Department of Economics, *Working Paper Series*, no. 9303

Barber, J., Harrison, M. (1991), *The Soviet home front, 1941–1945: a social and economic history of the USSR in World War II*, London

Beaumont, J. (1980), *Comrades in arms: British aid to Russia, 1941–1945*, London

Becker, A. S., Moorsteen, R. and Powell, R. P. (1968), 'The Soviet capital stock: revisions and extensions, 1961–1967', in *Two supplements to Richard Moorsteen and Raymond P. Powell, The Soviet capital stock, 1928–1962*, Yale University, The Economic Growth Center

Bergson, A. (1944), *The structure of Soviet wages*, Cambridge, MA

(1950), 'Soviet national income and product in 1937', part I, 'National economic accounts in current rubles', *Quarterly Journal of Economics*, vol. 64(2), 208–41; part II, 'Ruble prices and the valuation problem', *Quarterly Journal of Economics*, vol. 64(3), 408–41
(1953), *Soviet national income and product in 1937*, New York
(1961), *The real national income of Soviet Russia since 1928*, Cambridge, MA
Bergson, A. and Heymann, H. (1954), *Soviet national income and product, 1940–1948*, New York
Bergson, A. and Hoeffding, O. (1960), 'Soviet national income and product, 1928–1948, revised calculations', The RAND Corporation, Research Memorandum, RM-2544, Santa Monica, CA
Bialer, S. (ed.) (1970), *Stalin and his generals: Soviet military memoirs of World War II*, London
Birman, I. (1991), 'Ekonomicheskii detektiv', *Znanie - sila*, no. 3, 8–14
Bogart, E.L. (1920), *Direct and indirect costs of the Great World War*, 2nd edn, New York
Broadberry, S.N. and Howlett, P. (1994), 'Economic mobilisation for World War II: the United Kingdom', second meeting of the International Research Group on 'Economic mobilisation for World War II: the war economy and postwar perspectives of six great powers in international comparison', University of Warwick
Cairncross, A.K. (1991), *Planning in wartime: aircraft production in Britain, Germany and the USA*, Oxford
Chadaev, Ia.E. (1965), *Ekonomika SSSR v period Velikoi Otechestvennoi voiny*, Moscow
Chapman, J.G. (1963), *Real wages in Soviet Russia since 1928*, Cambridge, MA
Chenery, H.B. and Strout, A.M. (1966), 'Foreign assistance and economic development', *American Economic Review*, vol. 50, 679–733
Cherniavskii, U.G. (1964), *Voina i prodovol'stvie. Snabzhenie gorodskogo naseleniia v Velikuiu Otechestvennuiu voinu (1941–1945 gg.)*, Moscow
ChGK (Chrezvychainaia Gosudarstvennaia Komissiia) (1945), 'Soobshcheniie Chrezvychainoi Gosudarstvennoi Komissii po ustanovleniiu i rassledovaniiu zlodeianii nemetsko-fashistskikh zakhvatchikov', *Pravda*, 13 September
CIA (Central Intelligence Agency) (1990a), *Handbook of economic statistics, 1989*, Washington, DC
(Central Intelligence Agency) (1990b), *Measures of Soviet gross national product in 1982 prices*, a study prepared for the use of the Joint Economic Committee of the Congress of the United States, Washington, DC
(Central Intelligence Agency, Directorate of Intelligence) (1990c), *Measuring Soviet GNP: problems and solutions: a conference report*, SOV 90–10038, Washington, DC
Clark, C. (1939), *A critique of Soviet statistics*, London
(1957), *Conditions of economic progress*, 3rd edn, London
Cohen, J.B. (1949), *Japan's economy in war and reconstruction*, Minneapolis, MN
Court, W.H.B. (1951), *Coal*, London

Crafts, N.F.R. and Mills, T.C. (1995), 'Europe's golden age: an econometric investigation of changing trend rates of growth', *CEPR Discussion Paper Series*, no. 1087, forthcoming in van Ark, B. and Crafts, N.F.R., eds, *Quantitative aspects of Europe's postwar growth*, Cambridge

Davies, R.W. (1958), *The development of the Soviet budgetary system*, Cambridge

(1993), 'Soviet military expenditure and the armaments industry, 1929–33: a reconsideration', *Europe-Asia Studies*, vol. 45(4), 577–608

(1994), 'Industry', in Davies, R.W., Harrison, M. and Wheatcroft, S.G., eds, *The economic transformation of the Soviet Union, 1913–1945*, Cambridge, 131–57

Davies, R.W., Harrison, M. and Wheatcroft, S.G. (eds.) (1994), *The economic transformation of the Soviet Union, 1913–1945*, Cambridge

Dawson, R.H. (1959), *The decision to aid Russia, 1941: foreign policy and domestic politics*, Chapel Hill, NC

Degras, J., Nove, A. (eds.) (1964), *Soviet planning: essays in honour of Naum Jasny*, Oxford

Denison, E.F. (1967), *Why growth rates differ: postwar experience in nine western countries*, Washington, DC

EC–IMF–OECD–UN–WB (Commission of the European Communities – Eurostat, International Monetary Fund, Organisation for Economic Cooperation and Development, United Nations, World Bank) (1993), *System of national accounts 1993*, Brussels/Luxembourg, New York, Paris, Washington, DC

Ehrlich, E. (1991), 'Contest between countries: 1937–1986', *Soviet Studies*, vol. 43, 875–96

Ellis, J. (1990), *Brute force: allied strategy and tactics in the Second World War*, London

Ellman, M. and Maksudov, S. (1994) 'Soviet deaths in the Great Patriotic War: a note', *Europe-Asia Studies*, vol. 46(4), 671–80

Emerson, M., Aujean, M., Catinat, M., Goybet, P. and Jacquemin, A. (1988), *The economics of 1992: the European Commission's assessment of the economic effects of completing the internal market*, Oxford

Erickson, J. (1994), 'Soviet war losses: calculations and controversies', in Erickson, J. and Dilks, D., eds, *Barbarossa: the Axis and the Allies*, Edinburgh, 255–77

Ericson, R.E. (1988), 'The Soviet statistical debate: Khanin vs TsSU', Columbia University, Harriman Institute, *Occasional Papers*, no. 1

Evans, L.T. (1995), 'What can univariate models tell us about Canadian economic growth, 1870–1985?', *Explorations in Economic History*, vol. 32, 236–52

Fussell, P. (1989), *Wartime: understanding and behavior in the Second World War*, Oxford

Gatrell, P. and Harrison, M. (1993), 'The Russian and Soviet economy in two World Wars', *Economic History Review*, 2nd ser., vol. 46(3), 425–52

Gerschenkron, A. (1948), Review of *Voennaia ekonomika SSSR v period otechestvennoi voiny* (N.A. Voznesenskii), *American Economic Review*, vol. 38, 649–57

(1951), 'A dollar index of Soviet machinery output, 1927–28 to 1937', The RAND Corporation, Report, R-197, Santa Monica, CA

Gladkov, I.A. (1970), *Ekonomicheskaia pobeda SSSR v Velikoi Otechestvennoi voiny*, Moscow

Goldsmith, R. (1946), 'The power of victory: munitions output in World War II', *Military Affairs*, vol. 10, 69–80

Goskomstat (Gosudarstvennyi komitet statistiki SSSR) (1990), *Narodnoe khoziaistvo SSSR v Velikoi Otechestvennoi voiny 1941–1945 gg.*, Moscow

Granger, C.W.J. (1986), 'Developments in the study of cointegrated economic variables', *Oxford Bulletin of Economics and Statistics*, vol. 48, 213–28

Gregory, P.R. (1982), *Russian national income, 1885–1913*, Cambridge

(1994), *Before command: an economic history of Russia from Emancipation to the first Five-Year Plan*, Princeton, New Jersey

Gregory, P.R. and Stuart, R.C. (1990), *Soviet economic structure and performance*, 4th edn, New York

Hancock, W.K., and Gowing, M.M. (1949), *The British war economy*, London

Hanson, P. (1988), 'Navrozov versus the Agency', in Wiles, P.J.D., ed., *The Soviet economy on the brink of reform: essays in honor of Alec Nove*, Boston, MA, 153–64

Harrison, M. (1985), *Soviet planning in peace and war, 1938–1945*, Cambridge

(1988), 'Resource mobilization for World War II: the USA, UK, USSR and Germany, 1938–1945', *Economic History Review*, 2nd ser., vol. 41(2), 171–92

(1989a), 'Total output and the productivity of labour in Soviet industry, 1940–1945', University of Warwick, Department of Economics, *Warwick Economic Research Papers*, no. 319

(1989b), 'Soviet national income and the burden of defence, 1937 and 1940–1944', University of Warwick, Department of Economics, *Warwick Economic Research Papers*, no. 320

(1990a), 'The volume of Soviet munitions output, 1937–1945: A reevaluation', *Journal of Economic History*, vol. 50(3), 569–89

(1990b), '1941–5', panel on 'The economic transformation of the Soviet Union, 1913–1945,' Fourth World Congress for Soviet and East European Studies, Harrogate

(1990c), 'Mobilizatsiia Sovetskoi ekonomiki v 1941–1944 gody. K pereotsenke', paper to International Conference on 'Russia and the USSR in the XX Century', Moscow

(1991) 'New estimates of Soviet production and employment in World War II: a progress report', University of Birmingham, Centre for Russian and East European Studies, *Soviet Industrialisation Project Series*, no. 32

(1992), 'Russian and Soviet GDP on the eve of two World Wars: some international comparisons, 1913 and 1938–40', University of Birmingham, Centre for Russian and East European Studies, *Soviet Industrialisation Project Series*, no. 33.

(1993a) 'Soviet production and employment in World War II: a 1993 update', University of Birmingham, Centre for Russian and East European Studies, *Soviet Industrialisation Project Series*, no. 35

(1993b) 'Soviet munitions output in World War II in the light of new data', University of Warwick, Department of Economics, *Working Paper Series*, no. 9317

(1993c), 'Soviet economic growth since 1928: the alternative statistics of G.I. Khanin', *Europe-Asia Studies*, vol. 45(1), 141–67

(1994a), 'National income', in Davies, R.W., Harrison, M. and Wheatcroft, S.G., eds, *The economic transformation of the USSR, 1913–1945*, Cambridge, 38–56

(1994b), 'The Second World War', in Davies, R.W, Harrison, M. and Wheatcroft, S.G., eds, *The economic transformation of the Soviet Union, 1913–1945*, Cambridge, 238–67

(1994c), 'GDPs of the USSR and eastern Europe: towards an interwar comparison', *Europe-Asia Studies*, vol. 46(2), 243–59

(1994d), 'Russian and Soviet economic growth reassessed in the light of new growth theory', University of Warwick, Department of Economics, *Working Paper Series*, no. 9404

(1994e), 'Defence mobilisation and the military burden on the Soviet economy in World War II: an input/output approach', University of Warwick, Department of Economics, *Working Paper Series*, no. 9406

(1994f), 'Soviet economic losses in World War II: towards a balance sheet', University of Warwick, Department of Economics, *Working Paper Series*, no. 9411

(1994g), 'The Soviet defense industry complex in World War II', in Sakudo, J. and Shiba, T. (eds.), *World War II and the transformation of business systems*, Tokyo, 237–62

(1995a), 'Soviet national accounting for World War II: an inside view', in Cooper, J.M., Perrie, M. and Rees, E.A. (eds.), *Soviet history, 1917–1953: essays in honour of R.W. Davies*, London and Basingstoke, 219–42

(1995b), 'The Soviet economy and relations with the USA and Britain', in Temperley, H. and Lane, A. (eds.), *The rise and fall of the Grand Alliance, 1941–1945*, London and Basingstoke, 69–89

Herring, G.C. (1973), *Aid to Russia, 1941–1946: strategy, diplomacy, the origins of the Cold War*, New York

Higgs, R. (1992), 'Wartime prosperity? A reassessment of the U.S. economy in the 1940s', *Journal of Economic History*, vol. 52(1), 41–60

Hodgman, D.R. (1954), *Soviet industrial production, 1928–1951*, Cambridge, MA

Hoeffding, O. (1954), *Soviet national income and product in 1928*, New York

Hoeffding, O. and Nimitz, N. (1959), *Soviet national income and product, 1949–1955*, The RAND Corporation, Research Memorandum, RM-2101, Santa Monica, CA

Howlett, P. (1994), 'The wartime economy, 1939–1945', in Floud, R. and McCloskey, D. (eds.), *The economic history of Britain since 1700*, 2nd edn, vol. 3, Cambridge, 1–31

Hunter, H. and Szyrmer, J.M. (1992), *Faulty foundations: Soviet economic policies, 1928–1940*, Princeton, NJ

Illarionov, A.N. (1995), 'Pochemu pobediteli v voine proigrali mir?', *Segodnia*, 2 July

IMEMO (Institut mirovoi ekonomiki i mezhdunarodnykh otnoshenii) (1987), 'Sovetskii soiuz v mirovoi ekonomiki (1917–1987 gg.)', *Mirovaia ekonomika i mezhdunarodnye otnoshenii*, no. 11, 145–57

Inwood, K. and Stengos, T. (1991), 'Discontinuities in Canadian economic growth, 1870–1985', *Explorations in Economic History*, vol. 28, 274–86

(1995), 'Segmented trend models of Canadian economic growth', *Explorations in Economic History*, vol. 32, 253–61

ISE, vol. 5 (1978), *Istoriia sotsialisticheskoi ekonomiki SSSR*, Moscow

IVMV, vol. 4 (1975), vol. 6 (1976), vol. 11 (1980), vol. 12 (1982), *Istoriia Vtoroi Mirovoi voiny 1939–1945 gg.*, vols. 1–12, Moscow

IVOVSS, vol. 6 (1965), *Istoriia Velikoi Otechestvennoi voiny Sovetskogo Soiuza*, vols. 1–6, Moscow

Jasny, N. (1949), *The socialized agriculture of the USSR: plans and performance*, Stanford, CA

(1951a), *The Soviet economy during the plan era*, Stanford, CA

(1951b), *The Soviet price system*, Stanford, CA

(1951c), 'Labor and output in Soviet concentration camps', *Journal of Political Economy*, vol. 59(5), 405–19

(1952), *Soviet prices of producers' goods*, Stanford, CA

(1961), *Soviet industrialization, 1928–1952*, Chicago, IL

Jones, R.H. (1969), *The roads to Russia: United States Lend-Lease to the Soviet Union*, Norman, OK

Kaldor, N. (1946), 'The German war economy', *Review of Economic Studies*, vol. 13, 33–52

Kaplan, N., Blackman, J., Heymann, H., Redding, D. and Rodin, N. (1952), 'A tentative input–output table for the USSR, 1941 plan', The RAND Corporation, Research Memorandum, RM-924, Santa Monica, CA

Kaplan, N. and Moorsteen, R. (1960), 'Indexes of Soviet industrial output', vols. 1–2, The RAND Corporation, Research Memorandum, RM-2495, Santa Monica, CA

Kaser, M. (1970), *Soviet economics*, London

Katz, B.G. (1975), 'Purges and production: Soviet economic growth, 1928–1940', *Journal of Economic History*, vol. 35, 567–90

Khanin, G.I. (1988), 'Ekonomicheskii rost: al'ternativnaia otsenka', *Kommunist*, no. 17, 83–90

(1991), *Dinamika ekonomicheskogo razvitiia SSSR*, Novosibirsk

(1993), *Sovetskii ekonomicheskii rost: analiz zapadnykh otsenok*, Novosibirsk

Khrushchev, N.S. (1971), *Khrushchev remembers*, London

Klein, B.H. (1959), *Germany's economic preparations for war*, Cambridge,

Kornai, J. (1992), *The socialist system: the political economy of communism*, Oxford

Kosiachenko, G. (1944), 'Voennoe khoziaistvo SSSR', *Planovoe khoziaistvo*, no. 1, 3–16

Kostyrchenko, G. V. (1994), 'Aviatsionnaia promyshlennost' nakanune i v gody Velikoi Otechestvennoi voiny (1939–1945 gg.)', in Biushgens, G.S., ed., *Samoletostroenie v SSSR*, vol. 2, Moscow, 197–238

Kovalev, A.P. (1988), 'V Gosplane v to pamiatnoe vremia', *EKO*, no. 5, 19–24

Kravchenko, G.S. (1970), *Ekonomika SSSR v gody Velikoi Otechestvennoi voiny*, 2nd edn, Moscow, 1970

Krivosheev, G.F. (ed.) (1993), *Grif sekretnosti sniat. Poteri Vooruzhennykh Sil SSSR v voinakh, boevykh deistviiakh i voennykh konfliktakh*, Moscow

League of Nations (1938), *Statistical yearbook of the League of Nations, 1937/38*, Geneva

Linz, S.J. (1980), 'Economic origins of the Cold War? An examination of the carryover costs of World War II to the Soviet people', unpub. PhD thesis, University of Illinois at Urbana–Champaign

(1985), 'World War II and Soviet economic growth, 1940–1953', in Linz, S.J., ed., *The impact of World War II on the Soviet Union*, Totowa, NJ, 11–38

Liubimov, A.V. (1968), *Torgovlia i snabzhenie v gody Velikoi Otechestvennoi voiny*, Moscow

Lucas, R.E. (1988), 'On the mechanics of economic development', *Journal of Monetary Economics*, vol. 22, 3–42

Maddison, A. (1991), *Dynamic forces in capitalist development: a long-run comparative view*, Oxford

Maksudov, S. (1993), 'O frontovykh poteriakh Sovetskoi Armii v gody Vtoroi Mirovoi voiny', *Svobodnaia mysl'*, no. 10, 117–19

Malafeev, A.N. (1964), *Istoriia tsenoobrazovaniia v SSSR (1917–1963 gg.)*, Moscow

Mankiw, N.G., Romer, D. and Weill, D. (1992), 'A contribution to the empirics of economic growth', *Quarterly Journal of Economics*, vol. 107, 407–37

Marer, P. (1985), *Dollar GNPs of the USSR and eastern Europe*, London

Martel, L. (1979), *Lend-Lease, loans, and the coming of the Cold War*, Boulder, CO

Martynov, V. (1990), 'SSSR i SShA po materialam mezhdunarodnykh sopostavlenii OON i SEV', *Vestnik statistiki*, no. 9, 10–15

Millar, J.R. (1980), 'Financing the Soviet effort in World War II', *Soviet Studies*, vol. 32

Millar, J.R. and Linz, S.J. (1978), 'The cost of World War II to the Soviet people', *Journal of Economic History*, vol. 38(4), 959–62

Milward, A.S. (1977), *War, economy and society, 1939–1945*, London

Minvneshtorg (Ministerstvo Vneshnei Torgovli SSSR) (1967), *Vneshniaia torgovlia SSSR. Statisticheskii sbornik. 1918–1966*, Moscow

Mitrofanova, A.V. (1971), *Rabochii klass SSSR v gody Velikoi Otechestvennoi voiny*, Moscow

Mitrofanova, A.V. (ed.) (1984), *Rabochii klass SSSR nakanune i v gody Velikoi Otechestvennoi voiny. 1938–1945 gg.*, vol. 3 of *Istoriia sovetskogo rabochego klassa* (Khromov, S.S., editor-in-chief), vols. 1–6, Moscow

Moorsteen, R. (1962), *Prices and production of machinery in the Soviet Union, 1928–1958*, Cambridge, MA

Moorsteen, R. and Powell, R.P. (1966), *The Soviet capital stock, 1928–1962*, Homewood, IL

Moskoff, W. (1990), *The bread of affliction: the food supply in the USSR during World War II*, Cambridge

Mowat, C.L. (1956), *Britain between the wars, 1918–1940*, 2nd edn, Cambridge

Munting, R. (1984a), 'Lend-Lease and the Soviet war effort', *Journal of*

Contemporary History, vol. 19, 495–510
(1984b), 'Soviet food supply and Allied aid in the war, 1941–1945', *Soviet Studies*, vol. 36, 582–93
Nove, A. (1965), *The Soviet economy: an introduction*, 2nd edn, London
(1972), *An economic history of the USSR*, 1st edn, Harmondsworth
(1985), 'Soviet peasantry in World War II', in Linz, S.J., ed., *The impact of World War II on the Soviet Union*, Totowa, NJ, 77–90
Nutter, G.W. (1962), *The growth of industrial production in the Soviet Union*, Princeton, NJ
Ofer, G. (1987), 'Soviet economic growth: 1928–1985', *Journal of Economic Literature*, vol. 25, 1767–833
Overy, R.J. (1994), *War and economy in the Third Reich*, Oxford
Perron, P. (1989), 'The Great Crash, the oil price shock, and the unit root hypothesis', *Econometrica*, vol. 57(6), 1361–1401
Pitzer, J. (1990), 'Alternative methods of valuing Soviet gross national product', in Central Intelligence Agency, *Measuring Soviet GNP: problems and solutions: a conference report*, SOV 90–10038, Washington, DC, 1–28
Plotnikov, K.N. (1955), *Ocherki istorii biudzheta Sovetskogo gosudarstva*, Moscow
Powell, R.P. (1957), 'A materials input index of Soviet construction, 1927/28 to 1955', The RAND Corporation, Research Memoranda, RM-1872, RM-1873, Santa Monica, CA
(1968), 'The Soviet capital stock and related series for the war years', in *Two supplements to Richard Moorsteen and Raymond P. Powell, The Soviet capital stock, 1928–1962*, Yale University, The Economic Growth Center
Rebelo, S. (1991), 'Long-run policy analysis and long-run growth', *Journal of Political Economy*, vol. 99, 500–21
Richardson, J.D. (1989), 'Empirical research on trade liberalisation with imperfect competition: a survey', *OECD Economic Studies*, vol. 12, 7–50
Romer, P.M. (1986), 'Increasing returns and economic growth', *Journal of Political Economy*, vol. 94, 1002–37
Rosefielde, S. (1981), 'Knowledge and socialism: deciphering the Soviet experience', in Rosefielde, S., ed., *Economic welfare and the economics of Soviet socialism: essays in honor of Abram Bergson*, Cambridge, 5–23
(1991), 'The illusion of material progress: the analytics of Soviet economic growth revisited', *Soviet Studies*, vol. 43, 597–611
Rybakovskii, L. (1989), 'Dvadtsat' millionov ili bol'she?', *Politicheskoe obozrenie*, no. 10, 96–8
Samsonov, A.M. 9ed.) (1985), *Sovetskii Soiuz v gody Velikoi Otechestvennoi voiny*, 2nd edn, Moscow
Sheviakov, A.A. (1991), 'Gitlerovskii genotsid na territoriiakh SSSR', *Sotsiologicheskie issledovaniia*, no. 12, 3–11
(1992), 'Zhertvy sredy mirnogo naseleniia v gody otechestvennoi voiny', *Sotsiologicheskie issledovaniia*, no. 11, 3–17

SNK-TsK (Sovnarkom SSSR, Tsentral'nyi komitet VKP(b)) (1941), *Gosudarstvennyi plan razvitiia narodnogo khoziaistva SSSR na 1941 god*, reprinted by the American Council of Learned Societies (1947), Baltimore, MD

Sokolov, B.V. (1988), 'O sootnoshenii poter' v liudiakh i voennoi tekhniki na Sovetsko-Germanskom fronte v khode Velikoi Otechestvennoi voiny', *Voprosy istorii*, no. 9, 116–27

Sokolov, P.V. (1968), *Voenno-ekonomicheskie voprosy v kurse politekonomii*, Moscow

Sorokin, G.A. (ed.) (1971), *Po edinomu planu*, Moscow

Stalin, J. (1940), *Leninism*, London

(1945), *The Great Patriotic War of the Soviet Union*, New York

Sukharevskii, B. (1945a), 'Pobeda v Otechestvennoi voine i sovetskaia ekonomika', *Planovoe khoziaistvo*, no. 3, 3–20

(1945b), *Sovetkaia ekonomika v Velikoi Otechestvennoi voine*, Moscow

Summers, R. and Heston, A. (1988), 'A new set of international comparisons of real product and price levels: estimates for 130 countries, 1950–1985', *Review of Income and Wealth*, vol. 34, 1–25

(1991), 'The Penn World Table (Mark 5): an expanded set of international comparisons, 1950–1988', *Quarterly Journal of Economics*, vol. 106, 327–68

(1994) 'The Penn World Tables (Mark 5.5)', available from nber.harvard.edu

Tamarchenko, M.L. (1967), *Sovetskie finansy v period Velikoi Otechestvennoi voiny*, Moscow

Terpilovskii, M.V. (ed.) (1967), *Finansovaia sluzhba Vooruzhennykh Sil SSSR v period voiny*, Moscow

Titley, P.J. (1991), 'Royal Air Force assistance to the Soviet Union, June 1941 to June 1942', unpub. MA thesis, University of Kent

TsSU (Tsentral'noe statisticheskoe upravlenie SSSR) (1956), *Narodnoe khoziaistvo SSSR*, Moscow

(1958), *SSSR v tsifrakh. Statisticheskii sbornik*, Moscow

(1959), *Narodnoe khoziaistvo SSSR v Velikoi Otechestvennoi voiny 1941–1945 gg.*, Moscow

(1961), *Narodnoe khoziaistvo SSSR v 1960 gody*, Moscow

(1962), *Narodnoe khoziaistvo SSSR v 1961 gody*, Moscow

(1966), *Narodnoe khoziaistvo SSSR v 1965 gody*, Moscow

(1968), *Narodnoe khoziaistvo SSSR v 1967 gody*, Moscow

(1977), *Narodnoe obrazovanie, nauka i kul'tura SSSR*, Moscow

Tupper, S.M. (1981), 'The mobilisation of Soviet industry for defence needs, 1937–1941', went European conference on Soviet industry and the working class in the Inter-Wars years, Birmingham

(1982), 'The Red Army and Soviet defence industry, 1934–1941', unpub. PhD thesis, University of Birmingham

Uchastie (1962), 'Uchastie kolkhoznikov v obshchestvennom khoziaistve kolkhozov za gody Otechestvennoi voiny (po godovym otchetam kolkhozov za 1940–1944 gg.)', *Istoricheskii arkhiv*, no. 6, 19–68

United States Department of Commerce (1945), 'United States trade with Russia (USSR) during the war years', *International Reference Service*, vol. 2, no. 41

United States President (1944), *Report to Congress on Lend-Lease operations*, no. 14, Washington, DC

(1945a), *Report to Congress on Lend-Lease operations*, no. 19, Washington, DC

(1945b), *Report to Congress on Lend-Lease operations*, no. 20, Washington, DC

(1945c), *Report to Congress on Lend-Lease operations*, no. 21, Washington, DC

United States War Production Board (1945), *American industry in war and transition, 1940–1950*, part II, *The effect of the war on the industrial economy*, Washington, DC

UNSO (United Nations, Statistical Office) (1953), *A system of national accounts and supporting tables*, Studies in Methods, series F, no. 2, New York

(1968), *A system of national accounts*, Studies in Methods, series F, no. 2, rev. 3, New York

(1971), *Basic principles of the system of balances of the national economy*, Studies in Methods, series F, no. 17, New York

Urlanis, B. (1971), *Wars and population*, Moscow

van Creveld, M. (1977), *Supplying war: logistics from Wallenstein to Patten*, Cambridge

(1985), *Fighting power: German and U.S. Army performance, 1939–1945*, London

van Tuyll, H.P. (1989), *Feeding the Russian bear: American aid to the Soviet Union, 1941–1945*, Westport, CT

Vneshniaia politika, vol. 1 (1952), *Vneshniaia politika Sovetskogo Soiuza*, vols. 1–2, Moscow

Voznesenskii, N.A. (1947), *Voennaia ekonomika SSSR v period Otechestvennoi voiny*, Moscow

(1948), *The war economy of the USSR in the period of the Patriotic War*, Moscow

Weitzman, M. (1970), 'Soviet postwar growth and capital–labor substitution', *American Economic Review*, vol. 60, 676–92

Wheatcroft, S.G. and Davies, R.W. (eds.) (1985), *Materials for a balance of the Soviet national economy, 1928–1930*, Cambridge

Wheatcroft, S.G. and Davies, R.W. (1994a), 'The crooked mirror of Soviet economic statistics', in Davies, R.W., Harrison, M. and Wheatcroft, S.G., eds, *The economic transformation of the Soviet Union, 1913–1945*, Cambridge, 24–37

(1994b), 'Population', in Davies, R.W., Harrison, M. and Wheatcroft, S.G., eds, *The economic transformation of the Soviet Union, 1913–1945*, Cambridge, 57–80

Wiles, P.J.D. (1955), 'Are adjusted roubles rational?', *Soviet Studies*, vol. 7(2), 143–60

(1956), 'A rejoinder to all and sundry', *Soviet Studies*, vol. 8(2), 134–43

(1962), *The political economy of communism*, Oxford

(1964), 'The theory of international comparisons of economic volume', in Degras, J. and Nove, A., eds, *Soviet planning: essays in honour of Naum Jasny*, Oxford, 77–115

(1987), 'How Soviet defence expenditures fit into the national income accounts', in Jacobsen, C.G., ed., *The Soviet defence enigma: estimating costs and burdens*, Oxford, 59–94

Zaleski, E. (1980), *Stalinist planning for economic growth, 1933–1952*, London

Zamagni, V. (1993), *The economic history of Italy, 1860–1990: recovery after decline*, Oxford

Zelkin, I.I. (1969), *Kuznetskii ugol'nyi bassein v gody Velikoi Otechestvennoi voiny*, Moscow

Zemskov, V.N. (1991), 'Gulag (istoriko-sotsiologicheskii aspekt)', *Sotsiologicheskie issledovaniia*, no. 6, 10–27

(1992), '"Kulatskaia ssylka" nakanune i v gody Velikoi Otechestvennoi voiny', *Sotsiologicheskie issledovaniia*, no. 2, 3–26

Zinich, M.S. (1994), *Budni voennogo likholet'ia. 1941–1945* (2 parts), Moscow

Zverev, A.G. (1958), *Voprosy natsional'nogo dokhoda i finansov SSSR*, Moscow

Index

84 GEORGE O. LIBER
Soviet nationality policy and social change in the Ukranian SSR 1923–1934
The urban harvest

83 CHRISTOPH BLUTH
Soviet strategic arms policy before SALT

82 JOHN P. WILLERTON
Patronage and politics in the USSR

81 JAMES HUGHES
Stalin, Siberia and the crisis of the New Economic Policy

80 ILIANA ZLOCH-CHRISTY
East–West financial relations
Current problems and future prospects

79 MICHAEL D. KENNEDY
Professionals, power and Solidarity in Poland
A critical sociology of Soviet-type society

78 GARETH M. WINROW
The foreign policy of the GDR in Africa

77 JOZEF M. VAN BRABANT
The planned economies and international economic organizations

76 WILLIAM MOSKOFF
The bread of affliction: the food supply in the USSR during World War II

75 YAACOV RO'I
The struggle for Soviet Jewish emigration 1948–1967

74 GRAEME GILL
The origins of the Stalinist political system

73 SANTOSH K. MEHROTRA
India and the Soviet Union: trade and technology transfer

72 ILYA PRIZEL
Latin America through Soviet eyes
The evolution of Soviet perceptions during the Brezhnev era 1964–1982

71 ROBERT G. PATMAN
The Soviet Union in the Horn of Africa
The diplomacy of intervention and disengagement

70 IVAN T. BEREND
The Hungarian economic reforms 1953–1988

69 CHRIS WARD
Russia's cotton workers and the New Economic Policy
Shop-floor culture and state policy 1921–1919

68 LASZLO CSABA
Eastern Europe in the world economy

67 MICHAEL E. URBAN
An algebra of Soviet power
Elite circulation in the Belorussian Republic 1966–1986

66 JANE L. CURRY
Poland's journalists: professionalism and politics

65 MARTIN MYANT
The Czechoslovak economy 1948–1988
The battle for economic reform

64 XAVIER RICHET
The Hungarian model: markets and planning in a socialist economy

63 PAUL G. LEWIS
Political authority and party secretaries in Poland 1975–1986

62 BENJAMIN PINKUS
The Jews of the Soviet Union
The history of a national minority

61 FRANCESCO BENVENUTI
The Bolsheviks and the Red Army, 1918–1922

60 HIROAKI KUROMIYA
Stalin's industrial revolution
Politics and workers, 1928–1932

59 LEWIS SIEGELBAUM
Stakhanovism and the politics of productivity in the USSR, 1935–1941

58 JOZEF M. VAN BRABANT
Adjustment, structural change and economic efficiency
Aspects of monetary cooperation in Eastern Europe

57 ILIANA ZLOCH-CHRISTY
Debt problems of Eastern Europe

56 SUSAN BRIDGER
Women in the Soviet countryside
Women's roles in rural development in the Soviet Union

55 ALLEN LYNCH
The Soviet study of international relations

54 DAVID GRANICK
Job rights in the Soviet Union: their consequences

53 ANITA PRAZMOWSKA
Britain, Poland and the Eastern Front, 1939

52 ELLEN JONES AND FRED GRUPP
Modernization, value change and fertility in the Soviet Union

51 CATHERINE ANDREYEV
Vlasov and the Russian liberation movement
Soviet reality and émigré theories

50 STEPHEN WHITE
The origins of détente
The Genoa Conference and Soviet-Western relations 1921–1922

49 JAMES MCADAMS
East Germany and détente
Building authority after the Wall

48 S. G. WHEATCROFT AND R. W. DAVIES (EDS.)
Materials for a balance of the Soviet national economy 1928–1930

47 SYLVANA MALLE
The economic organization of war communism, 1918–1921

46 DAVID S. MASON
Public opinion and political change in Poland, 1980–1982

45 MARK HARRISON
Soviet planning in peace and war 1938–1945

44 NIGEL SWAIN
Collective farms which work?

43 J. ARCH GETTY
Origins of the great purges
The Soviet Communist Party reconsidered, 1933–1938

42 TADEUSZ SWIETOCHOWSKI
Russian Azerbaijan 1905–1920
The shaping of national identity in a muslim community

41 RAY TARAS
Ideology in a socialist state
Poland 1956–1983

39 DAVID A. DYKER
The process of investment in the Soviet Union

35 WILLIAM J. CONYNGHAM
The modernization of Soviet industrial management

34 ANGELA STENT
From embargo to Ostpolitik
The political economy of German–Soviet relations 1955–1980

32 BLAIR A. RUBLE
Soviet trade unions
Their development in the 1970s

30 JOZEF M. VAN BRABANT
Socialist economic integration
Aspects of contemporary economic problems in Eastern Europe

22 JAMES RIORDAN
Sport in Soviet society
Development of sport and physical education in Russia and the USSR